Windows Server® 2008 For Dummies

P9-DWU-986

Cheat Sheet

Windows Server 2008 Administrative Tools

You can access any of these programs by using the Start➪Administrative Tools menu or by typing the name of the launch file in the Run dialog box (Start➪Run).

Name	Launch File	Description
Active Directory Domains and Trusts	`domain.msc`	Manages trusts between domains.
Active Directory Sites and Services	`dssite.msc`	Manages sites involved in Active Directory replication.
Active Directory Users and Computers	`dsa.msc`	Manages users, groups, computers, and other objects.
Component Services	`comexp.msc`	Manages COM+ applications.
Computer Management	`compmgmt.msc /s`	Starts and stops services, manages disks, and provides access to other computer management tools for local and remote administration.
Data Sources (ODBC)	`odbcad32.exe`	Manages ODBC drivers and data sources.
DHCP	`dhcpmgmt.msc /s`	Manages DHCP, which assigns TCP/IP settings to clients.
Disk Defragmenter	`%systemRoot%\system32\dfrgui.exe`	Starts the Disk Defragmenter utility.
Distributed File System	`dfscmd`	Manages DFS, which creates a single shared hierarchy of resources from multiple hosts.
DNS	`dnsmgmt.msc /s`	Manages DNS, which resolves host names into IP addresses.
Event Viewer	`eventvwr.msc /s`	Accesses various log files under Windows Server.
Internet Services Manager	`%systemRoot%\system32\iis.msc`	Manages Web and FTP Internet services.
Licensing	`llsmgr.exe`	Manages licenses and client use.
Performance	`perfmon.msc /s`	Monitors the performance of a system or network.
Routing and Remote Access	`rrasmgmt.msc /s`	Manages remote connections and routing activities.
Terminal Services Licensing	`licmgr.exe`	Manages client access to terminal services.

Windows Server® 2008 For Dummies®

Cheat Sheet

Important TCP/IP Command Line Utilities

Each of these utilities performs some useful function. The Help String column shows how to get online help for syntax details on each command.

Name	Help String	Description
ARP	`arp /h`	Displays and modifies the address translation table maintained by the TCP/IP Address Resolution Protocol.
IPCONFIG	`ipconfig /?`	Displays all current TCP/IP network configuration data.
NETSTART	`netstat /?`	Displays protocol statistics and current TCP/IP network connections.
NSLOOKUP	`nslookup`	Displays information about known DNS servers.
PING	`ping`	Verifies connections to local or remote computers. (Ping stands for Packet Internet Groper, and it's an excellent IP troubleshooting tool.)
ROUTE	`route`	Displays and manipulates network routing tables.
TRACERT	`tracert`	Displays the route from your machine to a specified destination.

Windows PowerShell Quick Reference

Each of these script commands lets you automate tasks or guide users through specific system activities. For examples, manuals, and more visit the Script Center at www.microsoft.com/technet/scriptcenter.

Activity	Description
Access arguments.	Use the automatic `$args` variable.
Run a script.	Type full path to script (or script name, if script resides in a folder on your directory path). `.ps1` is the usual extension for PowerShell script files.
Use colored text.	Use the `Write-Host` cmdlet with `–foregroundcolor` or `–backgroundcolor` settings.
Insert a paragraph break.	Use the newline char `` `n `` in the `Write-host` cmdlet.
`Get-Help` gives help.	Use the `Get-Help` cmdlet with `–full` parameter plus any cmdlet name to retrieve help file details.
Use a comment marker.	Add a pound sign (#) to create inline comments.
Use multi-command lines.	Separate individual statements with semicolons (;) in a single line of text.
Use comparison operators.	`–lt` = less than; `–le` = less than or equal to; `–gt` = greater than; `–ge` = greater than or equal to; `–eq` = equal to; `–ne` = not equal to; `–like` (use wildcards for matching); `–notlike` (use wildcards for not matching).
Use a conditional.	Use `if`, `elseif`, and `else` with their own conditional statements, or `switch` for arbitrary value matches with single conditional.

Use looping constructs.	Set up loops to repeat instructions using For, For Each, and Do While.
	`for ($a = 1, $a -le 10; $a++) {$a}`
	`foreach ($i in get-childitem c:\scripts)`
	`{i.extension}; $i = 1; do {$i; $i +=1} while`
	`($i -le 15)`

Wiley, the Wiley Publishing logo, For Dummies, the Dummies Man logo, the For Dummies Bestselling Book Series logo and all related trade dress are trademarks or registered trademarks of John Wiley & Sons, Inc. and/or its affiliates. All other trademarks are property of their respective owners. Copyright © 2008 Wiley Publishing, Inc. All rights reserved. Item 8043-3. For more information about Wiley Publishing, call 1-800-762-2974.

For Dummies: Bestselling Book Series for Beginners

Windows Server® 2008
FOR DUMMIES®

by Ed Tittel and Justin Korelc

WILEY

Wiley Publishing, Inc.

Windows Server® 2008 For Dummies®

Published by
Wiley Publishing, Inc.
111 River Street
Hoboken, NJ 07030-5774

www.wiley.com

Copyright © 2008 by Wiley Publishing, Inc., Indianapolis, Indiana

Published by Wiley Publishing, Inc., Indianapolis, Indiana

Published simultaneously in Canada

No part of this publication may be reproduced, stored in a retrieval system or transmitted in any form or by any means, electronic, mechanical, photocopying, recording, scanning or otherwise, except as permitted under Sections 107 or 108 of the 1976 United States Copyright Act, without either the prior written permission of the Publisher, or authorization through payment of the appropriate per-copy fee to the Copyright Clearance Center, 222 Rosewood Drive, Danvers, MA 01923, (978) 750-8400, fax (978) 646-8600. Requests to the Publisher for permission should be addressed to the Legal Department, Wiley Publishing, Inc., 10475 Crosspoint Blvd., Indianapolis, IN 46256, (317) 572-3447, fax (317) 572-4355, or online at http://www.wiley.com/go/permissions.

Trademarks: Wiley, the Wiley Publishing logo, For Dummies, the Dummies Man logo, A Reference for the Rest of Us!, The Dummies Way, Dummies Daily, The Fun and Easy Way, Dummies.com, and related trade dress are trademarks or registered trademarks of John Wiley & Sons, Inc. and/or its affiliates in the United States and other countries, and may not be used without written permission. Microsoft and Windows Server are registered trademarks of Microsoft Corporation in the United States and/or other countries. All other trademarks are the property of their respective owners. Wiley Publishing, Inc., is not associated with any product or vendor mentioned in this book.

LIMIT OF LIABILITY/DISCLAIMER OF WARRANTY: THE PUBLISHER AND THE AUTHOR MAKE NO REPRESENTATIONS OR WARRANTIES WITH RESPECT TO THE ACCURACY OR COMPLETENESS OF THE CONTENTS OF THIS WORK AND SPECIFICALLY DISCLAIM ALL WARRANTIES, INCLUDING WITHOUT LIMITATION WARRANTIES OF FITNESS FOR A PARTICULAR PURPOSE. NO WARRANTY MAY BE CREATED OR EXTENDED BY SALES OR PROMOTIONAL MATERIALS. THE ADVICE AND STRATEGIES CONTAINED HEREIN MAY NOT BE SUITABLE FOR EVERY SITUATION. THIS WORK IS SOLD WITH THE UNDERSTANDING THAT THE PUBLISHER IS NOT ENGAGED IN RENDERING LEGAL, ACCOUNTING, OR OTHER PROFESSIONAL SERVICES. IF PROFESSIONAL ASSISTANCE IS REQUIRED, THE SERVICES OF A COMPETENT PROFESSIONAL PERSON SHOULD BE SOUGHT. NEITHER THE PUBLISHER NOR THE AUTHOR SHALL BE LIABLE FOR DAMAGES ARISING HEREFROM. THE FACT THAT AN ORGANIZATION OR WEBSITE IS REFERRED TO IN THIS WORK AS A CITATION AND/OR A POTENTIAL SOURCE OF FURTHER INFORMATION DOES NOT MEAN THAT THE AUTHOR OR THE PUBLISHER ENDORSES THE INFORMATION THE ORGANIZATION OR WEBSITE MAY PROVIDE OR RECOMMENDATIONS IT MAY MAKE. FURTHER, READERS SHOULD BE AWARE THAT INTERNET WEBSITES LISTED IN THIS WORK MAY HAVE CHANGED OR DISAPPEARED BETWEEN WHEN THIS WORK WAS WRITTEN AND WHEN IT IS READ.

For general information on our other products and services, please contact our Customer Care Department within the U.S. at 800-762-2974, outside the U.S. at 317-572-3993, or fax 317-572-4002.

For technical support, please visit www.wiley.com/techsupport.

Wiley also publishes its books in a variety of electronic formats. Some content that appears in print may not be available in electronic books.

Library of Congress Control Number: 2008922653

ISBN: 978-0-470-18043-3

Manufactured in the United States of America

10 9 8 7 6 5 4 3 2 1

WILEY

About the Authors

Ed Tittel is an increasingly grizzled, if not wizened, veteran of the publishing game, with over a thousand magazine articles and more than 140 books to his credit. Ed has worked on numerous *For Dummies* books, including *HTML 4 For Dummies,* 5th Edition (with Mary Burmeister) and *XML For Dummies*, 4th Edition (with Lucinda Dykes), as well as books on many other topics. Ed runs a small professional IT practice in Round Rock, TX, that specializes in network-oriented training, writing, and consulting. When Ed's not busy writing, he likes to spend time with his wife, Dina, and son, Gregory. He also likes to shoot pool, cook, and read sci-fi. You can reach Ed by e-mail at etittel@ yahoo.com or through his Web page at www.edtittel.com.

Justin Korelc has been working with computers and technology for over 15 years. Justin is an independent consultant working as a writer and trainer. His work focuses on security, Windows and Linux operating systems, and PC hardware. Justin has coauthored several books on media PCs, including *Build the Ultimate Home Theater PC* (an *ExtremeTech BuildIt Guide*) and *Hacking MythTV* (an *ExtremeTech* title). He has developed online training materials on information security, PC tune-ups, file transfer technologies, and more. Justin's computer knowledge is self-taught and based on nearly 20 years of hands-on experience. He spends his spare time practicing the fine art of bricolage, playing with computers, and improving his culinary skills. You can reach Justin by e-mail at jusphikor@yahoo.com.

Authors' Acknowledgments

As always, thanks to my agent, Carole McClendon at Waterside Productions, for hooking me up with *For Dummies* in the first place. Has it really been 15 years now? On the Wiley side, special thanks to Katie Feltman, Kim Darosett, and Heidi Unger. I'd also like to thank Justin Korelc for rolling up his sleeves and digging into the former Longhorn Server as far back as Beta 1. Personally, I want to thank my Mom and Dad for making my career both possible and attainable. Finally, I want to thank my wife, Dina Kutueva, for coming into my life rather later than sooner, and for giving me our wonderful son, Gregory.

—ET

Thanks to my coauthor, Ed Tittel, for including me in this book.

—JPK

Publisher's Acknowledgments

We're proud of this book; please send us your comments through our online registration form located at www.dummies.com/register/.

Some of the people who helped bring this book to market include the following:

Acquisitions and Editorial

Project Editor: Kim Darosett

Senior Acquisitions Editor: Katie Feltman

Copy Editor: Heidi Unger

Technical Editor: Christian Mayoros

Editorial Manager: Leah Cameron

Editorial Assistant: Amanda Foxworth

Sr. Editorial Assistant: Cherie Case

Cartoons: Rich Tennant
(www.the5thwave.com)

Composition Services

Project Coordinator: Lynsey Stanford

Layout and Graphics: Stacie Brooks, Reuben W. Davis, Andrea Hornberger, Shane Johnson, Christine Williams

Proofreaders: Laura Albert, Broccoli Information Management

Indexer: Broccoli Information Management

Publishing and Editorial for Technology Dummies

Richard Swadley, Vice President and Executive Group Publisher

Andy Cummings, Vice President and Publisher

Mary Bednarek, Executive Acquisitions Director

Mary C. Corder, Editorial Director

Publishing for Consumer Dummies

Diane Graves Steele, Vice President and Publisher

Joyce Pepple, Acquisitions Director

Composition Services

Gerry Fahey, Vice President of Production Services

Debbie Stailey, Director of Composition Services

Contents at a Glance

Table of Contents

Introduction

*W*elcome to *Windows Server 2008 For Dummies,* the book that helps anyone who's unfamiliar with Windows Server 2008 (or Windows-based networks) find his or her way around a Windows Server 2008–based network. In a wired world, networks provide the links that tie all users together. This book tells you what's going on, in basic, straightforward terms.

Although a few fortunate individuals may already be acquainted with Windows Server 2008 and the networks it supports, many more people are not only unfamiliar with server-based networking but downright scared of it. To those who may be concerned about facing new and difficult technologies, we say, "Don't worry. Be happy." Using a server-based network isn't beyond anyone's wits or abilities — it's mostly a matter of using a language that ordinary people can understand.

Ordinary folks are why this book talks about using Windows Server 2008 and networks in simple — and deliberately irreverent — terms. Nothing is too highfalutin to be mocked, nor too arcane to state in plain English. And when we do have to get technical, we warn you and make sure to define our terms to boot.

This book aims to help you meet your needs. You'll find everything you need to know about Windows Server 2008 in here, so you'll be able to find your way around — without having to learn lots of jargon or obtain an advanced degree in computer science along the way. We want you to *enjoy* yourself. Because server-based networking really is a big deal, it's important that you be able to get the most out of it. We really want to help!

About This Book

This book is designed so you can pick it up and start reading at any point — like you might read a reference book. In Parts I and II, we cover server basics: concepts and terminology in Part I, and the installation and deployment of Windows Server 2008 in Part II. In Parts III through V, you'll find tons of information on how to run or build a Windows Server 2008–based network. Part III covers running a Windows Server 2008–based network, whereas Part IV describes how you might design, build, and use a do-it-yourself network server PC. Part V includes tips and tricks to help smooth out installing, configuring, and using Windows Server 2008.

Each chapter is divided into freestanding sections, each one relating to the chapter's major theme. For example, the chapter on installing Windows Server 2008, contains the following collection of information:

- ✔ The differences between an upgrade install and a clean install
- ✔ How to make sure your hardware is suitable for use as a server
- ✔ A step-by-step walkthrough of the installation process
- ✔ What to do when installation completes
- ✔ Troubleshooting installation problems
- ✔ Automating the Windows Server 2008 installation process

You don't have to memorize the contents of this book. Each section supplies just the facts you need to make networking with Windows Server 2008 easy to use. On some occasions, however, you may want to work directly from the book to make sure you keep things straight.

How to Use This Book

This book works like a reference, so start with a topic that interests you. You can use the table of contents to identify general areas of interest or broad topics. The index, however, is your best tool for identifying detailed concepts, related topics, or particular Windows Server 2008 capabilities, tools, or controls.

After you find what you need, you can close the book and tackle whatever task you've set for yourself — without having to grapple with unrelated details.

If you've never worked with a Windows Server operating system before, it's a good idea to read Parts I and II in their entirety. Likewise, if you're new to administering a Windows Server 2008–based network, you might want to read all of Part III. If the idea of building your own server PC from scratch sounds interesting, you'll definitely dig Part IV. Otherwise, dig in wherever your fancy moves you!

When you need to type something at the keyboard, you'll see text that looks like this: **Type this**. You're expected to enter this text at the keyboard and then press the Enter key. Because typing stuff can sometimes be confusing, we always try to describe what it is you're typing and why you need to type it.

This book occasionally suggests that you consult the Windows Server 2008 online help, printed manuals, Resource Kit, and even Microsoft's Web site for additional information. In most cases, though, you find everything you need to know about a particular topic right here — except for some of the bizarre details that abound in Windows Server 2008.

If there's a topic we don't cover in this book that you need to know more about, we suggest you look for a book on that subject in the *For Dummies* series, published by Wiley Publishing. In addition, a whole world of Web information about Windows Server 2008 is available on the Internet, and the Microsoft Web site (at `www.microsoft.com/windowsserver2008/ default.mspx`) isn't a bad place to start looking for such information.

Foolish Assumptions

We're going to climb out on a limb and make some potentially foolish assumptions about you, our gentle reader. You have or are thinking about getting a computer, a network, and at least one copy of Windows Server 2008. You know what you want to do with these things. You might even be able to handle all these things yourself, if somebody would only show you how. Our goal with this book is to decrease your need for such a somebody, but we don't recommend telling him or her that out loud — at least, not until you've finished this book!

How This Book Is Organized

The book is divided into five major parts, each of which consists of two to six chapters. Each chapter covers a major topic and is divided into sections, which discuss particular issues or concerns related to that topic. That's how things in this book are organized, but how you read it is up to you. Choose a topic, a section, a chapter, or a part — whatever strikes your fancy or suits your needs — and start reading.

Part 1: Servers at Your Service

Part I provides an introduction to Windows Server 2008. You'll find a detailed description of Windows Server 2008 in Chapter 1 that includes its important features, functions, capabilities, and requirements. Chapter 2 takes a more general look at server-based networking and explains what makes servers special, hardware-wise; what kinds of things servers do; and what services they provide. Chapters 3 and 4 provide a speedy primer on network design and construction to help you decide where to put the pieces and parts that go into a network, including your server, and what to do with them when they're all interconnected. If you're already a seasoned networker or have worked with another Windows Server operating system, you can skip this part if you'd like, although you may still want to check out Chapter 1 to see what's new and interesting in this latest and presumably greatest of Windows Server operating systems.

Part II: Servers, Start Your Engines

Part II tackles Windows Server 2008 head on, starting with its installation and configuration. It covers the issues involved in installing and configuring network hardware specifically for Windows Server 2008. It also covers how to install and manage print servers and services on a Windows Server 2008–based network, how to handle Transmission Control Protocol/Internet Protocol (TCP/IP) addresses, and how to set up and manage directory services in a Windows Server 2008–based environment. Part II is where you figure out how to put the basic pieces of a network together using Windows Server 2008.

Part III: Running Your Network

Part III picks up where Part II leaves off — that is, it talks about living with and managing a Windows Server 2008–based network after the initial installation and configuration phase is complete. It begins with a discussion of how to manage users and groups on a Windows Server 2008–based network, including details on profiles, policies, and local and global groups. Next, it covers how Windows Server 2008 controls access to NTFS files and directories and how to manage network-accessible file system resources called *shares.*

After a network's users, groups, and data assets are in place, rebuilding such a setup from scratch can be a real pain. That's where a backup comes in handy, so Part III covers the ins and outs of backing up and restoring a Windows Server 2008 machine, plus other aspects of fault tolerance. After that, a review of network security principles and practices should help to prepare you to protect your data from accidental loss and from would-be hackers and crackers.

Part IV: Serve It Yourself

Part IV takes a detour away from the software side of servers to dig deeply into the hardware on which such software must run. You'll find out what kinds of pieces and parts go into a PC and what kinds of selections make the most sense when that PC is going to act as a network server. You'll also dig into the specifics involved in building a basic Intel-based PC for use with Windows Server 2008, where we guide you through options and selection rationales for choosing specific processors, motherboards, memory, disk drives, and so forth. Then we repeat that process for AMD-based PCs for those who might choose to opt for an Opteron processor instead.

Part V: The Part of Tens

Part V follows the grand tradition of *For Dummies* books, all of which include "The Part of Tens." Here, you'll find lists of information, tips, tricks, and suggestions, all organized into short and convenient chapters. This supplemental information is designed to be both helpful and informative and is supplied at no extra charge.

Part VI: Appendixes

If you'll recall, we said earlier that this book is divided into five major parts. By definition, that means the appendixes must be a minor part of the book, although there's nothing minor about the content you'll find covered here. In fact, we decided to include this material to provide our readers with additional information and resources on server hardware and developing good troubleshooting skills to help provide users with the best networking experiences possible.

Bonus Chapter

You'll find a bonus chapter titled "What Makes Servers Special" at this book's companion Web site at www.dummies.com/go/winserver2008. This chapter will quickly get you up to speed on server capabilities.

Icons Used in This Book

The icons used in this book point you to important (and not so important) topics in the text.

This icon lets you know that you're about to encounter information that's important to understand if you really want to *get* what's going on with Windows Server 2008. It may be painful at times, but you have to slog through it.

Oh gee, we're getting so old that we can't recall what this one means. Maybe you should check one out and see whether it's worth watching for!

This icon lets you know that you're about to be swamped in technical details. We include this information because we love it, not because we think you have to master it to use Windows Server 2008. If you aspire to nerdhood, you probably want to read it; if you're already a nerd, you'll want to write us about stuff we left out or other information we should put in!

This icon signals that helpful advice is at hand. We also use it when we offer insights that we hope make using Windows Server 2008 more interesting or easier. For example, whenever we include a shortcut that improves your productivity, it's usually marked with the Tip icon.

This icon means what it says — you'd better be careful with the information it conveys. Nine times out of ten, it's warning you not to do something that can have nasty or painful consequences, as in accidentally wiping out the contents of an entire hard drive. Whoops!

Where to Go from Here

With this book at your side, you should be ready to wrestle with Windows Server 2008 and the networks it connects to. Find a subject, turn to its page, and you're ready to jam. Feel free to mark up this book, fill in the blanks, dog-ear the pages, and do anything else that might make a librarian queasy. The important things are to make good use of it and enjoy yourself while you're at it.

Please check out the Web page at www.dummies.com. Be sure to take the opportunity to register your purchase online or send us e-mail with feedback about your reading experience.

Part I
Servers at Your Service

The 5th Wave   By Rich Tennant

"I'm not saying I believe in anything. All I know is
since it's been there our server is running 50% faster."

In this part . . .

In this part of the book, you get an introduction to the big star in this production — namely, Windows Server 2008 — as you dig into its features, functions, and requirements. But we also introduce you to the whole server circus as we explain what makes servers so special and why taking care of clients is both a joy and a chore. You even get a chance to meet and make sense of the network pieces and parts necessary to bring clients and servers together to help bring home the bacon.

Each chapter presents its information in small, easy-to-read sections. If information is really technical (mostly worth skipping, unless you're a glutton for punishment), it's clearly marked as such. Even so, we hope you find this information useful — and maybe even worth a giggle or two.

Chapter 1

Making Windows Server 2008 Serve You

*W*indows Server 2008 is the latest and greatest version of Microsoft's flagship server platform and the successor to the hugely popular Windows Server 2003. Prior to its debut, Windows Server 2008 was code-named Longhorn, a platform that shared common client features also found in Windows Vista, much like the relationship between Windows Server 2003 and Windows XP. In fact, Windows Server 2008 even shares a common code base with Windows Vista and therefore carries much of the same architecture and core functionality.

Both Windows Server 2008 and Windows Vista share common technical, security, management, and administrative features; an improved IPv6-capable networking stack; native wireless utilities; and a revamped image-based installation format (among many other exciting new features). However, Windows Server 2008 is a total departure from the desktop/workstation realm and offers enterprise and server-specific features and functionality above and beyond anything Windows Vista offers. In this chapter, we explore some of these features from a 10,000-foot view and then focus on specific topics in the chapters that follow.

Large-scale deployment options, improved self-diagnostic tools, advanced reliability and performance monitoring, and enhanced security features are just some of the benefits that inhere to the new Windows Server 2008 platform. First, we take a look at server hardware and make some important distinctions between workstation and server roles and responsibilities.

Any Server Must Do This

The term *server* speaks to a broad classification of computers that combine hardware components and software services to handle a variety of tasks maintained through network relationships. A server takes many shapes and sizes, covers a wide range of form-factors, and includes numerous components and services. Embedded server platforms are used in network attached storage (NAS) devices, included in network print servers, and scale all the way up to giant mainframes capable of handling millions of simultaneous transactions and resource-intensive processing.

The terms *form-factor* refers to a specific design, layout, size, and shape of component or device. A form-factor can refer to several mutually independent devices, from the power supply and its interface types to motherboards and their various dimensions, pinouts, and connection types.

In fact, if you take a good look around your office environment, or just about any other office IT infrastructure, you can probably identify several otherwise-overlooked servers and server applications that you use on a regular basis. Modern technology puts the power of servers and server applications in the hands of mere mortals, and nowhere is this more evident than in the consumer market, where multimedia home theater PCs (HTPCs) are part of daily life for many. But back to the business world. . . .

Essentially, any server must serve a network — either clients or other servers, or some combination of the two. The term *server* also includes the actual server operating system that makes the computer do its job. Commercial server software products such as Windows Server 2008 are designed to handle a greater frequency and variety of tasks than are typical in either the desktop or workstation realms. Server platforms are an entirely different breed of PC, as compared to their desktop and workstation brethren, which is why they perch atop the hierarchy and the marketplace when it comes to buying an operating system.

Specifically, a server is designed and intended to provide services and run server applications under heavy workloads, left unattended and self-managing most of the time. For the most part, servers are self-contained, self-regulated core network entities in an enterprise or business IT environment. Larger amounts of memory (upwards of 8GB or more), larger storage capacity (terabytes, petabytes, and beyond), special storage methods (mirroring, striping, and multiple disk aggregation), redundant power supplies, and server-specific form-factors all typically distinguish specialized server hardware components from other, more ordinary computer components. That said, plenty of servers use desktop and workstation hardware such as optical drives, disk drives, and peripheral or display devices.

See Appendix A for more details on server hardware components and check out the Bonus Chapter at dummies.com/go/winserver2008 for a more in-depth discussion of server technologies.

Choosing Windows Server 2008

The Windows Server 2008 platform is further subdivided into multiple packages designed specifically for particular forms and functions. Understanding the distinctions among these market offerings and then understanding how they do or don't meet your requirements will help you choose the right offering for your budget and your computing needs.

In this section, we give you a look at some of the different offerings available under the Windows Server 2008 umbrella.

Meeting the Windows Server 2008 family

Microsoft follows the usual format for marketing its server family offerings, which include both 32-bit and 64-bit varieties. Some of these editions remain functionally identical to the Windows Server 2003 family. These offerings include the following:

- **Windows Server 2008 Web Edition:** Designed as a basic Internet Information Services (IIS) server platform to build and host Web applications and pages and provide eXtensible Markup Language (XML) services including Active Server Pages (ASP) and the .NET framework.

- **Windows Server 2008 Standard Edition:** Designed for small to medium businesses, this version supports file and print sharing, works with up to four processors, and accommodates up to 4GB RAM.

- **Windows Server 2008 Datacenter Edition:** Designed for infrastructures that demand greater security and reliability features, supportive of up to 64 processors and 512GB for high-availability, high-demand processing applications and processes.

- **Windows Server 2008 Enterprise Edition:** Designed for medium- to large-size businesses as a fully-functional server platform capable of operating eight processors and 64GB RAM, with enterprise-class features including clustering and virtualization.

- **Windows Storage Server 2008:** Designed as a specialized platform for network attached storage (NAS) implementations and optimized for use with file- and print-sharing services in storage area network (SAN) scenarios.

- **Windows Server 2008 for Itanium-Based Systems:** 64-bit Intel Itanium-based computers require a special version of Windows Server 2008 entirely its own.

You might be thinking, "Wow, what a diverse group of systems! You can't possibly get any better than that!" Well, that's what Microsoft was aiming for: To expand and proliferate its new 2008 platform, Microsoft has reformulated many of its top products to encompass many diverse business computing environments. In the preceding list, the items up to and including Enterprise are listed by increasing cost and capability; we don't yet have information about the cost for Storage Server and Itanium versions, so we left those for the end of the list.

Why use Windows Server 2008?

There are dozens of compelling reasons to explore Windows Server 2008 as a viable platform for any business. In the list that follows, we give you a look at some highlights and expand on features and functions provided in Microsoft's latest flagship product:

✔ **More control:** Windows Server 2008 empowers IT professionals with greater control and management over servers and network infrastructure with enhanced scripting and task-automation capabilities. Improved self-diagnostics and remote control tools create field-serviceable platforms that also may be supported across the network or via the Internet. These features are described in some detail in the section entitled "Benefits of Windows Server 2008" in the Microsoft Product Overview at www.microsoft.com/windowsserver2008/evaluation/overview.mspx.

When we speak of *field-serviceable parts,* we mean those components and devices that can be operated and fixed onsite, or *in the field.* Many computer-related issues can be resolved onsite, but there are certain circumstances where a part must be sent to a well-equipped service department or parts distributor.

Role-based, image-driven platform installation streamlines large-scale deployment processes and includes new utilities to facilitate creation of custom installation images and custom recovery images, all under one umbrella. The new Server Manager console delivers a consolidated, centralized control center for managing server configurations and related system information. See Chapter 6 for more information on the all-new Server Manager console.

✔ **Greater flexibility:** Windows Server 2008 supports custom modifications to better adapt to ever-changing business needs. Enhanced flexibility for mobile users, *integrated virtualization* (which means that one server can look and act like a bunch of servers, as far as its users are concerned), centralized application access, and new deployment options create a workable platform to suit a variety of enterprise networking scenarios.

You can create a custom installation image, or several, based on a core set of necessary applications and configurations and then roll it out to an entire enterprise in a completely automated, unattended fashion to expedite upgrades and new installations.

✔ **Better tools and utilities:** The new Windows PowerShell command line interpreter and scripting language facilitates more administrative control and productivity and better monitoring and analysis of system performance with its new Reliability and Performance Monitor. Plus, you can manage and secure multiple server types using the new Server Manager console, which provides centralized access to common administrative tools. PowerShell functionality is beyond the scope of this book and remains in beta status at the time of this writing, so we don't include material on this subject. See `www.microsoft.com/windowsserver2008/ powershell.mspx` for more details on PowerShell.

✔ **Increased protection:** Windows Server 2008 delivers improved security features that increase platform protection, reduce attack surfaces, and provide a firm foundation on which to construct and operate a business. The very core, or *kernel,* of the operating system is now better protected against various forms of attack. Windows Service Hardening makes Internet-facing services more resilient to Internet attacks, and a variety of access protections and cryptography services strengthen the Windows system. See Chapter 14 for more information on security topics related to Windows Server 2008.

✔ **New and improved TCP/IP features:** Windows Server 2008 includes many changes and enhancements to the Next Generation TCP/IP stack, such as IPv6 enhancements and policy-based Quality of Service (QoS) for enterprise networks. The Next Generation TCP/IP stack is a total redesign of traditional network stack functionality for both IPv4 and IPv6 protocol versions. Receive window auto-tuning, neighbor reachability, dead gateway detection, black hole router detection, routing compartments, and explicit congestion notification are just a few of its newly added and updated capabilities. (See Chapter 2 for more on the Next Generation TCP/IP stack.)

✔ **Self-healing NT File System (NTFS):** In the past, file system errors often required that a disk volume be taken offline for service, which clearly impacted business flow. A new feature and added benefit of the Windows Server 2008 platform is its inclusion of a real-time recovery or self-healing process for the NTFS storage format. That way, businesses can remain operational even in the face of file-system-related issues.

✔ **Server Message Block version 2 (SMB2):** The de facto standard for network file systems in the Windows realm is SMB, now revamped to handle scalable increases in server workloads more expeditiously.

✔ **Windows Server virtualization:** Windows Server 2008 provides a built-in *virtualization capability* to enable multiple separate operating system instances operating at the same time, using the same hardware. Users see multiple servers, each with their own data sets, services, and access controls, but IT departments can manage multiple virtual servers on a single set of server hardware.

✔ **Server Core:** A new installation option for Windows Server 2008 includes a stripped-down, graphical interface-free server platform that contains only those components and subsystems necessary for a high-availability server that requires fewer updates and less servicing. Envision a cluster of low-overhead, virtualized, highly optimized server operating systems running stripped-down core roles like DHCP or DNS in protected environments, completely autonomous, managed only by a single terminal, and you've got the right idea.

These are just some of the exciting new things going on with Windows Server 2008. You'll find out about many of these capabilities in more detail in the chapters that follow.

Exploring Windows Server 2008 Networking Features

Generally speaking, from a networking perspective, it's safe to assume that Windows Server 2008 does everything that previous versions of Windows Server have done — including automatic client addressing (DHCP), directory services (Active Directory), network name resolution (DNS, WINS, and so forth), as well as a whole slew of networked applications such as e-mail, databases, transaction processing, and so forth. In fact, Windows Server 2008 does more for networking than previous versions have done, especially where advanced network performance (auto-tuning and optimization), network security, network-based offload and acceleration technologies, and simplified management and diagnostics are concerned. For the complete Microsoft version of this story, see "Windows Server 2008 Networking Features" at `www.microsoft.com/windowsserver2008/platnetworking/default.mspx`.

Providing services through your server

The client-server paradigm operates largely on client requests for server services. Such requests require both server and client hardware and compatible software, which are necessary to facilitate network functionality between the two. At the most basic level, a client must have a network connection available to transmit a request for services. Likewise, the client must have the correct software installed to formulate an intelligible request and pass it to the network, where a server can notice and respond to such a request.

Servers respond to client requests through a *listener process* represented by application services such as File Transfer Protocol (FTP) and Telnet. This process runs continuously, dispatching inbound client connections as they arrive and managing transitional connection states through the native TCP/IP stack implementation.

On the software side, servers require the following elements to make services available across the network:

- ✔ **Network drivers** enable the server to communicate with its network interface. This software lurks in the background and exists only to tie the computer to the network interface.

- ✔ **Protocol stacks** send and receive messages across the network. This software also lurks in the background and provides a common language shared with clients used to ferry information across the network.

- ✔ **Service applications** respond to requests for service and formulate replies to those requests. This software runs in the foreground and does the useful work. The service application includes the listener process, the temporary execution threads, and some type of configuration or management console so that it can be installed, configured, and altered as necessary.

Most software that resides on a server is network aware because delivery of information via network is a server's primary function. Some application and protocol services that are performed on behalf of a server computer include Active Directory, SQL Server database engines, Exchange e-mail servers, and Quality of Service networking.

Three improvements to existing services and one additional service in Windows Server 2008 include:

- ✔ **Failover clustering:** Improvements to failover clusters (previously called *server clusters*) simplify setup and management and better secure cluster deployment and enhance operational stability. In addition, both networking and communication to storage devices are improved to increase availability of applications and services.

The concepts and terminologies known as *failover* and *clustering* aren't something you'll encounter with only casual computing experiences, so don't feel threatened if these are entirely foreign to you. A *cluster* is a set of servers running one or several applications and services. A *failover cluster* is one in which several server computers operate cohesively so that in the event that one fails, another takes over processing of applications and data in its place.

- ✔ **Network load-balancing:** Advances include support for IPv6 and Network Driver Interface Specification (NDIS) 6.0, Windows Management Instrumentation (WMI) enhancements, and improved functionality with Internet Security and Acceleration (ISA) Server. *Network load-balancing* redistributes the load for networked client/server application requests across a set of cluster servers.

- ✔ **802.1X authenticated wired and wireless access:** Authenticated access for both networking technologies relies on 802.1X-compatible Ethernet switches and access points (APs) to provide port-based network access control. This prevents unauthenticated or unauthorized accesses and packet transmission to user and computer resources.

Managing the user experience

Windows Server 2008 provides a single central source for managing server identities, system information, server status, configuration problem identification, and role management through the new Server Manager console. Server Manager is an expanded Microsoft Management Console (MMC) snap-in that enables you to view and manage virtually all information and tools affecting server productivity.

Server Manager replaces features included with Windows Server 2003, such as Manage Your Server, Configure Your Server, and Add or Remove Windows Components. It also eliminates the requirement for the Security Configuration Wizard to run prior to server deployment, because roles are configured with security settings by default and easily deployable once installed and configured. See Chapter 6 for more on Server Manager.

Keeping it all safe and secure

Windows Server 2008 includes an impressive array of new security applications and features that further enhance enterprise deployments, particularly within hostile environments or under potentially threatening scenarios. Today's Internet is a brightly illuminated world that casts shadows, and from those shadows arise criminal aspirations that seek to infiltrate, pilfer, and undermine Internet-accessible businesses. Microsoft has stepped up its Windows Server 2008 defenses to better serve the computing public that can't always defend against unforeseen, persistent, or stealthy attack.

The following paragraphs briefly summarize some of the new and newly enhanced security features of the Windows Server 2008 family:

- **BitLocker Drive Encryption** is a security feature of both Windows Vista and Windows Server 2008 (again sharing a common base) to provide strong cryptographic protection over stored sensitive data within the operating system volume. BitLocker encrypts all data stored in the Windows volume and any relevant configured data volumes, which includes hibernation and paging files, applications, and application data. Furthermore, BitLocker works in conjunction with Trusted Platform Module (TPM) frameworks to ensure the integrity of protected volumes from tampering, even — and especially — while the operating system isn't operational (like when the system is turned off).

- **Windows Service Hardening** turns Internet-facing servers into bastions resistant to many forms of network-driven attack. This restricts critical Windows services from performing abnormal system activities within the file system, registry, network, or other resources that may be leveraged to install malware or launch further attacks on other computers.

- **Microsoft Forefront Security Technologies** is a comprehensive solution that provides protection for the client operating system, application servers, and the network edge. In the Forefront Client Security role, you may provide unified malware protection for business notebooks, workstations, and server platforms with easier management and control. Server security can fortify Microsoft Exchange messaging environments or protect Office SharePoint Server 2007 services against viruses, worms, and spam.

- **Internet Security and Acceleration (ISA) Server** provides enterprise-worthy firewall, virtual private network (VPN), and Web caching solutions to protect IT environments against Internet-based threats. Microsoft's Intelligent Application Gateway is a remote-access intermediary that provides secure socket layer (SSL) application access and protection with endpoint security management.

- **User Account Control (UAC)** enables cleaner separation of duties to allow non-administrative user accounts to occasionally perform administrative tasks without having to switch users, log off, or use the Run As command. UAC can also require administrators to specifically approve applications that make system-wide changes before allowing those applications to run. Admin Approval Mode (AAM) is a UAC configuration that creates a split user access token for administrators, to further separate administrative from non-administrative tasks and capabilities.

- ✓ **Windows Firewall and Advanced Security** is an MMC snap-in that handles both firewall and IP Security (IPSec) configurations in Windows Sever 2008. This edition is the first to have the Windows Firewall enabled by default. It can create filters for IPv4 and IPv6 inbound or outbound traffic and protect information entering or exiting the computer through IPSec. This component replaces both the firewall applet and the IPSec and IPSec-related tool sets.

- ✓ **Network Access Protection (NAP)** is a policy enforcement platform built into Windows Server 2008 that maintains a social health order for the network environment by specifically requiring that connecting client computers meet certain criteria. Such requirements include having a current, functional firewall enabled with recent operating system updates already in place. NAP helps create custom health code requirements driven through policy enforcement to validate compliant computers before making any connections to the protected network.

Microsoft has also gone to great lengths to improve and expand upon many other security features, management and configuration applets, applications, and tools. We cover network security topics more in-depth in Chapter 14.

The Very Basics of Windows Server 2008

Windows Server 2008 is built with components that draw on the Windows Vista family of features and functionality, with added components and capabilities that extend platform coverage to encompass medium and large business computing needs. From NT's humble beginnings in the early 1990s to Windows Server 2003, Microsoft's premier network operating system server product has come a long way.

Today, Windows Server 2008 offers a reliable and scalable platform for deploying complex intranet solutions by integrating Internet and local network capabilities. In other words, this product will let you play multiplayer, first-person shooter games with people across the office or spread across the globe.

Most of the advantages and benefits you enjoy with Windows Server 2003 are contained in Windows Server 2008, along with some changes, additions, and enhancements to existing features and functionality. Most of these improvements are found under the hood, such as changes to how Active Directory works, an expansion of command line management and scripting tools, improvements to domain management, improved security mechanisms and services, greater accessibility and authentication, and some convenient new prepare and repair options in the way installations are handled.

A can't-miss interface change is the Windows Server Manager (formerly called Manage Your Server), which appears automatically when you log on. In the Server Manager window, you can manage server roles and features, and access Diagnostics, Configuration, and Storage utility categories and much more. It's up to you whether you want to use Windows Server Manager or start programs and utilities the old-fashioned way (by choosing Start). We chose to bypass the Windows Server Manager by selecting the Do Not Show Me This Console at Logon check box at the bottom of the Computer Information window pane.

The entire 2008 platform does offer some interesting promises that just might be realized. The most important of these is the reduced effort required to develop and deploy complex e-commerce Web sites, stand-alone server core application services, and large-scale simultaneous roll-outs. Windows Server 2008 (as well as the rest of the .NET OS family) is tuned to provide better Internet and network service support to clients. When used with the .NET editions of Microsoft programming languages and networking services, you can create an impressive online presence.

In the next chapter, we expand more on networking concepts, covering topics that range from multiple network interfaces to load-balancing and protocol offload processing, application services, client-based management, and wide-scale software deployment.

Chapter 2

Server Networking Principles

*F*or most applications, using Windows Server 2008 in a networked environment means buying into the client/server model. To help you understand this networking model, which explains why it's necessary for Windows Server 2008 to exist, we explore the client/server model in detail in this chapter. Along the way, you discover more about the types of capabilities and services that client-server networks provide and the various ways that clients and servers interact on such networks.

Understanding the Differences between Server and Client Networking

The client-server networking paradigm describes the basic nature of operation between two computers that establish a connection and exchange data or share resources. The process typically begins when a client caller makes a request to a server application or service — this typifies a normal client-server transaction.

Now, the server may have something to give to the client, or the client may have something to give to the server, but that aspect doesn't alter the relationship (although it may superimpose roles, particularly where a server is actually the client to another server). This is the *push/pull concept,* which describes the nature of data that is either *pushed* or *pulled* from source to destination.

Characteristically, the client will follow this process:

1. **Initiate a request.**

   The client caller requests access to some resource or information from the remote server.

2. **Wait for a reply.**

   A participating server issues a reply, either permitting or forbidding the connection, which may require authentication in some cases.

3. **Connect and interact.**

   If access is granted, the client possibly authenticates and then begins interacting in some fashion with the server.

Likewise, the characteristic behavior pattern for a server includes these steps:

1. **Listen for a request.**

   Calling clients come and go as they please, requesting to initiate and interact with hosted services.

2. **Process the request.**

   Once received, the client request may optionally require authentication.

3. **Connect and interact**.

   At this point, both client and server are connected on a common channel and able to share resources or information.

What isn't always apparent is that a single client connection may potentially involve several different servers to fulfill a single client request. Simple examples are all around you:

- ✔ E-mail clients send and receive messages from e-mail servers.

- ✔ Web browser clients broker data connections to FTP and Web servers.

- ✔ Even simple numeric dots-and-decimals addresses to human-readable hostname resolutions (and vice versa) require that your computer act as a client to a Domain Name Server (DNS).

An alternative to the client/server model that you'll hear from time to time, which we don't discuss at great length, is the peer-to-peer (P2P) network model. In this model, participants act as both clients and servers, sometimes sharing multiple parts of a single piece of data or establishing an open network of client-server hybrids capable of either sending and receiving data or sharing resources without a formal client/server role.

More Is Better: Multiple NICs (No Cuts)

Redundancy is one way of handling heavy workloads and network traffic for a single server servicing multiple clients. Multiple NICs (network interface cards) or network adapters provide separate network stacks that are better able to process a higher volume of traffic, create joined or separate subnets, or serve as an immediate fail-over when one interface goes down. You can even bind, load, and prioritize settings for one interface over another.

Redundancy also enables future network expansion without the added cost of new servers and lets administrators logically separate networks according to the network interfaces they use. Administrators can establish and maintain server gateways that firewall inbound Internet connections from outbound internal endpoint computers, interconnect otherwise separate networks and subnets, and perform a variety of other tasks.

In fact, if you take stock of the server-worthy hardware currently available on the market, you're likely to see at least two integrated network adapters on many motherboards. Cheaper manufacturing costs and constant consumer demand put those dual interfaces on board and have thus far kept them there. However, these are limited-capability network interfaces that offer only basic functionality — mostly, they just do networking. Additional features are available from some add-in cards and stand-alone network appliances that can perform other tasks generally not feasible with integrated hardware, as described in the next section of this chapter.

Networking lingo

Network stack: We use the term *network stack* in this chapter, which is the basis of any operating system's networking capability. In Chapter 1, we called this the *protocol stack,* which is the same as *network protocol stack* (or TCP/IP, mentioned later in this chapter), so the two are used interchangeably. Hopefully you won't be confused when encountering these variations in the field.

NIC: A *NIC* is the hardware component that establishes network capability and connectivity through its software applications and drivers. This is the add-in or integrated interface card where you plug in the network cable from a router, switch, or broadband modem.

Windows Server 2008 Enhances Networking

Several underlying changes to the Windows Server 2008 networking infrastructure can enhance the capability and performance of an existing (or design-phase) network, regardless if it's at home or at work. Many of these substantial changes, including total redesigns and new additions, are enterprise-oriented, where the primary emphasis is on capability, performance, and security features, and where advanced options are in the greatest demand. But that doesn't mean you can't take advantage of them, too!

In this section, we make a connection to some of these enhancements to explore what you can do with your Windows Server 2008 network environment.

Next Generation TCP/IP stack

Windows Server 2008 includes a new implementation (a complete redesign) of the original TCP/IP protocol stack called the *Next Generation TCP/IP stack*. This new framework is a total rewrite of TCP/IP functionality for both IPv4 and IPv6. It's designed to better meet connectivity and performance needs in various networking environments using various networking technologies.

For the benefit of those stuck in a cave in Patagonia since the early 1980s, TCP/IP is the de facto standard network protocol stack for most server and workstation computers you'll encounter, but it's by no means the only one. It expands to Transmission Control Protocol/Internet Protocol and serves as the foundation for network traffic shuttled across the Internet. It's become a nearly universal means for networked communications of all kinds.

The core network stack framework is improved and enhanced to increase existing functionality, complement it with supplementary performance-enhancing functionality, and further expand that framework through additional features and components.

The following section covers much of the material that's both directly and indirectly related to advances in the Next Generation TCP/IP network protocol stack in Windows Server 2008.

Here's the deal with IPv6

The new kid on the netblock is IPv6, the designated successor to IPv4 and touted as the *next best thing*.

Primary improvements provided in IPv6 include a much larger (128-bit) address space capable of addressing 2^{128} unique hosts, eliminating stopgap measures to deal with IPv4 address space limitations and enhancing security and mobility for networked computers. Despite these improvements, little actual real-world deployment of IPv6 in a general sense limits the accessibility and availability of this new protocol framework to reserved, designated working groups in the technical field.

Outside the scope of experimental and prototype networks in Europe and branches in high-tech companies, nobody is really using IPv6. Not even Cisco has shifted its internal infrastructure entirely over to IPv6 yet, so it's no surprise (to us, anyway) that not too many other organizations are charging aggressively into IPv6 deployment, either.

That said, we certainly won't deny you the privilege of exploring this new technology and experiencing the advantages, benefits, and contributions of IPv6 deployment in your personal networking environment. We will, however, encourage you to experiment entirely at your own expense of time and money. (There's just too much ground for us to reasonably cover.)

Here are a few pointers to some online resources where you may begin your journey:

✔ **"Everything You Need to Know about IPv6":** This is an Ars Technica article explaining IPv6 in (almost) plain English, complete with block-assignment diagrams. See `http://arstechnica.com/articles/paedia/IPv6.ars` for more information.

✔ **IPv6 Running, Understanding IPv6 & Advanced Implementation of Protocol:** This daily blog is dedicated to IPv6 topical discussion. Visit `http://ipv6-tips.blogspot.com` for more information.

✔ **IPv6 to Standard:** This Web page, devoted to the IETF IPv6 working group standardization process, lists and identifies vendors whose products are IPv6-enabled. See `www.ipv6-to-standard.org` for details.

Receive window auto-tuning

In TCP, a *receive window size* defines the amount of data that a TCP receiver permits a TCP sender to push onto the network before requiring the sender to wait for acknowledgement of its receipt. Correctly determining the maximum receive window size for a connection is now automatically handled by *receive window auto-tuning*, which continuously determines the optimal window size on a per-connection basis using real-time bandwidth calculations.

Improved receive window throughput increases network bandwidth utilization during data transfers. If all receivers are optimized for TCP data, Quality of Service (QoS) can help reduce congestion for networks operating at or near capacity.

Quality of Service (abbreviated QoS) refers to the ability to shape and control the characteristics of ongoing network communications services. This idea operates on the notion that transmission and error rates (along with other traffic characteristics) can be measured, improved, and guaranteed — to some extent, anyway.

Compound TCP

The Next Generation TCP/IP network stack also treats connections with large receive window sizes and large bandwidth delays to Compound TCP (CTCP), a function that aggressively increases the amount of data sent in real-time by monitoring current traffic conditions.

CTCP also ensures that it doesn't negatively impact other existing TCP connections and complements receive window auto-tuning support to provide substantial performance gains appreciable in any high-delay, high-throughput network environment.

Explicit Congestion Notification support

Lost TCP segments are assumed to be lost, probably owing to router congestion, which triggers a congestion control mechanism that dramatically reduces a TCP sender's transmission rate. With Explicit Congestion Notification (ECN; see RFC 3168, which you can find at `www.faqs.org/rfcs/rfc3168.html`) support, both TCP peers and routers experiencing congestion accordingly mark packets they forward. On receipt of such packets, a TCP peer will scale back its transmission rate to ease congestion and reduce segment loss. Windows Server 2008 now includes core support for this protocol feature.

Quality of Service (QoS) support

Windows Server 2003 and Windows XP provide QoS functionality to applications through QoS APIs, which are leveraged to prioritize time-sensitive network data delivery functions. Windows Server 2008 and Windows Vista include new facilities for network traffic management on Windows networks so that high-priority traffic is handled first, which helps with streaming media, voice over IP, video conferencing, and other applications where quick response times are needed.

Policy-based QoS for enterprise networks allows IT staff to either prioritize or manage the send rate for outbound connections, which can be confined to applications, source/destination IPv4 or IPv6 addresses, and source/destination or a range of ports.

Enhancements for high-loss environments

The Next Generation TCP/IP stack also improves network conditions in high-loss environments through several optimization features that include:

- ✔ **(RFC 2582) The NewReno Modification to TCP's Fast Recovery Algorithm:** The NewReno algorithm provides faster throughput by changing the way a sender can increase its sending rate when multiple segments in a given window are lost, and the sender receives partial acknowledgement only for segments actually received.

- ✔ **(RFC 2883) An Extension to Selective Acknowledgement (SACK) Option for TCP:** SACK allows a receiver to determine when it has retransmitted a segment unnecessarily and adjust its behavior on-the-fly to prevent further unnecessary retransmissions. Fewer retransmissions result in more optimal overall delivery.

- ✔ **(RFC 3517) A Conservative Selective Acknowledgement (SACK)-based Loss Recovery Algorithm for TCP:** Windows Server 2003 and Windows XP use SACK information only to determine those TCP segments that have yet to arrive. Windows Server 2008 includes a method defined in RFC 3517 to use SACK information for loss recovery in the event duplicate acknowledgements are received, which is maintained on a per-connection basis by the Next Generation TCP/IP stack.

- ✔ **(RFC 4138) Forward RTO-Recovery (F-RTO):** Spurious retransmissions can occur as a result of increases in round trip time (RTT). The F-RTO algorithm prevents unnecessary retransmissions, particularly in wireless environments where client adapters may roam from point to point, to return quickly to normal send rates.

These represent only some of the many additions, enhancements, and inclusions to the core network components in Windows Server 2008. For a more complete list, visit the Microsoft TechNet article at `www.microsoft.com/technet/network/evaluate/new_network.mspx`.

Offloading protocol processing

Certain specialized network interfaces and hardware are capable of offloading the often resource-intensive burden of processing TCP/IP network stack information, which requires handling of a multilayered protocol framework to deliver encapsulated data. This frees up local CPU and RAM to process other general-purpose tasks and moves the strain of ongoing network connection processes to specially-designed hardware designated for that purpose.

By *encapsulated data*, we refer to the way data is packaged as it travels down the TCP/IP network protocol stack. Higher-level protocols are *encapsulated* within header (and sometimes trailer) information so that lower-level routing and switching devices can process (and in some cases interpret) protocol data.

Protocol offload processing is supported through software that is called the TCP Chimney in Windows (discussed next) and hardware that is called the TCP Offload Engine (discussed in Chapter 3).

TCP Chimney

The TCP Chimney is a feature introduced first in Windows Vista and second — by extension — in Windows Server 2008. It's the result of Microsoft's Scalable Networking initiative, which encompasses a number of changes to the core network infrastructure of every new platform product. The goal is to reduce operational overhead associated with establishing, maintaining, and terminating *connection state* — the status of a given network connection — and all requisite state information throughout the lifetime of a connection. By removing such overhead from general-purpose resources and delegating the responsibility to special-purpose network interfaces, additional computing resources are freed up, especially on servers.

A *chimney* is a collection of offloaded protocol state objects and any associated semantics that enable the host computer to offload network protocol processing to some other network device, usually the network interface. Since NDIS 6.0, Windows Server has included an architecture that supports full TCP offload, called a *chimney offload architecture* because it provides a direct connection between applications and an offload-capable network adapter. This enables the network adapter to perform TCP/IP stack processing for offloaded connections, as well as to maintain the protocol state.

Changes to NDIS

Microsoft's Network Driver Interface Specification (NDIS) defines a standard application programming interface (API) for network adapters. The details of a network adapter's hardware implementation are wrapped by a MAC device driver so that all devices for the same media are accessed in a common, predictable way.

NDIS provides the library of functionality necessary to drive network interactions for the Windows platform that both simplifies driver development tasks and hides the ugliness of platform-specific dependencies. Some of the new features provided by NDIS specification version 6.0 are described below.

New offload support

NDIS 6.0 now supports new offloading network traffic processing functionality to compatible network adapters that includes:

- ✔ **IPv6 traffic offload:** NDIS 5.1 (Windows XP, Windows Server 2003) already supports IPv4 protocol offload processing; NDIS 6.0 also includes IPv6 traffic.

- ✔ **IPv6 checksum offload:** Checksum calculations for IPv6 can now be offloaded to compliant network adapters.

- ✔ **Large send offload (version 2):** NDIS 5.1 supports large send offload (LSO), which offloads the segmentation of TCP protocol data into 64K blocks. Large send offload 2 (LSOv2) in NDIS 6.0 now offloads much larger blocks.

Support for lightweight filter drivers

Intermediate filter drivers are replaced by lightweight filter (LWF) drivers, a combination of an NDIS 6.0 intermediate driver and a miniport driver. LWF improves performance, consolidates protocol driver support, and provides a bypass mode where LWF examines only select control and data paths.

Receive-side scaling

Multiprocessor computers running Windows Server 2003 or Windows XP associate a given network adapter with a single processor. That individual processor must handle all traffic for that interface, despite the fact that other processors may be available. This impacts Web- and file-server performance when client connections reach the serviceable limit of that associated processor.

Incoming traffic that can't be handled by either network interface or server processor will be discarded, which is undesirable in just about every situation. This increases the number of TCP/IP-oriented session serialization and sequence identifiers and amplifies performance penalties as a result of network stack retransmissions.

Both *session serialization* (sessions encoded as a sequence) and *sequence identifiers* (unique numeric values associated with serialized sessions) are related to the protocol stack. These properties help identify what portions of data are assembled and in what order, such that portions arriving out-of-order are properly reordered and those that never arrive are requested again.

Windows Server 2008 no longer associates a network adapter to a single processor; instead, inbound traffic is distributed among the available processor array and processed accordingly. This feature is called *receive-side scaling,* which allows for more inbound traffic on high-volume network interfaces. A multiprocessor server computer can scale its ability to handle incoming traffic without additional hardware, so long as compliant network adapters are already in place.

Networking Is About Services, Too

In the first part of the chapter, our discussion of Windows Server 2008 principles covers mostly the new *features* included to core networking components, the NDIS 6.0 API, and protocol offload processing. Networking isn't just about these features — in fact, they represent the unseen or *transparent* infrastructure upon which all services are built and operate.

Networking is much more than the communications protocols, offload engines, and security frameworks that serve as the basis for connectivity. Networking might not have a purpose or place without the necessary application services that server computers host for client computers (comprised of workstations and servers), so that both may interact in some fashion.

A network, by and large, is for the people — the very endpoint representatives that create network connections. But it isn't entirely about what the people — or clients — want; much of the way a network infrastructure is designed, constructed, and maintained is dictated by what the business wants and needs.

In the following sections, we take a closer look at the very distinctions that differentiate client and server wants and needs in terms of application and background services.

What clients want

Client computers and personnel want a lot of things: easy access, worry-free reliability, unfaltering dependability . . . and probably some other things they aren't quite sure of or don't know how to articulate in techie terms. Who wants to configure an IP address every time a connection is made to the same, or any, network? What about sharing a common connection among other computers?

Simple naming schemes, remote Web-based application access, and transaction-driven database services are just some of what clients want. Let's delve a little further into these topics for your personal benefit.

DHCP

Dynamic Host Configuration Protocol (DHCP) is a set of rules used by network communications devices to request and obtain an IPv4 or IPv6 address lease assignment from the available pool of administrator-specified addresses. DHCP alleviates the need for network administrators to actually make such assignments by hand, freeing them up to handle other tasks.

A DHCP server ensures that uniquely-generated, dynamically allocated IP assignments are made to connecting clients, along with whatever preferential server settings may apply to the client connection. However, it can also ensure that the same IP is given only to a specific machine every single time it connects. DHCP is successor to an older Boot Protocol (BOOTP), which achieved a very similar goal.

DHCP automates not only the assignment of IP addresses but also subnet masks, default gateways, and other lease-related parameters. On boot-up, a connecting client will issue a request to the network for its personal address assignment to the DHCP application service. In turn, the service applies a set of rules that govern the assignment and return the requested information back to the client.

DHCP provides three modes for allocating addresses:

- **Dynamic:** Clients are provided an address assignment lease that expires after some specified duration of time. Reconnecting client computers may or may not receive the same IP address, and no real concern is given to consistency.

- **Automatic:** Also known as DHCP Reservation, an automatic assignment is one where a given address is permanently assigned to a particular client. The DHCP server selects from a range specified by the administrator.

- **Manual:** Client-based address selection and DHCP protocol message response inform the server of the new address allocation. The DHCP server performs the allocation based on a table with interface hardware or MAC addresses, where administrators manually specify IP and MAC pairs for connecting clients.

Network administrators not only reduce the amount of repetitive and potentially unnecessary effort associated with manual address assignments, but also eliminate the potential for configuration mistakes when configuring multiple clients.

Windows Server 2008 enhancements to DHCP include IPv6 support (DHCPv6) and Network Access Protection (NAP) enforcement, which requires a connecting DHCP client to prove its system health status before receiving an address assignment.

NAT

Network Address Translation (NAT), *network masquerading*, and *IP masquerading* are all terms used to describe rewriting packets as they pass through an intermediary networking device to appear as if they originated from that device. There are many NAT arrangements, types, and variations, but all operate along the same lines.

NAT confers two profound advantages on outbound network traffic:

- ✔ It permits internal networks to use private IP addresses as per RFC 1918 and handles incoming and outgoing traffic to make that arrangement work.
- ✔ It hides the details of internal network addresses, whether public or private — which explains the masquerading terminology used in the preceding paragraph.

There are several distinct advantages to this kind of arrangement. For starters, NAT insulates internal computers from external probes, keeping crime out like a security fence. At the same time, NAT enables many internal computers to utilize a single external network connection where only a single IP address is assigned. NAT originally began as a response to the IPv4 address space shortage but has proven useful in many other ways.

Sometimes, communications protocols can be sensitive to alterations in packet header data. NAT mangles the original data contained in a packet, which can disrupt certain types of security protocols that absolutely require a packet to pass from sender to receiver unaltered. This was the case for IPSec when it first arrived on the scene because critical portions of header elements were modified by NAT, upon which IPSec relied. As a result, connections failed, and trouble followed close behind. Today, such traffic is handled without much difficulty, thanks to innovations in how NAT works and how security protocols are used.

Internet Protocol Security, abbreviated IPSec, is an addition to the TCP/IP framework that includes more reliable security mechanisms for an otherwise insecure network environment. Such capability is usually involved with large-scale environments spread across geographically diverse networks, or anywhere sensitive business applications and services are privately shared over the Internet.

NAT can be used for load-balancing for connection redirection, as part of a failover design to establish high-availability, as a transparent proxy for content caching and request filtration, or to connect two networks with overlapping addresses.

Name services

Windows Internet Naming Service (WINS) is Microsoft's implementation of NetBIOS Name Server (NBNS) on Windows and is very similar to the relationship between DNS and domain names. This is a basic service for NetBIOS computer names, which are dynamically updated and mapped through DHCP. WINS allows client computers to register and request NetBIOS names and IP addresses in a dynamic, distributed fashion to resolve locally-connected Windows computer resources.

A single network may have several WINS servers operating in push/pull replication, perhaps in a decentralized, distributed hub-and-spoke configuration. Each WINS server contains a full copy of every other WINS server's records because there's no hierarchy as with DNS — but the database may still be queried for the address to contact (rather than broadcasting a request for the right one).

WINS is only necessary if pre-Windows 2000 clients or servers or Exchange 2000/2003 clients are present and resolving NetBIOS names. Realistically, most networking environments are better served by DNS as a preferable alternative to WINS, particularly in Windows Server 2003 or 2008 environments. However, WINS remains an integral function in Windows network to support older clients using legacy software.

Application access

Terminal Services (TS) in Windows Server 2008 implements Microsoft's most powerful centralized application access platform and offers an array of new capabilities that reshape administrator and user experiences alike.

TS provides centralized access to individual applications without requiring a full-fledged remote desktop session (although that's still an option). Applications operating remotely are integrated on local user desktops, where they look and feel like local applications. An organization can employ HTTPS over VPN to secure remote access to centralized applications and desktops.

Using TS in a Windows Server 2008 environment enables you to:

✔ Deploy applications that integrate with the local user desktop.

✔ Provide central access to managed Windows desktops.

✔ Enable remote access for existing WAN applications.

✔ Secure applications and data within the data center.

Windows Server 2008 TS includes the following features:

- ✓ **TS RemoteApp:** Programs accessed through TS behave as if they run locally on a remote user's computer. Users may run TS RemoteApp programs alongside local applications.

- ✓ **TS Gateway:** Authorized remote users may connect to TS servers and desktops on the intranet from any Internet-accessible device running Remote Desktop Connection (RDC) 6.0. TS Gateway uses Remote Desktop Protocol (RDP) via HTTPS to form a secure, encrypted channel between remote users.

- ✓ **TS Web Access:** TS RemoteApp is made available to remote end users through TS Web Access, which can be a simple default Web page used to deploy RemoteApp via the Web. Resources are accessible via both intranet and Internet computers.

- ✓ **TS Session Broker:** A simpler alternative to load-balancing TS is provided through TS Broker, a new feature that distributes session data to the least active server in a small (two to five) farm of servers. IT administrators can even map several TS IP addresses to a single human-addressable DNS name, so end users needn't be aware of any specific settings to connect and reconnect TS broker sessions.

- ✓ **TS Easy Print:** Another new feature in Windows Server 2008 enables users to reliably print from a TS RemoteApp program or desktop session to either a local or network printer installed on the client computer. Printers are supported without any installation of print drivers on the TS endpoint, which greatly simplifies the network sharing process.

In addition, the Application Server role in Windows Server 2008 provides an integrated environment for customizing, deploying, and running server-based business applications. This supports applications that use ASP.NET, COM+, Message Queuing, Microsoft .NET Framework 2.0/3.0, Web Services, and distributed transactions that respond to network-driven requests from other applications and client computers.

The Application Server role is a requirement for Windows Server 2008 environments running applications dependent upon role services or features selected during the installation process. Typically, this role is required when deploying internally-developed business applications, which might be database-stored customer records interfaced through Windows Communication Foundation (WCF) Web Services.

Data-based services

Centralized application and data access helps secure sensitive and/or personally identifying information to the remote working environment. Less data leaving the corporate network reduces the risk of accidental or incidental data loss through the interception, theft, or misplacement of company note-books. Through TS Gateway and TS RemoteApp, participants can be limited to a single application or several resources, without exposing any more infor-mation than necessary to do their jobs.

For those mobile users out in the field, BitLocker Drive Encryption provides a complete cryptographic solution to safely and securely store sensitive data at rest. Everything up to core Windows operating system data and files gets cryptographic coverage so that tampering by unauthorized parties is thwarted, even if the hard drive is removed and the notebook is manipulated in any way.

Windows Server 2008 File Services are technological provisions that facilitate storage management, file replication, folder sharing, fast searching, and accessibility for UNIX client computers. See Microsoft TechNet articles for information on these features.

Web-based services

Task-based Web server management is handled in Internet Information Services (IIS) 7.0, a powerful, modular platform for remote applications and services with enhanced security, featuring health monitoring for Web services. IIS 7.0 and .NET Framework 3.0 provide the basis for application and user connectivity, enabling users to distribute and visualize shared information.

Windows Server 2008 SharePoint Services is a scalable, manageable platform for the collaboration and development of Web-based business applications. This can be installed as an integrated server role through the new Server Manager console — no more downloading and running Setup. The SharePoint Products and Technologies Configuration Wizard runs you through the instal-lation process for server farm configurations, dramatically easing the deploy-ment options for large-scale enterprise networks. Consult Microsoft TechNet articles for more information on SharePoint Services.

What enterprises want

Enterprise wants and needs far exceed anything the desktop or workstation consumer group can possibly offer. Most of those wants and needs center around managing resources or maintaining connections among desktops, workstations, and other server computers.

Active Directory

Active Directory (AD) is an implementation of the Lightweight Directory Access Protocol (LDAP), a protocol and service framework that delivers directory services to Windows-based networks. AD provides central authentication and authorization services, global policy assignment, widespread software deployment, and large-scale updates for an entire organization.

AD Directory Service (DS) is used to centrally store and manage information about the network resources spread across a given domain. The framework itself holds a number of levels that include forests, domains, and trees, as described in fuller detail in Chapters 7 and 8.

Access controls

Employees are defined by their roles or capacities within an organization. There are leadership roles, management roles, and general occupational roles to fulfill, each defined by separate duties, privileges, and responsibilities. Among those privileges and responsibilities are varying layers of access to business-related information. For example, a general employee has no real reason to access or modify management-related information, such as work schedules or other employees' contact information.

In much the same way, users are defined in a system by their access privileges on that system. Access controls are captive restrictions set in place on server computers necessary to prevent accidental, intentional, and unauthorized use of data, files, and settings, particularly those critical to system operation.

One feature Windows Server 2008 brings to the table is Network Access Protection (NAP), which enforces strict *health checks* on all incoming client connections. That is, it inspects the state of the client to make sure it meets requirements for antivirus and antispyware coverage and currency, Windows update currency, and so forth.

Policy-based controls

Policy-based controls on the Windows Server 2008 platform are evident virtually anywhere a user or process interacts with the system. Active Directory (AD) Domain Services are a global configuration policy-driven framework used to define various Windows network parameters for an entire organization. Policy-based control is also apparent in protective access mechanisms deployed on the network to enforce certain requirements for connecting computers.

Microsoft's Network Policy Server (NPS) is an implementation of Remote Authentication Dial-In User Service (RADIUS), a network-policy checking server and proxy for Windows Server 2008. NPS replaces the original Internet Authentication Service (IAS) in Windows Server 2003 and performs all the same functions for VPN and 802.1x-based wired and wireless links, and performs health evaluations before granting access to NAP clients.

Policy-based controls also encompass the variety of various Windows Server 2008 core components and features like network protocol-oriented QoS and system-wide directory services provided through AD.

Client management

In addition to NAP features that ensure an optimal level of health for Windows Server 2008 networks, a number of other useful client management tools are natively available on the platform. TS Remote Desktop Connection (RDC) 6.0 remotely verifies that clients are connecting to the correct computers or servers. This prevents accidental connections to unintended targets and the potential to expose sensitive client-side information with an unauthorized server recipient.

TS Gateway also provides for endpoint-to-endpoint sessions using the Remote Desktop Protocol (RDP) with HTTPS for a secure, encrypted communications channel between various clients that include FreeBSD, Linux, Mac OS X, and Solaris.

Software deployment

There's a lot of redundancy in virtually every modern computing and networking environment. There are multiple workstation computers for multiple employees, possibly built with dual memory banks, dual-core processors, and doubled-up RAID drives and NICs, communicating with load-balanced servers operating in round-robin fashion — just to give a thumbnail perspective of a much bigger portrait. Chances are good that in an environment like this, when you configure, install, or modify something once, you'll have to repeat that same action elsewhere.

Large-scale software deployments are one clear instance of this observation. Generally, you don't install just one computer but several. It may be a few dozen, or it may be several hundreds or thousands. Either way, do you really want to process each case individually by hand? We didn't think so, and neither do most administrators, which is why you hear things like "unattended" or "automated" installation.

Windows Server 2008 further enhances the software deployment cycle by realizing a simple principle: Build a modular, easily modified, unified image format through which all subsequent installation images are created, each unique only in the features it removes or adds to the base. The Windows Imaging Format (WIF) creates an abstract modular building block for operating system deployment so that you can create in-house install images that incorporate whatever applications, configurations, or extensions you deem necessary. Then, you can roll out multiple installs at a time in a completely self-contained, automated fashion that can even include previously backed-up personal user data and settings.

Chapter 3

Building Your Network

*W*hether you're constructing a complete network or simply renovating an existing network, the basic approach is the same. You begin by planning what you want to implement, and then you gather the ingredients necessary to realize your plans. Next, you have to execute those plans according to the blueprint that you devised. The execution of any successful network project plan involves bringing all the pieces together, applying solid organizational principles to your network, and documenting what you add (and what's already in place) to your network.

Developing a Network Implementation Plan

Whenever you set forth on a network project, start by analyzing your requirements. If you're building a network from scratch, this phase can take weeks or even months of effort; if you're simply extending or repairing an existing network, planning may take a day of your time or less.

Whatever your project's scope, your plan should contain the following:

> ✔ **A brief statement of your overall objectives, plus a more lengthy statement of requirements that addresses the following:**
>
>   • *What applications and services users need to access*

- *Estimates of user-to-server bandwidth requirements*

- *Estimates of server-to-server bandwidth requirements (where applicable)*

For example: The new XYZ Inc. network will provide 60 users with access to Windows Server 2008 file and print services, plus access to a SQL Server sales and inventory database. Each user will require no more than 6 Mbps bandwidth, and there are no server-to-server bandwidth requirements during business hours because all backups are scheduled for after-hours and weekends.

✔ **A complete list of all the elements that you must purchase or otherwise acquire to meet those objectives.**

For example: At, XYZ Inc., three different department servers (Accounting, Manufacturing, and Sales) will act as routers to link two network segments of 10 users each, for a total of six user segments based on 100 Mbps Ethernet. The three servers will be connected with a 1000 Mbps Ethernet backbone using Gigabit Ethernet (GbE). We will purchase six 16-port 10/100 Ethernet hubs (one per user segment, each with two GbE links for the corporate backbone) to leave room for growth, and three dual-core 2.13 GHz Intel Xeon 3050 server machines, each with 8GB RAM and 2TB of disk space, along with a 16-port GbE switch to handle the backbone itself. We will also attach three Buffalo TeraStation Pro II network attached storage (NAS) units so that we can back up all three servers across the backbone.

✔ **A description of the role each element will play on the network, the location of each element on the network, the configuration of each element, and the time during the installation process in which you plan to add each element to the network.**

You should use a map or a set of plans to help you place cables, computers, and other components, and a timeline to indicate the order in which you have to install everything.

For example: The Accounting server will handle users from the Accounting and Purchasing departments; the Manufacturing server will handle users from the Manufacturing and Engineering departments; the Sales server will handle users from Administration as well as from the Sales and Marketing departments. All servers, the backbone, and all hubs will be installed when the company is closed between Christmas and the new year. The network should be operational when normal business operations resume. A map of this network appears in Figure 3-1.

✔ **A test plan that describes how you plan to test individual elements, individual cable segments, and the entire network (including who is responsible for specific tasks) to make sure everything functions properly after you finish the installation.**

For example: The three servers will be installed first and tested individually the weekend before the Christmas break. On December 23 and 24, the GbE backbone will be installed. On December 28, the backbone will be tested. On December 28 and 29, the hubs will be installed and tested. On December 30, workstations on all existing 10-Mbps cable segments will be connected to the new 10/100 hubs and tested individually. From December 31 to January 2, automated testing software will exercise the entire network. On January 3, a network technician will visit our site with Bob, the site administrator, and any last-minute changes, repairs, and adjustments will be performed. We believe the network will be ready for use on January 4.

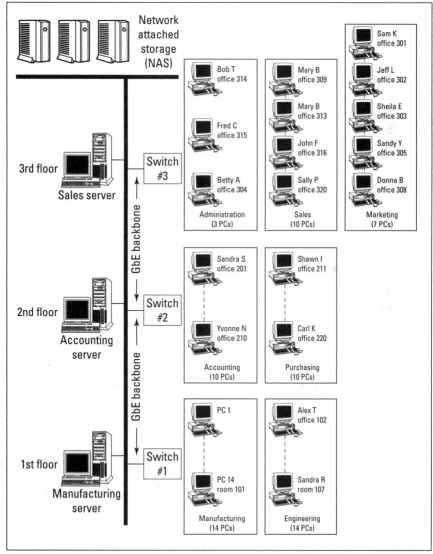

Figure 3-1:
A simple map of XYZ Inc.'s network shows all switches, servers, and cable segments laid over a simple floor plan.

This plan helps you to decide where you must place key network elements, such as servers, switches, routers, and other network devices. More importantly, the plan also helps you determine what type of network technology and bandwidth you need to deploy to meet your objectives. Because most businesses work on a budget, building a plan also helps you make sure that you won't try to spend more than you're allowed to spend or incorporate more exotic technologies than you can afford. Your network implementation plan should also help you evaluate your current network backbone or plan a new one to be able to carry all the traffic that normally comes together on such critical network segments.

Understanding Network Design's Barest Basics

The possible implementations from which you can choose when designing a network are innumerable. To help you distinguish between what's improbable, possible, feasible, and recommended when designing your network, here's a set of helpful guidelines:

- **Select a network technology:** When adding to or expanding an existing network, this decision is easy — it simply requires choosing something identical to or compatible with whatever you're using. For new networks, you need to analyze what kinds of applications and services users require:

  - *For ordinary office work* (e-mail, word processing, spreadsheets, basic database access, and so on), 10/100 Mbps Ethernet works well.

  - *For high-traffic or real-time applications* — such as Computer Aided Design (CAD), imaging, video conferencing, and voice over network — either 100 Mbps Ethernet or GbE to the desktop makes sense, depending on end-user bandwidth requirements.

  - *For high-availability or mission-critical business applications* — such as on-demand services and business-to-business applications — both redundant network configurations and failover clustering (first introduced in Chapter 1) should be part of your initial IT infrastructure design.

  It's seldom necessary to deploy GbE to all desktops, but some may need it. So plan carefully to provide gigabit connections to those who do need it, and likewise, plan your backbone carefully to make sure it can handle all the aggregated bandwidth needs. (In some rare cases, a 10 GbE backbone might be required, but usually not for most small- to medium-sized operations.)

✔ **Position office equipment close to users:** When designing a network, the smartest thing you can do is minimize the distance between users and the resources they use most. This applies to printers (so users enjoy easy access to output), servers (so cable runs needn't be too long), and other resources (such as fax machines, scanners, and copiers) that users need to access to do their jobs.

✔ **Closely situate mutually-dependent servers:** Keep in mind that some servers act as front-end clients to other servers, which stands in contrast to the typical client-server role. Maintain close proximity for these servers to minimize bandwidth utilization to a reasonable level and leave the longer pathways between client and server.

✔ **Build an online work environment:** When designing a network, you also have to take into account current working patterns and arrangements in your offices. (For example, if the Accounting and Purchasing departments work together all the time and use the same applications, perhaps they should share a server.) This also applies to the type of network you build. For small companies, centralized control and tight security may hamper your workers; in large companies, centralized control and tight security are the norm. You must serve the communities that currently exist in your organization and use the network to help users communicate and be as productive as possible.

✔ **Arrange servers, hubs, and other key resources:** The places where wiring congregates — namely at punchdown blocks, wiring centers, and equipment rooms (or closets) — sometimes dictate where certain equipment must be placed. Be sure to check the distance between those locations and the areas where workers reside. In most cases, offices are designed to support cabling from a centrally located wiring center or equipment room for groups of offices. If that isn't the case in your workspace, you may have to add new equipment rooms and wiring centers or move workers to bring them closer to existing facilities. Either of these solutions takes time and costs serious money, so be sure to get management involved in deciding which options make the most sense for your organization.

✔ **Build better backbones:** Depending on your network technology choice, you'll probably want to arrange your network to include a special highway for data to travel across when multiple network cables come together. This can happen between servers, as with the XYZ Inc. example in this chapter. Such portions of the network are called *backbones*.

A backbone can be something as simple as a so-called *collapsed backbone*, in which a high-speed switch links multiple cable segments and provides a single, high-speed connection between all cable segments. A backbone can also be as complex as a *staged backbone*, in which intermediate segments jump from switched 100 Mbps-Ethernet to switched GbE at the server (as in the XYZ Inc. example in this chapter). More complex backbones might even include a segment of 10 GbE on the innermost segment, where traffic is heaviest.

✔ **Plan for growth:** When planning a network, include at least 30 percent spare, unused capacity in your design. This spare capacity should include *network ports* (unused ports on switches), unused network cables in offices and cableways, and bandwidth on individual network segments and switches. That way, you can grow within your current environment for a while without having to redesign your network on a regular basis. If your annual growth rate exceeds 30 percent, design at least one year's planned growth into your network — better yet, one year's planned growth *plus* 30 percent.

✔ **Work within the system:** As you discover when you start deploying a network in any organization, networks have a political as well as a technical side. When you plan a network, you should work within your system in at least two ways:

1. *Make sure that management knows about and approves of what you plan.*

2. *Make sure that you handle the work, contracts, purchases, and so on within the rules and regulations of your organization.*

If you neglect either of these guidelines, the only thing you'll learn how to network is trouble!

✔ **Check your design:** After you put a network design down on paper, review that design against what you know about the network technologies it uses. Be especially careful to check maximum cable lengths, maximum number of devices per segment, and maximum number of cable segments and devices between any two ends of the network against the rules that apply to the technologies you plan to use. You don't want to build a network that tries to break these rules. If you do, your network may not work, or worse, it may work for a while and then quit working when you add users or devices. If you check your work before you build, you won't try to build something that can't work or that's inherently prone to trouble.

✔ **Ask for a sanity check:** After you've put a network design down on paper and checked your work, you should also solicit input from one or more networking experts. Redesigning a network is always easier while it's still on paper; you don't want to fix a flawed design after you've built a network. The more qualified advice you get before you start building, the better off you'll be in the long run. In fact, this advice is worth paying for because it can save you a world of hurt (or your job, for that matter).

Although this list of network design principles isn't exhaustive, it should lead you toward designing a network that works best for your organization. Because these guidelines consider work patterns, politics, and organizational rules as well as technology, the resulting network should serve your organization well for more than just technical reasons.

Deciding Where Networking Devices Must Go

You must purchase the necessary equipment, cables, connectors, and so on and start deploying the components that make a network work. When you start situating key network equipment — including servers, storage or backup devices, switches, and routers — you need to make some important decisions about how to situate them particularly as they fit into your existing network plan.

For small organizations of 25 people or less, using separate locked facilities to store hubs and servers may not make sense. Small organizations tend to be more informal and are less likely to have the kind of budget that supports a full-time information systems (IS) staff. In these circumstances, you usually want to situate your networking gear along with all your other gear — out in the open with other equipment for easy access to one and all. If you do put the networking gear out in the open, make sure that only users with valid passwords can log on to such equipment. Otherwise, we highly recommend locking it up.

Larger organizations tend to be more concerned about security and control, and therefore, they usually situate key networking components in locked equipment rooms and in locked wiring closets or wiring centers at various locations around their offices. Because the equipment has to be close to the wiring, it isn't uncommon for servers to reside in wiring closets along with punchdown blocks, switches, and other networking equipment.

Only authorized personnel should be allowed to access these facilities. Likewise, only authorized personnel should be allowed to add users or equipment to the network, usually within a system of regularly scheduled updates or maintenance. In office buildings, for example, this usually means one or two wiring closets or equipment rooms per floor, where only authorized personnel have keys or access codes to get into these rooms.

Choose an approach to situating your servers that makes sense for your organization, and stick with it. If you're going to follow rules for placing equipment, share those rules with employees so that they know what's going on. In fact, formulating a security policy for most networks is a smart move, and you should regularly explain that policy to your employees in detail. (For more information on this subject, see Chapter 14.)

Most small- to medium-sized companies — such as the fictitious XYZ Inc. mentioned in this chapter — put their servers into small, locked rooms at each end of the floors they occupy in an office building. This keeps the distances between users' desktops and the wiring centers acceptably low and puts their servers alongside the punchdown blocks and switches they use, which helps manage wiring. This approach also provides controlled access to the equipment and software that makes their networks work in a small number of closely managed locations. Finally, it addresses the need for adequate ventilation and power control that hubs and servers require for proper operation, which many wiring closets don't offer.

Consider Hiring an Expert to Install Cable and Equipment

Normally, you install cable and equipment at the same time you build a network. You may run your own cables for your network and perform all equipment installation and configuration yourself; you may contract both the cable and equipment installation out to third parties, or you may choose some point between these two extremes. Whichever way you go, somewhere along the way you'll be ready to put the finished pieces of your network together.

When it comes to installing cable, we highly recommend that you employ experienced cable installers with good references. The company that owns or operates your office building may even require a licensed cable installer to perform any such work. Here's why this is a good idea:

- ✔ Adherence to building and fire codes is mandatory, but it can also be tricky; working with an experienced professional is a good way to avoid trouble.

- ✔ Cable placement and routing are sensitive; trained professionals know how to avoid potential trouble spots and always test their work to make sure that the network will behave properly.

- ✔ High-speed networks are much more finicky and prone to installation difficulties than lower-speed networks. The faster you want your network to go, the better off you'll be if you leave the cabling to an expert.

- ✔ Consult with network installers and professionals to acquire an accurate concept as to how to lay your cable. They don't necessarily have to install your network if you already have capable hands onboard, but in the event you receive outside assistance, make sure they provide you with the cabling plans for your organization.

Always Check Your Work!

If you decide to install cable and/or equipment yourself, we strongly advise that you bring up your network in small, manageable pieces. When installing multiple cable segments, as when linking one wiring closet to another or each wiring closet to the backbone, bring up individual segments one at a time and test them to make sure each one works before connecting all of them. Likewise, if you're installing a backbone or a server cluster, test individual components separately before trying them out en masse.

When you install equipment, apply the same principles. After you install and configure a machine, check it by itself to make sure it works before attaching it to the network. This is as appropriate for switches and routers as it is for server and desktop computers, as well as network attached storage devices.

 Our suggestions on piecewise checking and gradually increasing the complexity of your network come from experience. We found out the hard way that throwing everything together at once can cause problems that are too hard to troubleshoot because you have to deal with too many unknowns.

Evaluating Your Network's Performance and Usefulness

After you build a network, you may be tempted to rest for a while to enjoy your success. After all, you've earned it, right? Well, although you should certainly pat yourself on the back, you should also realize that the real work begins as soon as users start using the network (or a new portion of an existing one). If you're responsible for a network, you must not only keep things running for the moment, but also keep them running — and running well — over time.

Whereas the network you build or extend may meet your users' initial needs, any network's capability to meet users' continuing needs diminishes over time. Growth, change in technologies, and new applications and services guarantee that nothing stays the same for long in the workplace — this includes your network as well as the systems and services that the network delivers to your users.

Therefore, you need to conduct regular reviews of how well your network meets users' needs. In small or slow-growing organizations, you may have to review the network only once a year. In large or fast-growing organizations, you should review the network on a quarterly basis.

Your network review should include at least these three elements:

✔ **Traffic analysis and usage review:** You can conduct this yourself by using the built-in Windows Server 2008 tools and facilities, such as System Monitor, and third-party software tools. The idea is to take a performance and behavior snapshot of your network during ordinary-load, light-load, and peak-load conditions. If any of these loads encroach on the boundaries of what the current design can reasonably support, start planning to extend and expand your network.

✔ **User interviews:** You can interview selected users on a one-on-one basis in your organization or hold meetings with individual workgroups and departments. The idea is to give employees a chance to share their observations, gripes, and wishes regarding the network. This can give you a great opportunity to not only gauge user satisfaction and networking knowledge, but also determine whether you should give employees additional training on how to use the network more effectively.

✔ **Management review:** You should meet with members of management regularly to find out what they're planning and what future information-processing needs they're considering. You can also gauge management's impressions of and beliefs about the network as you report your findings from the previous two items to them.

If you perform these reviews and keep in touch with upcoming changes and requirements, you can keep your network and your organization better synchronized. Planning for change and growth is essential to modern networks because they've become critical business tools that organizations depend on to do their work. If you take an active approach and plan, you can stay ahead of the curve!

Creating a Network Map

Earlier in this chapter, we introduce you to most of the basic principles involved in designing and building a network. By now, you have a pretty good idea about how networks work. As you spend more time around networks, however, you may realize that what they do isn't nearly as important as what you know about what they do.

Whether you wrestle with networks only occasionally or full-time, you may discover that there's nothing like a network map to help you find and keep track of routers, switches, and other network appliances on your network.

It isn't a map; it's the whole enchilada

Calling the collection of data that describes your network a *map* doesn't do this concept justice. A network map is certainly more than a mere drawing that shows where network components live on your network, but creating such a drawing is a great way to start building a network map. If you look at the following list of devices and properties that a network map should contain, you'll see why such a map is more than a mere depiction:

- A list of all computers on your network, with supporting documentation

- A list of all network equipment — such as servers and switches, plus any routers, firewalls, and so on — with supporting documentation

- A list of all printers and other similar equipment on the network — such as scanners and fax machines — with supporting documentation

- Lines to indicate where cables run and where punchdown blocks, wall plates, and other media-related elements are located

Capturing data for your network map

Because a network map is so important and such a powerful tool, pause right here and start one immediately. Be prepared to spend some time and energy on this project because most of the data that makes up a network map is scattered all over the place.

Building a detailed network map is a worthwhile investment. It can pay for itself many times over as you come to depend on it. At worst, you discover more about your network than you ever wanted to know (but not more than you'll ever need to know). At best, you get to know your network so well that it will seldom throw you a curve ball — and you may even find some things to tweak and tune while building that map.

Starting at the foundation

Obtaining a set of your building's architectural drawings or engineering plans can help a great deal. If you can find any drawings or plans, take them to an architect's supply store and make copies that you can mark up and use as a base map. (Most plans are created using an old-fashioned, ammonia-based copying system called *blueline.* You can copy even large-sized plans for less than $25 per plan.)

If a professional cabling outfit installed your network, you should be able to get a copy of their cabling plans, which work even better than architectural drawings or engineering plans because they probably already show where the cable is laid and how much of it you have. This is another good reason that do-it-yourself may not be the best way to cable your network.

If no such plans are available, you can sketch a room-by-room layout on rectangular grid paper (such as an engineering pad) to make it easy to draw to scale. Be sure to mark the location of machines, devices, approximate locations for cable runs, and so on. A network map drawn to scale enables you to visualize the network layout, including any potential problem areas or unforeseen complications in the final design.

Anything on your network should be on the map

Anything that merits attention or costs money is worth recording on your map. You don't need to go into great detail about each and every connector or note the exact length of every cable. (Approximate lengths within a meter or so are useful, however.) Indicate every major cable run, every computer, and every piece of gear attached to the network.

Taking stock of your network

The information you gather while producing a network map creates a detailed inventory of what's on your network and where everything's located. Unfortunately, you quickly find out that this is a lot of information.

To make keeping an inventory easy for yourself (and for anyone who follows in your footsteps), build a template or form that you can fill out for each item on the network. This approach forces you to collect consistent information and makes delegating information gathering to others easier. Include all of the following information for each computer on the network:

> ✓ **The hardware configuration for each machine:** Include a list of all interfaces and their settings, information about installed RAM and drives, and the make and model of the keyboard, display, and so on. If you can find out who sold you the equipment, write that down, too.

> Keeping track of equipment is typically the accounting department's responsibility. Check with those folks for a copy of your company's capital assets or a depreciable items inventory (if available). This type of documentation normally includes serial numbers and other identification for hardware on the network. If no one in your company has gathered such information, collect it yourself. It's valuable.

✔ **The software configuration for each machine:** Include lists of configuration files, operating system data (including version number, most recent Service Pack applied, and so on), as well as a list of programs and versions installed on the machine.

✔ **The network configuration for each machine:** Include the make and model of each *network interface card* (NIC), plus a list of driver files with names, version numbers, dates, and sizes. You can capture such data to a file easily on Windows systems by choosing Start➪Programs➪Accessories➪System Tools➪System Information➪Hardware Resources; use this as the basis for this inventory. (On Windows XP, Windows Vista, and Windows Server 2003/2008 systems, the menu selection begins with Start➪All Programs.)

In addition to information on each computer, your inventory should also include the following data:

✔ **A list of other equipment, such as switches, routers, storage devices, and printers:** Include the manufacturer, model, make, and serial number for each piece of equipment. If the equipment includes memory modules, disk drives, or plug-in interface cards, get information about them, too. If the equipment uses software or firmware, record the name, version, release date, and any other information you can garner about such items.

✔ **A list of all the cable segments on the network:** Give each segment a unique name or number and associate your records with whatever type of identifier you use for those segments. Record the type and make of cable, its length, the locations of its ends, and any significant connections or intermediate locations that you may have to visit in the future.

✔ **A list of all the vendors who've worked on your network or its machines:** Include names and phone numbers of contacts at each operation. This can be a valuable resource for technical support and troubleshooting. Over time, add the names and phone numbers of tech support or other individuals at these organizations who prove to be knowledgeable and helpful.

Essentially, the information gathered while creating and maintaining a network map forms a database of everything anyone needs to know about your network. To improve access to and usability of this data, consider storing the text for your network map in an honest-to-gosh database engine. If this is too labor-intensive, a file- or paper-based approach works, but it takes more effort to maintain over time. Whichever method of recording data for your map you use, be sure to keep your inventory complete and up-to-date.

Applications such as Visio (Microsoft Office's diagram and visualization application that can be found at `http://office.microsoft.com/en-us/visio/default.aspx`) and Cheops (an active network visualization tool that can be found at `http://cheops-ng.sourceforge.net/`) can help you create network maps. Search your favorite search engine using the keywords *network visualization* to find other applications and companies that can help you with this process. If you don't want to spend money on such a tool, add the words *free* or *open source* to the front of the search string.

When the network changes, so does the map!

One thing that you can always be sure of when it comes to networks: They're always changing. Your map is only as good as the information it contains. And the map remains useful only if that information is an accurate reflection of the real network in your organization.

Whenever anything changes on your network, make updating the map and its associated database a priority. Sitting down and checking your map is much less work than walking around and looking at the real objects that the map shows. If the map is current, you can keep on top of things from the comfort of your office. If it's out of date, you'd better start walking!

Network Interfaces: Built-ins versus Extender Cards

Integrated and add-in components continue to define the basic classifications for most computer hardware. Some consumers, consultants, and computer geeks swear by and base buying decisions purely and solely on this distinction. Why, then, is this distinction so incredibly special?

The advantages and disadvantages for built-in versus extender cards used to be much different only a few years ago, when components and technologies just weren't up to speed with the best-of-breed, high-speed network capabilities. As internal processing power and speed continue to increase, so does networking power — albeit separately and for its own reasons. Point being, these two computing properties are beginning to find that happy medium, which is perhaps best illustrated by the fact that GbE network interfaces are built into most contemporary retail motherboards, and server motherboards usually have two or more built-in GbE interfaces.

One primary difference remains unchanged: serviceability. Clearly an integrated network solution is an island unto itself when damaged, even though it's physically very much a part of the motherboard. That's actually the crux of the problem — it can't (easily, if at all!) be removed, and replacement can be costly, up to whatever the price of the same or similar motherboard replacement costs. Usually it isn't so bad — a simple GbE replacement NIC costs an average of $50 as we update this chapter, whereas fancy but very fast GbE NICs can cost from $100 to as much as $800.

As mentioned earlier, a Network Interface Card (NIC) is the basic physical component that enables you to have network capability on any given computer. This also requires a network stack and driver software and may involve a third-party configuration utility or application.

Don't knock your NIC

Don't underestimate the worth of your NIC, and certainly don't overestimate the capability of a cheap store-bought generic card. The problem with cheap network cards is the same as anything else: cost-saving, corner-cutting, conservative-thinking manufacturers skimp on form and feature to produce a market-ready, low-budget offering. Sure, these generic cards are okay for mundane machines handling lightweight, mundane chores. But we aren't even operating on that level — we have Windows Server 2008 to empower and embolden our network, and there's no sense in cutting cost on the NIC because the difference in price is negligible to savings that can be realized elsewhere.

Here are a few points to consider when researching NICs for your network:

- Which computers will connect to the network
- Connection types (wired, wireless) and interfaces (UTP, fiber)
- Network interface properties and services (TOE, Quality of Service, and so on)
- Security principles and procedures (encryption and encapsulation protocols)
- Server- or workstation-specific roles and responsibilities

For the most part, NICs are all the same for workstations, servers, and notebook computers. Their packaging, features, and capabilities are all specific to the particular needs and uses for the computers they go into. The interfaces for Ethernet and GbE are exactly the same — it's mainly in the way that the medium is used that makes up the biggest difference. However, a fiber interface is incompatible with a GbE interface and requires some intervening piece of network hardware to connect the two. While many such technologies can and often do intermix on the same network, there may be performance bottlenecks that occur with each transition between separate interface types and technologies. Such bottlenecks are unavoidable because there will always be some transition between several network technologies and protocols in a large-scale network environment, especially the Internet.

Remember that a computer is for computing and a router is for routing. Although a computer can perform the same tasks as a router (and then some), it may be considerably wasteful in some circumstances and just plain overkill in others. When given the option, always buy a router for routing purposes and leave the computing tasks to computers (and vice versa).

Don't stub your TOE (TCP Offload Engine)

Why make something your responsibility if it doesn't have to be? After all, offloading responsibility is how a lot of managers — ahem, we mean management applications — operate in the network world. The TCP Offload Engine (TOE) is one such technology built into network interfaces that offloads processing of the entire TCP/IP network stack directly onto a specialized NIC controller. This process no longer has to be the typical burden to your main CPU and RAM!

This tactic is employed within high-speed NICs and networks (typically Gigabit Ethernet and 10 Gigabit Ethernet) where handling network stack overhead is most significant. Because TCP is a *connection-oriented* protocol, this increases the complexity and processing overhead related to the establishment of serially-controlled connections, checksum and sequence number calculations, sliding window recalculations, and eventual connection teardown and termination. In short, there's a lot of computation and tracking required while TCP is busy at work, and that workload increases with network speed and increased demand.

TOE is a response to the increased load and network resource demand imposed by GbE hardware and the invariable increase in resource utilization. When the computer carries this burden, the CPU is interrupted repeatedly from processing normal applications and processes, which slows performance gradually to the point that perceptible signs of performance degradation can appear. As the network expands coverage and aggregates multiple GbE links, even the most powerful servers will eventually suffer performance penalties under intense load. Clustering, virtualization, Internet SCSI (iSCSI), and Remote Direct Memory Access (RDMA) have all contributed to the increasing use of TOE-enabled network interface cards because they leave more server oomph to deliver services and handle requests outside the network communications realm.

The ever-popular ping test

Perhaps nowhere is groping more appreciated than within an unresponsive network environment, where it's perfectly okay and even warranted to reach out and touch your neighbor — or several of them. *Packet Internet Groper (ping)* is a basic network diagnostic command that enables you to check link state and troubleshoot connectivity problems by sending stimulus packets to another endpoint or intermediary device on the network, which elicit responses from participating network devices and computers.

Ping is an essential first resort when testing network connectivity — it establishes a baseline and jump-off point for further investigation or immediate resolution. You usually precede issuance of the ping command only by an obligatory physical cable connection check to ensure sanity and eliminate any silly probable causes.

Ping works by issuing Internet Control Message Protocol (ICMP) echo request packets to a destination and then awaits echo reply response packets. This is sometimes dubbed *ping* and *pong* in honor of tabletop tennis. Ping uses interval timing and response rates, estimates round-trip time, and reports any packet losses that might occur.

Chapter 4

Hooking Up Your Network

. . . .

. . . .

*B*uying computers doesn't make a network! You have to interconnect computers to enable them to communicate. You can set up communications among computers in several ways; the one you choose depends on your budget and bandwidth needs. Okay, most of it depends on your budget!

Transmission media is a fancy, generic term for cabling and wireless transmission technologies. The media provide the means by which computers talk to each other across a network. In fact, computers can communicate through the airwaves using broadcast transmissions, through the wiring in a building, or through fiber-optic cabling across a campus. Linking long-distance or Internet connections to local networks means that there's almost no limit to what your network can access!

In this chapter, you also examine different methods to interconnect networks using cables and other media. You find out which media are appropriate for desktop access and which work best for server-to-server activity. You also discover more about network anatomy as we tackle two ticklish subjects — namely, backbones and wide area network (WAN) links.

Make a Network Medium Happy!

A happy network medium has nothing whatsoever to do with a TV psychic. Rather, finding the right *network medium* means implementing network cabling that won't cause bottlenecks. Depending on whether you're building a network from the ground up or starting from scratch, you may need to take a different approach to evaluating cabling options for your network:

✔ If you step into a job where a local area network (LAN) is already in place, cabling is probably in place, too. Evaluating the type, capabilities, and usability of an inherited network is almost always a good idea. That way, you can decide whether you can live with what you have, or whether some change will do the network good. You may learn, for example, that old cabling causes so many difficulties that you're better off replacing or upgrading it. (We've popped out ceiling tiles and found badly spliced cables hidden from view.)

✔ If you're planning a brand-new network, one of your concerns is to determine your cabling needs. Decide which network cabling you're going to use *before* ordering equipment for your network because you can often order computers and peripherals with the appropriate network interface cards (NICs) preinstalled and preconfigured. (Of course, NICs are preinstalled and preconfigured on an existing network, which means your choices have already been made for you.) The more work you save yourself, the better!

✔ If a contractor handles your cabling maintenance, don't assume that every old cable gets replaced if it isn't completely up to snuff. A contractor may choose to reuse substandard cables to save on material costs. Without proper wiring, your network may be in constant trouble. (Or it may not work at all.)

If you work with a cable contractor, require the contractor to test each network cable and insist that the contractor provide you with those test results. In fact, many companies hire one contractor to install cables and another to test them. By doing so, they ensure that the common tendency to overlook errors or potential sources of problems on a network can be avoided — plus, it never hurts to get a second opinion.

The most common cabling technology for LANs is *baseband cable,* which is cable set up for baseband transmission. For this reason, we concentrate on baseband cable in this book. Check out the sidebar titled "Use the right pipes in your network's plumbing" for a description of baseband transmission and how it differs from broadband transmission.

If you know what to look for, the name of a particular type of cable can tell you all about its transmission properties. Ethernet cable notation (set down by the Institute of Electrical and Electronic Engineers, or IEEE) breaks down as follows:

✔ The speed of the Ethernet in Mbps

✔ The cable's technology — broadband or baseband

✔ The cable's rated distance in hundreds of meters or the type of cable — twisted-pair or fiber-optic cable

KEY CONCEPT

Use the right pipes in your network's plumbing

Wiring in a network is like plumbing in a house. Just as pipes form the pathways through which water flows to and from your plumbing fixtures, a network's wiring provides the pathways through which computers transmit data using electrical signals. The amount of data that computers can move through a wiring system at any one time depends on the characteristics of the wires, or pipes, installed. The larger the pipes, the more data the computers can send simultaneously.

You can think of a network's *bandwidth* as the size of a network's pipes. Bandwidth represents a range of usable frequencies and is measured in hertz (Hz). A higher hertz rating for a network medium means higher available bandwidth. Higher bandwidth translates into bigger pipes to carry data. Just because you have big pipes, however, doesn't mean you always get to fill them completely. Therefore, it makes sense to try to measure the actual amount of data (called *throughput*) flowing through the pipes.

Different types of cabling are rated for different amounts of data flow at different distances. Remember, however, that even if a pipe is big enough to handle all the water you send through it, that pipe can still get clogged. As a result, although a given amount of data can theoretically flow through a cable, in the real world you may see less data flow than the maximum bandwidth indicates. Plumbers will tell you that mineral deposits and other obstructions can often restrict the water flow in pipes. In keeping with our metaphor, we can say that noise, cross-talk, electromagnetic interference (EMI), and other network maladies can often degrade the actual performance of your cable. *Throughput,* commonly measured in bits per second (bps), describes the actual amount of data that's flowing through a cable at any one time.

If you take one pipe and divide it into little pipes, you've just reinvented the concept of *broadband transmission* (in which multiple transmissions at different frequencies use the same networking medium simultaneously). If the pipe is kept whole instead of subdivided, you end up with the concept of *baseband transmission* (in which the entire bandwidth is used to carry only one set of frequencies and one transmission at a time).

Whew! Got all that? Maybe it's time to call Roto-Rooter!

For example, 10Base5 is an Ethernet designation that stands for [10 Mbps] [baseband] [5 x 100 meters = 500 meters]. From the name alone, you can tell that the baseband cable is rated to handle up to 10 Mbps on a segment up to 500 meters (1,640 feet) long.

Any time you see a T or an F in such a name, replace that letter with either *twisted-pair* or *fiber-optic,* respectively. For example, *10BaseT* means that this particular baseband Ethernet cable is rated at up to 10 Mbps using twisted-pair cables. Likewise, *10BaseF* means the same thing, except that it uses fiber-optic media instead of twisted-pair.

Fiber and coax make a seriously twisted pair

Fiber-optic cable is different from twisted-pair and coax cable because it transmits data using light signals instead of electrical impulses. When you look at the layout of the cable, it appears similar to coax but has a glass or plastic fiber as its inner conductor instead of a copper wire. Figure 4-1 shows you what the inside of a fiber-optic cable looks like.

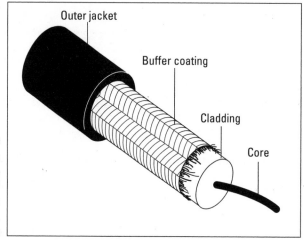

Figure 4-1:
An inside view of fiber-optic cable.

Notice that the inner glass core is sometimes called *buffer coating,* and the entire cable has another strong jacket around it. The outer jacket is designed to be thick enough to protect the inner fiber from being broken when the cable is handled (with care, that is).

Fiber-optic cable

Although it has a higher price tag than electrical cables, fiber-optic cable can also handle greater bandwidth, which means that it can transfer more data over longer distances. Fiber-optic cable is largely immune to electromagnetic interference (EMI) and other sources of noise that affect electrically conductive cables. One factor that adds to the expense of fiber-optic cable is the care required during installation. A knowledgeable technician must carefully polish each glass fiber with specialized tools and then add special connectors to the cable.

You often find fiber-optic cable installed between buildings in campus environments or between floors in a building. You rarely see fiber pulled to the desktop because of the expense involved — you must use fiber-optic NICs, and you must attach two cables to each workstation because one cable transmits outbound signals and the other receives inbound signals. Although the appetite for bandwidth is always increasing, don't expect your desktop to have a high-fiber diet anytime soon!

In some locations, such as hospitals, it's necessary to run fiber-optic cable to some desktops because X-ray and MRI equipment can interfere with electrical cables. Also, the bandwidth requirements for medical imaging equipment can be so extreme that conventional electrical cables can't handle the traffic involved.

For light signals to pass through a fiber-optic cable, you have to attach a transmitter to one end of the cable and a receiver to the other end. This is why you need two cables to permit any one device to send and receive signals. On the transmitting end, an injection laser diode (ILD) or a light-emitting diode (LED) sends light pulses down the cable. These light pulses reflect within the glass core and bounce against the mirror-like cladding through the length of the cable until they reach a photo diode receiver at the cable's other end. Notice that data flows in only one direction. The receiver converts incoming light pulses into electrical signals and passes the data to the NIC.

Because of the way that light pulses travel through fiber-optic cable, splicing two such cables requires great care so that the cable's signal-carrying capabilities aren't reduced. Otherwise, a light pulse may arrive at the splice but may not make it through to the other end of the cable. We call this situation a *bad splice*, but your users will call it much worse names!

Coaxial cable

Coaxial cable, also called *coax*, was once the most popular transmission medium for networks. However, with the cost of unshielded twisted pair (UTP) dropping significantly in the last few years, it's hard to justify supporting legacy coax cabling, NICs, and other network connection devices. Older networks used coaxial cable exclusively before UTP arrived in the mid-1980s. Initially, only thick coaxial cable (which we like to call "frozen yellow garden hose") was available. Thick coax is quite cumbersome to handle and a real pain in the neck to install. Imagine pulling a frozen garden hose through the ceiling and then having to connect *transceivers* (a portmanteau or combination of two words *transmitter* and *receiver)* to that cable! Maybe a frozen garden hose is easier after all. . . .

Coaxial cable incorporates two layers of insulation. Beginning in the middle of the cable and spanning outward, the cable has a copper wire surrounded by a foam insulator, which is surrounded by a wire mesh conductor that is then surrounded by an outer jacket insulation. This jacket, in turn, is surrounded by a plastic casing, called *cladding*. Figure 4-2 shows a cross section of a well-dressed piece of cable.

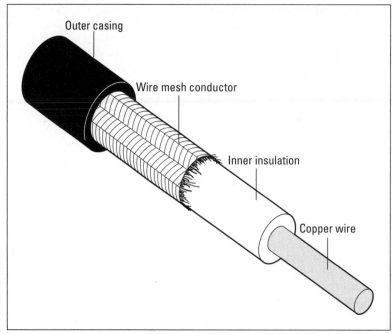

Outer casing

Wire mesh conductor

Inner insulation

Copper wire

Figure 4-2:
An inside
view of coax
cable.

Suffice to say, coaxial cable types are a dying breed in the local network segment, apart from the hybridized technology described in the next section,
but remains steadfast in its behind-the-scenes placement as a provider of
multimedia networking, television, and telephony service. We won't go into
their distinctions and differentiations, but we will leave you with one last
remark.

If you have a small network and a highly restricted budget, 10BaseT Ethernet
is absolutely the way to go. It's standardized, well-utilized here and abroad,
and is plentiful and cheap on the open market. There really is no cost justification for legacy coaxial equipment, only the operational justification to support existing legacy coaxial applications and services within the organization.

Hybrid networking

Hybrid fiber-coaxial (HFC) is the telecom industry term for networks that
incorporate both optical fiber and coaxial cable to produce a broadband network medium for handling high load and large subscriber traffic. This seriously twisted pair is capable of carrying and delivering a wealth of features
and services that include analog and digital television signals, video-on-demand
programming, and switched digital video, telephony, and high-speed data.

HFC network coverage extends from the cable operator's point of presence to
a through point at a neighborhood hub site, which terminates at a node that

services from 25 to 2,000 homes. This cable operator's master location also houses telephony equipment for providing telecom services to the community, which is individually delivered via coax. Therefore it's common to have the same provider supply both phone and Internet services (and possibly public television access, where applicable) to the same location.

HFC is the primary technology used to service many modern cable modem communities, so the technology is very widespread and widely utilized. In fact, it's likely you're already using the technology at home or work without even knowing it. That's the beauty behind transparent technologies — they work diligently for us, sight unseen, as long as we continue to rely upon them.

Wireless is media, too!

Speaking of things unseen, a relative newcomer to the high-speed network interface assortment is another IEEE design, the 802.11 wireless (WiFi) family of multiple over-the-air standards and modulation techniques. There are a number of competing technologies and substandards to the 802.11 specification, but they all essentially operate in much the same fashion. Instead of using hard, physical network links to transmit data, WiFi pushes and pulls information through the air using radio frequencies. While this brings a lot of eye-popping reactions to those previously unfamiliar with the technology, it does give those of us with some working knowledge and experience of these devices a moment to reflect and relate the reality of such devices operating in a business network environment.

First and foremost is the fact that no physical medium is present. This defies the logic built into most CSMA/CD-type of access methods, where you can satisfy line contention by merely listening on the wire for any ongoing communications and waiting some period of time before trying to transmit or retransmit data. (See the "Carrier sensing access methods" sidebar for more on CSMA/CD.) Instead, participant WiFi devices must request to speak before opening the lines for communication, which is a more active role than the more passive eavesdropping approach employed by 802.3 Ethernet. This creates extra overhead that increases with the number of participating devices in the effective vicinity of the radio.

This lack of physical medium also opens the network to other, unintended listeners. An eavesdropper can more easily observe, record, and potentially intrude upon wireless network traffic. In fact, the would-be attacker need not be inside the building to observe wireless traffic. There is also a limited effective range for such equipment, since radio signal has a difficult time permeating dense walls full of thick, absorbent material like metal, wood, and other elements. Shade trees can also deflect radio signals and cause connectivity problems for courtyard or outside network coverage. Additionally, any competing RF devices in the area will cause distortion, noise, and contention, which also reduces the effective reach and range for most WiFi devices. So you have to deliberately and thoughtfully design the WiFi network to fit the environment and its signal- or quality-reducing attributes.

Data transfer rates are typically half (or less!) of the manufacturer's rated speed for any given WiFi device operating under normal conditions:

- ✔ Early 802.11b devices operate on the 2.4 GHz frequency (which incidentally coincides with common cordless phones and causes much interference) and tend to realize around 4 Mbps, or much less than their rated 11 Mbps transfer rate.

- ✔ 802.11g, the next step up, also operates on 2.4 GHz and realizes around 19 Mbps versus a 45 Mbps maximum throughput rating.

    Fortunately, each device is backwards compatible in that an 802.11g device can and will work with an 802.11b device, but only at the maximum effective throughput of the slower (802.11b) performer.

- ✔ The 802.11n standard, which has remained in draft status for quite some time now, operates on 2.4 or 5 GHz channels at speeds between 74 Mbps and 248 Mbps, which easily eclipses anything previously seen in an airborne data-bearing communications medium. However, this technology is pricey and adds more cost than actual value to networks with existing GbE or better network infrastructures.

Of all the available options, 802.11g and 802.11n are the best suited for high-speed multimedia networks, especially where multiple users are involved.

Windows Server 2008 includes several changes and enhancements to 802.11 wireless support, such as a native Wi-Fi architecture that features user interface improvements for wireless connections; wireless Group Policy enhancements and auto-configuration capability; and Wi-Fi Protected Access 2 (WPA2) support. The new wireless architecture also integrates with Network Access Protection (NPA) when using 802.1X authentication, provides Wi-Fi diagnostics, and supports command-line settings configuration.

A final note about cabling

If you're going to install cable yourself instead of hiring a cable contractor, here are a few final notes we'd like to share with you:

- ✔ **Obtain a copy of the blueprints for your building or floor and make sure that all the electrical devices and outlets are clearly marked.**

    This map assists you in placing cable away from electrical devices or motors that can interfere with your network. You don't want to install cable near elevator motors, transformers, or other heavy-duty electrical devices (unless you're using fiber-optic cable, and even then, you need to protect it from potential sources of damage or wear and tear).

✔ **Obtain all relevant local, state, and federal building code regulations and make sure that your plans conform to such ordinances.**

You need to evaluate these requirements before purchasing any cable because some codes require you to purchase plenum-rated, fire-retardant cable. Other codes require you to use plenum-rated cable only when you run cable through locations that are likely to catch fire rapidly. In any case, it behooves you to know the rules before you purchase and install a network.

Plenums are the air-handling spaces between the ceiling of one floor and the bottom of the floor above where cable is often strung. Fires spread more rapidly in these areas because air carries fire rapidly; therefore, plenum-rated cable is mandated for use in such spaces to keep fire and smoke from spreading through a building.

✔ **Determine which parts of the network you can build and maintain on your own and which parts you need to subcontract.**

For example, if you have the time and inclination to build cables and also have the time to troubleshoot the network when those cables don't work, so be it. We recommend that you buy as much prefabricated cable as possible and make cables only when you absolutely must. Why? Because companies that make cables do it all the time, and they're good at it. If you make cables for your network only occasionally, you may introduce problems.

✔ **Try to hire a contractor to install cable for your LAN.**

The wiring is your network's infrastructure. If the wiring isn't installed properly, it can cause endless network snafus. Wiring contractors should provide you with bids, install the cabling, label all cables, test and certify all cables, and provide you with final documentation. You're responsible for keeping them on track. Don't assume that a contractor will follow local ordinances unless you make him or her do it. Put all expectations in writing and keep tabs on the work.

Raising the Bandwidth Ceiling

As organizations have come to depend on LANs and WANs, they've put more applications and information on their networks. Speedy retrieval of such information becomes critical to such organizations. This retrieval is where the need for additional bandwidth most often manifests itself.

Conventional text-only documents don't normally put much strain on a network. But today, data often takes the form of audio, video, graphics, and other types of multimedia. Such files or data streams are much larger than plain-text files and often impose delivery deadlines on networks. If this is hard to picture, think how frustrating it is when the audio track and the video track get out of synch on your TV, and then multiply this frustration by several orders of magnitude. Then consider what delivering time-sensitive audio, video, or multimedia data over a network really requires.

Such complex forms of data can easily consume the full bandwidth of an ordinary 10 Mbps network while handling only one or two users' needs. That's why an increasing appetite for higher-bandwidth networks is emerging in the workplace. Such added bandwidth is increasingly necessary to handle the more complex types of data traversing the network and to prepare the infrastructure to deal with emerging applications, such as network teleconferencing, network telephony, collaborative development, and all kinds of other gee-whiz technologies now under construction.

This is why we feel compelled to tell you about some of the cabling alternatives available for today's networks that might be able to handle tomorrow's bandwidth needs.

Carrier sensing access methods

Networks use sets of rules, called *protocols*, to communicate with one another. Some network technologies operate in a free-for-all, in which any computer can send and receive data whenever the shared network medium isn't already in use.

Computers must listen to the media to determine whether it's in use (indicated by active signals on the media). If a computer wants to transmit, it stops and listens, like the well-mannered little computer it is, to see whether someone else is talking. If the computer doesn't hear any signals, it can go ahead and transmit right away. When another computer does the same thing at more or less the same time, data from one computer collides with data from

another, and both computers must back off and try again.

You want to have something in place to deal with these kinds of collisions. Ethernet implements *Carrier Sense Multiple Access/Collision Detection* (CSMA/CD), whereas 802.11 wireless uses CSMA/Collision Avoidance (CSMA/CA) to monitor radio channels and wait for an opportunity to broadcast or transmit data. Because there is no physical medium for 802.11 transmission, compliant network devices must be designed to listen for radio signals on designated channels.

The names that describe how these technologies access network media are called *access methods*.

100 Mbps Ethernet

Two flavors of 100 Mbps Ethernet are available today, each with its own particular access method: CSMA/CD (this means Carrier Sense Multiple Access with Collision Detection; we discuss it in detail in the sidebar titled "Carrier sensing access methods") and demand priority (as described later in this chapter). When proposals for 100 Mbps were solicited, two factions emerged: one that used the same CSMA/CD access method used in conventional Ethernet (now known as *Fast Ethernet*, or *100BaseT*) and another that used a demand priority access method (now known as *100BaseVG-AnyLAN*).

Both factions put proposals forward to implement their approaches. Curiously, both proposals were ultimately accepted as standards, but each one fell under different IEEE committees. Today, the Fast Ethernet standard falls under the 802.3 standards family, and the 100BaseVG-AnyLAN standard falls under the IEEE 802.12 standards family.

100BaseT is similar to 10BaseT except that it runs 10 times faster. When implementing 100BaseT, you need to use equipment designed for 100BaseT throughout your network. But otherwise, designing and building the network is pretty much the same as for 10BaseT. It's even possible to mix and match 10BaseT and 100BaseT technologies on a single network, but you need to include hubs that have 10 Mbps and 100 Mbps capabilities to bring these two worlds together.

100BaseVG-AnyLAN offers the same bandwidth as 100BaseT but uses four pairs of wires instead of two pairs in each cable. Doubling the number of pairs enables a different access method, called *demand priority,* to control access to the network medium. In addition, 100BaseVG-AnyLAN permits devices on the network to receive and transmit at the same time. (That's one reason that the number of pairs doubles.)

100BaseVG-AnyLAN hubs help manage the demand priority scheme and provide arbitration services when multiple requests for network access occur at more or less the same time. When using the CSMA/CD access method, workstations listen before sending, and they transmit as soon as they recognize that the medium isn't in use. This arrangement leads to collisions when two or more stations begin to broadcast at more or less the same time, especially as network utilization increases. When a demand priority device wants to transmit data across the network, it signals the hub, and the hub determines when that device may access the network. This setup eliminates collisions and allows networks to function at higher utilization rates than CSMA/CD can support.

On the downside, networking equipment and cabling for 100BaseVG-AnyLAN is more expensive than that for 100BaseT, even though 100BaseVG-AnyLAN offers better performance. Perhaps that's why 100BaseT has proven more popular in the marketplace than 100BaseVG-AnyLAN has.

Gigabit Ethernet

You're probably wondering what you can implement on your network when you start running out of bandwidth even with 100 Mbps technology. From there, the next step up is to Gigabit Ethernet. Although Gigabit Ethernet technologies are currently available, they aren't yet in broad use. However, because the need for speed will never decrease, we want to give you a taste of this technology so you can salivate over it — even if it's unlikely to show up in your office any time soon.

To begin with, Gigabit Ethernet isn't typically used as a networking solution for the desktop. (In fact, no conventional PC or other desktop machine can come close to saturating a Gigabit Ethernet network.) Rather, Gigabit Ethernet is used primarily as a backbone technology, especially in large networks where certain pathways need to carry huge amounts of traffic. Ideally, Gigabit Ethernet helps boost server-to-server communications and permits ultra-fast data transfers between switches on a network backbone.

Gigabit Ethernet uses the CSMA/CD access method and the same frame size and formats as conventional Ethernet. Therefore, you can integrate this technology into existing Ethernet networks easily, and you don't need to buy new protocol analyzers, network management software, and so forth.

To jump on the Gigabit Ethernet bandwagon, the devices you need to add to your network include

✔ Suitable NICs and connectors for your servers

✔ Proper cables (fiber-optic, in most cases, though twisted-pair options are under development)

✔ Upgrades to the routers and switches that handle Gigabit Ethernet traffic

In some cases, this emerging standard may require you to replace certain pieces of equipment; but modern routers and switches need only new EPROM chips and upgrades for certain interface cards. Eventually, as the price of the technology drops, you may even consider adding Gigabit Ethernet interfaces into your high-end workstations. This probably won't be necessary for a few more years, however.

3com offers a terrific white paper on this technology. You can download it at www.3com.com/other/pdfs/solutions/en_US/10g_whitepaper.pdf. It gives a great overview of Gigabit Ethernet and describes what types of applications demand this kind of network speed.

The Backbone's Connected to . . . Everything Else!

As mentioned in the previous section, 100BaseT and Gigabit Ethernet are both well suited for network backbones. If networks have backbones, do they also have hip bones and tailbones? How about it?

In networking, the *backbone* is a particular cable segment that connects other cable segments or that provides a high-speed link to accommodate high-volume network traffic on cable segments where large quantities of traffic aggregate. If you think about this situation for a minute and take a quick look at Figure 4-3, you should begin to understand that saying "a cable segment that connects other cable segments" and "a cable segment where large quantities of traffic aggregate" are two ways of saying the same thing.

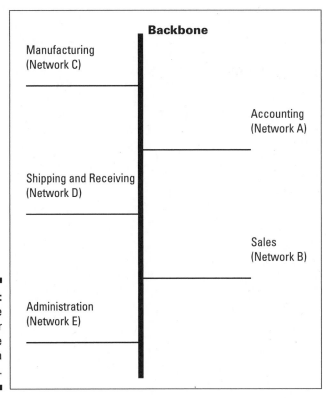

Figure 4-3:
A backbone ties together all the pieces of a network.

Simply put, a backbone provides a link to tie together many other cables. As the demand for network bandwidth goes up for individual users, the amount of traffic that backbones must carry increases accordingly. Backbones also often provide links to outside resources, such as the Internet, or access to massive centralized data collections, such as mainframe databases and their ilk.

Part II
Servers, Start Your Engines

The 5th Wave   By Rich Tennant

"Configuring it has been a little tougher than we thought."

In this part . . .

*H*aving covered server basics and introduced the star of the show in Part I, we try to cover something more tangible in Part II — installing and setting up a network infrastructure built around Windows Server 2008.

Starting with the methods for and steps involved in installing Windows Server 2008, you'll see and understand what makes it tick and how to get it up and running on a system of your careful choosing. You also learn how to organize your server-based network and set up and populate the directory services that are so essential to a satisfactory server situation.

Along the way, you also discover how to install and use print services with Windows Server 2008 and how to manage those pesky network addresses that enable PCs to communicate with each other. As you unfurl the grand structures that support a well-designed Windows network, you'll come to appreciate the many things it can do for you and your users.

Chapter 5

Ready, Set, Install!

*I*nstalling Windows Server 2008 is relatively easy, but getting from start to logon takes a while. Fortunately, you can reduce many of the delays with just a little planning. And by following our suggestions in this chapter, we hope that you can avoid some common installation problems, many of which relate to a lack of correct equipment. We also provide a troubleshooting section to smooth out any ruffles you encounter along the way.

Windows Server 2008 further streamlines the installation process by putting all site-specific configuration data at the *end* of the installation process, on your first boot-up to a fully installed desktop. You'll know when you reach that point because you'll see the Initial Configuration Tasks dialog box.

Planning the Installation: Upgrade or New?

Whether you're installing Windows Server 2008 from scratch or upgrading from a previous version, planning helps to ensure a smooth installation:

> ✔ **Upgrading**, as the term implies, means that you want to install Windows Server 2008 over an existing operating system on your computer and, in the process, retain as many settings as possible. Windows Server 2008 provides numerous upgrade paths from Windows Server 2003. (See

Table 5-1 for a complete list of upgrade paths. This table applies equally to 32-bit and 64-bit versions; however, cross-platform [32-bit to 64-bit and vice versa] upgrades aren't supported.)

Note that there's also an upgrade path from beta versions of Windows Server 2008. If you elect to perform an upgrade installation of Windows Server 2008 from a beta, we strongly urge you to begin by backing up all the data on every machine that you plan to upgrade. (We cover backups in Chapter 13.) Although you can upgrade to Windows Server 2008 without losing data, hardware and software sometimes have minds of their own and mess things up. A smidgen of prevention can prevent some real headaches!

✔ **Installing** means you're adding Windows Server 2008 to a computer that may or may not already have an existing operating system. On systems with existing operating systems, you have the option to replace the current one or create a multiboot system. A *multiboot system* is a computer with two or more operating systems installed. You can choose which operating system you wish to load at bootup. In some multiboot configurations, data from one operating system isn't accessible from other operating systems. For example, you can't access NTFS partitions from Windows Server 2008 from Windows 95 or Windows 98.

Rest assured that Windows Server 2008 will install in a multiboot configuration with Windows Vista because they share the same code base — particularly the unique Boot Configuration Data capability. So you won't have to put forth any extra effort with these two; previous editions of Windows (or other OS platforms) are an entirely different matter.

Table 5-1	Windows Server 2008 Upgrade Paths		
If You're Running . . .	*. . . Upgrade to This 2008 Edition*		
	Standard	*Enterprise*	*Datacenter*
Windows Server 2003 R2 Standard Edition	X	X	
Windows Server 2003 SP1 Standard Edition	X	X	
Windows Server 2003 SP2 Standard Edition	X	X	
Windows Server 2003 R2 Enterprise Edition		X	
Windows Server 2003 SP1 Enterprise Edition		X	
Windows Server 2003 SP2 Enterprise Edition		X	
Windows Server 2003 R2 Datacenter Edition			X
Windows Server 2003 SP1 Datacenter Edition			X
Windows Server 2003 SP2 Datacenter Edition			X

If you're installing Windows Server 2008 for the first time, you need to make some decisions about how you're going to set up the server *before* you install the software. You can install Windows Server 2008 in the following three basic ways:

- ✔ **DVD-ROM:** This installation requires that you have a computer with a local DVD-ROM drive installed. DVD-ROM installations don't require a network interface, but if you plan to connect the system to a network, it's best to have the network interface in place during installation. We focus on this type of installation in this chapter.

- ✔ **Across the network:** This type of installation requires network access, where the DVD-ROM files are available. Network access can be gained either from an existing operating system or a boot floppy.

- ✔ **Automated:** This type of installation requires you to input installation information into a data file that you can then merge into a script file for execution.

You can also start installing Windows Server 2008 in several ways:

- ✔ **DVD-ROM boot installation:** If your computer allows the DVD-ROM drive to participate in the boot sequence, you can boot the Windows Server 2008 installation program right from the DVD.

- ✔ **DVD-ROM from operating system installation:** If the operating system on your computer lets you access the DVD-ROM drive, you can launch the Windows Server 2008 setup without much hassle. (See the "Step by Step: Installing Windows Server 2008" section, later in this chapter, for details.)

- ✔ **Across the network installation:** Do this if the Windows Server 2008 installation files are available from another computer on the network. You can share the files on a shared DVD-ROM drive, or copy the contents of the distribution DVD onto a shared network drive. See the "Installing across a Network" section, later in this chapter, for details.

- ✔ **Remote installation:** Microsoft offers its Remote Installation Services (RIS) to enable network administrators to push a Windows Server 2008 installation out to network systems. (*Pushing an installation* means that an administrator can deploy Windows Server 2008 on a network without going to every target machine to launch its setup by hand.)

Handling preinstallation tasks

Before installing Windows Server 2008, you must perform a few preparatory preinstallation tasks. These include the following:

- ✔ **Check for application compatibility.** Use the Microsoft Application Compatibility Toolkit (ACT) to ascertain compatibility information about network applications and also to prepare Windows Server 2008 for installation. See the Microsoft TechNet Web site about Windows Application Compatibility at `http://technet.microsoft.com/en-us/windowsvista/aa905066.aspx`

✔ **Disconnect uninterruptible power supply (UPS) devices.** Setup automatically attempts to detect serially-connected devices, and UPS devices cause issues with the hardware-detection process.

✔ **Back up your servers.** Include all data and configuration settings necessary for function, especially with servers that provide network infrastructure services. Also include boot and system partitions and system state data. You may alternatively create a backup set for the Automated System Recovery process.

✔ **Disable virus protection software.** Virus detection and prevention applications can interfere with installation tasks, particularly in the form of performance penalties because every locally copied file is scanned for signs of infection.

✔ **Run the Windows Memory Diagnostic tool.** Test the RAM in your target computer for error-free reliability and operation. Follow the instructions detailed in the Windows Memory Diagnostics User Guide at `oca.microsoft.com/en/windiag.asp`.

✔ **Copy mass storage device drivers.** Manufacturer-specific driver files should be stored to an easily-accessible storage medium in the root directory or in a specifically named amd64, i386, or ia64 folder, whichever is most suitable for the target hardware.

✔ **Prepare the Active Directory environment.** Before adding a domain controller based on Windows Server 2008 to an existing Active Directory (AD) environment based on either Windows 2000 or Windows Server 2003, you need to update all older domain controllers. You can do this before installing the operating system — or after running Setup and before installing AD Domain Services.

Windows Server 2008 Server Core installation provides only the binaries necessary for certain server roles to function. The traditional Windows interface will not be installed; instead, configuration and management are handled through the crude but effective command prompt. This installation option reduces server management requirements and reduces the overall attack surface. If you've heard the expression "running headless" applied to monitor-free server computers, this is akin to running *faceless*.

Installation of multiple operating systems on the same server to include Windows Server 2008 should be handled through separate partitions. For best results, Microsoft recommends that you start Setup from within Windows rather than booting from the install medium, and then perform a clean custom installation onto a separate partition.

Preparing for the battle

We offer the following list to help you gather information and equipment you need for your setup. The setup program in Windows Server 2008 doesn't require all the items that we list in the following sections, but we like to have everything handy when we perform an install so that we don't need to run around looking for things during that process.

Manuals

The following is a list of books that you may want to have within arm's reach. (This book, of course, is the most important.)

- ✔ **Windows Server 2008 manuals:** In some cases, the manuals you receive with Windows Server 2008 are in print form; in others, they're available only in electronic form from the distribution DVD or online at the Microsoft Windows Web site at www.microsoft.com/windowsserver2008/default.mspx.

- ✔ **Computer hardware manuals:** These are the manuals for the base machine on which you plan to install Windows Server 2008, plus all additional components or peripherals. You especially want manuals for your network interface(s) and video cards.

- ✔ **Modem manual (optional):** Grab this manual only if you plan to install one or more modems on the server.

Software

If you don't want to hunt around halfway through the installation, make sure that you have the following software handy:

- ✔ **Windows Server 2008 DVD-ROM:** This disc is the DVD-ROM that ships with **Windows Server 2008.** You also need the DVD key from the sticker on the jewel case, or some other legitimate license key.

- ✔ **Windows Server 2008 Service Pack DVD-ROM or downloaded file:** Don't expect a service pack for Windows Server 2008 for at least three months after it's officially released. Until then, you can skip the "Windows Server 2008 service packs" section later in this chapter. After that, it's wise to let the OS update itself during the installation process.

- ✔ **Network driver:** Windows Server 2008 Setup should find the network interface(s) in the server, but keep a floppy or a USB flash drive with the necessary drivers handy in case it doesn't.

✔ **Small Computer System Interface (SCSI) drivers:** Windows Server 2008 Setup should recognize all SCSI devices if they're listed in the Windows Server Hardware Platform info at `www.microsoft.com/whdc/system/platform/server/default.mspx`. Again, keep the drivers handy just in case.

Hardware

Of course, setting up Windows Server 2008 also requires some hardware, particularly the following:

✔ **Computer:** Make sure that the computer complies with the Hardware Platform criteria. Remember that you'll need at least a 1 GHz CPU, but we don't think you'll be satisfied with anything slower than 2 GHz. You also want to have a mouse attached to the computer — it just makes life easier!

✔ **RAM:** The more memory that you can afford, the better. You must have at least 512MB, but you'll get better results with 2GB at the very least, if not 4GB (more for 64-bit installations).

✔ **DVD-ROM drive:** If you're installing Windows Server 2008 from a DVD-ROM, you need a DVD-ROM drive. Newer computers can recognize it as a boot drive; if so, you can start Windows Server 2008 installation from the DVD.

✔ **Hard disk:** You must have at least 10GB of free space, but we think you shouldn't even begin with less than 40GB of available disk storage space. Even better, 80GB is closer to ideal — unless you absolutely won't be storing large amounts of data for short-term or long-term periods. For what it's worth, you will seldom see drives smaller than 400GB on new servers these days.

✔ **Modem:** If the server connects to the Internet or provides access to remote users, a modem (either internal or external) can provide this connection. We prefer at least a cable or DSL modem, particularly where a multiple user network server is involved.

✔ **Video:** You need a Video Graphics Array (VGA) or higher-resolution video adapter and monitor. We recommend Super Video Graphics Array (SVGA) as a minimum.

✔ **Cables:** Depending on the components you install, you may need modem/network cables, telephone cables, power cords, monitor cables, and so forth.

Information

You must make several choices as you work through the setup process. You're better off if you already have an idea of what you're going to answer before you begin the installation. Consider the items in the following list:

✔ **NTFS:** *NTFS* is the Windows Server 2008 native file system and is much more secure than the File Allocation Table (FAT) file system. Unless you need backward compatibility with older Microsoft operating systems on the same machine in a multiboot configuration, there's really no need to use FAT.

✔ **Licensing:** You need to know how you purchased your Windows Server 2008 and client licenses because the Windows Server 2008 Setup program asks you whether you want per-seat or per-server licensing.

✔ **Computer name:** Each computer needs a unique name that you can identify easily on the network.

✔ **Workgroup/domain name:** If this is the first domain controller installed in a network, you must create a domain name. If this computer joins a current domain where a domain controller already exists, plan to connect this computer to a network with access to that domain. If you're installing Windows Server 2008 in a workgroup, you need the workgroup name. Remember it's an either/or setting, but you can always change your mind later.

✔ **Protocols:** Determine which protocols the server uses (or will use) to communicate. If you plan to use the Transmission Control Protocol/Internet Protocol (TCP/IP), see Chapter 10 for details. Decide whether you must configure TCP/IP manually or automatically through a Dynamic Host Configuration Protocol (DHCP) server. If this server connects to the Internet, it must have at least one valid public IP address (unless you have a NAT server handling address translation between the server and the Internet).

✔ **Remote connectivity options:** Determine whether the server connects (or will connect) to the Internet or will host a Web server. If so, you can install Internet Information Services (IIS) to provide Web services and Remote Access Services (RAS) for connectivity. RAS also enables your users or customers to dial into the network. You can always install RAS and IIS later. In either case, you need a working Internet connection.

✔ **Server roles:** The game has changed for roles that servers can play when maintaining a domain. The function of your server may affect how you install Windows Server 2008, but it's no longer a life-threatening decision because the server isn't configured until after initial installation is complete.

Got Enough Horsepower?

Before you install Windows Server 2008 (whether you're upgrading or creating a new installation), you must meet Microsoft's minimum hardware requirements. If your server doesn't match these requirements, your installation can halt midway and leave you stuck in the mud.

Microsoft goes easy on its minimum requirements, so we provide more realistic numbers to meet real-world needs. If you follow Microsoft's lead, expect a doo-dah server that lacks the zip-a-dee part. Table 5-2 shows a comparison between Microsoft's numbers and our real-world numbers.

Table 5-2 Minimum Requirements: Microsoft versus For Dummies		
Item	*Microsoft Says*	*Real World Says*
Processor	1 GHz	2 GHz or better
RAM	512MB	4GB or better
Monitor	VGA	SVGA or better
NIC	None*	One (at least 32 bit)
DVD-ROM	DVD-ROM	DVD-ROM (12X or better) or DVD
Hard disk	40GB+	120GB or better

Note: A network interface of some kind (wired or wireless) is required for direct network access. If a network interface isn't present at the time of installation, you can install it later.

You can squeak by with Microsoft's minimum requirements, but many of your server's capabilities will end up terribly slow or intractable. For example, even though Windows Server 2008 supports low-resolution monitors, you should use a higher-resolution monitor (SVGA or better) because of the Windows Server 2008 graphical user interface (GUI) — except for the case of Server Core installation. In many cases, more (disk space, RAM, processor power, and so on) is better. Buy as much as your budget allows so you don't need to upgrade too soon.

Take a trip to Microsoft's Web site, particularly the Windows Server 2008 pages at www.microsoft.com/windowsserver2008/default.mspx. There you can find white papers and Frequently Asked Questions (FAQs) that answer common questions to many issues, such as licensing, minimum requirements, and upgrades. If you don't find enough answers there, head to www.windowsitpro.com/windowsnt20002003faq for a searchable Windows FAQ site — it includes Windows Server 2008 information.

Another important item to check is whether your server (or its components) appears in Microsoft's Windows Server Hardware Platform or related criteria. Microsoft's test lab tests innumerable products for compatibility with Windows Server 2008. Obtaining Microsoft lab certification means an organization can display Microsoft's logo on its products. Also, Microsoft puts listings for certified products in a hardware catalog it maintains for Windows Server 2008–compatible items.

Selecting a network server from those listed in the catalog helps ensure the smoothest installation because you know Microsoft has already tested and certified that product. Certifying products for the catalog is an ongoing task at Microsoft, and the company maintains an updated catalog for all of its current server operating system releases on its Web site at `www.microsoft.com/whdc/system/platform/server/default.mspx`.

If you're unsure about the compatibility of an entire system or a specific component, look it up in the catalog or employ the automatic system compatibility checker on the DVD. Just insert the DVD into a system with an existing Windows OS. (If the Welcome screen doesn't appear automatically, run `setup.exe` from the root of the DVD.) Choose the Check System Compatibility option and then choose the Check My System Automatically option. The test wizard loads and prompts you to download updated files. If you have Internet access, this tool can always update itself with the latest and greatest catalog before scanning your system. If any problems or incompatibilities are found, a list of problems is displayed.

Windows Server 2008 utilities aplenty

No single operating system can do everything. Programmers, and others adept at computing, typically develop small scripts or programs to perform functions that the basic operating system doesn't include. Utilities for Windows Server 2008 abound because of its popularity. You can find many of these utilities, especially installation tools, on the Internet at popular Windows Server 2008 and NT Web sites, such as `http://windowsnt.about.com` or `www.bhs.com`.

In some cases, the same tool used on Windows 9x, NT, or 2000 also works on Windows Server 2008. However, this isn't always the case. You should test applications on Windows Server 2008 before you use them in situations where data loss is possible.

Microsoft sells a Windows Server 2008 Resource Kit that you can purchase on the Internet or at a bookstore. The package includes utilities for installation, file management, troubleshooting, and planning. As we write this book, the full-blown Resource Kit isn't yet on the radar, but several subtitles are, including Windows Server Resource Kits for Active Directory, Security, and IIS 7.0. (Go to `www.microsoft.com/mspress/hop/` for details.)

Step by Step: Installing Windows Server 2008

In this section, we walk you through the whole Windows Server 2008 installation screen by screen. There's not enough space in this book to present screens for every possible type of installation, so in this section, we provide instructions for the most common type: from a bootable DVD-ROM drive.

Server: Are you ready?

The first major task in getting the software onto a system is to make the server ready for the process. Generally, these are the issues you must resolve before traveling into the Windows Server 2008 installation process:

1. **Ensure that all hardware is HCL compatible.**

   Although it's possible to install Windows Server 2008 on a system with some components not on the HCL, it's not always easy. In short, if it isn't HCL compatible, you don't want to keep it in your system.

2. **Install the network interface in the server (unless integrated).**

   Fortunately, Windows Server 2008 supports plug and play, so you can make most card changes on the fly — unless you have a card so old it still uses dual in-line package (DIP) switches or jumpers. Hopefully this isn't the case — even we aren't sure if those are still supported.

3. **If you need an internal modem and want to connect the server to external sources such as the Internet, install the modem.**

Windows Server 2008 Setup: A walk-through

The following steps detail the Windows Server 2008 installation process from a bootable DVD-ROM drive. Throughout this installation, we accept the default options.

Your system must be configured to boot from the DVD. This is accomplished by editing the CMOS. Consult your motherboard documentation on how to enter, edit, and save the CMOS settings.

Ready, set, here are the steps:

1. **Insert the Windows Server 2008 DVD-ROM into the DVD-ROM drive and boot the computer. If prompted to press a key to boot from the DVD, do so.**

   A gray GUI screen with an Install Now button appears. In addition, the Windows Setup Wizard starts automatically. You may optionally click the What to Know before Installing Windows link for further information on the installation process.

   Three other options also appear: Language Options, Time & Currency Format, and Keyboard Input Methods.

2. **Click Install Now.**

   The Install Windows screen appears with an option to get the latest updates prior to installation. This is a nice new feature you'll appreciate in time, if not instantly. If you elect to update the computer now, which we strongly recommend, your setup proceeds to search for installation updates. Our instructions from here on out follow that assumption.

   Optionally, you may elect to make the installation process better for sub-sequent users by selecting a check box that informs Microsoft of the installation process as it proceeds through your setup. Click the What Information Will Be Sent to Microsoft? link, which gives you the full scope of information collected and reported about your experience with the Windows Server 2008 installation wizard.

   Be careful when working through the GUI wizard. Often, after you click the Next button to continue, the system takes several seconds (some-times up to a minute) to change the display. Do *not* try to click the Next button again — even if you think you missed the button by accident. If you click the Next button twice, you skip screens, and the Back button doesn't always work; in some places, the Back button is grayed out or non-existent. If you wait two to five minutes and the system doesn't change the display, it's probably safe to click Next again.

3. **Click the Go Online to Get the Latest Updates button to proceed to the next screen.**

   The installation wizard searches online for updates, which requires an active Internet connection throughout the installation process.

   You can't choose a course of action until the next screen appears, which permits you to choose the version of Windows Server 2008 that matches your valid key. Trust us, the folks at Redmond are smart enough to write code to differentiate between the various full-install and upgrade keys, so you'll only be fooling yourself by trying to "upgrade" here.

4. Select the appropriate edition and click Next.

5. Type your product key for activation.

You may also choose to activate Windows when you're online.

6. Read or scroll through the license terms agreement and then select the I Accept the License Terms check box to enable the Next button — then click Next.

The installation options dialog box appears; choose between an upgrade or custom install. The distinction lies in both the license key and the process: One can only update an existing installation, and the other has both options available.

Sometimes an information box appears below, stating Upgrade Has Been Disabled, followed by an explanation. Here, we choose Custom because you need a full-install key on new hardware. Click the appropriate button to proceed.

You can usually find the Product Key on a sticker on the DVD case.

7. Choose how to install Windows when presented with multiple-choice answers; otherwise, the choice is clear. Click Next.

Two choices, Upgrade and Custom, appear in this dialog box. However, the type of license you have (upgrade or full-install) determines which options are available.

8. Choose the drive where you want to install Windows Server 2008.

In a single-drive build, you shouldn't have any questions about this; otherwise, you should know in advance which volume you designated for Windows Server 2008 installation.

9. Use the arrow keys to select a partition hosted by a physical hard drive and then click Next.

You may also click Refresh to update this list, or Load Driver to add any supportive files you need for the installation process.

After you click Next, the Install Windows dialog box appears with no options for you to select.

Setup begins processing Windows Server 2008 installation, and this dialog box indicates every step (from copying and expanding files to installing updates and completion) along the way.

Setup spends a considerable amount of time formatting the drive, especially for large partitions. After formatting is complete, Setup inspects your hard drives, builds a file list, and then copies lots and lots of files from the DVD to the newly formatted drive. This is a great time to stretch, change your oil, get coffee, or learn how to cross-stitch.

Setup copies and expands files, installs features and updates, and then completes installation by asking for all site-specific information at the very end — instead of throughout the entire process, as with previous Windows installations.

10. **When you see a message that says the system will be rebooted, you can press Enter to reboot immediately or wait 15 seconds for an automatic reboot.**

    Be sure there are no floppies in the drive. Also, don't press a key to boot to the DVD. If your DVD boots automatically instead of requiring a key press to initiate a DVD boot, eject the DVD before the reboot.

    After the reboot, Windows Server 2008 Setup reenters the GUI mode. Setup scans your computer for devices and installs drivers appropriately.

    When the system comes back up, you're presented with the Initial Configuration Tasks dialog box, which is where you fill in all the specific server details. We describe only the first three basic options.

11. **Click Set the Administrator Password and choose a strong password.**

    If you're using the server for personal use, you can leave the password blank, but even then, we don't advise it.

12. **Click Set the Timezone so that crucial timestamps are marked appropriately.**

13. **Click Configure Networking and specify the default values.**

14. **Click Close.**

    Setup delivers you to a screen that reads `Press CTRL + ALT + DELETE to login`.

15. **Press Ctrl+Alt+Del to display the Log On to Windows dialog box.**

16. **Type your password for the Administrator account and then press Enter to log on.**

    After several moments, the Windows Server 2008 desktop appears — a sure sign that you've successfully installed Windows Server 2008! (Just to keep you on your toes, Windows Server 2008 automatically launches the Server Manager Wizard in preparation for your next set of tasks. Jump to Chapter 6 to find out more about this wizard.)

Installing from an Existing OS

If your computer already has an operating system with access to the DVD-ROM drive — such as DOS, Windows 3.*x*, Windows for Workgroups, Windows 9*x*,

Windows NT, Windows 2000/2003, or Windows XP — you can launch the Windows Server 2008 setup from that OS. This is the only way to accomplish an upgrade install. If you launch an install from a bootable DVD, a full install is performed automatically.

Although you can begin the Windows Server 2008 installation from previous editions of Windows, you can't upgrade to Windows Server 2008 from many of these former operating systems. Regardless of the existing OS, you must meet the minimum hardware requirements to install Windows Server 2008 (refer to Table 5-2), which wouldn't ordinarily be found on a system running many such previous editions of Windows.

To install from the DVD-ROM drive, issue one of the following from a command prompt or a Run dialog box:

✔ If you're using a 16-bit operating system, such as DOS, Windows 3.1, or Windows for Workgroups, you need to use this command, replacing *drive letter* with the letter assigned to your DVD drive:

```
<DVD-ROM drive letter>:\i386\winnt
```

✔ If you're using a 32-bit operating system, such as Windows 9*x*, Windows NT, Windows 2000, or Windows XP, and you don't have autorun enabled, you need to use this command, replacing *drive letter* with the letter assigned to your DVD drive:

```
<DVD-ROM drive letter>:\i386\winnt32
```

If you try to run the wrong setup program, the tool will tell you — just run the other program.

If autorun is enabled, you see the Welcome to Windows Setup Wizard screen.

Manually launching Setup from DOS, Windows 3.*x*, or Windows for Workgroups requires you to do the following after the DOS, text-only display appears, asking for confirmation of the location of the distribution files:

1. **Make sure that the screen shows the correct path to the i386 directory on the distribution DVD-ROM and then press Enter.**

   Setup copies files from the DVD to your hard drive.

2. **After Setup informs you that all files have been copied, press Enter to reboot and continue.**

   After the machine reboots, the setup resumes at Step 9 of the "Windows Server 2008 Setup: A walk-through" section earlier in this chapter.

If you insert the Windows Server 2008 DVD into a DVD-ROM drive under an operating system with autorun enabled (for example, Windows NT), the Windows Server 2008 splash screen appears and asks whether you want to upgrade to Windows Server 2008. By clicking Yes, you don't need to manually locate and execute WINNT or WINNT32.

Launching Setup from an eligible Windows platform requires you to follow these steps:

1. **On the Install Windows Setup Wizard screen, click Next.**

2. **Choose whether to get important updates now or later, locate the corresponding option, and then click it.**

   Windows Setup will begin looking for updates if you so choose, which requires an Internet connection.

3. **Enter your product key and then click Next.**

   Alternatively, you can choose from a drop-down list of choices and omit the license key altogether at this stage, but they must match up for activation purposes.

4. **Accept the license agreement terms and click the Next button.**

5. **Choose between Upgrade or Custom installation options and click the corresponding text button.**

6. **To install Windows Server 2008 to a partition other than the one currently hosting an operating system (highly recommended), be sure to choose the appropriate partition from the menu displayed in this dialog box.**

7. **Click Next to continue.**

   Setup copies files from the DVD to your hard drive. Setup then offers a 10-second interval during which you can manually restart before automatically rebooting your computer.

   After the machine reboots, the setup resumes at Step 9 of the "Windows 2003 Setup: A walk-through" section earlier in this chapter.

Installing across a Network

Installing Windows Server 2008 across a network is almost the same as performing the installation from a local DVD-ROM. Both methods require access to the distribution files from the DVD (duh!), and you have to manually launch the Windows setup tools.

Manually launching setup over a network requires little change to the process described in the preceding section. However, you need to map a local drive letter to the network share. (This mapped letter tells Setup where the distribution files live.) Setup automatically copies all of the data files it needs before rebooting.

Installing Remotely

Microsoft has created an installation process called the Remote Installation Service (RIS). RIS enables network administrators to push a Windows Server 2008 installation out to network systems. Although this process simplifies multiple installations overall, it isn't a simple activity. It requires the installation and configuration of several key services, namely Domain Name Service (DNS), DHCP, and Active Directory, in addition to RIS.

The clients that will have the Windows Server 2008 installation pushed to them must have a Preboot Extension Environment (PXE)–compliant NIC or be booted with a special network client boot disk.

If you want to explore the remote OS installation procedure further, we highly recommend that you check out the RIS documentation in the operating system, TechNet, and the Windows Server 2008 Resource Kit.

Working through Post-Installation Stress Disorder

After you finish the basic installation, you've simply defined a basic server. You need to dress it up with things such as users, groups, domain controllers, Active Directory, applications, services, and printers, as we describe in Chapters 7 through 14. But, before you get excited and flip to those chapters, we want to mention three more issues: the activation process, service packs, and Automated System Recovery.

Understanding Activation

In an effort to curb pirating of software, Microsoft has implemented an installation control feature (first debuted in Windows XP) called *activation*. After the initial installation of a product, such as Windows Server 2008, Microsoft grants you a 30-day period within which you must contact Microsoft and activate that product. If you fail to activate the product, on day 31, the product ceases to function. In fact, the only activity you can perform from that point forward is activation. After a product has been activated, it functions normally.

The activation process requires your system to generate a 50-digit code. This code is unique to your system and is used to associate your product key with your computer hardware. If any other computer attempts to activate the same product key on a different computer, Microsoft will think you've pirated their software or at least attempted to install it on another system without purchasing another package. The gotcha to activation is this computer ID, which is generated by pulling unique IDs from ten different parts of your computer, including your motherboard, CPU, and hard drives.

If you change six or more of these parts, the system thinks you've changed computers, and your activated status will be terminated. You have to contact Microsoft and explain that you've only upgraded your existing system and that you're not just installing the product onto a completely new second system. Can we say major headaches ahead?

Activation can occur over the Internet, in which case it takes only a few seconds. Activation can occur also over a phone line, whereby you must read off the 50-digit computer ID to the auto-attendant or a customer service representative, and then you must enter an equally long confirmation key yourself.

To activate your system, you can click the reminder pop-up bubble that appears over your *notification area* (previously known as the *icon tray* or *system tray*), which is right beside the clock. Until you activate, the operating system reminds you every day, or every time you log on, about activating. You can initiate the activation process also by launching the Activation Wizard found in the Start menu. It appears in the top-level menu initially; after you activate, it appears only in the All Programs⇨Accessories⇨System Tools section.

Dealing with service packs

A *service pack* is a release of updates and patches for a software product. Microsoft is famous for releasing service packs to repair its software. This indicates to some cynics that Microsoft is concerned enough about its user community to maintain a product, but not concerned enough to get it right the first time. Be that as it may, the first service pack for Windows Server 2008 will probably be released three to nine months after Windows Server 2008 makes its debut in February 2008.

Microsoft has integrated two capabilities into Windows Server 2008 to ease the burden of maintaining an up-to-date version:

✔ You can configure the **Windows Update** tool to regularly check for new updates and prompt you to download and install them.

> ✔ You can slipstream **service packs** into distribution files so that an initial setup results in automagic application of the service pack. In other words, you can apply service packs to a distribution point so that new systems automatically get installations that include that service pack. After service packs are available for Windows Server 2008, read the accompanying documentation to learn how to slipstream them.

Windows Server 2008 service packs don't entangle you in the Catch-22 of installing files from the original distribution DVD after a service pack is applied. In other words, adding new services doesn't require reapplication of service packs, and application of service packs doesn't require reinstallation of services from the distribution DVD. What a relief!

Microsoft advertises releases of its service packs, making it easier for the typical user to locate, download, and apply these jewels. You'll usually find a link on the product-specific Web page at www.microsoft.com/windows server2008/default.mspx.

Using Automated System Recovery

Automated System Recovery (ASR) is partially designed to replace the function of the previous ERD repair process (remember that from Windows NT?). You can use ASR to restore a system to its stored configuration settings in the wake of a complete system failure. The only drawback to ASR is that it restores files found on only the system partition. Therefore, if you have applications or user data files on other partitions, ASR doesn't offer a safety net for these items.

To use the ASR restore process, you must first create an ASR backup set. You can create an ASR backup set from the Welcome tab of the Backup utility (Start⇨All Programs⇨Accessories⇨System Tools⇨Windows Server Backup). The ASR backup set consists of a single floppy and one or more backup tapes (depending on the amount of data stored on your system partition). To restore a failed system, you must boot to the original setup program either from a bootable DVD or the setup boot floppies, and then press F2 when prompted to initiate the ASR repair process. You'll then be prompted for the floppy and your backup tapes.

If you want to protect all your data, you have two options. You can use the full backup capabilities (which include the System State) of the native Backup utility. Or you can spend the money for a quality third-party backup solution that offers restoration from tape after simply booting from a floppy instead of requiring that the entire operating system be reinstalled before a restoration can be performed.

Oops, My Installation Didn't Take

In most cases, as long as your hardware is on the HCL, installation will be a breeze. (Well, how about a long, continuous gust?) For those other cases, here are some common problems and solutions:

- **DVD-ROM problems:** The entire Windows Server 2008 installation ships on a single DVD-ROM (unlike previous market releases that appear on CDs), so if you can't read the DVD, you can't install Windows Server 2008 (unless you're installing over a network, but even then, the distribution files have to come from a DVD at some point). DVD-ROMs are similar to music records or DVDs in that one little scratch or speck of dust on the surface can cause problems. On the other hand, the DVD may be okay, but the drive may not function correctly — or Windows Server 2008 may not recognize the drive. We hope that your drive appears on the HCL. To determine whether the drive or the DVD isn't functioning, take the DVD to another DVD-ROM drive and see whether you can read it there. After you determine which element is the culprit, you can replace it and retry your installation.

- **Hardware problems:** If Windows Server 2008 setup doesn't recognize a server's hardware, it's likely to stop. Make sure that the machine's hardware appears in the HCL and that you configured all devices correctly. If you have more than one SCSI device, for example, make sure that they're chained (connected) correctly.

- **Blue screen of death:** Sometimes, Setup simply crashes and gives you a blue screen; other times, it gives you a display of error codes that only a propeller head can understand. By itself, the blue screen simply means that you must reboot. If you get a fancy stop screen, however, you can look at the first few lines to determine the error code and then use it to look up the error message in the error-message manual. A stop typically occurs if a driver problem occurs; if you look beyond the first few lines of the error-message screen, it tells you which drivers were loaded at the time the crash occurred. A good idea is to write the first few lines of the stop screen down before attempting to reboot.

- **Connectivity problems:** Installing a machine into an existing domain requires that the new system be capable of communicating with a domain controller to create a domain computer account. If communication isn't possible for any reason (such as a wrong network interface, a wrong driver, a bad or missing cable, a domain controller offline, or too much network traffic), you can't join the domain. In some cases, you can resolve the problem by quickly replacing a cable or allowing the system to try the connection a second or third time. In other cases, you can delay confronting the problem by joining a workgroup instead. Then you can resolve any problems (such as network interface, driver, and configuration problems) with a functioning system.

✔ **Dependency problems:** Some services in Windows Server 2008 depend on other services loading correctly. If service A doesn't load, service B doesn't work, and you get error messages if service B is set to automatically start at bootup. For example, if a network interface isn't installed correctly, all services that use that network interface also fail to start. Your first order of business, therefore, is to get the network interface to function correctly. If you get this far in the installation process, you can view the error logs (Start⇨All Programs⇨Administrative Tools⇨Event Viewer) to see which service didn't start and then work your way from there.

✔ **Script file errors:** The Windows Server 2008 automated installation program (see the next section) isn't forgiving if you mistype a script. If a script stops midway and the Windows Server 2008 setup program asks you for manual input, you entered something incorrectly. Check the input file to look for transposed letters or anything else that may be out of place. Scripts expect to feed the computer exactly what you put in the script file. If you don't enter the right information, Setup doesn't receive the information it expects.

Exploring Automated Installation

An unattended installation feature enables you to install Windows Server 2008 without keyboard interaction. Just start the process and walk away. Unattended installation uses a script file that pipes in information and keyboard strokes from a data file that you compose in advance. If you already know all the answers to the questions that the installation program asks, you can answer these questions and place them in a data file. You can use more than one data file for different types of installations.

Unattended installation is great for organizations that install Windows Server 2008 over and over on machines with the same hardware configurations. Large enterprise networks that include remote offices can also take advantage of unattended installation because home office administrators can customize script files and transmit them to remote offices. The caveat here is that you must test the script files for accuracy thoroughly in the central office; otherwise, the folks in the remote office may soon be screaming for help!

Details on creating automation scripts are included in the Windows Server 2008 Resource Kit. You can also find information on this subject in the Windows Server 2008 Technical Library at `technet2.microsoft.com/windowsserver2008/en/library/`.

Chapter 6

Configuring Connections to the Universe

*E*ven after you complete the installation of Windows Server 2008, you still face numerous decisions and related activities before you can safely say, "Mission accomplished!" What role does this server play on your network? Does it host multiple network interfaces? Do you need remote access? In this chapter, you seek answers to all these questions and follow the steps to implement them properly.

Before you get too excited, we must warn you that certain topics covered in this chapter are just flat-out complex. We try to give a general overview of each topic, but in some cases, covering all the relevant details goes beyond the scope of this book. When that happens, we refer you to other resources and materials where you can find meaningful, reliable, and more detailed coverage of these topics, to supplement and complete what we provide you with here.

In this chapter, you go through the steps necessary to get your Windows Server 2008 installation up and running.

Completing the Initial Configuration Tasks

Starting at square one, the first time you log on to Windows Server 2008 after completing the initial installation, you're confronted with an Initial Configuration Tasks (ICT) dialog box, shown in Figure 6-1. This wizard appears by default the first time you log in, and every subsequent time, unless you select the Do Not Show this Window at Logon check box.

ICT assists administrators with Windows Server 2008 deployments by postponing platform settings previously encountered during the installation process to shorten the installation time. ICT does this by allowing administrators to specify relevant values at the end of the installation process, thereby bypassing lots of dialog boxes and related interruptions along the way.

Windows Server 2008 also brings a concept called *componentization* to the table, which is defined as breaking a complete system into interchangeable parts to create a standardized approach to assembly, interface, or operation. For Windows Server 2008, this translates into the ability to reuse components outside their usual frameworks. A simple analogy is the relationship between electronic components and electronic devices. A device is made of components, but it can also do things that individual components normally can't.

Figure 6-1:
The Initial Configuration Tasks dialog box.

The Initial Configuration Tasks dialog box allows administrators to configure a server with the following parameters:

- ✔ **Administrator password:** Set the administrator password (left blank by default).

- ✔ **Computer name:** The computer name is randomly generated and assigned during installation, but you get your first chance to change it here.

- ✔ **Time zone:** Configure the local time zone.

- ✔ **Configure networking:** Establish initial network interface settings.

- ✔ **Domain membership:** There is no default domain to join; however, the computer is automatically assigned to a workgroup, appropriately named WORKGROUP.

- ✔ **Enable Windows Update and feedback:** Choose whether to automatically update Windows and issue problem reports or receive feedback.

- ✔ **Add roles:** A *server role* describes the primary function of a server, which can be one or several roles (each with one or more separate services) on a single computer.

- ✔ **Add features:** A feature provides supportive functionality to servers, which typically means augmenting a configured server role with additional capabilities.

- ✔ **Enable Remote Desktop:** Remote desktop assistance is provided by an underlying Remote Desktop Protocol (RDP), which enables user computers to communicate with Microsoft Terminal Services.

- ✔ **Configure Windows Firewall:** The Windows Firewall is enabled by default, but you might want to spend some time familiarizing yourself with its features and capabilities, or configure it with site-specific settings.

These pre-deployment options are left for the end of installation to improve efficiency. Administrators can set these as soon as the install completes, which shortens time-to-launch for a fresh server installation. When you close the ICT dialog box, another configuration utility pops up: the Windows Server Manager, which we describe next.

Server Manager Configuration

Windows Server 2008 includes an all-new Server Manager application in GUI and command-line form that simultaneously replaces and consolidates the Windows Server 2003 interfaces called Manage Your Server, Configure Your Server, and Add or Remove Windows Components. Server Manager eliminates any need to run the Security Configuration Wizard prior to deployment because server roles come pre-configured with recommended security settings. Each separate application is consolidated into one utility for a better combination of features and functionality in a single centralized applet, which provides a holistic view of server configuration and related server components. This new management platform enables you to install, configure, and manage server roles specific to Windows Server 2008, including some capabilities that even work on Windows Server 2003 machines.

Getting to know the Server Manager console

You can use the expanded Server Manager MMC (Microsoft Management Console) to configure various applications, features, and roles on your Windows Server 2008 PC. A *role* describes a server's primary function; administrators may designate or dedicate an entire computer to one or more roles that can include DHCP and DNS services, among many others. A *feature* describes some supporting function in a server; for example: failover clustering indicates that multiple server computers function as a single logical server, and if one computer fails, another stands ready to take its place automatically.

The Windows Server Manager console provides a consolidated view that includes: server information, configured roles, services, and feature status. It puts all the easily accessible management tools together under one interface. Server Manager improves productivity so that you spend less time on deployment, management, and maintenance phases and more time adding and using new features in your network infrastructure.

Here are a few key highlights to the new Server Manager platform:

✔ Server Manager functionality incorporates snap-in extensions from Computer Manager (Reliability and Performance, and Windows Firewall) that are always available regardless of which roles are installed.

✔ Server Manager displays notifications linked to descriptive help topics atop role management homepages when constraints in the role model are violated. Help topics may include additional content, solutions, or tools to help resolve some particular issue.

✔ The Server Manager Add Roles Wizard provides configuration pages for many roles, including AD Federation Services (AD-FS), Network Policy and Access Services, Fax Server, AD Rights Management (AD-RM), File Services, and many others, as shown in Figure 6-2. See Table 6-1 for more information on Server Roles.

✔ The Server Manager Add Features Wizard supports installation of BitLocker Drive Encryption, Group Policy Management, Remote Server Administration Tools, and a variety of supplementary or supportive network and storage features. See Table 6-2 for more details about Server Features.

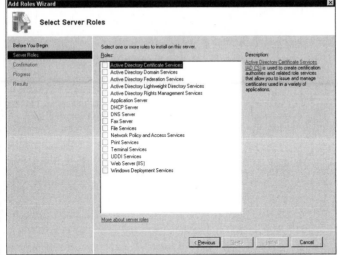

Figure 6-2:
The server roles that can be installed through the Server Manager Wizard.

> ✔ Server Manager provides Remote Server Administration Tools (RSAT) that enable remote management for specific roles, role-based services, and features on computers running Windows Server 2008 and Windows Server 2003.

> ✔ Server Manager supports automated deployment and scripting options for Windows Server 2008 roles from a command-line tool that can install or remove multiple roles, role services, or server features.

Table 6-1	Windows Server 2008 Server Roles
Role Name	**Description**
Active Directory Certificate Services (AD-CS)	AD-CS provides customizable services to create and manage public key certificates used in public cryptographic systems. Organizations may enhance their security posture by binding user identities, devices, or services to corresponding private keys. AD-CS also includes features for enrollment and revocation of certificates.
Active Directory Domain Services (AD-DS)	AD-DS stores user, computer, and other net-worked device information to help administrators securely manage and facilitate resource sharing or collaboration between users. AD-DS is also required for directory-enabled services such as Microsoft Exchange Server or Group Policy.

(continued)

Table 6-1 *(continued)*

Role Name	Description
Active Directory Lightweight Services (AD-LDS)	AD-LDS is a directory for storing application data that runs as a non-operating system service, which doesn't require deployment on a DC and permits multiple simultaneous instances to be configured independently to service multiple applications.
Active Directory Rights Management Services (AD-RMS)	AD-RMS is information protection technology that works with compatible applications to safeguard against unauthorized use of digital media. Content owners define how such data may be used, and organizations may create custom templates that apply directly to financial reports, product specifications, and other such materials.
Application Server (AS)	AS provides a turnkey solution for hosting and managing high-performance distributed business applications with integrated services such as .NET, COM+, and others.
Dynamic Host Configuration Protocol (DHCP)	DHCP allows temporary or permanent dynamic (and static) address assignments to computers and other network-addressable devices and gives administrators more flexible control over address assignments, duration, and type.
File Services	File Services provides storage management, file replication, a distributed namespace, and fast file-searching technologies for efficient client access to server resources.
Network Policy and Access Services (NPAS)	NPAS delivers an array of options to local and remote users, works across network segments, centralizes management tasks and enforces network health properties among client callers. NPAS facilitates VPN, dial-up server, router, and 802.11 protected access deployment, and other such capabilities.
Print Services (PS)	PS provides printer and print server management, which reduces administrative overhead by centralizing printer management tasks.
Terminal Services (TS)	TS enables users to access server-based Windows applications and desktops so that remote users can connect and utilize remote resources.

Role Name	Description
Universal Description, Discovery, and Integration (UDDI)	UDDI services enable information sharing via intranet-based Web services or between business partners that share an extranet or Internet connection. UDDI can help improve developer productivity and promote reuse of existing development work.
Web Server (IIS)	IIS 7.0, the Windows Web server, enables information sharing on intranets or over the Internet as a unified Web platform that integrates several key Microsoft components.
Windows Deployment Services (WDS)	WDS is used to remotely install and configure Windows installations using the Preboot Execution Environment (PXE).
Windows SharePoint Services (WSP)	WSP services allow end-user collaboration through documents, tasks, and events, enabling them to easily share contacts and other necessary information. WSP is designed to support flexible deployment, administration, and custom application development.

You can find more in-depth information about each of the server roles we introduce in Table 6-1 on Microsoft's Windows Server 2008 TechCenter page located at `http://technet.microsoft.com/en-us/windowsserver/2008/default.aspx`.

Table 6-2   Windows Server 2008 Server Manager Server Features

Feature Name	Description
.NET Framework 3.0	This latest version combines .NET 2.0 APIs with newer technologies for building user interface applications that help protect customer identities, enable seamless and security-enhanced communication, and model an array of business procedures.
BitLocker Drive Encryption	This new feature protects data-at-rest (stored information), whether the data is lost or stolen or inadvertently stored on decommissioned computers. Integrity is maintained through the Trusted Platform Module (TPM).

(continued)

Table 6-2 *(continued)*

Feature Name	Description
Background Intelligent Transfer Service (BITS)	BITS server extensions enable receipt of client file uploads that can be transferred in the foreground or background, asynchronously. It keeps other network applications more responsive and permits resumption of failed transfers.
Connection Manager Administration Kit (CMAK)	CMAK builds connection manager service profiles suitable for reducing the cost of providing remote access to all network service providers, whether you're part of a corporation or an Internet Service Provider (ISP).
Desktop Experience	The Desktop Experience includes portions of Windows Vista (Media Player, themes, and photo management) that aren't enabled by default.
Internet Printing Client (IPC)	IPC supports HTTP connectivity to Web-accessible printers to users in the same domain or on the same network, including roaming employees on mobile platforms.
Internet Storage Name Server (ISNS)	ISNS provides service discovery for Internet SCSI (iSCSI) storage area networks by processing registration/de-registration requests and queries from clients.
LPR Port Monitor (LPM)	LPR Port Monitor allows UNIX-based client computers to print on Windows computers with attached print devices.
Message Queuing (MQ)	MQ provides guaranteed message delivery, delivery prioritization, and efficient routing between applications running on different operating systems, using dissimilar network infrastructures, that may even be temporarily offline or scheduled to operate at different times.
Multipath I/O (MPIO)	MPIO combined with any Device Specific Module (DSM) provides multiple data path support to Microsoft-based storage devices.
Peer Name Resolution Protocol (PNRP)	PNRP enables applications to register and resolve names from individual computers sharing a common connection.

Feature Name	Description
Quality Windows Audio/Video Experience (qWave)	qWave is an enhanced streaming A/V platform that improves performance and reliability in IP-based networks. It ensures Quality of Service (QoS) and provides admission controls, run-time monitoring, and application feedback.
Recovery Disc (RD)	RD is a Windows utility that creates an OS installation disc, which you may use to recover data on a corrupted installation without the original installation medium, or where standard recovery tools are inaccessible.
Remote Assistance (RA)	RA enables support personnel to assist in problem resolution on remote client computers using the network or Internet. You can view, share, and control the end user's desktop, troubleshoot problems, and apply solutions.
Remote Server Administration Tools (RSAT)	RSAT provides remote management capability for Windows Server 2003/2008 computers, which includes the ability to run some management tools, role services, and server features on the remote server.
Removable Storage Manager (RSM)	RSM catalogs and manages removable media and operates automation for such devices.
Network File System (NFS) Services	NFS services provide a distributed file system protocol for network-driven access to server storage volumes, which are mounted remotely like local resources.
Simple Mail Transfer Protocol (SMTP)	SMTP server provides a basic foundation for e-mail messaging between client and server systems.
Telnet Client	The Telnet protocol permits clients to connect to remote computers running the Telnet server, providing remote control over server applications and resources.
Telnet Server	The Telnet Server aspect of the Telnet protocol permits different platform Telnet clients to connect and utilize remote server resources.
Trivial File Transfer Protocol (TFTP)	TFTP is a very basic file transfer protocol used between embedded devices and systems to obtain and update firmware, configuration settings, and other information.

(continued)

Table 6-2 *(continued)*

Feature Name	Description
Failover Clustering (FC)	FC enables several individual servers to work cohesively as one to provide high-availability applications and services, often as file and print or database services.
Network Load Balancing (NLB)	NLB distributes a workload among many other servers, which ensures scalable stateless TCP/IP applications under increased loads.
Windows Server Backup (WSB)	WSB permits backup and recovery for Windows platform files and other supportive applications and data.
Windows System Resource Manager (WSRM)	WSRM is an administrative tool that controls CPU and memory resource allocation for improved system performance and reduced runtime risk to applications, processes, and services that might otherwise interfere with or hinder performance.
Windows Internet Naming Service (WINS)	WINS is a distributed database used to register and query dynamic IP-to-name mappings for NetBIOS computers and workgroups on Windows networks, and it alleviates issues with NetBIOS name resolutions in routed environments.
Wireless LAN (WLAN) Service	WLAN service configures and starts the WLAN AutoConfig service, even when the host computer has no wireless network interface.
Windows Internal Database (WID)	WID is a relational data storehouse used only by Windows roles and features like UDDI or AD-Rights Management services.
Windows PowerShell	PowerShell is a command-line shell and scripting language used to achieve greater administrative control, a more powerful scripting language, and scripted automation.
Windows Process Activation Service (WPAS)	WPAS removes IIS dependency on HTTP, making it accessible to applications hosting non-HTTP protocols such as WCF services. WPAS also manages application pools, worker processes, and message-based activation via HTTP and non-HTTP requests.

Whether you're an IT administrator, planner, or technology evaluator for medium or enterprise-level network design, or an early adopter or architect and engineer responsible for daily management, you'll appreciate what Server Manager offers. It greatly simplifies and consolidates tasks so succinctly that you might oversimplify your personal assessment of its capabilities. Trust us: You'll learn a whole new appreciation for this consolidated capability in any large-scale server deployments you may undertake.

Establishing directory trees and forests

To get your Windows Server 2008 system up and running, the first bit of information you need to feed it is whether it's the first server in your domain. If it is the first server, the Server Manager console helps you install the core services required to maintain a domain. If it isn't the first server on the network, you can set the server up as another domain controller or a member server in a domain, but with no domain responsibilities. Or you can elect to make the server a stand alone server, which has no domain involvement at all.

New to Windows Server 2008 is the read-only domain controller (RODC), which allows organizations to deploy and utilize a DC in physically insecure locations, where absolute security can't be guaranteed. An RODC hosts read-only partitions of data under the AD-DS database that can't be altered directly. The first DC in the AD forest must be a fully capable global cataloging server, not an RODC, which you'll encounter during this setup process.

Prior to the advent of Windows Server 2008, users had no alternative but to authenticate with a DC via some wide area network (WAN) linkage if no local DC was available. Branch offices often can't provide or ensure adequate security measures to restrict physical access to writable DCs, which are often shared over limited network bandwidth connections to hub sites that increase delays and logon times. This model of operation is inefficient and underutilizes network resources. Windows Server 2008 improves all of these issues through RODC server deployments, which provide much finer-grain control over administrative access and data storage.

If you're setting up the first domain controller on the first domain for your organization, you're setting up more than just a domain; you're also defining the root of your first directory tree and the root of your first directory forest. In Active Directory domain lingo, a group of computers that shares a single namespace and DNS structure is called a *domain.* A group of domains linked in parent-child relationships (also like the roots of a tree) is called a *tree.* A domain tree is a set of domains connected through a two-way transitive trust, sharing a common schema, configuration, and global catalog. These domains also form a contiguous hierarchical namespace with one domain acting as the domain root.

The first domain installed in a tree is considered the root domain for that tree. It would be considered the forest root domain only if it was also the first domain in the forest, which we will discuss next.

Groups of trees may be linked together as a forest. The capability to organize a network into complex logical namespace structures gives Windows Server 2008 (and Windows Server 2003) its scalability and versatility as an enterprise-capable network operating system.

A *forest* is a collection of one or more domains that share a common schema, configuration, and global catalog. A forest may or may not have a common domain namespace. If the forest has only a single tree, it will have a common domain namespace because it's the only tree. Because a forest can have more than one domain tree (it isn't a requirement, but it's allowed), these different domain trees will have their own individual, contiguous namespaces.

All the domains in a domain tree and all the trees in a single forest have the connectivity benefit of a two-way transitive trust relationship, which is the default trust relationship between Windows 2000, 2003, and 2008 domains. A two-way transitive trust is the combination of a transitive trust and a two-way trust. This complete trust between all domains in an Active Directory domain hierarchy helps form the forest as a single unit through its common schema, configuration, and global catalog. The first Windows 2000, 2003, or 2008 domain installed in the forest is considered the *forest root domain.*

The first domain controller you create also defines the domain. If it's the first domain on your network, it's also the root of the first tree and the first tree in the forest. For more detailed information on the logical structure of domains, trees, and forests, please consult the Windows Server 2008 Resource Kit.

A Windows Server 2008 computer is just a stand alone system that acts like a workstation until you employ the configurations offered through the ICT and Server Manager wizards. Once those configurations are elected and put to work, your Windows Server 2008 machine can take on almost any role you want, including limited Server Core roles and capacities. Unlike Windows NT, in which you have either primary or backup domain controllers, all domain controllers on Windows Server 2008 are essentially the same. Each and every domain controller shares the responsibility of maintaining the domain, updating changes to the Active Directory, and distributing the authentication and communication load.

For now, we assume that your server is the first server on the network. To set up your server, follow these steps:

1. **Open Server Manager by choosing Start**⇨**Server Manager.**

   The Initial Configuration Tasks (ICT) dialog box appears by default on startup, until you configure it not to reappear. Close the ICT dialog box to automatically invoke the Server Manager applet; otherwise, the Server Manager applet appears by default, unless and until you configure it not to reappear unless manually triggered.

2. **Under the Roles Summary entry, select Add Roles.**

3. **Review the information on the Before You Begin page and then click Next.**

   A summary of changes to be made is displayed.

4. **On the Select Server Roles page, shown in Figure 6-3, select the Active Directory Domain Services check box and then click Next.**

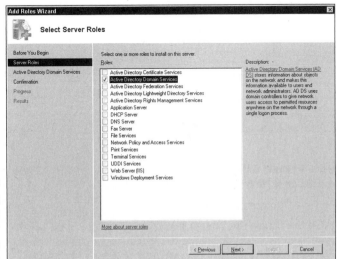

Figure 6-3:
The Select
Server
Roles page.

5. **Review the information on the Active Directory Domain Services page and then click Next.**

   A summary of changes to be made is displayed.

6. **On the Confirm Installation Selections page, shown in Figure 6-4, click Install.**

   The Installation Results page appears.

7. **Click Close This Wizard to launch the Active Directory Domain Services Installation Wizard (dcpromo.exe).**

8. **On the Welcome to the Active Directory Domain Services Installation Wizard page, click Next.**

9. **Select the Use Advanced Mode Installation check box.**

   The Domain NetBIOS Name page appears, enabling you to change the NetBIOS name that is otherwise generated as a default value.

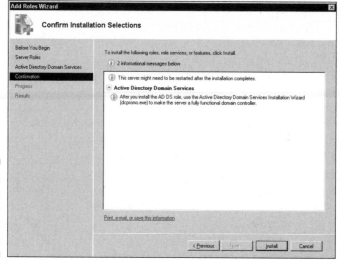

Figure 6-4:
The Confirm
Installation
Selections
page.

10. **Under Choose a Deployment Configuration, click Create a New Domain in a New Forest and then click Next.**

    The New Domain Name page appears.

11. **Under the Name the Forest Root Domain page, type the full Domain Name System (DNS) name for the forest root domain and then click Next.**

    The name must be in fully qualified domain name (FQDN) format, such as `mycompany.local` or `googleplex.com`. This isn't the name of your server; you define that when you first install Windows Server 2008, and again with Initial Configuration Tasks. Instead, this defines the top-level domain name.

    You can use the same name that will be used on the Internet to access your organization (such as `googleplex.com`), or you can use an internal, network-only domain name that won't be accessible from the Internet (such as `mycompany.local` or `mycompany.ad`).

12. **On the Set Forest Functional Level page, select the forest functional level that accommodates the domain controllers that you plan to install in the forest, and then click Next.**

    Windows 2000 and Windows Server 2003 forest functional levels are included with additional levels provided in Windows Server 2008. At this forest level, only the Windows Server 2008 DCs are supported.

13. **On the Additional Domain Controller Options page, DNS server is the default selection so that your forest DNS infrastructure can be created during AD-DS installation. Unless you intend to use AD-integrated DNS, deselect the DNS server check box. Click Next to continue.**

    A supportive DNS infrastructure must already exist to enable proper name resolutions within the new forest. By default, this wizard designates that this installation be delegated the zone to this DNS server in the authoritative parent zone prior to deployment.

If the wizard can't create a delegation, a message says that you may create one manually. Click Yes to continue. Otherwise, click No and let the wizard install DNS services with default settings on this, the first DC in the AD forest, which must be configured as a global catalog server (not an RODC). This server will hold five Operation Master roles and should be pre-configured for static IPv4 address assignment.

14. **If default values are unacceptable, type or point to the volume and folder locations for each element on the Location for Database, Log Files, and SYSVOL page; then click Next.**

15. **Type and confirm the restore mode password on the Directory Services Restore Mode Administrator Password page and then click Next.**

    The DS Restore Mode Administrator Password page appears, requesting a unique password to be used to start AD-DS in Directory Services Restore Mode for tasks that are performed offline following a system error. This mandatory provision is new to Windows Server 2008, and failure to supply a strong choice will prohibit you from continuing further with the AD-DS installation process.

16. **On the Summary page, review your selections. Click Back to change any necessary selections.**

    At this time, you may save a copy of your configuration settings by clicking the Export Settings button. This is especially useful for deploying RODC servers elsewhere, where installation is entirely command-line oriented. Such deployment relies on correct syntax and layout of a crucial answer file where all settings are acquired for installation.

    Accuracy of this information is crucial to a successful automated, unattended installation process.

17. **Select the Reboot on Completion option box to invoke an automatic restart, or manually restart the server and the AD-DS installation when prompted by clicking Restart Now.**

At this point, you can decide which network or application components, server roles, or features you want to install on the new server. The second, third, and fourth servers installed on a network can each have a different network role, including serving as one of the following:

✔ A peer domain controller hosting Active Directory

✔ A network management server hosting DHCP, DNS, WINS, Routing and Remote Access, or any other of a myriad of network services

✔ A file or print server

✔ A Web, media, or application server

We cover Active Directory details in Chapters 7 and 8, file servers in Chapter 12, and print servers in Chapter 9. Everything you must know about these Server Manager options appears in these chapters.

Getting the word out

Windows Server 2008 includes Internet Information Services (IIS) 7.0 and supports streaming media server, also known as Windows Media Services (WMS), now at version 9.5. IIS allows you to host Web and File Transfer Protocol (FTP) sites to intranet and Internet users. With WMS, you can create stunning multimedia presentations, combining audio, video, slides, interactive media, and more — all delivered by means of streaming connection.

You can use the IIS and WMS items on the Server Manager Wizard to jump directly to the administrative tools for IIS 7.0 and Media Services. You can also access Internet Information Services Manager (also known as the IIS MMC snap-in), shown in Figure 6-5, by choosing Start⇨Control Panel⇨Administrative Tools⇨Internet Information Services (IIS) Manager.

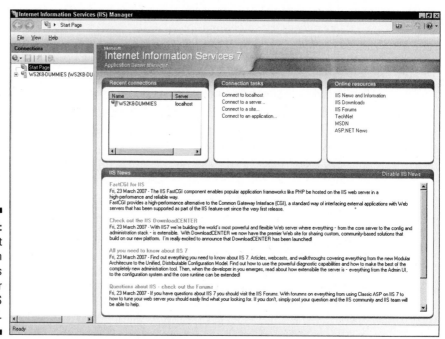

Figure 6-5:
Internet
Information
Services
Manager
for IIS
version 7.0.

To host Windows Media Services on your Windows Server 2008 system, you first need to configure it as a streaming media server by choosing Start⇨ Control Panel⇨Administrative Tools⇨Server Manager Wizard. Next, choose Add Roles under Roles Summary, and then select Streaming Media Wizard in the Add Roles Wizard. This installs the streaming media server role, which allows you to complete the setup of your server to stream audio and video content to clients over the Internet or your company's intranet.

IIS 7.0 is its own application, and its features go far beyond the scope of this book. If you really want to set up this service on your server, see the Windows Server 2008 Resource Kit or TechNet.

Organizing the neighborhood

The Configure Your Server Wizard's Networking option offers you quick access to the configuration tools used to manage DHCP, DNS, Remote Access, and Routing.

DHCP is a method for automatically configuring TCP/IP settings on clients and non-critical servers upon bootup. *DNS* is a method of resolving host names into IP addresses. We cover both DHCP and DNS in Chapter 10.

Although DHCP and DNS qualify as neat stuff, they're fairly complex topics that aren't covered in great detail in this book. Please look into the Windows Server 2008 Resource Kit for complete instructions on their configuration and management.

Routing and Remote Access is a service that combines two functions: routing and remote access (duh!):

- ✔ **Routing** is the capability to direct network communications across a local area network (LAN) or — with the help of a remote access link — across a wide area network (WAN).

- ✔ **Remote Access** is the capability to establish network connections using either telephone or Integrated Services Digital Network (ISDN) lines.

Windows Server 2008 can act as a client to connect to remote systems, or it can act as a server to accept inbound calls. The Remote Access and Routing selections under the Networking option (in the Configure Your Server Wizard) offer a link to the Routing and Remote Access management console shown in Figure 6-6. With this console, you can install and configure Routing and Remote Access.

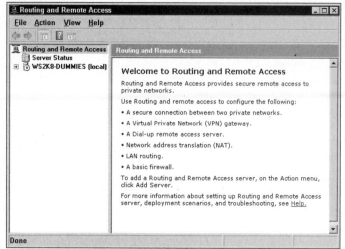

Figure 6-6:
The Routing
and Remote
Access
management
console.

Here are the basic steps to enable this service:

1. **Open the Routing and Remote Access management console (Start⇨ Administrative Tools⇨Routing and Remote Access).**

2. **Click the Routing and Remote Access item in the left pane.**

   The list of servers on the network is displayed.

3. **Right-click your server and choose Configure and Enable Routing and Remote Access.**

   The Routing and Remote Access Server Setup Wizard appears.

4. **Click the Next button to continue.**

   The wizard provides a selection list of common configurations and the option to manually define settings. The options available in the Common Configurations windows are as follows:

   - *Remote Access (dial-up or VPN)*

   - *Network Address Translation (NAT)*

   - *Virtual Private Network (VPN) Access and NAT*

   - *Secure Connection between Two Private Networks*

   - *Custom Configuration*

5. **Choose the option that best matches your needs or choose Custom Configuration and set things up manually.**

6. **Click Next.**

   Each of the four common configuration suggestions prompt you for further details to fine-tune the system. For more information on these selections, consult the Windows Server 2008 Resource Kit.

7. **Just follow the prompts through the rest of the wizard to complete the configuration.**

Keep in mind that to enable routing, you need at least two network interfaces. These can be NICs, specialized connections to the Internet, or even modems.

Although it looks like everything has been enabled, we recommend that you reboot before you make any further modifications. After the reboot, Routing and Remote Access is configured and functioning. All it needs now are network interfaces and a bit of configuration. The Routing and Remote Access interface is a graphical user interface (GUI), which — compared to the previous command-line, text-only control and display — is a great improvement. Furthermore, this management tool allows you to install routing protocols, monitor interfaces and ports, watch dial-up clients, define access policies, and modify logging parameters. You'll never want to use the ROUTE command again!

However, routing isn't a subject for the timid. For this reason, we recommend that you consult the Windows Server 2008 Resource Kit for more information. We don't want to leave you completely in the dark, so we list a few more features of Remote Access in the "Other frills" section a little later in the chapter.

Establishing Remote Connections

Remote communications consist of two distinct elements: the client and the server. Windows Server 2008 can either establish a connection to a remote system (as a dial-up client) or accept connections from remote clients (as a dial-up host). For more information on using Windows Server 2008 as a dial-up host, please see the Windows Server 2008 Resource Kit or consult Microsoft TechNet articles.

Getting connected

Using Windows Server 2008 as a dial-up client isn't terribly difficult. In most cases, you dial out to an Internet Service Provider (ISP) to make an Internet connection. We can take you step-by-step through the process of establishing such a connection if you have the following pieces of information at hand:

✔ Phone number of the ISP

✔ Logon name

✔ Logon password

For this type of connection, we assume that you have a modem, not an ISDN line or other connection device. If you don't have a modem, you definitely need one for this exercise. You can install a modem using the Add/Remove Hardware applet from the Control Panel. If you follow the prompts, you'll be amazed at how easy it is to do the installation.

We also assume that your ISP has a simple logon procedure. If you require special characters to be prefixed to your logon name, must traverse a logon menu, or must execute a logon script, you need to consult your ISP for instructions on how to configure Windows Server 2008 to properly establish a connection. Fortunately, most ISPs have a simple logon process.

Here's how to get things rolling:

1. **Choose Start⇨Connect To to display the Network Connections screen, as shown in Figure 6-7.**

   You should have a modem installed before you follow these steps.

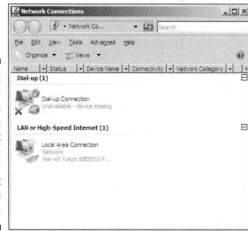

Figure 6-7: The Network Connections management console (after a dial-up object has been defined).

2. **Click the Set Up a Connection or Network link.**

3. **Under Choose a Connection Option, select Set Up a Dial-Up Connection and then click Next.**

4. **Fill in the Telephone Number and Destination Name entries, select whether this object is shared among other users, and click Next.**

5. **Type the User Name and Password into each corresponding field, choose an optional Domain, and click Create.**

6. **When the connection is ready to use, you may click Connect; otherwise, click Close.**

That's it! An icon now appears in the Network Connections window with the name you provided. Double-click this icon to display the Connection dialog box. Click the Dial button to establish the connection. After a few noisy moments, you'll establish a connection and be ready to surf!

You can view the status of the connection by placing your mouse cursor over the connection icon (the one with the two overlapping computers) in the icon tray. You can also double-click the icon to display a dialog box with more information.

You can change the parameters of the dial-up connection by right-clicking the icon in the Network Connections window and choosing Properties. In the dialog box for the Network Connections Property page, you can change every aspect of the connection.

To end the connection, right-click the connection icon in the icon tray and choose Disconnect — or double-click the connection icon to display the Details box and then click Disconnect.

Other frills

Windows Server 2008 includes all the latest capabilities that you would expect in a Windows-based remote access server. You'll recognize most of these from Windows Server 2003, and some from Windows 2000 and Windows NT. But even with the latest enhancements, Windows Server 2008 has retained nearly all of its old capabilities and functions. That means if you could accomplish something using Windows NT 4.0, Windows 2000, or Windows Server 2003 RAS, you can do it better using Windows Server 2008 Remote Access.

These features include but aren't limited to the following:

✔ Point-to-Point Protocol (PPP) for dial-out and dial-in connections. Serial Line Internet Protocol (SLIP) is still retained for outbound connections to non-PPP systems. (Windows XP Professional doesn't support SLIP for incoming connections; only Windows Server 2008 can use TCP/IP to connect through SLIP.)

✔ Multilink PPP for aggregating similar connections into a single pipeline.

✔ Point-to-Point Tunneling Protocol (PPTP) for link establishment over the Internet for secure communications.

- ✔ Authentication encryption to secure logon passwords.
- ✔ VPN security features: IPSec and L2TP. (See the Windows Server 2008 Resource Kit or TechNet for more information.)
- ✔ Support for *smart cards* (which are small cards added to the system to store security information).
- ✔ Full Remote Authentication Dial-in User Service (RADIUS) support.
- ✔ Shared connections (a single computer sharing its connection with other network clients).

For an in-depth discussion of Remote Access, check out the Windows Server 2008 Resource Kit.

Chapter 7

Doing the Directory Thing

*I*n this chapter, you look at the updates made to the directory service known as Active Directory. You find out what a directory service is, why it's required for a Windows domain and forest structure, and how to plan for and install the Windows Server 2008 Active Directory. It may not be the greatest thing since sliced bread, but it's at least as good as cracked pepper crackers!

What you won't find here, but might benefit from knowing, is that Active Directory cleanly integrates with virtual machines in Virtual Server capacities. This level of integration enables delegated administration and secure, authenticated guest access. And for those of you not already in the know, *Windows Server Virtualization* is the logical partitioning of server software resources so that multiple instances of an operating system (such as Windows Server 2008) can operate simultaneously, side by side.

What Is a Directory Service?

You may not know it, but you use directory services all the time. When you get hungry and crave pizza, you open your telephone directory and look under P for this peerless paragon of sustenance. That telephone book is a kind of directory service — namely, it contains the information you need, along with a way to locate the information you require. (In this case, it's in alphabetical order.) A computerized directory service works pretty much the same way: It contains information about numerous aspects of your company, organizes that information, and provides one or more tools to help you explore the information it contains.

The first operating system from Microsoft to offer directory services was Windows Server 2000. Novell NetWare has its own native directory service — Novell Directory Services (NDS) or eDirectory in NetWare 6 — and it's been offered in all the released Novell versions of Network Operating System (NOS) since 1993. Microsoft bases the entire Windows Server 2003/2008 domain structure (which started with Windows Server 2000) around its directory services, rather than simply offering them as an add-on to previous domain implementations. Microsoft's directory service is called *Active Directory*.

Although Active Directory and Novell Directory Services don't interact directly, you can synchronize Active Directory with Novell Directories using Microsoft Directory Synchronization Services (MSDSS). MSDSS is included with Services for NetWare 5 and up, and enables Active Directory synchronization with NDS and NetWare 3.*x* binderies so that system administrators can reduce overall directory management by administering one, rather than two, separate directory services.

When it comes to names, Microsoft seems obsessed with the word *active.* There's Active Desktop, ActiveX, and Active Directory. However, the term is accurate — indeed, Active Directory *is* active (when used correctly).

Meeting Active Directory

To do its job properly, a directory service must meet three primary requirements:

- ✔ It must include a structure to organize and store directory data.
- ✔ It must provide a means to query and manage directory data.
- ✔ It must supply a method to locate directory data and the network and server resources that might correspond to such data. (For example, if the directory data includes a pointer to a file and a printer, the directory service must know where they reside and how to access them.)

Windows Server 2008's Active Directory fulfills all these requirements using various technologies. For more information about Active Directory, pick up a copy of *Active Directory For Dummies* (Wiley Publishing).

Organizing and storing data

The structure of Active Directory follows the *ISO X.500 protocol* guidelines. (ISO stands for International Organization for Standardization.) Figure 7-1 shows the hierarchical structure of an X.500 directory. This is a common standard used in nearly all directory services, including not only Microsoft's

Active Directory but also Novell Directory Services (NDS), Netscape products, and other implementations. X.500 has proven to be useful for this application because it organizes data in a hierarchy that breaks directory information into a variety of useful containers, such as countries, organizational units, subunits, and resources. The example in Figure 7-1 organizes the directory down to the user object level.

The two X.500 standards most commonly used today are the 1988 and 1993 X.500 versions. The 1993 version includes a number of advances over the older 1988 version. Happily, the 1993 version is the standard upon which Microsoft built Active Directory for Windows Server 2008.

Managing data

A special-purpose protocol known as the Lightweight Directory Access Protocol (LDAP) provides the second ingredient for the Active Directory service. LDAP normally utilizes TCP port 389 as its main network transport connection. As the latter part of its name suggests, LDAP is designed specifically to retrieve and access directory data. (The *Lightweight* part of its name stems from the fact that it's a stripped-down version of an older, more cumbersome X.500 Directory Access Protocol.)

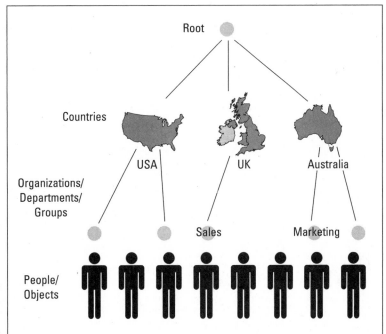

Figure 7-1:
The hierarchical structure of an X.500 directory.

The terminology used in this chapter may seem familiar to those of you who are acquainted with Microsoft Exchange Server's directory service. This is because the Active Directory service in Windows Server 2008 shares a common heritage (and common technology) with the Exchange Server directory service. In fact, an Exchange connector is supplied with Windows Server 2008 to link these two directory services and to replicate data between them. Not surprisingly, this software component is called the Active Directory Connector.

More information on LDAP appears on the RFC 1777 (Request For Comments) page at www.ietf.org/rfc/rfc1777.txt.

Locating data and resources

If Windows Server 2008 directory data is structured using the X.500 protocol and this data is accessed using LDAP, there also must be a way to locate directory data. Time for the missing third ingredient! How does Active Directory meet the third and final requirement for a working directory service? We're glad you asked. Active Directory relies on the well-known and widely used Internet standard called the Domain Name Service (DNS) as its locator service.

Of Domains and Controllers

Behind every great domain is a great domain controller (so the Aretha Franklin song goes), but before you look at how Windows Server 2008 uses domain controllers, a quick recap of Windows NT 4.0 usage is in order.

The Windows Server 2008, Windows Server 2003, and Windows 2000 way of doing the domain controller thing is quite different from the Windows NT 4.0 way — mainly because of Active Directory. Okay, so we don't have to repeat it over and over, Windows Server 2003/2008 and Windows 2000 all support Active Directory in the same way, so what you see here for Windows Server 2008 is also true of Windows Server 2003 and Windows 2000. (Those few small differences concern mainly high-level schema control and naming management and are too detailed for this book.)

In the beginning . . .

In Windows NT 4.0, 15-character NetBIOS (Network Basic Input-Output System) names represent domains. These domains revolve around a single user/group/policy database called the Security Accounts Manager (SAM) database, stored in writable format on a single, primary server known as the primary domain controller (PDC).

NetBIOS names can be a total of 16 characters long. On Microsoft operating systems, the NetBIOS name is limited to 15 characters. The 16th character is hidden from view and is used as a NetBIOS suffix by Microsoft Networking software to identify services installed on a given system. Additional information on Microsoft NetBIOS suffixes is available at `http://support.microsoft.com/default.aspx?scid=KB;en-us;q163409`.

Access to the domain database is required to access a domain's resources, so any model that depends on a single domain controller introduces a single point of failure. To improve availability and reliability of the domain database, Microsoft added a second type of server to this mix, known as a backup domain controller (BDC), which stores a read-only version of the SAM database. Users can access the BDC to log on to a domain and to investigate user, group, or account information, but changes to the database can be applied only to the PDC.

In this kind of domain environment, the PDC must periodically update the SAM database on all BDCs in its domain to keep them synchronized. Should a PDC ever fail, a BDC can be promoted to become the PDC and to write-enable its copy of the SAM database. However, there's an unbreakable master-slave relationship between PDCs and BDCs, because changes to the SAM database must be applied to the PDC first, then copied from the PDC to all BDCs. Therefore, if the PDC goes down, no changes can be applied to the SAM database unless the PDC is brought back up or a BDC is promoted to become the new PDC instead. Phew! Got all that?

Although this sounds like a form of subjugation, a master-slave relationship is computerese for "everything that changes on the master is copied to all slaves" and "only a master accepts changes and copies all changes to its slaves."

Windows Server 2008 no longer uses NetBIOS to name its domains; instead, it uses DNS domain names. (See Chapter 10 for more information on DNS domain names.) For example, rather than a `Dummies` domain, you might have `sales.dummies.com` as a legal domain name. However, you can still use a NetBIOS name to refer to a domain, which is a requirement for all non–Active Directory systems, such as the Windows 98 and Windows NT client operating systems, sometimes called *legacy clients*. (That's why you define one when you install Active Directory in Chapter 6.) Likewise, the concept of a SAM is no longer used in a Windows Server 2008 domain. All information about users, passwords, and groups is stored in Active Directory. Therefore, instead of servers that read from or write to the SAM, servers must supply the LDAP service that's needed to interface with Active Directory.

On Windows Server 2008, network servers that host the LDAP service are domain controllers. As in Windows NT–based networks, these servers are responsible for authentication and other domain activities. In Windows Server 2008–based networks, however, servers use Active Directory to provide the services that their older counterparts delivered using the SAM database.

Wherefore art thou, BDC/PDC?

The concept of PDCs and BDCs isn't used in the Active Directory domain structure of Windows 2000 and Windows Server 2003/2008. In this brave new world, all domain controllers are equal (although some are indeed more equal than others). How is this equality maintained? A process known as *multimaster replication* ensures that when changes occur on any domain controller in a domain, these changes are replicated to all other controllers in that domain. Therefore, instead of the older master-slave relationship between PDC and BDCs, you have a peer-to-peer relationship among all domain controllers in a Windows Server 2008 domain (and beyond) where trust relationships exist. (A *trust relationship* is a special interdomain access arrangement that you define when users in one domain require access to resources in another domain.)

Because you can't upgrade all your domain controllers from Windows NT 4.0 to Windows Server 2008 in one fell swoop, Windows Server 2008 allows you to operate your domains in a mixed mode. This allows Windows NT 4.0 BDCs (but not PDCs) to participate in a Windows Server 2008 domain. The idea is that you begin by upgrading the NT4 PDC to Windows Server 2008 and then proceed on to other server-based systems in the enterprise. This will often include the upgrading or total demotion of all existing NT4 Server class BDCs.

For a Windows NT 4.0 BDC to function properly, it needs to obtain updates from a PDC. Therefore, a single Windows Server 2008 domain controller impersonates a Windows NT 4.0 PDC, which allows changes to be replicated to any Windows NT 4.0 BDCs in that domain. This capability of a Windows Server 2008 domain controller is known as a Flexible Single Master Operations (FSMO) role (also known as operations master role). This specific server role is called PDC emulator.

Even in a full-fledged, Windows Server 2008–only environment, the PDC emulator operations master still plays an important part in the scheme of things. It performs certain duties that no other DCs in the domain handle. The PDC emulator receives preferential replication of password changes performed by other domain controllers in the domain. When passwords are changed, it takes time to replicate the change in every domain controller in the domain. That synchronization delay might cause an authentication failure at a domain controller that hasn't yet received the change. Before that remote domain controller denies access to whatever is trying to perform the access, it forwards the authentication request to the PDC emulator because the PDC emulator may have different information (for example, a new password).

In a mixed mode domain operation, clients can use NetBIOS names to access old-style domain services, or they can use Active Directory to access Windows Server 2008 domain services. To find a Windows Server 2008 domain controller, clients must query a DNS server for a service record that takes the general form that follows:

```
_ldap._tcp.<domain name>
```

where `_ldap._tcp.dummies.com` represents the domain controllers for the `dummies.com` domain, for example.

Windows Server 2008 domain controllers don't have to run the DNS service locally. The only requirement is that the DNS servers support the service record types required so that those domain controllers can be located as needed.

Knowing What Makes Active Directory Tick

To put things in a technobabble nutshell, Active Directory is implemented using an X.500 structure for directory data, an LDAP interface to access directory data, and Dynamic DNS as a locator mechanism for directory data. So, now that you know all this stuff about Active Directory, what does it give you? The following list recounts some of the main features and advantages of Active Directory:

- ✔ **Security:** Information is stored in a secure form. Each object in Active Directory has an access control list (ACL) that contains a list of resources that may access it along with which access privileges are granted to each such resource.

- ✔ **Query capabilities:** Active Directory generates a global catalog to provide a flexible mechanism for handling queries. Any client that supports Active Directory can query this catalog to request directory data.

- ✔ **Replication:** Replication of the directory to all domain controllers in a domain means easier access, higher availability, and improved fault tolerance.

- ✔ **Extensibility:** Active Directory is *extensible,* which means that new object types can be added to a directory or existing objects can be extended. For example, you could easily add a salary attribute or an employee ID to the user object. (An *attribute* is extra information about an object.)

✔ **Multiple protocols:** Communication between directory servers or across directories from multiple vendors can use numerous networking protocols because of Active Directory's X.500 foundation. These protocols currently include LDAP Versions 2 and 3 and the HyperText Transfer Protocol (HTTP). Third parties can extend this capability to include other protocols as well, if needed.

✔ **Partitioning:** In an Active Directory environment, information may be partitioned by domain to avoid the need to replicate large amounts of directory data. Each such domain is called a *tree* because of the way that X.500 structures directory data into an interlinked hierarchy with a single root. In a large and complex network, a collection of domains forms a group of trees that is called — you guessed it — a *forest!*

When you partition Active Directory data into different trees, it doesn't mean that Active Directory can't be queried for information from other domains. Global catalogs contain a subset of information about every object in an entire domain forest, which allows such searches to be performed on the entire forest through the agencies of your friendly local domain controller.

What replication means

In a Windows Server 2008 domain, all domain controllers are equal. Therefore, if you apply changes to any domain controller, the complete domain directories of all other domain controllers must be updated (through a process called *multimaster replication)* to record those changes.

Domain trees

A *domain tree* is a set of Windows 2000 domains or Windows Server 2003/2008 domains (or both) connected by a two-way transitive trust and sharing a common schema, configuration, and global catalog. To be considered a true domain tree, all domains must form a contiguous hierarchical namespace. A single domain by itself with no child names is still considered a tree.

The first domain installed in a domain tree is the *root domain* for that tree. It is considered the *forest root domain* if it is also the first domain in the forest. An *Active Directory forest* is a collection of one or more Windows 2000 domains

or Windows Server 2003/2008 domains (or all three) that share a common schema, configuration, and global catalog. Active Directory forests have a noncontiguous namespace.

All domains in a domain tree and all trees in a single forest have the connectivity benefit of the two-way transitive trust relationship, which is the default trust relationship between Windows 2000 and Windows Server 2003/2008 domains. This complete trust between all domains in an Active Directory domain hierarchy helps to form the forest as a single unit through its common schema, configuration, and global catalog.

Here's how multimaster replication works: Active Directory uses an update sequence number (USN) to track changes and updates made to Active Directory objects. As changes are made to the objects, this number is incremented by 1 on each object affected by the change. For example, a user account object that was updated to include a home telephone number would have its USN incremented by 1 to reflect that it had been modified. This modification is then sent to the other domain controllers in the domain. The object with the highest USN — that is, the most recently updated object — overwrites any object with a lower USN.

USN increments are *atomic operations;* in English, this means that the increments to the USN's value and the actual change to directory data occur at the same time. If one part fails, the whole change fails; therefore, it isn't possible to change any Active Directory object without its USN being incremented. Thus, no changes are ever lost. Each domain controller keeps track of the highest USNs for the other domain controllers with which it replicates. This allows the domain controller to calculate which changes must be replicated during each replication cycle. In the simplest terms, the highest-numbered USN always wins!

At the start of each replication cycle, each domain controller checks its USN table and queries all other domain controllers with which it replicates for their latest USNs. The following example represents the USN table for Server A.

Domain Controller	USN
DC B	54
DC C	23
DC D	53

Server A queries other domain controllers for their current USNs and gets these results:

Domain Controller	USN
DC B	58
DC C	23
DC D	64

From this data, Server A can calculate the changes it needs from each server:

Domain Controller	USN
DC B	55–58
DC C	Up to date
DC D	54–64

It would then query each server for the updates it needs.

Up-to-date vectors are two different segments of data that contain a globally unique identifier (GUID) and the Update Sequence Number (USN). The Up-to-date vector is made up of server USN pairs held by the two domain controllers containing the highest originating updates. (This is usually the domain controller in which the originating update occurred and then its immediate replication partners.) The *high watermark vector* contains the highest attribute USN for any given object. By using both of these vectors, domain controllers can calculate that a given replication of data has already been received to prevent further replication of any particular update.

Because objects have properties, they also have property version numbers (PVNs). Every property of an object has a PVN, and each time a property is modified, its PVN is incremented by 1. (Sound familiar?) These PVNs are used to detect collisions, which happen when there are multiple changes to the same property for an object. If a collision occurs, the change with the highest PVN takes precedence.

If PVNs match, a *time stamp* is used to resolve any such conflicts. Time stamps are a great second line of defense in avoiding collisions. They explicitly mark when each change to the directory data is made, thus enabling the system to determine whenever one change takes precedence over another.

In the highly unlikely event that the PVNs match *and* the time stamp is the same, a binary buffer comparison is carried out and the larger buffer size takes precedence. PVNs (unlike USNs) are incremented only on original writes, not on replication writes. PVNs aren't server specific but travel with the object's properties.

A propagation-dampening scheme is also used to stop changes from being repeatedly sent to other servers. The propagation-dampening scheme used by Windows Server 2008 prevents logical loops in the Active Directory structure from causing endless proliferation of updates and prevents redundant transmission of updates to servers already current.

The grand schema of things

Every object in an Active Directory forest is part of the same schema. The schema defines the different types of information that Active Directory objects can contain and store. The two main data definitions outlined in the schema are attributes and classes.

For example, a user object takes attributes such as name, address, and phone number. This collection of attributes and their definitions is called the *schema*. You may think of an object's schema as a laundry list of its attributes or a checklist of its capabilities. The default schema supplies definitions for users, computers, domains, and more. You can have only one schema per domain per object because only one definition per object is permitted.

The default schema definition is defined in a file named SCHEMA.INI, which also contains the initial structure for the NTDS.DIT file in which Active Directory data is stored. SCHEMA.INI is located in the %systemroot%\ntds directory: It's an ASCII file, so you can view it or print it as you like.

By default, the Active Directory schema can't be edited easily. For example, you can add a salary attribute or an employee ID to the user object. In most cases, you should leave schema editing to the most senior programmers or system administrators because changes made to the schema can't be undone, and incorrect edits can severely damage Active Directory and affect the entire forest. Some applications, such as Exchange, edit the schema for you when they're installed. If you feel the need to edit the schema for some reason, lie down and wait for that feeling to go away. If it comes back, hire a professional Active Directory programmer.

An entire *enterprise forest* (a collection of Active Directory trees in a single organizational container) shares a single schema. If you change that schema, it affects every domain controller in every linked domain. Therefore, you'd better be sure that any changes you make are both correct and desirable. Only experienced programmers or schema administrators should be allowed to change the schema. For more information on extending the schema, search the Microsoft Web site (www.microsoft.com) for *Active Directory Programmer's Guide*.

Global catalogs

The *global catalog* contains entries for all objects in a single *Active Directory forest* (which is a collection of domain trees that may or may not explicitly share a single, contiguous namespace). It contains all the properties for all the objects in its own domain, and it contains a partial subset of properties from all the remaining objects in the forest. The entire forest shares a single global catalog. Multiple servers hold copies of the entire catalog; these servers are domain controllers called *global catalog servers.* To hold a copy of the global catalog, a server must maintain a copy of the Active Directory, which automatically makes the server a domain controller.

Searches across the entire forest are limited to the object properties that appear in the global catalog. Searches in a user's local domain can be for any property when you perform a so-called *deep search* on properties not in the global catalog.

Don't configure too many global catalogs for each domain because the replication needed to maintain such catalogs can levy a burden on a network. One global catalog server per site is usually sufficient.

Although any given search can encompass a specific container or organizational unit (OU) in a domain, a specific domain, a specific domain tree, or the entire forest, in most cases full searches involve querying the entire Active Directory forest through the global catalog.

Planning for Active Directory

If you're using some version of Windows NT, you may have multiple domains with several trust relationships between individual pairs of domains. Theoretically, you could just upgrade each domain, keep existing trust relationships, and make no changes. If you did that, however, you'd lose the advantages of Active Directory.

If you're running a Windows 2000 domain, a bit of planning is still necessary to upgrade. Even though Windows Server 2003/2008 and Windows 2000 can both be domain controllers in the same domain, we generally don't recommend using two versions of a product to perform a single function. In most cases, using the same version of operating system (including upgrades and patches) keeps unexpected hiccups from corrupting your domain and bringing down your network.

That said, you can deploy Windows Server 2008 systems into a domain as domain controllers. You can even perform an upgrade installation on a Windows 2000 domain controller to convert it to a Windows Server 2003/2008 ("Longhorn") domain controller. Just be careful. Don't upgrade every system at once. Upgrade one or two, and then test everything to make sure your network still performs as you expect it to. Always leave yourself an out — the ability to roll back to a previous configuration, when things were working properly.

In some cases, businesses using Windows 2003 won't move to Windows Server 2008 in a hurry. The most likely candidates for Windows Server 2008 migration are Windows Server NT or 2000 shops that have been waiting for the latest and greatest generation of Active Directory servers from Microsoft before jumping on the bandwagon. Therefore, the remainder of the discussion of Windows Server 2008 migration focuses on upgrading from Windows NT or 2000. If you need to upgrade from Windows Server 2000 or 2003 and are already using Active Directory, some of the following applies, but the details will differ somewhat from case to case.

Before you upgrade a single domain controller, you should create a plan for your domain. Then, you should use this plan to govern the order and method for your migration from Windows NT domains to Windows Server 2008 Active Directory.

What's in a namespace?

A *namespace* is a logically bounded region that contains names based on a standardized convention to symbolically represent objects or information. Specific rules guide the construction of names within a namespace and the application of a name to an object. Many namespaces are hierarchical in nature, such as those used in DNS or Active Directory. Other namespaces, such as NetBIOS, are flat and unstructured.

In Windows Server 2008, domains use full-blown DNS names rather than NetBIOS names. This creates *interdomain parent-child relationships* — where one domain may be created as a child of another — that Windows NT can't support. For example, sales.dummies.com is a child of the dummies.com domain. (A child domain always contains the full parent name within its own name.)

It's important to remember that parent-child relationships can be created only from within a parent domain using DCPROMO, the Active Directory Installation Wizard. The parent domain must exist before you create any child of that parent. Thus, the order in which you create or upgrade domains is crucial!

In the next section, you find more reasons why it's important to create your domains in a certain order. But even before you concern yourself with site issues, you need to be aware that you should always create an enterprise root domain before creating any other domain. For example, if you begin by creating the dummies.com root domain, the sales.dummies.com domain and all other dependent domains can then be created as children of the dummies.com root domain. This structure helps when searching other domains and enables the possibility of moving domains around in future versions of Windows Server.

Making sites happen

Sites in Active Directory are used to group servers into containers that mirror the physical layout of your network. This organization lets you configure replication between domain controllers. Actually, sites are primarily used for replication control over slower wide area network (WAN) links between separate sections of the same network. A number of TCP/IP subnets can also be mapped to sites, which allows new servers to join the correct site automatically, depending on their IP addresses. This addressing scheme also makes it easy for clients to find the domain controller closest to them.

When you create the first domain controller, a default site called Default-First-Site is created, and the domain controller is assigned to that site. Subsequent domain controllers are added to this site, but they can be moved. You can also rename this site to any name you prefer.

Sites are administered and created using the Active Directory Sites and Services Microsoft Management Console (MMC) snap-in. To create a new site, do the following:

1. **Start Active Directory Sites and Services, shown in Figure 7-2. (Choose Start⇨Control Panel⇨Administrative Tools⇨Active Directory Sites and Services.)**

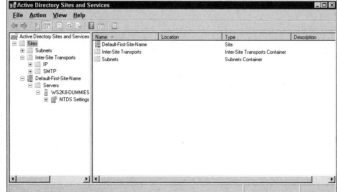

Figure 7-2: Active Directory Sites and Services.

2. **Right-click the Sites branch and choose New Site.**

   The new object Site dialog box appears.

3. **Type a Link Name for the site (for example, NewYork).**

   The name must be 63 characters or less and can't contain "." or space characters. You must also select a site link from the list. By default, DEFAULTIPSITELINK is created during the DCPROMO process. If you haven't created additional sites manually, this is the only one listed.

4. **Select a site link to contain the new site and then click OK.**

5. **Read the confirmation creation dialog box and then click OK.**

You must be a member of the Enterprise Admins group in the forest or the Domain Admins group in the forest root domain. Otherwise, unless you're delegated the appropriate authority, you can't make these changes.

For best security practice, use Run as Administrator from your lowest-level user account and use administrative credentials.

Now that the site is created, you can assign various IP subnets to it. To do so, follow these steps:

1. **Start Active Directory Sites and Services. (Choose Start⇨ Administrative Tools⇨Active Directory Sites and Services.)**

2. **Expand the Sites branch.**

3. **Right-click Subnets and choose New Subnet.**

   The New Object — Subnet dialog box appears.

4. **Type the name of subnet in the form <network>/<bits masked>.**

   For example, 200.200.201.0/24 is network 200.200.201.0 with subnet mask 255.255.255.0.

5. **Select the Site with which to associate the subnet (for example, New York).**

6. **Click OK.**

You now have a subnet linked to a site. You can assign multiple subnets to a site if you like. For more information on subnets, see Chapter 10. For even more details, search the Windows Server 2008 Help menu for subnets.

Oh, you organizational unit (OU), you

The *organizational unit* (OU) is a key component of the X.500 protocol. As the name suggests, organizational units contain objects in a domain that are organized into logical containers, thus allowing finer segregation and control within a domain. Organizational unit containers can contain other organizational units, groups, users, and computers.

OUs may be nested to create a hierarchy to match the structure of your business or organization closely. Using OUs, you can eliminate cumbersome domain models developed for Windows NT Server–based domains (the master domain model, for example, in which several resource domains use accounts from a central user domain). Using Active Directory, you can create one large domain and group resources and users into multiple, distinct OUs.

The biggest advantage of OUs is that they allow you to delegate authority. You can assign certain users or groups administrative control over an OU, which allows them to change passwords and create accounts in that OU but grants no control over the rest of the domain. This capability is a major improvement over Windows NT domain administration, which was an all-or-nothing affair.

Installing Active Directory

In Windows NT, you set up each server's type during installation. The server's function can fill one of the following roles:

- ✓ Stand-alone/member server
- ✓ PDC
- ✓ BDC

With the exception of PDC/BDC swapping, a server's role can't be changed without reinstalling the operating system. For example, you can't change a member server to a domain controller without reinstalling Windows NT.

Windows Server 2008 has left all that behind by allowing you to install all servers as normal servers. You can use a wizard (covered in the following section) to convert normal servers to domain controllers, or domain controllers to normal servers. This facility also gives you the ability to move domain controllers from one domain to another by demoting a domain controller to a member server and then promoting it to a domain controller in a different domain. In the Windows NT environment, demoting and promoting domain controllers typically requires reinstalling the operating system or jumping through some pretty major hoops.

Promoting domain controllers

Windows Server 2008 allows you to convert servers from normal servers to domain controllers and vice versa. To do this, you use the Active Directory Installation Wizard. You can access this wizard through the Configure Your Server tool (Start⇨Server Manager — see Chapter 6) or by executing DCPROMO from the RUN command (or command prompt). You can use the Active Directory Installation Wizard also to remove Active Directory from a domain controller; this returns the system to a member server state.

For the step-by-step of installing Active Directory and creating a domain controller, go to Chapter 6.

Active Directory's database and shared system volume

Although you can think of Active Directory as an information bubble, it's stored in file form on each domain controller in a file named `%systemroot%\NTDS\ntds.dit`. This file is always open and can't be backed up using a simple file copy operation. However, like old methods for backing up SAM in Windows NT 4.0, the new NTBACKUP program included with Windows Server 2008 includes an option to take a snapshot of Active Directory and back up that information. (This option is called System State.) There's even a special *directory restoration mode* you must boot into to restore an Active Directory backup! (Chapter 13 covers backups in detail.)

The *share system volume,* or SYSVOL, is the replication root for each domain. Its contents are replicated to each domain controller in the domain using the File Replication Service. The SYSVOL must reside on an NTFS 5.0 volume because that's a File Replication Service requirement.

SYSVOL is also a share that points (by default) to `%systemroot%\SYSVOL\`
`sysvol`, which contains domain-specific areas, such as logon scripts. For
example, the logon share NETLOGON for domain `savilltech.com` points to
`%systemroot%\SYSVOL\sysvol\savilltech.com\SCRIPTS`. You can
simply copy files used for logging on to or off this directory, and the change
is replicated to all other domain controllers in the next replication interval
(which by default is set to 15 minutes).

Modes of domain operation

Windows Server 2008 domains operate in four modes: mixed, native, .NET,
and .NET interim:

- ✔ **Mixed mode domains** allow Windows NT 4.0 BDCs to participate in a
  Windows Server 2008 domain.

- ✔ In **native mode,** only Windows Server 2008/2003–based and Windows
  2000–based domain controllers can participate in the domain, and
  Windows NT 4.0–based BDCs can no longer act as domain controllers.

- ✔ In **.NET mode,** only servers running Windows Servers 2008 can act as
  domain controllers.

- ✔ The **.NET interim mode** is used when upgrading a Windows NT 4.0
  domain to the first domain in a new Windows 2008 forest.

The switch from mixed to native mode or native mode to .NET mode can't be
reversed, so don't change mode until all domain controllers are converted to
Windows Server 2008, Windows Server 2003, or Windows 2000 for native
mode — or just Windows Server 2008 for .NET mode. Also, note that you can't
add more Windows NT 4.0–based BDCs after the domain mode is switched.

In addition, a switch to native mode allows the use of *universal groups,* which,
unlike global groups, can be nested inside one another. Older NetBIOS-based
clients remain able to log on using the NetBIOS domain name even in native
mode. Universal groups are also supported in .NET mode.

Changing a domain's mode is known as *raising a domain's functionality.* You
can choose to step up to native mode from mixed mode, step up to .NET
mode from native mode, or jump directly to .NET mode from mixed mode. Be
careful: This is a one-way switch. After you raise the functionality, you'll have
to reinstall Windows Server to return to a lower functionality.

To raise a domain's functionality, perform the following steps on a Windows
Server 2008 domain controller:

   **1. Start Active Directory Domains and Trusts. (Choose Start⇨
   Administrative Tools⇨Active Directory Domains and Trusts.)**

2. **In the console tree, select and right-click the domain you want to change.**

3. **Click Raise Domain Functional Level.**

   The Raise Domain Functional Level dialog box appears, as shown in Figure 7-3.

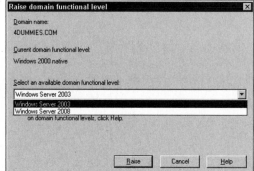

Figure 7-3:
The Raise
Domain
Functional
Level
dialog box.

4. **Under Select an available domain functional level, do one of the following:**

   • *Raise the domain functional level by selecting Windows Server 2003 and clicking Raise.*

   • *Raise the domain functional level by selecting Windows Server "Longhorn" and clicking Raise.*

5. **Click OK.**

   A warning is displayed stating that the domain mode change can take up to 15 minutes.

You can also raise the domain functional level by right-clicking a domain in the Active Directory Users and Computers snap-in, and then clicking Raise Domain Functional Level. The current domain functional level is displayed under a like-named entry in the Raise Domain Functional Level dialog box.

You also need to check all other domain controllers in the domain. Make sure each domain lists the correct mode on its properties dialog box. (Right-click the domain and select Properties.) If any domain controller isn't reflecting the change after 15 to 20 minutes, reboot it. This forces a replication.

If a domain controller can't be contacted when you make the change (for example, if it's located at a remote site and connects to the main site only periodically), the remote domain controller will switch its mode the next time replication occurs.

When Domains Multiply

In this section, you look at new methods available in Windows Server 2008 to interconnect domains. In Windows NT 4.0 domains, you're limited to simple unidirectional or bidirectional trust relationships to interconnect two domains explicitly at a time. Windows Server 2008 has many more sophisticated, functional models to create relationships and connections among its domains.

Trust relationships across domains

Windows NT 4.0 trust relationships aren't transitive. For example, if domain *A* trusts domain *B,* and domain *C* trusts domain *B*, domain *C* doesn't automatically trust domain *A*. (See Figure 7-4.)

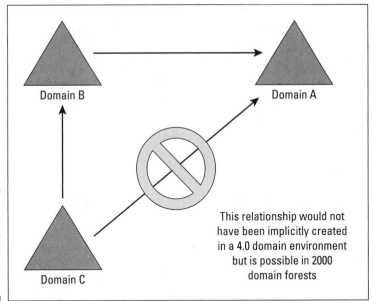

Domain B

Domain A

Domain C

This relationship would not have been implicitly created in a 4.0 domain environment but is possible in 2000 domain forests

Figure 7-4:
An example of a trust relationship in Windows NT 4.0.

This lack of transitivity is no longer the case with the trust relationships used to connect members of a tree or forest in Windows Server 2008/2003 or Windows 2000. Trust relationships used in a Windows Server 2008/2003 or 2000 tree are two-way, transitive trusts. This means that any domain in the forest implicitly trusts every other domain in its tree and forest. This removes the need for time-consuming administration of individual trusts between pairs of domains because such trusts are created automatically whenever a new domain joins a tree.

The security of Windows Server 2008 trusts is maintained by Kerberos. Kerberos Version 5.0 is the primary security protocol for Windows Server 2008, but it isn't a Microsoft protocol. Kerberos is a security system developed at the Massachusetts Institute of Technology (MIT). It verifies both the identity of the user and the integrity of all session data while that user is logged in. Kerberos services are installed on each domain controller, and a Kerberos client is installed on each workstation and server. A user's initial Kerberos authentication provides that user with a single logon to enterprise resources. For more information about Kerberos, see the Internet Engineering Task Force's (IETF's) Requests for Comments (RFCs) 1510 and 1964. These documents are available on the Web at `http://rfc-editor.org`.

Building trees

In Windows Server 2008, one domain may be a child of another domain. For example, `www.legal.savilltech.com` is a child of `savilltech.com` (which is the root domain name and therefore the name of the tree). A child domain always contains the complete domain name of the parent. As shown in Figure 7-5, `dev.savillCORP.com` can't be a child of `savilltech.com` because those domain names don't match. A child domain and its parent share a two-way, transitive trust.

When a domain is the child of another domain, a *domain tree* is formed. A domain tree must have a *contiguous namespace* (which means all namespaces share a common root — that is, have the same parent).

Domain trees can be created only during the server-to-domain-controller-promotion process with `DCPROMO.EXE`.

Here are some advantages to placing domains in a tree:

✔ All members of a tree enjoy Kerberos transitive trusts with their parent and all of its children.

✔ These transitive trusts mean that any user or group in a domain tree can be granted access to any object in the entire tree.

✔ A single network logon can be used at any workstation in the domain tree.

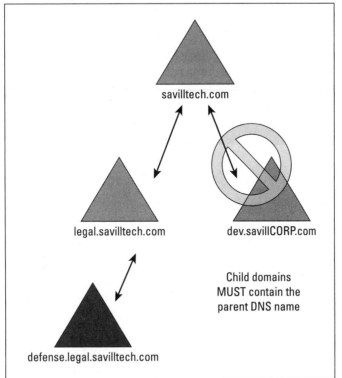

savilltech.com

legal.savilltech.com

dev.savillCORP.com

Child domains
MUST contain the
parent DNS name

defense.legal.savilltech.com

Figure 7-5:
Parent/child
relationship
example.

Understanding forests

You may have a number of separate domain trees in your organization with which you'd like to share resources. You can share resources between domain trees by joining those trees to form a forest.

A *forest* is a collection of trees that doesn't explicitly share a single, contiguous namespace. (However, each tree must be contiguous.) Creating a forest may be useful if your company has multiple root DNS addresses.

For example, in Figure 7-6, the two root domains are joined via transitive, two-way Kerberos trusts (like the trust created between a child and its parent). Forests always contain the entire domain tree of each domain, and you can't create a forest that contains only parts of a domain tree.

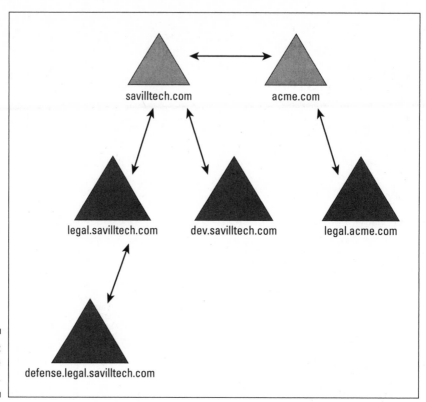

Figure 7-6:
An example
of a forest.

Forests are created when the first server-to-domain-controller-promotion process using DCPROMO is initialized and can't currently be created at any other time.

You aren't limited to only two domain trees in a forest. (You can have as few as one because a single domain by itself is technically considered both a tree and a forest.) You can add as many trees as you want, and all domains in the forest will be able to grant access to objects for any user in the forest. Again, this cuts back the need to manage trust relationships manually. The advantages of creating forests are as follows:

- All trees have a common global catalog containing specific information about every object in the forest.

- The trees all contain a common schema. Microsoft has not yet confirmed what will happen if two trees have different schemas before they're joined. We assume that the changes will be merged.

- Searches in a forest perform deep searches of the entire tree of the domain from which the request is initiated and use the global catalog entries for the rest of the forest.

Chapter 8

Working with Active Directory, Domains, and Trusts

*A*ccess to Active Directory's sheer power is useless unless you can configure and manage its content. Only then can you get the most out of its
powerful (but sometimes cryptic) environment. In this chapter, you take a
long hard look at Active Directory. Before you enter into this staring contest
with your computer screen, however, we want to show you how manipulating
and configuring content is tied to manipulating and configuring domains.
That's right; you get to tackle domains one more time. So once more into the
breach, dear friend, so that you too can master your own domain(s).

For details on domain controllers and their changing roles in Windows 2008,
see Chapter 7. We also suggest you pick up a copy of *Active Directory For
Dummies* (Wiley Publishing).

Master of Your Domain

Domain controller roles aren't defined during the installation of Windows
Server 2008 but rather while running the Active Directory Installation Wizard.
(For more information about the Active Directory Installation Wizard, see
Chapter 7.) Windows Server 2008 borrows the concept of a primary domain
controller (PDC) from Windows NT through the use of the PDC emulator for
certain domain functions, though it has jettisoned Windows NT's concept of a

backup domain controller (BDC). In Windows 2008, all domain controllers are equal and share peer-to-peer relationships, rather than acting either as master (PDC) or slave (BDC).

To support older Windows NT Server 4.0 and 3.51 BDCs in a mixed mode environment, one of the Windows Server 2008 domain controllers must emulate a Windows NT Server 4.0 PDC. Then it must replicate changes to those old-fashioned BDCs so that they can keep up with changes to Active Directory, such as password modifications.

Keeping lots of peers around can cause problems if you don't watch out. (Ever hear the expression, "Too many cooks spoil the soup"?) Windows Server 2008 uses five special roles to keep peers in line. One role is specifically designed to support any Windows NT vintage clients and domain controllers. The other four roles work to minimize the risk that multiple domain controllers will make changes to the same object, thereby losing or confusing attribute modifications.

These roles are called Flexible Single Master Operation (FSMO) roles, where each of the five roles manages a particular aspect of a domain or forest. Some of the Flexible Single Master Operation domain controllers, sometimes referred to as *operations masters,* have a role that is domain wide, so their effect percolates throughout the given domain. When a forest has multiple domains, each domain has a domain-wide FSMO domain controller. Other FSMO domain controllers have a forest-wide role. Each forest-wide FSMO domain controller is the only one of its type in the entire forest, regardless of how many domains reside within that forest.

The *flexibility* of the Flexible Single Master of Operation domain controllers indicates that these roles can move between domain controllers within a domain if the role of the original FSMO DC is domain wide, or between other domain controllers in the forest if the role of the original FSMO DC is forest wide. However, it does take some effort on your part to move them.

You assign FSMO roles using the NTDSUTIL utility. For more information on the NTDSUTIL utility, see the Windows Server 2008 Server Help files or the Resource Kit.

The following list gives you an idea how these five roles work with domains in Active Directory:

   ✔ **Schema master:** At the heart of Active Directory, the *schema* is a blueprint for all objects and containers. Because the schema has to be the same throughout an entire forest, only one domain controller can be used to make modifications to the schema. If the domain controller that holds the role of schema master can't be reached, no updates to the Active Directory schema may be performed. You must be a member of the schema administrators group to make changes to the schema. (See Chapter 7 for a more detailed definition of the schema.)

✓ **Domain naming master:** To add a domain to a forest, its name must be verifiably unique. The domain naming master of the forest oversees the domain name operation and ensures that only verifiably unique names are assigned. It also functions to add and remove any cross-references to domains in external directories, such as external Lightweight Directory Access Protocol (LDAP) directories. Only one domain naming master exists per forest. You must be a member of the enterprise administrators group to make changes to the domain naming master, such as transferring the FSMO role or adding domains to or removing domains from a forest.

✓ **Relative ID (RID) master:** Any domain controller can create new objects (such as user, group, and computer accounts). The domain controller contacts the RID master when fewer than 100 RIDs are left. This means that the RID master can be unavailable for short periods of time without causing object-creation problems. This ensures that each object has a unique RID. There can be only one RID master per domain.

✓ **PDC emulator:** The PDC emulator domain controller acts as a Windows NT primary domain controller when there is a domain environment that contains both NT4 BDCs and Windows 2000 DCs or Windows 2003/2008 DCs (or all three). It processes all NT4 password changes from clients and replicates domain updates to the down-level BDCs. After upgrades to the domain controllers have been performed and the last of the BDCs are upgraded or removed from the environment, the Windows 2000 domain or Windows Server 2003/2008 domain (or all three) can be switched to native mode. After the domain is in native mode, the PDC emulator still performs certain duties that no other DCs in the domain handle.

Each domain in the forest, including child domains, has only one PDC emulator domain controller.

✓ **Infrastructure master:** When a user and a group are in different domains, there can be a lag between changes to a user profile (a username, for example) and its display in the group. The infrastructure master of the group's domain is responsible for fixing the group-to-user reference to reflect the rename. The infrastructure master performs its fix-ups locally and relies on replication to bring all other replicas up to date. (For more information on replication, see the "When replication happens" section, later in this chapter.)

Trusts Are Good for NT 4.0 and Active Directory Domains

In the good old days before the need for FSMO roles (that is, during Windows NT's prime), there was exactly one main domain controller (a primary domain controller, or PDC) that could make changes to the Security Accounts Manager (SAM) database. Those changes were then replicated to other backup domain controllers (BDCs). In this model, the SAM database was simply a file stored on each PDC that contained information about the domain's security objects, such as users and groups. To support authentication across domains (and thus stymie unauthorized access to the network), you created one-way trust relationships between domains that would allow users and groups from the trusted domain to be assigned access to resources in the trusting domain.

The concept of trusting and trusted is confusing, so we're going to try to shed some light on the subject. Imagine a trust between two domains: A and B. Domain A trusts domain B, so domain B is the trusted domain, and domain A is the trusting domain. Because domain A trusts domain B to correctly authenticate its users, users from domain B can be assigned access to resources in domain A. (You could create a bidirectional trust relationship, where domain A trusts domain B with its resources and domain B trusts domain A with *its* resources. However, what you really have with a bidirectional trust is two unidirectional trusts that have been joined.) Before you get the idea that we're all one happy, trusting family, don't forget that Windows NT 4.0–based trusts aren't transitive; therefore, if domain C trusts domain B, and domain B trusts domain A, domain C doesn't implicitly trust domain A. For domain A to trust domain C, you must establish an explicit trust relationship between domain A and domain C. Got all that? Remember it; we'll come back to it later.

Windows Server 2008 makes use of Active Directory to keep domains in line when it comes to trust relationships. Windows Server 2008 domain controllers store the directory service information in a file (NTDS.DIT), and trust relationships are still needed to authenticate across multiple domains. Windows Server 2008 automatically creates trust relationships between all domains in a forest just as it did under Windows 2000, but the real change from the older NT4 model to the Active Directory approach lies in how modifications are made and replicated to the domain database and how all automatically created trusts are two way and transitive by default. Now if A trusts B and B trusts C, A trusts C — and the reverse is true as well.

Before you get too flabbergasted, don't forget that Windows 2000 and Windows Server 2003/2008 use trusts in the same way. All operating systems create two-way and transitive trusts.

How Domain Controllers Work Together

In the days of Windows NT, domains had it easy. You made changes at only one domain controller, and the changes were copied at regular intervals to any other controllers for the domain.

Now, with Windows Server 2008, you can make changes at any domain controller and remain confident that Windows Server 2008's left hand always knows what its right hand is doing. How does this work, you ask? The answer, dear friend, is multimaster replication. (And you thought we were going to say "blowing in the wind.") How multimaster replication works is discussed in Chapter 7, but here you look at the concept at a higher level.

With multimaster replication, any domain controller can make changes to the Active Directory database. Those changes are then replicated to all other domain controllers in that domain.

When replication happens

Replication between domain controllers in a Windows NT 4.0 domain is configured using a couple of Registry settings. That's it. Fairly useless really. Windows Server 2008 is *much* cooler!

A *site* is a collection of machines and domain controllers connected by means of a fast network and grouped by IP subnets. What do sites have to do with replication, you ask? Well, everything. They allow us to define different replication schedules depending on the domain controllers' site membership.

There are essentially two types of replication: *intrasite replication* (between domain controllers in the same site) and *intersite replication* (between domain controllers in different sites).

Intrasite replication

When a change is made to the Active Directory, such as adding or deleting a user or changing an attribute of an object (say, adding properties to a printer), this change must be replicated to other domain controllers in the domain. The change is called an *originating update*. The domain controller where the originating update was made sends a notification to its replication partners (other domain controllers in the site) that a change is available. After replication occurs, the replication partners will have a copy of the change that was made on the other domain controller. This updating of the Active Directory on the partner domain controller is called a *replicated update* because it originated elsewhere.

Replication is initiated between domain controllers at a defined regular interval (five minutes, by default), and urgent replication using notification can be initiated for any of the following:

- ✔ **Replication of a newly locked-out account:** Prevents users from moving to another part of a domain to log on with a user account that has been locked out on a domain controller.

- ✔ **Modification of a trust account:** Enables all members of a domain to take advantage of a new trust with another domain.

This replication methodology has some problems. In the good ol' days (in other words, with Windows NT 4.0), you changed your password at the PDC to avoid the problem of a new setting not being replicated for a long time. With Windows 2008, password changes are initially changed at the PDC FSMO; in the event of password failure, the PDC FSMO is consulted in case the password has been recently changed but hasn't yet been replicated.

If replication partners don't receive any change notifications in an hour (the default setting), they initiate contact with their replication partners to see whether any updates were made remotely and whether the subsequent change notifications were missed.

Intersite replication

Intersite replication takes place between particular servers in one site to particular servers in another site. This is where Windows Server 2008 shines. You can configure a timetable of how often to replicate for every hour of every day. All you need to do is follow these steps:

1. **Navigate to the Active Directory Sites and Services MMC snap-in. (Choose Start⇨Control Panel⇨Administrative Tools⇨Active Directory Sites and Services.)**

2. **Go to the Inter-Site Transport branch and select IP.**

3. **In the right-hand pane, select a site link (for example, a remote domain), right-click, and choose Properties.**

4. **Make sure that the General tab is selected and then click Change Schedule.**

   The dialog box used to change replication times appears, as shown in Figure 8-1.

5. **Change the replication schedule as desired.**

   For example, you can set it to replicate only on Sundays from 6 p.m. to 7 p.m.

You can have different replication schedules for every pair of sites, so depending on the network connectivity and geographical location, different schedules may be appropriate. For example, if a slow WAN link exists between two sites, a replication with less frequent updates may be necessary to prevent bandwidth consumption.

One other area of replication crosses domains: global catalog information. The global catalog contains all the information about all the objects in its own domain and a subset of information for every object in the forest. However, Windows Server 2008 performs all the calculations needed to optimize this replication, so mere mortals like us don't need to worry about it.

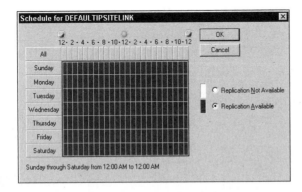

Figure 8-1:
This is where you change replication times.

Know your database limits

In Windows 2008, there's really no limit to the number of objects per domain — your organization will never get that big! Windows NT 4.0 domains are limited to around 40,000 objects per domain. This forces some companies to acquire multiple master domains joined by bidirectional trust relationships.

Windows 2008, on the other hand, extends this to around 10,000,000 objects per domain. HP has performed tests and created 16,000,000 user objects in a single domain with no significant performance problems. However, it had some *very* powerful hardware — probably much more powerful than your home PC or even your company's primary server!

These objects have to be replicated at some point. Windows Server 2008 uses *property* rather than *object* replication, which means that only the property change is replicated, not the entire object. In other words, if you change just one property of an object (a user's phone number, for example), only the property change (the new phone number) is replicated.

Your database size is governed by your domain controller hardware and the physical network infrastructure. But if you have enough money to invest in the proper hardware, we doubt that you would need more than a single domain (unless your company is really big). There are, however, other reasons for needing multiple domains and forests, such as needing different schemas. (See Chapter 7 for more on schemas.)

The backup and restoration needs of your enterprise may govern database size because a huge directory database is no good if it takes days to back it up.

Administrivia Anyone? (Controlling Domains and Directories)

If you don't have sufficient tools available to manipulate and manage Active Directory, its power won't do you much good. Fortunately, not only does Windows Server 2008 come with a complete set of ready-made tools, but you can also write your own tools and scripts using the Active Directory Scripting Interface (ADSI).

Exploring the directory management console

As with everything else in Windows 2008, management of Active Directory is accomplished using a Microsoft Management Console (MMC) snap-in. The snap-in you'll use most often is the Active Directory Users and Computers snap-in (shown in Figure 8-2), which is what you use to create, manage, and delete everything from users to computers. It includes some of the features of the old User and Server Manager from Windows NT.

Figure 8-2:
The Active
Directory
Users and
Computers
MMC
snap-in.

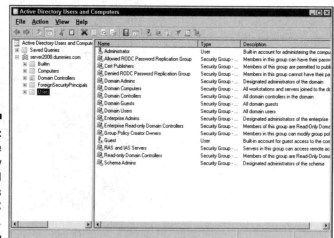

To access the Active Directory Users and Computers snap-in, choose Start⇨Administrative Tools⇨Active Directory Users and Computers. When you first start the snap-in, you see your domain name (represented as a DNS domain name) at the top of the directory. You'll also notice several containers (known more commonly as folders). Some of these containers are built-in organizational units (OUs), which contain objects in a domain that are organized into logical containers, thus allowing finer segregation and control in a domain. Certain container objects appear in all typical Active Directory installations:

- **Built-in:** By default, the details of the old Windows NT 4.0 groups, such as Administrators and Backup Operators.

- **Computers:** The computer accounts that were managed using Windows NT's Server Manager. Computer objects in other organizational units aren't listed in this container.

- **Domain controllers:** A built-in organizational unit that contains all domain controllers.

- **Users:** The default store for all domain users. Again, users in other organizational units aren't listed.

In a fully functional domain, you'll find various organizational units, depending on the services you have installed and the organizational units you create.

Everything is *context driven* in Windows Server 2008. This means that if you right-click an object or container, a menu specific to that object or container is displayed. This is much better than hunting through huge standard menus for options relevant to the chosen object.

Creating directory objects

Windows Server 2008 has tons of objects, such as computer, user, group, and shared folder objects. In this section, we concentrate on the creation of only the first two (computer and user objects) because the others are fairly intuitive and don't support many configuration options.

In a Windows NT 4.0 domain, it never took too much planning to create new user or computer objects. You just did it. In Windows Server 2008, however, you can't be quite so spontaneous. You first need to think about where you want to create such an object. Placement is important because, although you can still move objects around, it's much easier in the long run if you create an object in the correct location from the get-go. However, because you may not always have the time to plan and do it right the first time, you can always move the object later if you have to. (Just don't say we didn't warn you.)

Use OUs to help you organize your data into logical containers. First you create an OU for the various departments in your organization (for example, one for accounting, one for engineering, one for personnel, and so on). Then you can put all user and computer objects in a particular department in its OU. In addition, you can lighten your administrative load by assigning a person in each department the rights necessary to manage his or her OU and that OU only. Pretty nifty, huh?

You can create a user object in one of two places: in the default User/Computer container or in some organizational unit they or someone else has already created. If you delegate the ability to create objects, you can set it up so that the delegated users can create objects in only one location, or certain selected locations.

To create a user object, perform the following steps:

1. **Start Active Directory Users and Computers. (Choose Start➪Control Panel➪Administrative Tools➪Active Directory Users and Computers.)**

2. **In the Active Directory Users and Computers console tree, right-click the container (such as Users) in which you want to create the user object, point to New, and click User.**

   The first page of the User Creation Wizard (the New Object – User dialog box) is displayed, as shown in Figure 8-3.

   For interoperability with other directory services, you can click InetOrgPerson instead of the user object type, which is nearly identical. You can find information regarding InetOrgPerson in the "Understanding user accounts" article in the Windows Help files.

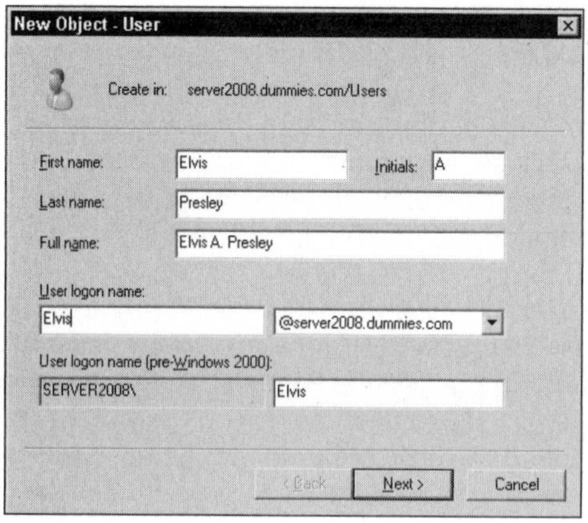

Figure 8-3:
The first page of the User Creation Wizard.

New Object - User

Create in: server2008.dummies.com/Users

First name: Elvis   Initials: A
Last name: Presley
Full name: Elvis A. Presley

User logon name:
Elvis   @server2008.dummies.com

User logon name (pre-Windows 2000):
SERVER2008\   Elvis

< Back   Next >   Cancel

3. **Type the user's first and last name, initials, and a logon name, and then click Next.**

   The next page of the Wizard allows you to set the new password and the following options:

   - *User Must Change Password at Next Logon*
   - *User Cannot Change Password*
   - *Password Never Expires*
   - *Account Is Disabled*

4. **In the Password and Confirm Password text boxes, type the user's password and select the appropriate password options.**

5. **Click Finish.**

That's it; you've created a new user. You're probably thinking, "What about all the other user attributes, such as security features?" Well, you no longer define those settings during the creation of the user. After you create the user object, you right-click it and select Properties. The Properties dialog box for the user appears.

Each tab pertains to various aspects of the selected user object. These tabs vary depending on the Windows Server 2008 subsystems in use, on other back office applications such as Exchange Server or SQL Server, and even on what third-party software you might have installed.

Computer account creation is much simpler and doesn't bombard you with quite so many tabs. Again, in Active Directory Users and Computers, right-click the container in which you want to create the new computer object (such as computers), and choose New⇨Computer. The New Object – Computer dialog box appears, as shown in Figure 8-4. You have to only type a computer name and select who can add the computer to the domain.

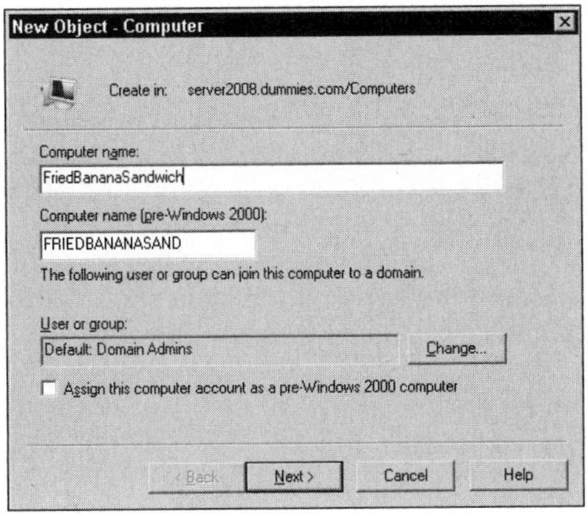

Figure 8-4:
We're
creating
a new
computer
object
named
FriedBanana
Sandwich.

Finding directory objects

Finding objects is one of Active Directory's greatest pluses. Using the global catalog, you can find an object anywhere in an enterprise forest by querying Active Directory.

You can search for anything — a user, a computer, even a printer — and you can search for many attributes. (The attributes presented vary depending on the type of object you're searching for.) For example, you can ask Active Directory to find the closest color-capable, double-sided printer at your site. You don't even have to tell Active Directory where you are. It figures that out automatically.

On a Windows Server 2008 system, there's a Search component that you can access from the Start menu. (Choose Start⇨Search.) Under this menu, you can use a number of options to search for users, folders, and printers. The available options are as follows:

- ✔ For Files or Folders
- ✔ On the Internet
- ✔ Find Printers
- ✔ For People

For example, if you want to search for a color printer, choose Start⇨Search⇨ Find Printers. There are three available tabs: Printers, Features, and Advanced. You want to choose the Advanced tab because it allows you to specify that you're searching for a color printer. After you enter all your details, click Find Now, and your results appear. In a large enterprise, many listings that meet your requirements may appear, so always try to be as specific and detailed as possible when performing a search.

A word on ADSI

Active Directory Scripting Interface (ADSI for short) allows you to manipulate the directory service from a script. You can use Java, Visual Basic, C, or C++ scripts. With ADSI, you can write scripts that automatically create users, including their setup scripts, profiles, and details.

If you need to manage a medium or large domain, you should learn ADSI. In the long run, it'll save you a great deal of time and aggravation.

Search the Microsoft Web site at www.microsoft.com/windows for ADSI, and you'll find loads of great information (more than you'd want!). Also check the Windows Server 2008 Resource Kit for details.

Permission to Proceed? Handling Directory Permissions

An old concept says, "You're the administrator; administrate no longer." And it does have some truth to it in Windows Server 2008. Although some tasks still require a full-fledged domain administrator, the common management of a domain may be more easily accomplished when you grant different sets of user permissions to manage different sets of users and user properties. In English, this means you can delegate the responsibility for managing low-level users to slightly higher-level users, and so on, until you, as the administrator, need to get involved only to manage more weighty constructs, such as domain forests and trees or intrasite access.

About Active Directory permissions

If you're familiar with the Windows NT security model, you probably know all about Access Control Lists (ACLs). ACLs allow a set of permissions to be applied to a file, directory, share, or printer (and more), thus controlling which users can access and modify these particular objects.

Windows Server 2008 takes this to the next level by assigning an ACL to every single attribute of every single object. This means you can control user access to such a fine degree that you can micromanage your users into the nearest insane asylum. You could insist, for example, that "User group Personnel Admin may change the address, phone number, and e-mail attributes of all users but nothing else."

Assigning permissions

You can assign permissions to Active Directory objects in various ways. Here, we present an extreme case, so everything else looks like a piece of cake!

Remember Active Directory Users and Computers? Well, earlier in this chapter, in "Exploring the directory management console," you saw a nice, basic view of this utility. However, it has other options that are shown only when it's in Advanced Features mode. To turn on Advanced Features, start Active Directory Users and Computers (choose Start⇨Administrative Tools⇨Active Directory Users and Computers) and then choose View⇨Advanced Features.

Some new branches are added to the basic domain root: LostAndFound and System. We don't care about that, though. Instead, we're interested in the new tab added to the objects — the Security tab.

In Active Directory Users and Computers, find a user, any user. Right-click the user and then select Properties. In the user's Properties dialog box, click the Security tab, and then click the Advanced button. The Permissions tab for the Advanced Security Settings dialog box appears, as shown in Figure 8-5. You see a list of permission entries that includes a type (Allow/Deny), a user or group, and the permission and its scope.

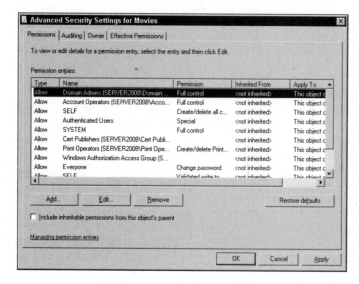

Figure 8-5:
The
Advanced
Security
Settings
dialog box
for an object
used to
control user
access.

Obviously, assigning permissions explicitly to every object takes forever. Thankfully, Active Directory uses an inheritance model so that you need to make changes only at the root; the changes propagate down from there. The following section spells out how this works.

Permissions inheritance

There are two types of permissions: explicit and inherited. *Explicit* permissions are assigned directly to an object, and *inherited* permissions are propagated to an object from its parent (and so on). By default, any object in a container inherits permissions from its container.

Sometimes, you don't want permissions to be inherited — for example, you're working with a directory structure in which different permissions are defined on each contained object, such as with a multiuser File Transfer Protocol (FTP) site or a shared folder that contains user home directories. The default setting in Active Directory specifies that permissions are inherited, but you can change this default behavior.

Remember the Advanced Features view for Active Directory Users and Computers? Well, you need it again. When you turn on the Advanced Features from the View menu and check out the advanced security properties of a user (right-click the user, choose Properties, click the Security tab, and then click the Advanced button), notice the Include Inheritable Permissions from This Object's Parent check box, which is selected by default. If you deselect it, any changes made to the parent container no longer propagate to the objects it contains. You disable inheritance for the object.

If you do disable inheritance, you're given the following options:

- ✔ Copy Previously Inherited Permissions to This Object
- ✔ Remove Inherited Permissions
- ✔ Cancel (Disable) the Inheritance

Of course, you can enable inheritance later if you want. It's not a one-way operation, so don't panic!

Delegating administrative control

Delegating administration over certain elements of your domain is one of the great things about Active Directory — no more administrator or non-administrator. Different people or groups can be delegated control over certain aspects of a domain's organizational unit. The following steps can be employed to delegate administration on objects:

1. **Open Active Directory Users and Computers. (Choose Start⇨Control Panel⇨Administrative Tools⇨Active Directory Users and Computers.)**

   Another way of accessing Active Directory Users and Computers is to click Start and type **dsa.msc** into the Start Search bar.

2. **In the console tree, right-click the organizational unit (OU) for which you want to delegate control.**

3. **Click Delegate Control to start the Delegation of Control Wizard.**

   This is accomplished by clicking the Add button to access the Active Directory search tool to locate users and groups. Make your selections. (Hold down Ctrl to select multiple users at the same time.)

   The users are now displayed in the selected user's area. The people you've selected are the ones who can perform the tasks you're about to choose.

4. **Click Next.**

   A list of common tasks is displayed for which you can delegate control (reset passwords and modify group membership, for example).

5. **Make your selections and then click Next. If you choose to create a custom task to delegate, follow the steps presented by the wizard.**

   A summary screen is displayed (as shown in Figure 8-6), giving you the option to change your mind.

6. **When you're happy with the changes you've made, click Finish.**

That's it; a few mouse clicks and you've delegated control of a container to a specific person or groups of people.

Figure 8-6: The summary screen of the Delegation of Control wizard.

Managing Trusts

In Windows NT 4.0, trust management was a big problem in a large enterprise. In Windows Server 2008, however, trust management is simple because all trusts are set up by default between all domains in a forest, and these trusts are two-way transitive trust relationships.

Two-way transitive trusts are created automatically between all domains in a forest when you run DCPROMO. You can, however, still create the old-style Windows NT 4 trusts for any domains that aren't part of the same enterprise forest.

Establishing trusts

You can create old-style trusts by following these steps:

1. **Open Active Directory Domains and Trusts by choosing Start⇨ Control Panel⇨Administrative Tools⇨Active Directory Domains and Trusts.**

2. **Right-click the domain of choice in the Active Directory Domains and Trusts interface and then choose Properties.**

3. **Click the Trusts tab (see Figure 8-7) to create one-way trusts.**

One-way external trusts aren't transitive and work the same as the old Windows NT 4.0 trusts.

You can delete a trust by selecting the trust and choosing Remove.

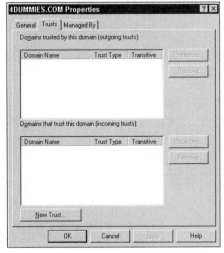

Figure 8-7:
This is where you create one-way trusts between domains.

If you open the door to trusts, who gets to come through?

In a forest, when you open the trust door (which happens automatically between all domains in the same forest), anyone gets to come in. All trusts are transitive, so anyone in any domain in the forest can be granted permission to any resource.

For old-style trust relationships (which are created manually between domains in different forests or in a Windows NT domain), the trust isn't transitive. Only users in the two domains for which the trust is defined can be assigned access to resources and only in the direction of the trust.

There's no need to panic, though, because users can't access resources without permission. Therefore, although they *can* be given access, they won't be able to gain access until specifically given permission to do so.

Chapter 9

Printing on the Network

· ·

· ·

*N*ext to not being able to access network resources, nothing freaks out users more than not being able to print their work. We bet you can't find a network administrator who can say that he or she hasn't struggled with print devices at one time or another. (If you've seen the movie *Office Space,* you can imagine the kind of frustration we're talking about.)

Windows Server 2008 includes a new printer architecture that provides a better print-server platform with improved performance and a strong foundation for future application development. It simultaneously maintains compatibility with existing print applications and drivers and enables them to use features found only in the newer XPSDrv printer drivers, which are built upon a modular design that enables more efficient print queue operation.

In addition to TS Easy Print capabilities, Windows Server 2008 integrates the XML Paper Specification (XPS) throughout to provide efficient, compatible, and high-quality document delivery to the entire print subsystem. The XPS document format is based on fixed-layout technology and, along with Open Packaging Conventions (OPC), defines a new format and specification built on industry standards like XML and ZIP.

In this chapter, you discover the specifics for setting up print devices on your network and avoiding common printing problems.

Throughout this chapter, we use the Microsoft terminology *print device* and *printer,* which may be confusing in the real world. Microsoft defines a *print device* as the physical printer, such as an HP LaserJet 2605, and a *printer* as the software on the server where you configure settings for the physical print device. We use Microsoft's terms in this chapter to be technically accurate. However, this terminology may be confusing if this is your first time working with Windows Server 2008.

Windows 2008 Has a Print Model

When a user prints, the print data follows a particular path from the user to the print device. One such example is the new XPS print path, which uses the XPS document format throughout the entire print path, from application to printer, and creates the possibility for true WYSIWYG output.

In Windows Server 2008, the basic pieces of this print scheme are as follows:

- ✔ **Print users:** *Print users* are the people who want to send print jobs to a print device on the network, on the Internet, or attached to their PC. To actually print, users must have a *print device driver* (called a *print driver* in non-Microsoftspeak) installed on their PC.

- ✔ **Graphics Device Interface (GDI):** The already expanded GDI is a software program that finds the appropriate print device driver and works with the driver to render print information into an appropriate printer language. After the information is rendered, the GDI sends it to the client-side spooler. (A Windows client application would call the GDI the *print process.*)

- ✔ **Print device driver:** This software piece is provided by either the manufacturer (for the latest version) or by Microsoft (not always the latest) and corresponds directly to a particular print device make and model. It's the interface between the software application and the print device, which is called a *print driver* in non-Microsoftspeak. You may also hear it referred to as a *printer driver.* The print device driver need not be installed on the client. Instead, if the client is a Windows 98, SE, ME, NT, 2000, or XP system, it can download the print device driver from the print server when it wants to print a document. However, this does require that the print server be configured to host print device drivers for these operating systems.

- ✔ **Printers:** This is also called a *logical printer,* and it isn't the physical piece of machinery you sometimes want to kick, but rather the bundle of settings you need to make a print device run. It exists as software on the server that you use to configure settings for print job processing and routing for the physical print device.

- ✔ **Print jobs:** *Print jobs* are files you want to print. Print jobs are formatted at the workstation by the GDI and a print device driver and submitted for output on a local or networked print device. If the print device is local (attached to the PC), the output is printed right there and then. If a network print device and print server are involved, the output is sent (spooled) to a queue on the print server until a print device is available to service the request.

- ✔ **Print servers:** *Print servers* are computers that manage network print devices attached to them. A print server can be any computer located on a network (or the Internet) that has a print device attached and runs some Microsoft operating system, such as Windows 2000/2003/2008, NT, or 9*x*. (Even a user workstation can function as a print server — but we don't like this approach because it typically brings too much traffic to some user's PC.) When a user submits a print job, the print server stores the job in a queue for the print device and then polls the print device to check for its availability. If the print device is available, the print server pulls the next job out of the queue and sends it to the print device.

  Any network administrator or user with appropriate access rights can manage print servers from anywhere on the network. By default, in Windows 2008, all members of the Everyone group can *print* to a device, but only those members specifically given rights can *manage* the device.

- ✔ **Print queues:** A *print queue* is a location on the hard disk where spooled files wait in line for their turn to print. Each print device has at least one corresponding print queue (although additional queues are possible). As users submit print jobs, those jobs go into the queue to wait for their turn. You define a queue for a print device when you add a printer to the Printers and Faxes folder and assign it a name. Print jobs enter the queues on a first-come, first-serve basis.

  Only someone with appropriate access rights to manage queues (administrators, print operators, and server operators) can alter print order in a print queue. You can assign users on your network permission to manage print queues for you. Windows 2008 includes a built-in user group called Print Operators, and you can add users to this group to give them the proper access rights for the task by choosing Start⇨ Administrative Tools⇨Active Directory Users and Computers, selecting a domain, and opening the Built-in folder.

  Giving some users print-queue management rights rather than others may be seen as playing politics if you don't exercise great caution in making such assignments. Some folks may accuse others of playing favorites when print jobs are rearranged in the queue. We've seen this happen a lot. If you choose people who are neutral, your life will be easier!

- ✔ **Print devices:** *Print devices* are physical devices or physical printers, such as HP laser printers. Print devices can be attached locally to a workstation or server or directly to the network. In the real (non-Microsoft) world, this is what we normal people call a printer!

Physical print devices

We call print devices *physical print devices* because you can walk up to these devices and touch them. Print devices come in different categories, including laser, plotter, inkjet, and bubble jet. You can attach a physical print device locally to a PC, server, or print server, or directly to the network (as shown in Figure 9-1).

A print server is just a network-attached PC that services print jobs — so, technically, we could lump PCs and print servers in the same category. We list them separately in this case because we want to distinguish between a PC where a user does work and a dedicated print server located on the network.

Logical assignments

A *logical printer assignment* isn't a print device — it exists intangibly, in the form of a Windows Server 2008 definition. It's sort of like a name that Windows 2008 uses to identify a physical print device (or a group of physical print devices, as you see later in this section). Each time you define a print device and its properties in Windows 2008, the operating system assigns a logical printer definition to the physical print device so that it knows to which physical print device you want to send your jobs.

When you first install a print device, a one-to-one correlation exists between the physical print device and the logical definition. You can expand the use of logical printer assignments, however, so that one logical printer assignment serves as the definition for several physical print devices. This use is known as *print device pooling,* and you set it up through print device properties by adding ports to the print device's definition.

You don't need to be too concerned about defining logical printers unless you intend to pool print devices. Pooling happens whenever you attach a print device to the server (as explained later in the "Attaching print devices to servers" section). Just understand that Windows 2008 correlates a logical printer definition to one or more physical print devices attached to your network.

For example, you're likely to have several print devices connected to your network, and all or many of them may be the same type, such as HPLJ2605. If you don't define a logical printer for Windows 2008, how does it know to which HPLJ2605 print device to send your jobs? You could end up running all around the building looking for your expense report! Defining a logical printer definition keeps order in your world. You could name one logical printer

2FLWest and you'd know that your report is sent to the HPLJ2605 on the second floor of the west wing of your building. (The mechanics involved are covered in the next section, "Installing on the Server's Side.")

Another bit of magic that logical assignments can help you with is balancing print jobs. Suppose that you have three physical laser print devices (A, B, and C) located on your network in close proximity. If a user chooses to send a print job to print device A, which is printing a large print job, a lot of time and resources are wasted if print devices B and C sit idle at the same time.

You can help your users by setting up one logical printer definition and assigning it several different physical print devices to which to print. Therefore, your users print to the logical printer, which then figures out which physical print device is available. This takes decision-making and worrying away from users and transfers it to the operating system. The only caveat here is avoiding too much physical distance between print devices. Try to make sure that all physical print devices in any logical printer definition are in the same general area so users don't have to run around the building looking for printouts.

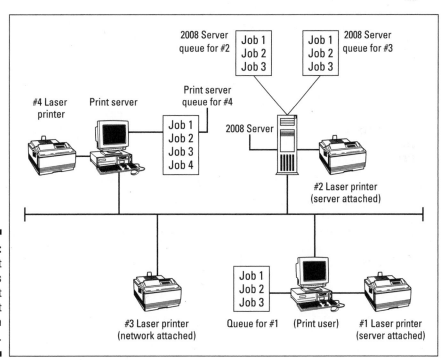

Figure 9-1:
Different
methods
to connect
print
devices on
a network.

Individual departments are typically arranged so that they share a common print device or print device group. Each group is logically labeled in some site-specific manner (hopefully accompanied by physical identifiers on each print device) that may or may not be descriptive of its assigned area or purpose. You will require advanced knowledge of what prints where whenever multiple devices are available in a pool.

When setting up logical assignments to service more than one physical print device, all physical print devices must be identical. The only changes you can make are to properties, such as bin number or paper size for each print device.

Conversely, you can assign several printer assignments to service one physical print device. You want to do this if users print special items, such as envelopes. Define one printer assignment to print to the envelope bin on the physical print device and define another printer assignment to print letter-size paper on the same print device.

If you give logical assignments descriptive names, users will know where the print device is and what type of function it performs. For example, using logical names such as *2FLWestEnv* and *2FLWest* tells users that 2FLWestEnv is on the second floor of the west wing and it prints envelopes, whereas the other is a normal print device on the second floor of the west wing. Both printer assignments service the same physical print device, but they may print to different bins, or one may pause the print device between pages, and so on. Here, you don't need to do anything other than define separate print devices that all print to the same port.

Installing on the Server's Side

Before you set up clients to print on your network, first make sure to go to the server and install all the print device definitions, drivers, and hardware, and then go to the client side. Doing so ensures that when you finally get to the user's workstation, you can submit a test print job right away because all the components are in place. If you start at the user's side first, you have to return later to check your work.

Meet the Printers folder

You can find nearly everything you want to do with print devices on the server in the Control Panel's Printers folder, which you can access by choosing Start⇨Control Panel⇨Printers. Previously, this applet was called Printers

and Faxes, but Microsoft has since reassigned faxing and scanning capabilities to a combined applet. We say *nearly* everything because the print device
drivers are stored outside the print devices folder. (Most of the drivers are
found on the Windows Server 2008 DVD.)

When you first install Windows Server 2008, the Printers folder contains only
an Add Printer icon, which is designed to help you install a physical print
device (or logical printer definition). Each time you install a new print device
by clicking the Add Printer icon (as described later in this chapter), Windows
2008 assigns it a separate icon in the Printers folder, as shown in Figure 9-2.

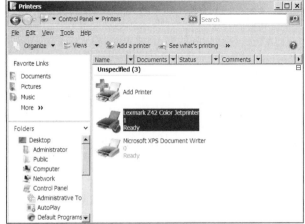

Figure 9-2:
The Printers
folder
showing an
installed
print device,
a Microsoft
XPS
Document
Writer icon,
and the Add
Printer icon.

When you click the Add Printer icon, the Add Printer Wizard appears,
bringing with it a set of default policies that it uses to guide you through
the process of adding each new print device to the Printers folder.

After you've installed the print devices you want, you can make changes
to the print devices' settings by visiting the Printers folder. Right-click the
print device you added and choose Properties from the pull-down list that
appears. A window with numerous tabs appears. You make all the changes
to the particular print device's settings in this Properties dialog box, so take
some time to familiarize yourself with the available settings.

Adding a networked print device

In an ideal world, your network and users would allow you to set up one type
of print device in one manner (such as all laser print devices of the same
make and model with network interface cards). In the real world, however,

things don't pan out like that. Therefore, the engineers at Microsoft designed Windows Server 2008 to provide you with four ways to attach print devices to your network:

- ✔ Windows Server 2008
- ✔ Print server
- ✔ Networked (as shown in Figure 9-1)
- ✔ PC (a workstation, in Microsoft-speak)

In the following sections, we show you the four approaches to installing print devices on your network. Three of the four installations are similar; they're just performed on different machines. For example, the steps for installing print devices attached to networks are similar to the steps for installing print devices attached to workstations. Both machines have print devices connected to their local ports, and they both share print devices on the network.

Attaching print devices to servers

You may find a need to attach a print device directly to your server. We don't recommend that you use this method unless your organization can't afford to spare a machine for you to use as a dedicated print server. Why? Because any time you attach a device to a file server, you run the risk that it may get hosed and crash the server — and we've seen this happen often.

To attach a print device to a Windows Server 2008, you need a print device, a Windows Server 2008 computer, a cable, the Windows Server 2008 installation DVD (if you didn't copy it to your server's hard disk), and any print device drivers you want automatically downloaded to the clients.

Connect the print device directly to one of the ports on the server (for example, LPT1) and install the print device on this machine in its Printers and Faxes folder by choosing Start⇨Control Panel⇨Printers. Then follow these steps:

1. **Double-click the Add Printer icon, which invokes the Add Printer Setup Wizard, and click Next.**

2. **Choose Add a Local Printer and then click Next. (USB devices are automatically detected and installed by Windows.)**

   The printer detection window of the wizard appears, searching for and installing attached Plug and Play print devices. If the print device isn't Plug and Play, you must follow the rest of the steps in this section.

3. **From the Use an Existing Port drop-down list, select the port to which you attached this print device (such as LPT1) and click Next.**

   A window appears for choosing the manufacturer and model of the print device.

4. **In the Manufacturer area, highlight the print device manufacturer; In the Printers area, highlight the model of the print device and click Next.**

   If you don't see your print device listed here, it means you have to provide the Add Printer Wizard with the driver. Click the Have Disk button and point the wizard to the location and path where the driver resides.

5. **In the Type a Printer Name window of the wizard, Setup suggests a name for this printer. Accept this name by clicking Next or type a new name for this printer in the Printer Name text box.**

6. **(Optional) Select the Set As the Default printer check box if you want this to be the default printer for users permitted to access the associated print queue.**

7. **Click Next to move on to the Printer Sharing window.**

8. **Indicate whether you'd like to share the printer.**

   By default, Windows furnishes a share name in the Printer Sharing window of the wizard.

   - *Share:* If you want to share the printer and you don't want to use the default name, you can type over it to change it. The share name is the name that your users will see when they print to this printer, so make it meaningful. (For example, create a name such as 2ndFLWestEnv to indicate that the printer is on the second floor of the west wing and it prints envelopes.)

   - *Do Not Share:* If you don't want to share the printer, choose the Do Not Share this printer option.

9. **Click Next.**

10. **Choose whether you want to print a test page (always a great idea) by clicking the Print a Test Page option. Next, to install drivers for the other client operating systems that will access the printer, click the Install Drivers button.**

11. **Click Finish.**

    Setup copies files from the Windows Server 2008 installation DVD to the Windows Server 2008 computer's hard disk. If you elected to print a test page, it also emerges from your newly defined printer at this point.

    If you chose to share the printer in Step 8, Windows may ask you to supply any missing operating system print drivers (see Step 10) so that it can automatically download those drivers to its clients. (However in most cases, Windows Server 2008 won't have to ask, because it comes equipped with a large library of client print drivers from which it can draw.)

12. **If you chose not to print a test page and not to install additional drivers, Setup presents you with a summary page of the choices you elected during the setup process. Click Finish if your choices are correct. Otherwise, use the Back and Next buttons to correct any invalid or incorrect info.**

If you're familiar with setting up printers on previous versions of Windows, you probably whipped through these steps because the print device setups are similar. At this point, you've set up the following:

✔ **One basic logical printer assignment that points to one physical print device on Windows Server 2008:** We say *basic* because you haven't yet customized any options, such as paper bins, dots per inch, and separator pages, for this print device. You probably weren't aware that as you defined this physical print device, you also assigned it a logical printer assignment. Remember that there's a one-to-one correlation between the two each time you install a physical device and define it — unless you add more physical devices.

✔ **A print queue for this print device:** Windows Server 2008 does this for you when you define the print device. To view the queue, double-click the print device icon. You won't see anything in the queue just yet.

✔ **Shared access to this print device by everyone on the network:** When you define a share name on the network for a print device, Windows Server 2008, by default, assigns the Everyone group access to this print device. You have to change this default policy if you don't want "everyone" to have access to this print device. If you have Active Directory installed, the print device is published to the Directory.

You can have multiple logical printer assignments pointing to one physical print device. If you want to assign another logical printer assignment that services this physical print device, you repeat the previous steps but assign a new computer and share name. You can assign different properties to this physical print device for each logical printer definition.

Attaching print devices to print servers

In the preceding section, we show you how to hook up a print device to a Windows Server 2008 computer so that your Windows Server 2008 functions as a print server on your network, in addition to its other duties. To help manage the load on the Windows Server 2008, you can offload this printing task to another computer on your network and have *it* function as your print server.

The print server is just another computer on your network, only with an attached print device that you set up to manage print spooling, print queues, and print jobs. We like this method because it frees up the Windows Server 2008 to perform other tasks. When your clients print to the print server, they bypass the Windows Server 2008.

You can install any Microsoft operating system that you like on the computer that will be your print server. We recommend at least Windows 9x, but we prefer a Windows NT, 2000, or XP workstation because you can download the print drivers to the client workstations from the print server automatically with no intervention on your part. This means that you don't have to install drivers manually on each of the client workstations.

After you've installed an operating system on your soon-to-be print server, follow Steps 1 through 12 from the "Attaching print devices to servers" section if you're using a Windows NT, 2000, or XP Workstation as the operating system. If you're using Windows 9x, repeat the same steps but exclude the downloadable print device drivers from Step 10. Instead, you must go to each client and install the corresponding print device drivers.

Attaching networked print devices to print servers

Some print devices, such as HP laser print devices, are neat because after you plug a network adapter into them, they're nearly ready to be placed anywhere on your network where there's an electrical outlet and an available network connection. Nearly, but not quite! You must still make all the physical connections and assign an IP address to the printer. After you do that, perform the following steps to add the networked print device to the print server:

1. **Choose Start⇨Control Panel⇨Printers.**

   The Printers applet window appears.

2. **Double-click the Add Printer icon to invoke the Add Printer Wizard and click Next.**

3. **In the Add Printer window, click Add a Network, Wireless, or Bluetooth Printer and then click Next.**

   Windows begins searching for available network-accessible print devices and displays the Searching for Available Printers window.

4. **Select the printer (print device) you want from the list of discovered printers (print devices) that appears in list form and then skip to Step 6. If the desired print device isn't found, you can find it by following these steps:**

   a. *Click The Printer I Want Isn't Listed.*

      The Find a Printer by Name or TCP/IP Address window appears.

   b. *Under Find a Printer by Name or TCP/IP Address, choose Browse for a Printer, Select a Shared Printer by Name (followed by the actual name), or Add a Printer Using a TCP/IP Address or Hostname.*

   c. *Click Next and follow the dialog boxes to find and select the printer.*

5. **Depending on what option you selected in Step 4, do the following:**

   • **If you clicked Browse for a Printer,** a browse list of all the local servers and workstations appears. Double-click those entries to find attached print devices, after which you can add them. If you supply a valid UNC name for a networked print device (for example, `\\library-srvr\HPLaserJ`), you can add it by using that name when you click Next.

   • **If you clicked Add a Printer Using a TCP/IP Address or Hostname**, the Type a Printer Hostname or IP Address window appears. Here you can explicitly identify (TCP/IP Device or Web Services Device) the device type or stick with the default Autodetect option. After that you must supply a valid hostname or IP address and a UDP port number to complete the print device connection.

6. **After completing these steps, click Next to see a Connect to Printer window, where you can change the printer name or leave it as is.**

7. **Finally, you can elect to print a test page (a good way to make sure your printer connection is working), or you can simply click the Finish button.**

   Congrats! You're done!

When installing a print device on a Windows Server 2008 with Active Directory installed, the Add Printer Wizard shares the print device and publishes it in the Directory — unless you change the policy rules. For more information on Active Directory, please read Chapter 7.

Attaching print devices to a workstation PC

Some users may have print devices on their desks that you may want to make available to other users on the network. Attaching a print device to a PC is the least desirable method because it involves users going to another user's PC to pick up print jobs. This can cause a disruption in workflow for the user who's unfortunate enough to have a print device on his or her desk. However, in smaller organizations where budgets are tight, this method is sometimes used.

To set this up, you must go to the user's desktop and share that print device on the network. If you'd like, you can restrict access to that share so that the entire organization isn't allowed to print there. Where do you find all this? In the Printers and Faxes folder on the user's desktop, of course! Right-click the Add Printer icon if no print device is installed, choose the print device to be a local print device connected to a local printer port (such as LPT1 or a USB port), and assign it a name. If a print device is already defined, right-click its icon and select Properties to give this print device a share name. After you share the print device on the network, other users can see it.

This method causes the user's workstation to manage the printing process. You can define this workstation-attached print device so that Windows 2008 Server will manage the print process instead. Here's how:

1. **Go to the user's computer desktop and define a share for this print device, but limit access to the username of "JoePrinter." This is a fabricated username you set up purely to manage this printer.**

   See the following section, "Sharing Printer Access," to find out how to define a share.

2. **Mosey back over to the Windows Server 2008 computer.**

3. **Add a user named "JoePrinter" in Active Directory Users and Computers. (Choose Start⇨Administrative Tools⇨Active Directory Users and Computers.)**

4. **Choose Start⇨Control Panel⇨Printers to open the Printers applet.**

5. **Follow the same steps in the "Attaching print devices to servers" section earlier in this chapter, except for the following changes:**

   • Click the Add Printer icon and choose the networked print device instead of the locally attached print device.

   • Let Windows search the network or choose The Printer I Want Isn't Listed to manually specify a share name. Either type the share name or use the Browse option to select and choose the share name you gave the print device on the client's desktop.

   • Give this print device a new share name that the rest of the users on the network will see.

Again, we don't recommend that you use this method unless your organization is tight on money. It can cause aggravation for the user who has to share the print device with other people on the network and can disrupt that user's work environment.

Sharing Printer Access

After you've installed a printer (software and a print device, that is) on your network (as we explain in the previous section), the next step is to create a share for it on the network. (See Chapter 12 for more details on Windows 2008 network shares.)

Until you share a print device, your users can't see it on the network. To share a print device, do the following:

1. **Open the Printers folder. (Choose Start⇨Printers and Faxes).**

2. **Right-click the print device you want to share and choose the Sharing option.**

3. **On the Sharing tab, choose the Share this Printer option and type a descriptive share name (for example,** 2ndFlWest**).**

4. **Unless you want to process print jobs locally on this computer, leave the Render Print Jobs on Client Computers option selected.**

5. **Click OK and you're finished!**

When you share a print device, it's available to everyone on the network by default. You must specifically restrict groups or users from accessing the print device if that's what you want.

If you have MS-DOS-based clients on your network, make sure that your share names for print devices are only eight characters long.

Bringing Printers and Clients Together

The final step in setting up networked printing involves setting up the print devices on the client side. Fortunately, not much is required in this process. Everything you need is on the Windows Server 2008, the print server, or in the user's Printers and Faxes folder on his or her desktop, depending on which client operating system is used.

If the client operating system is Windows XP, 2000, or NT, you need to only add the print device in the Printers and Faxes folder (Add Printer) and choose Networked Print Device. The reason is that the print device is attached to another computer somewhere on the network; it isn't local to this workstation. For the port, use the Browse option and find the share name of the print device to which you want to print. That's it!

If your clients have Windows 9x and are printing to a Windows Server 2008 (and you've installed the various client operating system drivers at the server), you simply add the print device in the Printers and Faxes folder (Add Printer) and select it as a networked print device. When you select the port as the share name of the networked print device, Windows Server 2008 automatically downloads the drivers.

Managing Windows 2008–Based Printers

You can view and manage your print servers, queues, and print devices (all of which are called printers in Microsoft-speak) from anywhere on the network, including your Windows Server 2008. From one location, you can view what's going on with all the print devices on your network. The only thing you can't do remotely is install hardware on the print device itself, such as memory or cables. But you knew that already!

The improved Print Management Console (PMC) that first appeared with Windows Server 2003 R2 is now enhanced to meet larger-scale network demands. PMC supports print server migration from Windows Server 2000/2003 to Windows Server 2008 installations and features an improved Network Printer Installation Wizard. The installation wizard reduces administrative overhead by automatically locating and — where applicable — deploying a compatible driver for hands-free automated setup.

The following list includes some issues to keep in mind as you manage print devices:

- ✔ **Make sure you don't run out of disk space on the server.** If you set up spooling on your network, you must keep a close eye on the hard disk space that print servers consume. The spooling process involves sending files from the print user to the print server. Remember that the print server can also be your Windows Server 2008. In either case, if your network handles high-volume print activity, it's possible to fill up a hard disk quickly with the spooling process.

  After files are spooled to the print server, they remain on the hard disk in the queue until an available print device is ready. If there's a problem with the print device, jobs can back up quickly. Remember that queues take up space on the hard disk, so if the queues back up, more and more space is needed. Be careful that you don't run low on disk space!

- ✔ **Make sure your print devices have enough memory.** When your users print graphics on the network, memory becomes an issue on the print devices. Large graphics files require more memory to print. You can find out how much memory is in a print device by performing a self test on the print device. Some organizations don't have a large budget for adding extra memory to all networked print devices, so they select one or more in strategic locations and then define logical print device setups just for graphics output.

✔ **Select the appropriate properties for print devices.** You can access the print device's Properties menu by right-clicking i icon in the Printers folder. (Figure 9-3 shows the various settings you can alter for any print device on your network.) We go through each of the tabs here to help you understand which print device properties you can change:

- *General tab:* Here's where you add information about the print device, such as comments, location, and whether to use a banner page. When defining a *banner page*, we recommend that you add some general comments about the print device and its location. In medium- to large-sized operations, adding a separator page so that print jobs may more easily be distinguished from each other is a good idea. The current print driver information is also found here. Change this only if you're going to install a new driver.

- *Sharing tab:* If you want users on the network to see this print device, you define the share name on this tab. (Remember to make it meaningful.) You can also tell Windows Server 2008 to allow this device to show up in the Directory. This is also where you tell Windows Server 2008 which client operating systems you have on your network and to which systems you want print drivers automatically downloaded.

- *Ports tab:* This is where you tell the system to which port your print device is attached. If it's a network-attached print device, you define it here using the Media Access Control (MAC) address; if it's a Transmission Control Protocol/Internet Protocol (TCP/IP) print device, you define it here using the IP address.

- *Advanced tab:* On this tab, you can schedule the print device's availability, priority, and spooling options. For example, you may opt to have print jobs run at night for a print device.

- *Security tab:* On the Security tab, you set up auditing of your print devices, which enables you to gather the information you'll need if something goes wrong with a device. You may want to use the Security tab for *charge-back purposes on a departmental basis* (where you audit the usage and charge users or departments for that use) or limit this print device's availability. You can also define who is allowed to manage this print device.

- *Device Settings tab:* On this tab, you define specific properties of the print device, such as paper size, dots per inch, and paper bin.

- *Color Management tab:* Adjust monitor or print device color-specific settings on this tab.

- *Cartridge Maintenance tab:* On this tab, you can view left and right ink cartridge levels and use clickable options to install/change cartridges, clean print nozzles, align cartridges, and order supplies. This last option actually opens the default Web browser and points it to your print device manufacturer's Web site. (This tab may not show up in every Properties window you examine; its presence or absence depends on your print device.)

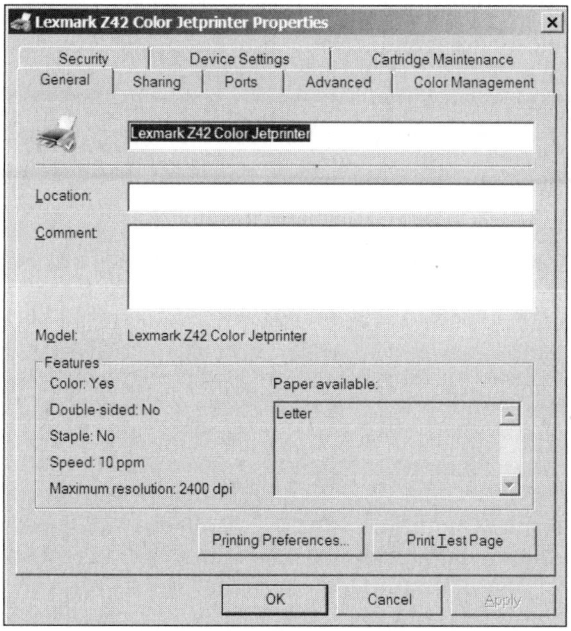

Lexmark Z42 Color Jetprinter Properties   ☒

| Security | Device Settings | Cartridge Maintenance |
| General | Sharing | Ports | Advanced | Color Management |

Lexmark Z42 Color Jetprinter

Location:

Comment:

Model: Lexmark Z42 Color Jetprinter

Features
Color: Yes
Double-sided: No
Staple: No
Speed: 10 ppm
Maximum resolution: 2400 dpi

Paper available:
Letter

Printing Preferences...   Print Test Page

OK   Cancel   Apply

Figure 9-3:
Print device
Properties
tabs in the
Printers
folder.

Preventing Printer Problems

Printing problems on a network can wreak havoc. Here are a few pointers to help you head off this type of trouble. If you do experience problems, see Chapter 20 for some troubleshooting help.

✔ **Purchase Windows Server Catalog compatible devices.** Purchase only network print devices listed in the Hardware Catalog for Windows Server 2008. Otherwise, you may spend hours trying to get a print device to work on the network — only to find that the device isn't compatible. And always remember to check Microsoft's site for the latest version of the Windows Server Catalog; you can find it at www. windowsservercatalog.com.

✔ **Get the latest print device drivers.** Be sure to obtain the latest print device driver associated with each print device on your network. Windows Server 2008 does its best to install print device drivers by itself where applicable, which may come from dated archives, online updates, or install media. Newer drivers often correct bugs found in older drivers. If you use an older driver, you may sometimes end up troubleshooting a known bug that has already been corrected in a newer driver.

✔ **Purchase a name brand.** We hope that your organization can afford to purchase name-brand print devices, such as Hewlett-Packard or Lexmark, for your network. We find that the biggest printing problems on networks stem from cheaper models. Even if you're able to hook these cheaper devices up, it may take so long to get all the pieces working that investing in brand-name print devices would be more cost effective.

✔ **Purchase from one manufacturer.** We like to stick with one type (brand name) of print device where possible. Notice we said *brand* and not *model.* We realize that some organizations need to print in both black and white and color. If you can purchase all your print devices from one manufacturer (for example, Hewlett-Packard), your life and your users' lives will be easier. If you have all Hewlett-Packard laser print devices on your network, don't buy another manufacturer's laser print device just because it's on sale that day at your local computer superstore. You can save time by working with one vendor and its equipment and drivers instead of having to hunt all over the Internet for various manufacturers' Web sites. Allow your users to become familiar with the one brand, and they won't have to learn how to use new equipment all the time.

✔ **Buy enough memory.** The influx of graphics software has upped memory usage in print devices to produce image-laden output. Don't wait until print jobs start fouling up before adding memory. If your budget is too low to do this up front, find a local vendor that stocks memory for your printers and keep their telephone number handy.

Faxing the Windows Server 2008 Way

Windows Server 2008, like Windows Server 2003 and Windows XP, includes native fax and scan support. This means you can now send and receive faxes using your computer without third-party software. The combined capabilities of Windows Server 2008 faxing and scanning are now controlled through (you might've guessed) the Windows Fax and Scan applet.

Windows Fax and Scan enables you to perform and manage all faxing or scanning tasks and documents from a central location. The new Windows Fax and Scan interface (shown in Figure 9-4) closely resembles Microsoft's Outlook interface — not coincidentally. Historically, Outlook stores calendar entries, contact entries, and e-mail messages; presently, the next-generation Exchange Server and Outlook client software utilize more expansive roles that encompass and accommodate many other types of information.

Figure 9-4:
Windows
Server 2008
Fax and
Scan
application.

For example, Unified Messaging in Exchange Server stores mailboxes, public folders, voice messages, and faxed documents in a central repository for clients. Windows Fax and Scan provides a limited scope of capability that interfaces with Exchange Server Unified Messaging.

Enabling faxing

Faxing isn't enabled by default. First, you must have a fax modem already installed and properly configured. (That means the driver is installed and things are working properly.) Next, follow these steps to enable faxing:

1. **Open the Windows Fax and Scan applet from the Start menu or Control Panel, and choose File⇨New Fax.**

   The Fax Setup Wizard launches.

2. **When the wizard asks whether you want to connect to a fax modem or fax server on the network, click OK.**

   The wizard installs the necessary components for faxing. After a few moments, you're returned to the Windows Fax and Scan applet.

3. **Follow the setup wizard's instructions to define the fax device name and location and decide how to receive faxes or incoming calls.**

Sending faxes

Faxing is like printing, but instead of sending the document's print job to a physical print device where the results are on paper, the print job is digitized and sent over the phone line to a receiving fax device (which can be a traditional fax machine or a fax-enabled computer). Other than needing to provide a phone number and the occasional cover sheet, faxing a document is just like printing a document. To send a fax, just select the New Fax option from the File menu of Windows Fax and Scan, begin formatting or typing your message, and then click Send.

The first time you attempt to send a fax, the Fax Configuration Wizard is launched. This wizard is used to define information about your fax system, such as the phone number, area code, and sender information.

Windows Fax and Scan is used to track and manage incoming and outgoing faxes, in much the same way as you might manage e-mail in Outlook. If you want to change your sender information, choose Tools⇨Sender Information from the Windows Fax and Scan console. To receive faxes, you have to enable incoming faxes and set the Answer After Rings control.

Keep in mind that you can have only one answering service per modem device. So, if you need a telecommuter to call in to connect to your system, don't set up that modem to wait for faxes. The device that is waiting for incoming faxes can still be used to send faxes or even for normal dial-out connections. If you find that you need more help with the fax capabilities of Windows 2008, check out the help file and the Windows Server 2008 Resource Kit.

Chapter 10

IP Addressing: Zero to Insane in Two Seconds Flat

*T*he Transmission Control Protocol/Internet Protocol (TCP/IP) drives the Internet and makes it accessible around the world. However, TCP/IP is a lot more than just a collection of protocols: Many elements in TCP/IP marry protocols to related services to provide complete capabilities. Important examples include dynamic address allocation and management, known as the Dynamic Host Configuration Protocol (DHCP), plus domain name to address resolution services, known as the Domain Name Service (DNS).

In this chapter, you find out about TCP/IP names, addresses, and related standard services, as well as other related services hosted in Windows Server 2008.

Resolving a Name: TCP/IP and NetBIOS

Whenever you issue a command in Windows Server 2008, you're expected to use the proper syntax. Otherwise, your efforts may not produce the desired results. For example, when you issue a `net use` command from a command prompt, you must enter the server name and a share name, as well as the drive to which you want to map. Therefore, a simple command such as

```
net use G: \\ORWELL\APPS
```

associates the drive letter G with a share named APPS on the ORWELL server. If you use the TCP/IP protocol to convey the data involved, the protocol doesn't know how to interpret the name ORWELL as a server. Instead, it understands Internet Protocol (IP) addresses, such as 172.16.1.7.

If you use TCP/IP on your network, you need some way to convert IP addresses into names and vice versa. Just as the United Nations requires translators so that everyone can communicate, so too does Windows Server 2008, which is why understanding naming conventions and name-to-address resolution are such an important part of working with TCP/IP on Windows Server 2008.

NetBIOS names

If you're like most folks, you freeze like a deer in the headlights when you hear the word *NetBIOS*. Don't worry. Only a small number of people really understand NetBIOS in detail, and figuring out what you need to know is easy.

A NetBIOS name is often called a *computer name.* When you install Windows Server 2008 on a network, each computer that runs Windows requires a unique computer name. This allows all NetBIOS-based utilities to identify each machine by name. When you enter a command that includes a computer name, Windows 2008 knows which computer you're talking about.

If you try to give two devices the same name, you run into trouble — like trying to use the same Social Security number for two people. Each time a computer joins the network, it registers its name with a browser service that keeps track of such things. When the second computer with the same name tries to register, it's rejected because that name is already taken. In fact, that machine will be unable to join the network until its name is changed to something unique.

When creating NetBIOS names, you need to work within some limitations, which are as follows:

✔ NetBIOS names must be between 1 and 15 characters long.

✔ NetBIOS names may not contain any of the characters shown in the following list:

   "   double quotation mark

   /   right slash

   \   left slash

   [left square bracket

   ]   right square bracket

:	colon
;	semicolon
		vertical slash
=	equal sign
+	plus sign
*	asterisk
?	question mark
<	left angle bracket
>	right angle bracket

In addition, dollar signs aren't recommended because they have a special meaning. (A NetBIOS name that ends in $ doesn't appear in a browse list.)

✔ Don't use lengthy names or put spaces in names. Windows Server 2008 doesn't care if you use longer names or include embedded spaces, but other networking clients or systems may not be able to handle them.

✔ Choose names that make sense to users and are short and to the point. Don't name machines after users or locations, especially if users come and go regularly or if machines move around a lot. When it comes to servers, name them to indicate their organizational role or affiliation (for example, Sales, Accounting, or Engineering).

What's in a NetBIOS name, you ask? A NetBIOS name should provide a short, clear indication of what's being named so users can recognize what they see. At best, this type of naming convention makes sense without further explanation. At the least, you can do what we do and put a sticker with the machine's name on each monitor or computer case for identification. You can view a list of your network's NetBIOS names by expanding the My Network Places section of Windows Explorer. See Figure 10-1 for a sample list of NetBIOS names taken from our network (such as Hush and Pentium_m).

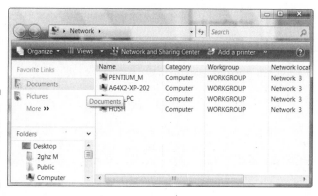

Figure 10-1:
NetBIOS computer names on our network.

TCP/IP names and addresses

TCP/IP uses a different naming scheme than NetBIOS does. TCP/IP uses 32-bit numbers to construct IP addresses (for example, 172.16.1.11). Each host or node on a TCP/IP network must have a unique IP address.

IP addresses aren't meaningful to most humans and are difficult to remember. Therefore, it's helpful to have some way to convert IP addresses to meaningful names. On a Windows Server 2008 network, you use computer names (also known as NetBIOS names). The Internet community uses a different naming convention called domain names. Translation methods, such as Windows Internet Name Service (WINS) and Domain Name Service (DNS), maintain databases to convert IP addresses to computer names (WINS) or domain names (DNS).

If you've ever used a Web browser on the Internet, you know that you can type a Uniform Resource Locator (URL), such as www.wiley.com, or an IP address, such as 208.215.179.146, to obtain access to a Web page. You can do so because the Internet uses DNS to resolve IP addresses to domain names and vice versa. If you type an IP address, the Web browser jumps straight to that address; if you type a domain name, your request goes through a DNS server that resolves the name to an IP address, and then the browser jumps to that address.

In the IP world, the naming scheme you can use is limited if you plan to connect your network directly to the Internet. VeriSign (www.verisign.com) is one of many domain name registrars in charge of approving and maintaining a database of *legal* Internet top-level domain names. You can request any domain name you want, but if someone else is using it or has a legitimate claim to a trade or brand name, you won't be able to use it. For example, you probably won't be able to use mcdonalds.com or cocacola.com as domain names. In fact, if someone else has already registered xyzcorp.com, you wouldn't be able to use that name, even if your company is named XYZ Corporation.

The format for a typical IP name is *host.domainname.suffix*. The domain name is something you can't guarantee, but typically represents your organization. The suffix, called a *top-level domain,* sometimes identifies the country of origin (for example, .ca is Canada and .de is Germany) or the type of organization (.gov is government, .edu is education, .com is a commercial business, .org is a nonprofit organization, and so forth).

Some domain names are more complex; they can take a form such as *host.subdomain.domainname.suffix*, as in jello.eng.sun.com, where the host name is jello, the subdomain is eng (for engineering), and the domain name is sun (the domain name for Sun Microsystems, Inc.), which is a commercial (.com) entity. The only parts of the name under control of the various Internet domain name registrars (such as VeriSign and other companies and organizations identified at `www.norid.no/domenenavnbaser/domreg.en.html`) are the domain name and the suffix — every domain name must be unique in its entirety to be properly recognized.

Names that include the host part, the domain name, and the suffix (plus any other subdomain information that may apply) are called Fully Qualified Domain Names (FQDNs). To be valid, any FQDN must have a corresponding entry in some DNS server's database that allows it to be translated into a unique numeric IP address. For example, the Web server for this book's publisher is named `www.wiley.com`, which resolves into an IP address of 208.215.179.146.

As long as you're completely isolated from the Internet and intend to stay that way, you can assign any names and IP addresses you like on your network. If you ever connect your network to the Internet, however, you'll have to go back and change everything! If your network will be — or simply *might ever be* — connected to the Internet, you have one of two options for assigning addresses:

> ✔ **You can obtain and install valid public IP addresses and domain names.**
>
>   Your Internet Service Provider (ISP) can provide these for you. When you obtain a range of IP addresses for your network — remember, each computer needs its own unique address, and some computers or devices need multiple addresses (one for each interface) —, make sure you get enough to leave some room for growth.
>
> ✔ **You can (and should) obtain a valid domain name from VeriSign or another domain name registrar, but you can use any of a range of reserved IP addresses, called *private IP addresses,* to number your networks.**
>
>   These addresses may not be used directly on the Internet; they've been set aside for private use. When used in concert with a type of software called Network Address Translation (or NAT for short), this approach requires you to obtain only a small number of public IP addresses but still allows Internet access for every computer on your network. This topic is discussed in more detail later in this chapter in the section "Address translation: The new magic."

To find out more about the process of obtaining a domain name, visit VeriSign's Web site at `www.verisign.com`. The form for researching domain names (determining whether a FQDN is already in use) and registering domain names (applying for a new FQDN) is on the main page. You'll find details on name registration services as well as on directory and database services that support the Internet's distributed collection of DNS servers.

Calling Everything a Node

A unique numeric identification tag, called an *IP address,* is assigned to each interface on a TCP/IP network. Every IP address in a TCP/IP network must be unique. Each device on a TCP/IP network is known as a *host.* Each host has at least one network interface with an assigned IP address. However, a host can have multiple network interface cards (NICs), and even multiple IP addresses, assigned to each NIC.

To network ID or host ID? That is the question

An IP address consists of two components:

- **Network ID:** Identifies the network segment to which the host belongs.

- **Host ID:** Identifies an individual host on some specific network segment. A host can communicate directly only with other hosts on the same network segment.

A *network segment* is a logical division of a network into unique numeric network IDs called *subnets.* A host must use a router to communicate with hosts on other subnets.

A *router* moves packets from one subnet to another. In addition, a router reads the network ID for a packet's destination address and determines whether that packet should remain on the current subnet or be routed to a different subnet. When a router delivers a packet to the correct subnet, the router then uses the host ID portion of the destination address to deliver the packet to its final destination.

A typical IP address looks like

```
207.46.249.222
```

(This example address matches the domain name www.microsoft.com.) This numeric IP address format is known as *dotted-decimal notation.* However, computers *see* IP addresses as binary numbers. This same IP address in binary form is

```
11001111 00101110 11111001 11011110
```

and is written in collections of eight bits called *octets.* Each octet is converted to a decimal number and then separated by periods to form the dotted-decimal notation format shown at the beginning of this paragraph.

The dotted-decimal version of IP addresses is more human-friendly than the binary version. As you may already know, domain names and NetBIOS names are even more friendly because they use symbolic names that make sense to humans.

An IP address requires 32 binary digits and defines a 32-bit address space that supports nearly 4.3 billion unique addresses. Although this seems like a lot of addresses, the number of available IP addresses is quickly dwindling. Consequently, several plans exist to expand or change the IP addressing scheme to make many more addresses available. For more information on such plans, search for *IPng Transition* in your favorite search engine.

IP designers carved the entire galaxy of IP addresses into classes to meet different addressing needs. Today, there are five IP address classes labeled by the letters A through E. Classes A, B, and C are assigned to organizations to allow their networks to connect to the Internet, and Classes D and E are reserved for special uses.

The first three classes of addresses differ by how their network IDs are defined:

✔ Class A addresses use the first octet for the network ID.

✔ Class B addresses use the first two octets.

✔ Class C addresses use the first three octets.

Class A addresses support a relatively small number of networks, each with a huge number of possible hosts. Class C addresses support a large number of networks, each with a relatively small number of hosts, as shown in Table 10-1. (Class B falls in the middle.) Therefore, branches of the military, government agencies, and large corporations are likely to need Class A addresses; medium-sized organizations and companies need Class B addresses; and small companies and organizations need Class C addresses.

Table 10-1	Address Classes and Corresponding Network and Host IDs			
Class	*High-Order Bits*	*First Octet Range*	*# Networks*	*# Hosts*
Class A	0xxxxxxx	1–126.x.y.z	126	16,777,214
Class B	10xxxxxx	128–191.x.y.z	16,384	65,534
Class C	110xxxxx	192–223.x.y.z	2,097,152	254

When it comes to recognizing address Classes A through C, the network ID for Class A addresses always starts its first octet with a 0. Each Class B network ID always starts with 10, and Class C network IDs always start with 110.

Consequently, you can determine address classes by examining an address, either in binary or decimal form. (See Tables 10-1 and 10-2.)

Table 10-2	Division of IP Address Component Octets According to Class		
Class	*IP Address*	*Network ID*	*Host ID*
A	10.1.1.10	10	1.1.10
B	172.16.1.10	172.16	1.10
C	192.168.1.10	192.168.1	10

Network ID 127 is missing from Table 10-1 because that ID is a loopback address. *Loopback addresses* are used when testing IP transmission — they transmit to themselves.

Subnetting: Quiet time for IP addresses

Subnets represent divisions of a single TCP/IP network address into logical subsets. The motivation for subnetting is twofold:

- ✔ It reduces overall traffic on any network segment by collecting systems that communicate often into groups.

- ✔ It makes it easier for networks to grow and expand and adds an extra layer of security control. Subnets work by "stealing" bits from the host part of an IP address and using those bits to divide a single IP network address into two or more subnetworks, usually called *subnets* — hence, the term in the preceding heading.

Network administrators typically use subnet masks to divide IP address blocks into smaller subnetworks. A *subnet mask* is a special bit pattern that takes over part of the host ID portion of an IP address and permits a larger network to be subdivided into two or more subnetworks, each with its own unique network address. The base subnet masks for Classes A, B, and C networks are 255.0.0.0, 255.255.0.0, and 255.255.255.0, respectively. You can create additional subset masks by adding extra bits set to 1 in the space occupied by the 0 that appears next to the rightmost 255 in any such number. This transformation is illustrated in Table 10-3, which shows some typical values for usable subnet masks.

Table 10-3	Subnet Masks and Results		
Binary Mask	*Decimal Equivalent*	*Number of New Subnets*	*Number of Hosts*
00000000	A: 255.0.0.0	A: 16,777,214	1
	B: 255.255.0.0	B: 65,534	
	C: 255.255.255.0	C: 254	
10000000	A: 255.128.0.0	A: Not valid	Not valid
	B: 255.255.128.0	B: Not valid	
	C: 255.255.255.128	C: Not valid	
11000000	A: 255.192.0.0	A: 4,194,302	2
	B: 255.255.192.0	B: 16,382	
	C: 255.255.255.192	C: 62	
11100000	A: 255.224.0.0	A: 2,097,150	6
	B: 255.255.224.0	B: 8,190	
	C: 255.255.255.224	C: 30	
11110000	A: 255.240.0.0	A: 1,048,574	14
	B: 255.255.240.0	B: 4,094	
	C: 255.255.255.240	C: 14	
11111000	A: 255.248.0.0	A: 524,286	30
	B: 255.255.248.0	B: 2,046	
	C: 255.255.255.248	C: 6	
11111100	A: 255.252.0.0	A: 262,142	62
	B: 255.255.252.0	B: 1,022	
	C: 255.255.255.252	C: 2	
11111110	A: 255.254.0.0	A: 131,070	126
	B: 255.255.254.0	B: 510	
	C: 255.255.255.254	C: Not valid	

What about IPv6?

Those who know a little bit about TCP/IP already are also likely to know it comes in two flavors. The current, predominant flavor (the one we describe at length in this very chapter) is called IPv4. It features 32-bit addresses broken into four 8-bit octets. There's a newer version of IP around, however. It's known as IPv6 and features 128-bit addresses (16 8-bit octets but seldom represented as such; these numbers are so big you see them primarily in hexadecimal or base 16 form if not plain old decimal form). In addition to a much bigger address space, IPv6 features enhanced security, multiple automatic addressing schemes, improved routing, and much more. But it's seldom used on small networks and despite a U.S. government mandate to switch over to IPv6 addressing in June 2008, that event looks increasingly unlikely as the date looms ever closer. Because it's very rarely used on small networks, we don't cover IPv6 in this book. Those readers who want to learn more, and work with IPv6 on Windows Server, should check out the TechNet IPv6 clearinghouse at `technet.microsoft.com/en-us/network/bb530961.aspx`.

Because routers are required to communicate across IP subnets, a router's IP address on each subnet must be known to every client on that subnet. This address is called the *default gateway* because it's where all out-of-subnet transmissions are directed by default. (It's the gateway to the world outside each local subnet.) If no default gateway is defined, clients can't communicate outside their subnets.

Hanging your shingle: Obtaining IP addresses

Deploying your own network or using a stand alone system with Network Address Translation (NAT) to connect to the Internet requires that you obtain one or more valid IP addresses. For some uses, you may simply contract with an ISP to use a dial-up connection. Each time you connect, you're assigned an IP address automatically from a pool of available addresses. After you disconnect from the ISP, that IP address is returned to the pool for reuse. This works equally well for stand alone machines and for the servers that might dial into an ISP to provide an on-demand connection for users who have private IP addresses but can attach to the Internet using NAT software.

One way to attach an entire network to the Internet is to lease a block, or subnet, of IP addresses from an ISP. However, leasing IP addresses can be expensive and can limit your growth. Also, many ISPs can no longer lease large blocks of IP addresses, so you may have to limit Internet access to specific machines or subnets.

For more information about taking this approach, you must contact your ISP to find out what it offers by way of available addresses and contiguous subnets. For some uses, public IP addresses are required because security needs dictate a true end-to-end connection between clients and servers across the Internet. In plain English, true *end-to-end connection* means that the IP address that a client advertises to the Internet is the same one it uses in reality. In the next section, you discover an alternate approach where an IP address advertised to the Internet is different from the private IP address that a client uses on its home subnet.

For some applications, particularly where secure IP-based protocols such as IP Secure (IPSec) or particular secure sockets layer (SSL) implementations are involved, network address translation techniques may not work! Make sure you understand your application requirements in detail before you decide whether to lease public IP addresses or use private IP addresses with network address translation.

Address translation: The new magic

If you don't want to pay to lease a range of IP addresses and your application requirements allow you to use private IP addresses, you can employ IP addresses reserved for private use in RFC 1918 on your networks. When used with network address translation software to connect to an ISP, a single public IP address (or one for each Internet connection) is all you need to service an entire network.

Routers move packets among subnets and networks

Only *routers* can transfer packets from one subnet to another, or from one network ID to another, in the TCP/IP world. *Routers* are specialized, high-end, high-speed devices from companies such as Cisco Systems or Extreme Networks. However, any computer with two or more NICs installed (where each NIC resides on a different subnet) can act as a router, provided that the computer can forward packets from one NIC to another (and thus, from one subnet to another). Right out of the box, in fact, Windows Server 2008 includes software and built-in capabilities to work as a router. Computer nerds like to call such machines *multi-homed computers* because the machines are "at home" on two or more subnets.

RFC 1918 (which you can find at www.faqs.org/rfcs/rfc1918.html) defines special IP addresses for use on private intranets. These addresses, which appear in Table 10-4, cannot be routed on the Internet. This approach provides improved security for your network as a fringe benefit because it means that any impostor who wants to break into your network can't easily masquerade as a local workstation. (Doing so would require routing a private IP address packet across the Internet.) Because all of these addresses are up for grabs, you can use the address class that makes sense for your organization. (And for Class B and Class C addresses, you can use as many as you need within the legal range of such addresses.)

Table 10-4	Private IP Address Ranges from RFC 1918	
Class	*Address Range*	*# Networks*
A	10.0.0.0–10.255.255.255	1
B	172.16.0.0–172.31.255.255	16
C	192.168.0.0–192.168.255.255	254

Using address translation software to offer Internet access reduces your costs and allows nearly unlimited growth. If you think private IP addresses combined with NAT software make sense for your situation, consult with your ISP for specific details and recommendations on how to use this technology on your network.

You've probably seen the terms *firewall* and *proxy* thrown about when reading about Internet access. Firewalls and proxy servers are network tools that are little more than special-purpose routers. A firewall may be used to filter traffic — both inbound and outbound.

Firewall filters may be based on a source or destination address, on a specific protocol, or port address, or even on patterns that appear in the contents of a data packet. A *proxy server* is an enhanced firewall, and its primary purpose is to manage communications between an in-house network and external networks such as the Internet. Proxies hide the identity of internal clients and can keep local copies of resources that are accessed frequently. (This is called *caching*, and it improves response time for users.)

You can check out several great online resources for firewalls, but online information on proxies is limited to product documentation. In addition to consulting the Windows Server 2008 Resource Kit and TechNet (http://technet.microsoft.com/en-us/default.aspx), here are several online resources you may want to check to discover more about these technologies:

✔ **NIST Guidelines on Firewalls and Firewall Policy:** `http://csrc.nist.gov/publications/nistpubs/800-41/sp800-41.pdf`

✔ **Microsoft's Internet Security and Acceleration Server (ISA) 2006:** `www.microsoft.com/isaserver`

✔ **Zone Lab's ZoneAlarm:** `www.zonealarm.com`

✔ **Cisco's Self-Defending Networks:** `www.cisco.com/en/US/netsol/ns643/networking_solutions_packages_list.html`

✔ **WinGate proxy server:** `www.wingate.com`

In addition to these excellent third-party products, Windows Server 2008 offers a built-in native firewall product known as the Windows Firewall (previously called the Internet Connection Firewall, or ICF), which is enabled and configured on the Advanced tab of a connection object. Windows Firewall is a host-based solution that can provide stateful filtering for inbound and outbound traffic with integrated IPSec protection settings, which may or may not offer the versatility and capabilities that your production network requires in a firewall. If you want to find out more about Windows Firewall, check the Help and Support Center and the TechNet article at `http://technet.microsoft.com/en-us/network/bb545423.aspx`.

Forcing IP Down the Throat of Windows Server 2008

Configuring TCP/IP on Windows Server 2008 can range from simple to complex. We review the simple process and discuss a few advanced items. For complex configurations, consult a reference such as the Windows Server 2008 Resource Kit or TechNet.

Three basic items are always required for configuring TCP/IP:

✔ IP address
✔ Subnet mask
✔ Default gateway

With just these three items, you can connect a client or server to a network.

Basic configuration

The protocol is configured on the Internet Protocol (TCP/IP) Properties dialog box. To access this dialog box, follow these steps:

1. **Choose Start➪Control Panel➪Network and Sharing Center.**

2. **Under Tasks, click Manage Network Connections.**

   The Network Connections dialog box appears.

3. **In the Network Connections dialog box, right-click Local Area Connection and select Properties.**

   The Local Area Connection Properties dialog box appears.

4. **In the list of installed components, select Internet Protocol (TCP/IP).**

   Note: If TCP/IP isn't already installed, follow these steps to install it:

   a. *In the Local Area Connection Properties dialog box, click Install.*

   The Select Network Component Type dialog box appears.

   b. *Select Protocol and then click Add.*

   The Select Network Protocol dialog box appears.

   c. *Select Internet Protocol Version 4 (TCP/IP) and then click OK.*

   d. *If prompted, provide a path to the distribution CD.*

5. **Click Properties to open the Internet Protocol Version 4 (TCP/IP) Properties dialog box, shown in Figure 10-2.**

   The Internet Protocol (TCP/IP) Properties dialog box offers fields to define the three IP configuration basics. Note the selection to obtain an IP address automatically. This setting configures the system to request IP configuration from a Dynamic Host Configuration Protocol (DHCP) server. Because most servers don't work well using dynamic IP addresses, you may want to define a static IP address for your Windows Server 2008 instead of using DHCP. (Or use DHCP to make a manual or static address allocation.)

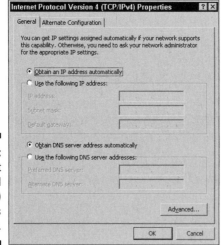

Figure 10-2:
The Internet
Protocol
(TCP/IP)
Properties
dialog box.

6. **To enter your IP settings, select the Use the Following Address option in the dialog box and fill in the fields as follows:**

   - *IP Address:* Either obtain a public IP address from your ISP or use a private IP address from one of the reserved address ranges defined in RFC 1918.

   - *Subnet Mask:* You must also calculate a subnet mask for your network. (That is, as long as you aren't using DHCP.) Here again, you may obtain this from your ISP if you're using public IP addresses, or you may calculate your own if you're using private IP addresses. In most cases where private IP is used, the default subnet mask for the address class should work without alteration or additional calculations, as described in Table 10-3.

   - *Default Gateway:* Finally, you must also provide a default gateway address for your server (unless you just don't want this system to communicate with other hosts outside of its subnet). The default gateway should be the address of the router on the local subnet to which the server is attached that can forward outbound traffic to other network segments. On networks using public IP addresses, this is probably a router, firewall, or proxy server that connects the local subnet to other subnets or to the Internet. On networks using private IP addresses, this is usually the machine on which the proxy and NAT software resides, which mediates between the local subnet and an Internet connection.

7. **The Internet Protocol (TCP/IP) Properties dialog box also offers fields to configure Domain Name Service (DNS). You can leave these fields blank — at least for now.**

   We talk more about DNS in the "DNS Does the Trick" section later in this chapter.

8. **After you define an IP address, a subnet mask, and a default gateway, click OK, and then close all the windows you've opened and reboot.**

   That's all there is to basic TCP/IP configuration on Windows Server 2008!

Advanced configuration

More complex configurations become necessary when your network is larger and, therefore, more complicated. To deal with such complexity, you have to do some advanced work. Click the Advanced button in the Internet Protocol (TCP/IP) Properties dialog box (we tell you how to open that dialog box in the preceding section) to reveal the Advanced TCP/IP Settings dialog box, complete with its four tabs (see Figure 10-3). The tabs (along with brief descriptions) are as follows:

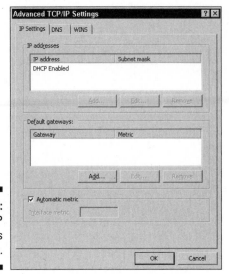

Figure 10-3:
The TCP/IP
Settings
dialog box.

✔ **IP Settings:** This tab allows you to define multiple IP address and subnet mask combinations for a single NIC. You can define also additional default gateways, as well as an interface metric, which is used by routers (or the routing service of Windows Server 2008) to determine which path to send data to — the path with the lowest metric is used first.

✔ **DNS:** This tab allows you to define additional DNS servers — the one or two you define on the Internet Protocol (TCP/IP) Properties dialog box appears here as well, so don't get confused. In addition, you can specify how to search or resolve issues based on DNS server, DNS domain, and DNS parent domains. The two check boxes at the bottom of the DNS tab allow you to use dynamic registration to automatically add your server's IP address and domain name to your local DNS. For more information about DNS, please consult the "DNS Does the Trick" section later in this chapter.

✔ **WINS:** This tab is where IP addresses for Windows Internet Name Service (WINS) servers are defined. WINS servers resolve NetBIOS names into IP addresses. WINS is convenient for Windows Server 2008 networks with multiple servers and network segments. This tab also offers you control over how or whether NetBIOS operates over TCP/IP. For more information about WINS, please consult the "Everyone WINS Sometimes" section later in this chapter.

✔ **Options:** This tab is where you can define alternate settings associated with TCP/IP. This tab offers access to only TCP/IP filtering by default, but the layout of the interface seems to hint that other optional features or services may be configured here if they're installed later. TCP/IP filtering allows you to define TCP, User Datagram Protocol (UDP), and protocol ports that will be allowed to function. In other words, it blocks all traffic except the traffic for the ports that you choose to allow in. This interface is rather limited because it doesn't tell you which ports you need to allow in. We recommend deploying a proxy or firewall to perform TCP/IP filtering because these devices are more user-friendly and tell you which ports you need.

Everyone WINS Sometimes

In a Microsoft Windows network, TCP/IP hosts can be called by NetBIOS names instead of IP addresses or domain names. Because NetBIOS names are more or less unique to Microsoft networks, there's no current standard for associating NetBIOS names with IP addresses. On a Microsoft network that uses TCP/IP as its only networking protocol, it's essential to be able to resolve NetBIOS names to IP addresses. This is where Windows Internet Name Service (WINS) comes in.

A glimpse at WINS

Because resolving NetBIOS names to IP addresses is the key to providing access to many of Windows Server 2008's built-in services and facilities, Microsoft provides two methods to handle this process:

- ✔ **LMHOSTS:** You can use a file named LMHOSTS to create a static table that associates specific NetBIOS names with specific IP addresses. (LM stands for LAN Manager and points to the network operating system that preceded Windows NT in the Microsoft product world.) Such a file must be present on every machine to provide the necessary name-to-address resolution capabilities.

  For small, simple networks, using LMHOSTS files is an acceptable method. On large, complex networks, the busywork involved in maintaining a large number of such files can quickly get out of hand.

- ✔ **WINS:** Larger, more complex networks are where WINS comes into play. WINS runs on Windows Server 2008 machines as a service that automatically discovers NetBIOS names and manages a dynamic database that associates NetBIOS names with TCP/IP addresses. As networks grow, multiple WINS servers sometimes become necessary to help speed up the time it takes to handle name resolution requests.

  A single WINS server can handle an entire network. On networks that include multiple sites or thousands of users, however, multiple WINS servers can distribute the load involved in providing name resolution, and speed users' access to NetBIOS-based resources.

WINS has several advantages over LMHOSTS files. For one thing, it's built on a dynamic database, which means that as networks change and names and addresses come and go, the database changes as the WINS server detects new name and address relationships or finds old names with new addresses. WINS can be especially important on networks where DHCP is used, if clients also share files or printers on their machines. Also, WINS is something like a Spanish-English dictionary that's constantly updated as new words — or in this case, names — are added.

WINS servers

A WINS server maintains a database that maps computer names to their respective IP addresses and vice versa. Rather than sending broadcasts for address information, which eats excess network bandwidth, a workstation that needs a NetBIOS name resolved makes a request directly to a designated WINS server. (That's the real purpose of the WINS tab in the Advanced TCP/IP Settings dialog box.)

This approach lets workstations take advantage of a well-defined service and obtain address information quickly and efficiently. Also, when workstations with NetBIOS names log on to the network, they provide information about themselves and their resources to the WINS server. Then, any changes automatically appear in the WINS server's database.

Although WINS is much simpler than DNS, it still isn't an easy process. You need to install WINS as a network service component through the Local Area Connections applet and corresponding network interfaces. We recommend seeking guidance from the Windows Server 2008 Resource Kit or Technet before starting on that journey.

WINS clients

When configuring workstations or servers (at least, those servers that don't play host to the WINS server software) on your network, you provide an IP address for one or more WINS servers on your network. When those machines boot, they provide the WINS server with their computer names, share names, and IP addresses. The WINS server handles everything else. If a workstation needs an IP address that corresponds to a NetBIOS name, it asks the WINS server to supply that information.

NetBIOS over TCP/IP

The bane of many security consultants, NetBIOS over TCP/IP is a piggyback application programming interface (API) employed by Windows Server 2008 for all of its internal and server-to-server communications. Within a secured environment, such as behind firewalls and proxies, NetBIOS over TCP/IP is beneficial because it supports many of the user-friendly features of Windows Server 2008 networking. But without adequate security, it's a gaping hole that devious individuals can exploit to overtake your network or stand alone system. The WINS tab offers you the ability to disable NetBIOS over TCP/IP on the current system (meaning NetBIOS will not be transmitted over network links from this computer) or allow it to mimic its DHCP server. (If the DHCP server disables NetBIOS, this system will as well.) You should consider disabling NetBIOS over TCP/IP only if all systems on the network are Windows 2000, Windows XP, or Windows 2003 and no application or service on the network requires NetBIOS to function. In other words, you'll need to live with NetBIOS for a bit longer.

DNS Does the Trick

One way to simplify TCP/IP host identification is to use Fully Qualified Domain Names (FQDNs) instead of IP addresses. An FQDN is the type of name used to identify resources on the Internet to make access easier for humans (such as `www.microsoft.com`). Resolving domain names and FQDNs to IP addresses is a crucial service on TCP/IP networks in general and especially on the Internet, where hundreds of millions of names and addresses can be found. This is where the Domain Name Service — sometimes called the Domain Naming Service or Domain Name System, but always abbreviated as DNS — comes into play.

As with NetBIOS names and IP addresses, the association between FQDNs and IP addresses can also be maintained in two ways:

✔ **HOSTS file:** You can create a HOSTS file on each system. The HOSTS file maintains a local table that associates specific FQDNs with specific IP addresses. When such associations change, the HOSTS file must be updated manually and copied to all machines on a network.

HOSTS files aren't suited for interaction with large IP-based networks, especially the Internet. This explains why HOSTS files are mostly relics of an earlier, simpler era of IP networking. Except as a fallback in case access to DNS fails, no one uses HOSTS files anymore.

✔ **DNS:** Access to a DNS server allows network machines to request name resolution services from that server instead of maintaining name-to-address associations themselves. Although DNS servers must be configured manually, a DNS server can handle the name resolution needs of an entire network with ease. DNS servers can also communicate with one another, so a name resolution request that the local server can't handle can be passed up the FQDN name hierarchy until it reaches a server that can resolve the name into an address or indicate that the name is invalid.

The Internet includes tens of thousands of DNS servers. ISPs manage many of these DNS servers; others fall under the control of special top-level domain authorities. To stake out an Internet presence, you must obtain a unique FQDN through the InterNIC (or let your ISP do it for you). After you obtain this name, it's associated with a special root IP address in some DNS server (probably at your ISP, unless you decide to set up a DNS server of your own).

Whether to DNS

Unless you manage a large, complex network, chances are better than average that you'll work with someone else's DNS server — probably your ISP's — rather than managing your own. However, if you have a large network with more than 1,000 computers, or if your network spans multiple sites using private wide-area links, a DNS server may be just the thing to help you stake out the right type of Internet presence.

One unique feature of Windows Server 2003 is that it automatically installs three services on the first server of a domain: Active Directory, DHCP, and DNS. Although you don't actually have to employ DHCP and DNS, they're still installed by default. Installing these services is therefore a breeze. (So much so that the Configure Your Server Wizard does it for you automatically.) The real headaches come when you try to configure DNS (or DHCP, for that matter).

The deans of DNS

If you think you may be interested in setting up a DNS server, you need to consult a technical resource, such as the Windows Server 2008 Resource Kit or TechNet. We also highly recommend *DNS on Windows Server 2003,* a book by Matt Larson, Cricket Liu, and Robbie Allen (published by O'Reilly

& Associates), as the ultimate resource for using Windows 2003 as a DNS server. Even though the title says Windows 2003, this is also a great resource for Windows Server 2008 because DNS is almost exactly the same. Paul Albitz and Cricket Liu also wrote a general DNS book called *DNS and BIND,* now in its fifth edition (also published by O'Reilly) that is widely regarded as the best general reference on DNS. Both of these books should be updated or revised soon to encompass new material for Windows Server 2008.

DHCP: IP Addressing Automation

DHCP, the Dynamic Host Configuration Protocol, is used to dynamically assign IP addresses and other configuration settings to systems as they boot. This allows clients to be configured automatically at startup, thus reducing installation administration. DHCP also allows a large group of clients to share a smaller pool of IP addresses, if only a fraction of those clients needs to be connected to the Internet at any given time.

What is DHCP?

DHCP is a service that Windows Server 2008 can deliver. In other words, a Windows Server 2008 can run DHCP server software to manage IP addresses and configuration information for just about any type of TCP/IP client. In fact, it can even perform this role in a completely stripped-down way if Windows Server 2008 is installed as Server Core with additional service roles.

DHCP manages IP address distribution using leases. When a new system configured to use DHCP comes online and requests configuration data, an IP address is leased to that system. (Each lease lasts three days by default.) When the duration of the lease is half expired, the client can request a lease renewal for another three days. If that request is denied or goes unanswered, the renewal request is repeated when 87.5 percent and 100 percent of the lease duration has expired. If a lease expires and isn't renewed, the client can't access the network until it obtains a new IP address lease. You can initiate manual lease renewals or releases by executing ipconfig /renew or ipconfig /release at the Windows Server 2008 command prompt.

You can view the current state of IP configuration using the ipconfig command. Issuing the ipconfig /all|more command at the command prompt displays all of a machine's IP configuration information, one screen at a time.

Is DHCP in your future?

We can think of two profound reasons why DHCP is a godsend to Windows Server 2008 administrators who need to use it:

✔ DHCP enables you to manage an entire collection of IP addresses in one place, on a single server, with little effort beyond the initial configuration of the *address pool* (the range of addresses that DHCP will be called upon to manage). In the old days (before DHCP), managing IP addresses usually required walking from machine to machine on a far too frequent basis.

✔ DHCP automates delivery of IP addresses and configuration information (including subnet mask and the default gateway addresses) to end-user machines. This makes it astonishingly easy to set up IP clients and to handle configuration changes when they must occur.

To configure IP on a new client, all an end user (or you) must do in Windows Server 2008, Windows Server 2003, Windows NT, or Windows 9*x* is click the single option in the Internet Protocol (TCP/IP) Properties dialog box that reads, Obtain an IP Address Automatically. DHCP does the rest!

When configuration changes occur, these changes are automatically introduced when IP leases are renewed. You can even cancel all existing leases and force clients to renew their leases whenever major renumbering or configuration changes require immediate updates to their IP configurations.

Enough TCP/IP to choke a hippo

If this chapter whets your appetite for TCP/IP, you can obtain more details and information from the following great resources:

✔ *Windows Server 2008 TCP/IP Protocols and Services,* by Joseph Davies (published by Microsoft Press)

✔ *The TCP/IP Guide,* by Charles Kozierok (published by No Starch Press; check out the complete online version at www.tcpguide.com.)

✔ *Internetworking with TCP/IP, Volumes I, II, and III,* by Douglas E. Comer, David L. Stevens, and Michael Evangelista (published by Prentice Hall) in various editions from 2nd through 5th

✔ *TCP/IP For Dummies,* 5th Edition, by Candace Leiden, Marshall Wilensky, and Scott Bradner (published by Wiley Publishing)

If that's still not enough, one of your authors pulled together a more comprehensive TCP/IP bibliography for NetPerformance.com. Check it out at www.netperformance.com/reading_tcpip.aspx.

The ultimate reason for using DHCP is that it makes your job much easier. DHCP is recommended for all networks that use TCP/IP with ten or more clients. The first Windows Server 2008 in a domain has DHCP installed automatically, but you still need to enable and configure it properly before it will do you any good. So, if you think you may be interested in setting up a DHCP server, consult a technical resource, such as the Windows Server 2008 Resource Kit or TechNet, for all the details of installation and configuration.

Ironing Out Problems

Problems that occur on TCP/IP networks are almost always associated with incorrect configurations. The wrong IP address, subnet mask, default gate-way, DNS server, WINS server, or DHCP server can bring a system, if not an entire network, to its knees. Therefore, you need to take extra caution to double-check your settings and changes before putting them into effect.

If you connect to an ISP, you should contact the ISP's technical support per-sonnel early to eliminate as much wheel-spinning as possible. You may dis-cover the problem isn't on your end, but theirs. If so, your only recourse is to wait it out, and then complain. If problems occur too often for your comfort, take your business elsewhere.

Windows Server 2008 includes a few TCP/IP tools that you can employ to help track down problems. We already mentioned ipconfig; here are the others:

- ✔ **ping:** This tool tests the communications path between your system and another remote system. If a PING returns, you know the link is traversal and the remote system is online. If the PING times out, either the link is down or the remote system is offline.

- ✔ **tracert:** This tool reveals the hops (systems encountered) between your system and a remote system. The results inform you whether your trace route packets are getting through and at what system a failure is occurring.

- ✔ **route:** This tool is used to view and modify the routing table of a multi-homed system.

- ✔ **netstat:** This tool displays information about the status of the current TCP/IP connections.

- ✔ **nslookup:** This tool displays DNS information that helps you manage and troubleshoot your DNS server.

- ✔ **telnet:** This tool is used to establish a text-based terminal emulation with a remote system. Telnet gives you access to a remote system as if you were sitting at its keyboard. Windows Server 2003 doesn't include an inbound Telnet server.

Complete details on these tools are included in the Windows 2008 help files, the Windows Server 2008 Resource Kit, and TechNet.

Part III
Running Your Network

The 5th Wave   By Rich Tennant

"I didn't know they made skins for mainframes."

In this part . . .

After Windows Server 2008 is up and running, the real fun — namely, maintaining the server and network you've so laboriously constructed — begins. Or at least, so goes the conventional wisdom. In a very real sense, therefore, Part III begins where Part II leaves off.

First, there's managing the users (and their groups) who will work on your network and use your server. Then, it's on to how to set up and handle NTFS and share permissions, with a heaping order of file systems and related topics on the side. Once you have data and users to protect, backing up your system is no longer an option — it's a downright necessity — so it's the next topic on our systems-management agenda. Part III closes out with an exercise in positive paranoia, where you find out about computer and network security in a discussion that covers the bases from physical security all the way up to how to build a solid password.

Thus, Part III covers all the key topics involved in managing a Windows Server 2008–based network to prepare you to live with one of your own (or to work on someone else's). Use these chapters to establish a systematic routine — not only will your users thank you, but you'll also save yourself some time and effort!

Remember this: Maintenance activities and costs usually represent 90 percent of any computer system's life cycle. That's why establishing a solid maintenance routine and sticking to it religiously are the keys to running a successful network. Do yourself a favor and don't learn this lesson the hard way. . . .

Chapter 11

Managing Users with Active Directory Users and Computers

*U*ser accounts are indispensable elements in the Windows Server 2008 environment. They're central management and control tools for the operating system to authenticate users and manage access to the resources on a local system and in the domain and forest as well. If you don't have a defined user account on a Windows Server 2008 stand-alone system or a Windows Server 2008 domain, you can't gain access to that system or to available resources in the forest. This chapter looks at managing domain user accounts and policies through the Active Directory Users and Computers console.

User Accounts Have Properties

Computers are typically used by more than one person. Even systems that workers use exclusively on their desks allow system administrators to log on locally. If these systems have computer accounts in the domain, it's possible for other users with domain accounts to log on to those systems as well. The computer distinguishes between one person and another by employing a security device called the *user account object.* Each user on a computer or a network has a unique user account that contains details about the user, such as his or her rights and restrictions to access resources and more.

A Windows Server 2008 domain-based user account contains, is linked to, or is associated with the following items:

- ✔ **Password security:** User accounts are protected by passwords so that only authorized persons can gain access to the systems.

- ✔ **Permissions:** *Permissions* are the access privileges granted to a user account. These include group memberships and user-specific settings to access resources.

- ✔ **Identification:** A *user account* identifies a person to the computer system and the network.

- ✔ **User rights:** A *user right* is a high-level privilege that can be granted to users or groups to define or limit their actions on a computer system.

- ✔ **Roaming:** You can define user accounts so that a user can log on to any system that is a member of a domain by using a *domain user account* (certain users may be able to log on to local accounts in certain situations), a Remote Access Service (RAS), or a gateway.

- ✔ **Environment layout:** Profiles are user-specific and store information about the layout, desktop, and user environment in general, unless they are specifically restricted through the use of mandatory profiles. You can define profiles so that they follow the user account no matter where the user gains access on the network.

- ✔ **Auditing:** Windows Server 2008 can track access and usage by domain user accounts if that level of auditing has been enabled in the domain.

Access to Windows Server 2008 requires that users successfully authenticate themselves with a domain user account. This means that when a user with the proper permission level (not everyone has permission to log on locally to all systems in a domain) sits down at a Windows Server 2008 system, he or she can log on at the local machine with a local account (called an *interactive logon)* by pressing Ctrl+Alt+Delete to start the logon process. Then the user must provide a valid username and password. He or she may also log on to a domain user account in the same manner if the server is a member of the domain. After the system verifies this information, the user is granted access.

When the user is finished, he or she can log out and leave the system available for the next user to log on.

With Windows Server 2008 installed, three user accounts are automatically created by default on stand-alone (non-domain-member) systems:

- ✔ The **Administrator account** is used to configure the system initially and to create other user accounts.

- ✔ The **Guest account** is a quick method to grant low-level access to any user — but is disabled by default.

✔ The **HelpAssistant**, often named Support_*<random characters>*, is the primary account used for Remote Assistance sessions. Remote Desktop Help Session Manager services manage this account, which is also disabled by default.

Administrators rule!

The Administrator account is the primary means by which you initially configure Windows Server 2008. It's also the most powerful local account on the Windows Server 2008 system; therefore, you should make sure that the password for the Administrator account is complex and secret. The Administrator account has full-control access to almost everything in Windows Server 2008 (the exceptions are a few system processes that the Administrator doesn't own and therefore doesn't have access to), such as managing user accounts, manipulating shares, and granting access privileges.

The Administrator account boasts the following features:

✔ You can't delete it.

✔ You can lock it out or disable it.

✔ You can (and should) rename it. (Right-click the account and choose Rename.)

✔ Although defining a blank password on a local Administrator account is allowed, it's actively discouraged as a bad security practice. In certain situations, some services don't function properly if you don't provide a password. Therefore, you should provide a valid, complex password for this account.

Renaming this account is a good security practice. Would-be hackers (that is, people who want to gain unauthorized access to your system) need only two bits of information to gain access to your system: a user account name and a password. Unless you rename this account, they already have half of what they need to gain access to the most powerful account on your system. That ends up being the only thing they need if you don't define a password for this account!

Guests can wear out their welcome

The Guest account is the second default account created by Windows Server 2008. You can use this account as a temporary public-access method. It has minimal access rights and restricted privileges to resources.

The Guest account boasts the following features:

 ✔ You can't delete it.

 ✔ You can disable it and lock it out. (It's disabled by default.)

 ✔ You can rename it.

 ✔ It can have a blank password. (It has a blank password by default.)

 ✔ Changes to the guest environment aren't retained by this account. (That is, the user profile is mandatory because user changes to the environment aren't retained.)

The Guest account can be a security hole. Good security practices suggest that you keep this account disabled, rename it, and assign it a valid password.

Creating Active Directory Accounts

Creating accounts in Active Directory for users to log on to the domain and forest to access resources is a common and simple task. You use the Active Directory Users and Computers console (see Figure 11-1) in Windows Server 2008 to create and manage domain user accounts and domain groups.

Creating user accounts isn't difficult, but you need to pay attention to lots of details. First, we walk you through creating a quick-and-dirty user account. Then, we talk about all the fine-tuning you can perform on this account:

1. **To get to Active Directory Users and Computers, choose Start⇨All Programs⇨Administrative Tools⇨Active Directory Users and Computers.**

2. **In the console tree, click the folder that corresponds to the domain or organizational unit to which you want to assign this new account.**

   You see all the default settings for this domain or organizational unit, including user accounts. If you're assigning the user account to the Users container, when you initially click it, you see the Administrator and Guest accounts, plus other accounts that Windows Server 2008 set up, depending on the services you installed.

   An *organizational unit* is an Active Directory container that holds other organizational units, computers, user accounts, and groups. For more information on organizational units, see Chapter 7.

3. **In the details pane, right-click the group and then choose Properties.**

4. **On the Members tab, click Add.**

   (You can also right-click the container and choose New⇨User from the pop-up menu.) This reveals the Create New Object – User Wizard, shown in Figure 11-2. When you create a user object from scratch, you should pay attention to every detail of that account.

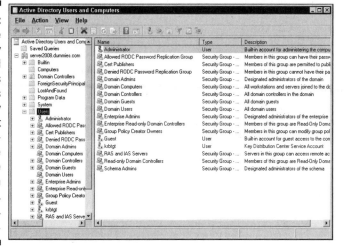

Figure 11-1:
The Active
Directory
Users and
Computers
console is
the primary
tool that
adminis-
trators use
to create
domain
users,
accounts,
and groups.

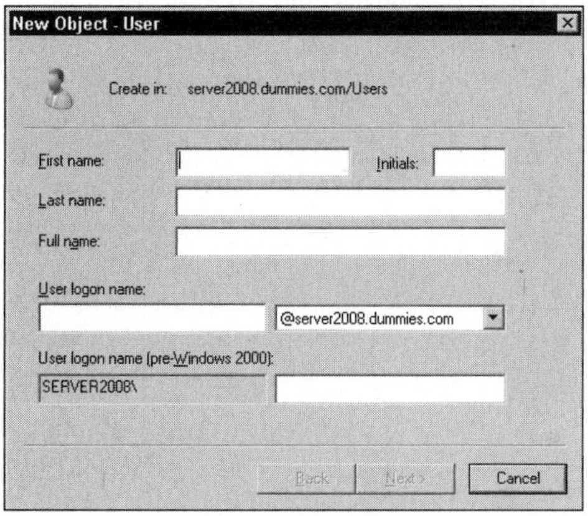

Figure 11-2:
Use the New
Object –
User Wizard
to create a
user object.

5. **Fill in the following information:**

   • *First Name; Last Name; Initial:* Type the user's first name, last name, and middle initial, if applicable.

   • *Full Name:* This is how the name will be displayed on the system. Notice that the Setup Wizard has entered the name for you. You can replace what's filled in for you and arrange the display of the full name any way you like. Usually, the first name is displayed, then the last name.

   • *User Logon Name:* Type the information you want the user to use to validate himself or herself to the network. You should create a company standard such as last name, first initial, or something similar. (See the "What's in a name?" sidebar later in this chapter.)

Pre–Windows 2000, the user logon name is the name given to the user for pre–Windows 2000 systems. Notice that the wizard fills in this information for you. You won't need to change this unless you're a tech head.

6. **Click the Next button to continue setting up this new user account object.**

   In the next screen, you'll enter information about the password.

7. **Type a password for this account and then confirm that password to the system by retyping it.**

8. **Configure the password settings using the options described in the following list:**

   - *User Must Change Password at Next Logon:* Forces users to change their passwords.

   - *User Cannot Change Password:* Prevents users from changing their passwords.

   - *Password Never Expires:* Exempts this account from the policy that can require a password change after a specified time period.

   - *Account Is Disabled:* Ensures that this account can't be used to gain access to the system. Chances are, if you're creating a new user, you don't want to select this option because you want the user to be able to access the system.

9. **Click the Next button when you're finished marking your selections.**

   You're presented with a confirmation screen about the choices you've made.

10. **Click the Finish button if everything is correct. If you think of something else that needs to be added, click the Back button to add it now.**

    If you need to add data later, you can edit the properties of the account as well.

You've just created a new domain user account object, and you'll see that object in the Active Directory Users and Computers console window. In Step 5, we mention the way the name is displayed, and that's how you should see the object's name listed.

If you right-click the new object and then click Properties, you'll see several tabs, including General, Address, Account, Profile, and many more. You can use these tabs to enter more information about the new user account object, such as the groups to which it belongs. You may see other tabs, depending on the services installed on your Windows Server 2008 system and whether the server is a stand-alone server, a domain member server, or a domain controller.

In the following sections, individually we go through some of the default tabs of a member server so that you'll know what to fill in and why.

What's in a name?

Windows Server 2008 doesn't actually use or even care about the human-friendly name assigned to a user account. Instead, Windows Server 2008 uses a Security Identifier, or SID, to recognize and track user accounts. But, because you're human, you should employ human-friendly names whenever possible. This reduces stress and makes user management easier.

What we're trying to say is that you should employ a naming convention. A *naming convention* is just a predetermined method for creating names for users, computers, resources, and other objects. The two key features of a naming convention are the capability to always create new names and that the names created provide descriptive information about the named object.

Small networks rarely need complex or even predefined naming conventions. However, when the number of named items on your network exceeds about 100 or so, you may find it increasingly difficult to remember who or what jackal, herbie, and 8675309 actually are. Therefore, starting a small network with a naming convention can ease the growth process later.

Windows Server 2008 doesn't impose or suggest a naming scheme. It just lets you define names as you please. If you decide to use a naming convention, you need to be diligent in enforcing and employing that scheme.

The naming convention you choose or create doesn't matter; as long as it always provides new names and those names indicate information about the objects they label. Here are some general naming-convention rules:

- ✔ The names need to be consistent across all element types (user names, computer names, share names, directory names, and so on).

- ✔ The names should be easy to understand. (If they're too complex or difficult, they won't be used.)

- ✔ The names should somehow identify the types of objects.

You can create new names by mimicking the structure of existing names. Here are some examples of partial naming conventions that you can customize for your network:

- ✔ Create user names by combining the first and last name of a user (for example, JohnSmith or JSmith).

- ✔ Create user names by combining the last name of a user and a department code (for example, SmithAcct and SmithSales5). With Active Directory, this type of design is less needed because, in many cases, the layout of your OU structure reflects the organizational areas of your company.

- ✔ Create computer names by combining the user name, a computer type code, and room number (for example, SmithW98 and JS102).

- ✔ Create group names by combining resource descriptor, location, project, or department names (for example, Tower12, Planning2, and Conference12).

- ✔ Create share or directory names by combining the content or purpose descriptor with a group or project name (for example, Documents, SalesDocs, and AcctSheets).

- ✔ Create printer names by combining the model type, location, department, and group names (for example, HP5Sales, CLJRm202, and HP4Acct).

As you can see, each of these suggested partial naming schemes always creates new names and provides enough information about the named object to determine where it is and whether it's a user account, computer, share, or printer.

General tab

When you click the General tab, you can type more information about the account, such as a description (additional location information, what the account is used for, or whatever you want), office address, telephone number, Web page address, and e-mail address. The more information you provide at this time, the more you'll appreciate it later when you need this information. The description information shows up in the Active Directory Users and Computers console if you have the detail view selected. (Choose View➪Detail to see it.)

Address tab

Click the Address tab to type information about the user's physical mailing address. Although this information isn't required, it's good to have handy.

Account tab

Click the Account tab to reveal the logon name, logon name for pre–Windows 2000 systems, logon hours, workstation restrictions (which can be set with the Log On To button), and account expiration information. Most of the options in this tab are self-explanatory — except the logon hours and expiration information, which are described as follows:

- ✔ **Logon hours:** Click the Logon Hours button to reveal the Logon Hours dialog box. (See Figure 11-3.) In this dialog box, you can define the hours during which a user can gain entry to the system. If this user account attempts to log on during off hours, the logon fails. If the user is already online when the hours expire, the user remains online but can't establish any new network connections. (That is, the user can't send a document to a printer or open a new file.) You define hours by selecting the day and hour sections and selecting the Logon Permitted or Logon Denied option. This option is mostly used for contractors who are allowed to use the system only during regular working hours.

- ✔ **Account expiration:** Select the Account Expires End Of option to define when (if ever) the account expires. This is useful for contract or temporary employees who have been granted access to the system for a specified period of time.

Profile tab

Click the Profile tab in the Properties dialog box to reveal current information about the user account's profile. (See Figure 11-4.) In this dialog box, you can define the following:

✔ **User Profile Path:** The location where the roaming profile for this user is stored. The roaming profile makes a user's working environment available to him of her on any workstation on the network. (See the "Giving Your Users Nice Profiles" section later in this chapter.)

✔ **Logon Script:** The filename of the script file to be executed at logon. Logon scripts are usually batch files that define paths, set environmental variables, map drives, or execute applications. You typically use logon scripts only in Windows Server 2008 for compatibility with older servers or DOS applications or to automatically configure settings for NetWare server access.

✔ **Home directory:** The default storage location for this profile as a local path or as a mapped drive letter to a network drive.

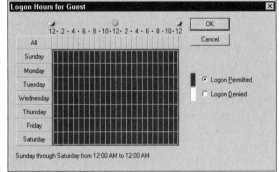

Figure 11-3:
Access can
be set by
time of day
and day of
week.

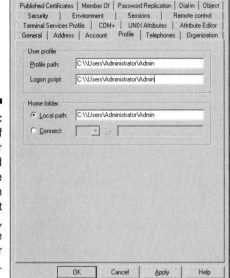

Figure 11-4:
Examples of
a User
Profile and
its profile
path, logon
script
location,
and Home
Folder
designation.

Telephones tab

Click the Telephones tab in the Properties dialog box to enter every imaginable phone number a person can have these days, such as pager, fax, and mobile. There's even a Comments section where you can add whatever you want.

Organization tab

Click the Organization tab in the Properties dialog box to enter information about the user's title in the organization and the names of the people to whom the person reports to directly. If your organization is prone to restructuring, you may opt to leave this tab blank.

Member Of tab

Clicking the Member Of tab in the Properties dialog box reveals information about the account's group membership status. This is where you can add a user account object to a group or remove a user account object from a group. (See Figure 11-5.) If you want to add this object to another group, click the Add button and select the group. As we discuss later in this chapter, group membership determines the resources to which you grant a user account access.

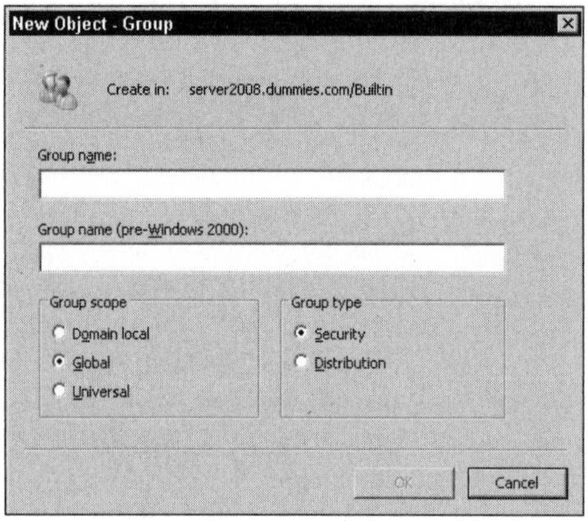

Figure 11-5:
Group membership are defined here.

New Object - Group

Create in: server2008.dummies.com/Builtin

Group name:

Group name (pre-Windows 2000):

Group scope
- Domain local
- Global
- Universal

Group type
- Security
- Distribution

OK   Cancel

Dial-in tab

Click the Dial-in tab in the Properties dialog box to enable or disable the account from dialing into the network. This is also where you can set any callback options. *Callback* means that, as users dial into the network, the server dials back a preset telephone number to verify that the users are in fact who they say they are. This number can be preset or set by the user. Callback is often used in security situations, but dial back doesn't work particularly well when a user is on the road and staying in different hotels, which all have different telephone numbers. Use this option with caution.

Getting Pushy with Users

At some point during your management lifetime, you may need to disable, rename, or delete user accounts. You can do all this using Active Directory Users and Computers, as described in the following list:

- **Disabling a user account** is when you turn off the account so that it can't be used to gain entry to the system. To disable an account, highlight the user account and then choose Action⟶Disable Account. When you create a user using the Setup Wizard (see the "Creating Active Directory Accounts" section earlier in this chapter), you can select the Account Disabled check box, and the user account is disabled until you enable it.

- **Renaming a user account** changes the human-friendly name of the account. Just select the user account and then choose Action⟶Rename. A dialog box prompts you for the new name. Note that a name change doesn't change the Security Identifier (SID) of the account.

- **Deleting a user account** removes the user account from the system. Highlight the user account you want to delete and then choose Action⟶Delete. You're prompted to confirm the deletion. When you delete an account, it's gone for good. The SID used by the deleted account is never reused. Creating a new account with the same configuration as the deleted account still results in a different account because a new SID is used; therefore, as far as the accounts database is concerned, it's a new account.

When users leave your organization, you need to decide whether you want to retain their old user accounts to use for their replacements. This is your best option because it retains all department and group settings, but it does mean that you have to change all the personal information so that it relates to the new user.

What about Groups?

A *group* is a collection of users who need similar levels of access to a resource. Groups are the primary means by which Windows Server 2008 domain controllers grant user access to resources.

Groups simplify the administration process by reducing the number of relationships that you have to manage. Instead of managing how each individual user relates to each resource, you need to manage only how the smaller number of groups relate to resources and to which groups each user belongs. This reduces the workload by 40 to 90 percent. Windows Server 2008 has a Best Practices section under its Help guide that encourages you to use groups in as many situations as you can.

Understanding group scopes

A group is nothing more than a named collection of users. There are two different types of groups, and each type can have any one of three scopes (described next):

- ✔ **Security groups** are used to assign user rights to objects and resources in Active Directory. A secondary function of a security group is that it can also be used to send e-mails to all the members of the group.

- ✔ **Distribution groups** are used only for sending e-mail to all the members of the group. Distribution groups can't be used to define permissions to resources and objects in Active Directory.

Both group types can have any of the following scopes:

- ✔ **Global groups** exist on a domain level. They are present on every computer throughout a domain and are managed by any Active Directory for Users and Computers tool hosted by Windows Server 2008. When the domain is running in Windows 2000 native mode or Windows Server 2008 mode, members of global groups can include accounts and global groups from the same domain. When the domain is running in Windows 2000 mixed mode, members of global groups can include accounts from the same domain.

- ✔ **Domain local groups** exist only on a single computer. They aren't present throughout a domain. When the domain is running in Windows 2000 native mode or Windows Server 2008 mode, members of domain local groups can include accounts, global groups, and universal groups from any domain, as well as domain local groups from the same domain. When the domain is running in Windows 2000 mixed mode, members of domain local groups can include accounts and global groups from any domain.

✔ **Universal groups** extend beyond the domain to all domains in the current forest. When the domain is running in Windows 2000 native mode or Windows server 2008 mode, members of universal groups can include accounts, global groups, and universal groups from any domain. When the domain is running in Windows 2000 mixed mode, security groups with a universal scope can't be created. When the domain is running in Windows 2000 native mode or Windows Server 2008 mode, universal groups can be created and used to house other groups, such as global groups, to facilitate the assignment of permissions to resources in any domain in the forest.

The three group scopes simplify the user-to-resource relationship. Using groups greatly reduces the management overhead for a medium or large network, but it may seem a bit complicated for a small network. You can use groups like this:

✔ Local groups are assigned access levels to resources.

✔ Users are assigned membership to a global group or a universal group.

✔ A global group or a universal group is assigned as a member of a local group.

Therefore, users are granted access to resources by means of their global or universal group membership, and, in turn, that group's membership to a local group has access to the resource. Whew, now it's time for a drink!

Here are a few important items to keep in mind about groups:

✔ A user can be a member of multiple global or universal groups.

✔ A global or universal group can be a member of multiple local groups.

✔ A resource can have multiple local groups assigned access to it. Using multiple local groups, you can define multiple levels of access to a resource from read/print to change/manage to full control.

Although it's possible to add user accounts directly to a universal group, best practices dictate that you should add them only to global groups and add global groups to universal groups. When membership changes in a universal group, such as the addition or removal of user accounts or groups, the change must be replicated throughout the forest through the global catalog servers. Adding and removing user accounts often from universal groups will cause a great deal of forest-wide replication traffic on the network.

If you add a global group to a universal group, user accounts and nested global groups can be added to and removed from the global group without causing a single replication. This is because the membership of the universal group hasn't changed. It still has the same global group or groups in it. Only the membership of the global group changes when you add or remove user accounts or nested global groups.

Although you can assign a user direct membership to a local group or even direct access to a resource, doing so subverts the neat little scheme that Microsoft developed to simplify your life. So, just follow this prescription, and you'll be vacationing on the beach in no time.

Whereas any other group can be a member of a local group, a local group can't be a member of any other group when the domain is running in mixed mode. Domain local groups can be placed in other domain local groups from the same domain when the domain is running in Windows 2000 native mode or Windows Server 2008 mode.

Creating and managing groups

You manage groups on Windows Server 2008 using Active Directory Users and Computers. To create a group using Active Directory Users and Computers, follow these steps:

1. **In the console tree, right-click the folder to which you want to add the group (Active Directory Users and Computers/*domain node*/*folder*) and choose New⇨Group.**

   The New Object – Group dialog box appears. (Refer to Figure 11-5.)

2. **Type the new group name.**

   The group name for pre–Windows Server 2008 machines is filled in automatically. By default, the name that you type is also entered as the pre–Windows 2000 name of the new group.

3. **In Group Scope, select one of the options: Domain Local, Global, or Universal.**

   Universal groups are powerful because they extend to all domains in the current forest.

4. **Select the group type: Security or Distribution.**

   You'll almost never use the Distribution group setting because it does not contain the access control list (ACL) information necessary for security purposes. The Distribution group setting is used mainly for e-mail operations, where you'd want to send an e-mail to a collective group of users and don't need security attached to it. We recommend always using the Security type.

5. **Click OK.**

After the group object is created, you can double-click the object to add more attributes to it. You see several new tabs called General, Members, Member Of, and Managed By. These tabs are fairly self-explanatory, but here's a little bit about them:

✔ **General:** This tab contains the same information you filled in when you created the group, such as group name, description, e-mail, group scope, and group type.

✔ **Members:** This tab shows the users who are members of the group. This is where you add users to the group.

✔ **Member Of:** This is where you can add this group to other groups.

✔ **Managed By:** This tab allows you to specify who manages the group. You can provide information about the user, such as name, address, and phone number.

Using built-in groups

You don't have to create your own groups: Windows Server 2008 domain controllers have several built-in security domain local groups that you can use. The groups are in the Builtin container, by default. The following lists just a few of them (the default members are in parentheses):

✔ Administrators (administrator, domain admin, Enterprise admin)

✔ Guests (domain guests, guests)

✔ Pre–Windows 2000 Compatible Access (anonymous logon, everyone)

✔ Users (domain users, authenticated users)

Note that your screen may show that these built-in groups have more members than we've listed, depending on which services are installed on your server. For example, if you've installed Internet Information Services (IIS), you'll see more members in the built-in Guests group.

These default, built-in security domain local groups have both predefined built-in capabilities (see Figure 11-6) and default user rights. You can modify the user rights of these groups (see this chapter's section titled "User Accounts Have Properties"), but you can't change the built-in capabilities.

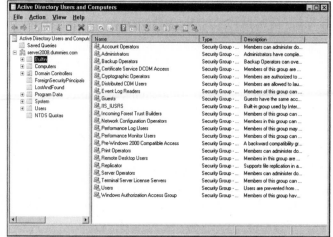

Figure 11-6:
The built-in
security
groups of
Windows
Server 2008.

Windows Server 2008 domain controllers include the following additional security groups as well, which can be found in the Users container by default:

- ✔ Cert Publishers (domain local)
- ✔ Debugger Users (domain local)
- ✔ HelpServicesGroup (domain local)
- ✔ RAS and IAS Servers (domain local)
- ✔ Telnet Clients (domain local)
- ✔ Domain Admins (global)
- ✔ Domain Computers (global)
- ✔ Domain Controllers (global)
- ✔ Domain Guests (global)
- ✔ Domain Users (global)
- ✔ Group Policy Creator Owners (global)
- ✔ Enterprise Admins (universal)
- ✔ Schema Admins (universal)

Other groups may exist, such as DnsAdmins, which would be created if the domain controller hosted DNS services. For the most part, however, the preceding list is inclusive for the forest root domain controller.

Windows Server 2008 has three more groups that it classifies as special identities: Everyone, Network, and Interactive. These are built-in groups that you can modify only indirectly. The following list describes these groups:

✔ **Everyone:** This group, for example, may reflect a membership of 20 user accounts until you add another account to the domain. The user is automatically added to the Everyone group with no intervention by you. Therefore, although you didn't specifically make the new account a member of the Everyone group, you did affect its membership. Guests are also added to the Everyone group, so be careful and modify the guest account to restrict access to the network. (See the "Guests can wear out their welcome" section earlier in this chapter for more information.)

✔ **Network:** This group is for those who use the network as a means to access resources. When you give users access to resources across the network, they're automatically added to the Network group.

✔ **Interactive:** This group represents users who access resources by logging on locally.

Again, you can't change who is a member of these groups in a direct sense. However, when you set permissions to resources, these groups will appear, and you should modify the access levels of these groups to specific resources. For example, when giving users access to the root level of a volume, you can restrict access to the Everyone group so those users have only Read permissions.

You should create groups that make sense to your organizational pattern, method of operations, or just common sense. Groups should be meaningful, and their names should reflect their purposes. Naming a group Sales isn't very useful, but a name such as SalesPrintOnly is very informative. You should create groups so that users are divided by purpose, access levels, tasks, departments, or anything else you consider important. Remember that groups exist for your benefit, so try to get the most out of them.

Giving Your Users Nice Profiles

A *user profile* is the collection of desktop, environment, network, and other settings that define and control the look, feel, and operation of the workstation or member server. Windows Server 2008 records profile information automatically for each user. However, unless you make them roaming profiles (which you find out about later in this chapter), these profiles are accessible only locally.

A user profile records lots of information about the user's environment and activities, including the following:

✔ Start menu configuration

✔ Screensaver and wallpaper settings

- List of recently accessed documents
- Favorites list from Internet Explorer
- Network mapped drives
- Installed network printers
- Desktop layout

In addition, a profile includes a compressed copy of the HKEY_CURRENT_ USER Registry key in a file named NTUSER.DAT. To find definitions for all the various Registry keys, you can use the Registry Tools utility in the Windows Server 2008 Resource Kit and access REGENTRY.HLP.

You can turn profiles into roaming profiles. (Note that a nonroaming profile is called a *local profile*.) A *roaming profile* is a profile stored on a network-accessible drive; therefore, no matter which workstation is used to gain access, the user's profile is available. As a result, the user's working environment follows him or her from one computer to the next. (You can also set the profile so that the user can't customize his or her roaming profile, which is called a mandatory user profile. See the last paragraph of this section for details.)

To create and enable a roaming profile for a specific user, follow these steps:

1. **On the domain controller, start Active Directory Users and Computers. (Choose Start⇨Control Panel⇨Administrative Tools⇨ Active Directory Users and Computers.)**

2. **In the console tree, right-click the domain or organizational unit for which you want to set a policy and choose Properties.**

3. **Click the Group Policy tab.**

4. **If you want to modify an existing group policy, select it in the Group Policy Object Links portion of the window and choose the appropriate option.**

5. **Click the Copy To button.**

6. **Define a network accessible path for the new storage location for the profile.**

   For example, *domain controller*\users\\<*username*>, where *domain controller* is the name of the domain controller, *users* is the share name, and *username* is the name of the user account that is tied to the profile.

7. **On the domain controller (or any domain member that has the ADMINPAK.MSI tools properly installed), launch the Active Directory Users and Computers. (Choose Start⇨Programs⇨Administrative Directory Users and Computers.)**

8. **Right-click the user object you just copied to the domain controller and then choose Properties.**

9. **Click the Profile tab.**

10. **In the Profile Path box in the User Profile section, type the same path from Step 6.**

11. **Click OK.**

The profile for the selected user is now a roaming profile. After a user has a roaming profile, the local profile is no longer used. It remains on the system, but the user account is now associated with the roaming profile.

By default, each time a user logs out, all changes made to his or her profile during that logon session (no matter which workstation he or she uses) are saved to the profile on the domain controller, unless you specifically made this a mandatory profile. The next time the user logs on, the work environment is exactly the same as when he or she logged off. Local and roaming profiles should be used only by a single user. If multiple users need to use a single profile, you should employ a mandatory profile.

A *mandatory profile* doesn't save customized or personal changes to the profile when a user logs out. Instead, the profile retains the same configuration at all times. This type of profile is used mainly when system or network administrators want to control or limit the end users' ability to modify their profiles beyond a standard one that may be employed throughout the enterprise.

You create a mandatory profile by simply renaming the NTUSER.DAT file to NTUSER.MAN in either a local or roaming profile. After this change is made, the profile remains consistent no matter who uses it. You can always reverse this process by renaming the NTUSER.MAN file back to NTUSER.DAT.

Where You Find Profiles, Policies Are Never Far Away

Group policies are the collections of rules governing, controlling, or watching over the activities of users. You can set group policies based on sites, domains, or organizational units. In Windows NT Server 4.0, this was known as the System Policy Editor. In Windows Server 2008 (as it was in Windows 2003 and 2000), you set these policies using the group policy and its snap-in extensions, such as Administrative Templates, Security Settings, and Scripts.

Administering a group policy

One way to administer (manage or modify) the group policy from Active Directory Users and Computers is to do the following:

1. **Start Active Directory Users and Computers. (Choose Start➪Control Panel➪Administrative Tools➪Active Directory Users and Computers.)**

2. **In the console tree, right-click the domain or organizational unit for which you want to set a policy and choose Properties.**

3. **Click the Group Policy tab.**

4. **If you want to modify an existing group policy, select it in the Group Policy Object Links portion of the window and choose the appropriate option.**

The following options are available on the Group Policy tab. (We list them in alphabetical order.)

- ✔ **Add:** This opens the Add Group Policy Object Link dialog box. If you want to add an existing group policy object to the domain or organizational unit you're viewing, you do so under this option.

- ✔ **Block Policy Inheritance:** Select this option to prevent the directory object you choose from inheriting its group policy from its parent object.

- ✔ **Delete:** Use this option if you want to remove the group policy object.

- ✔ **Edit:** Allows you to make changes to the selected group policy.

- ✔ **New:** Allows you to create a new group policy object.

- ✔ **Properties:** Opens the Group Policy Properties dialog box. You can find all sites, organizational units, and domains using the selected policy. In addition, you can set permissions on a user or group basis to this object.

In addition, there's an Options button. When you click it, the following options are available:

- ✔ **Disabled:** This temporarily disables the group policy from the directory object.

- ✔ **No Override:** This is similar to a veto. If this is selected, child directories must inherit group policy from their parent directory. Not even the Block Policy Inheritance setting can keep this group policy from being forced after No Override is set.

If more than one group policy object is listed, you can use the Up and Down buttons to change the group policy order. Policies are enforced from the bottom of the list to the top. The one at the top is enforced last and thus takes priority over any of the others in the list or any of the others processed at higher points in the inheritance scheme, such as at the parent OU or domain or site levels.

Understanding how group policies are processed

A group policy is processed in the following manner:

1. **All Windows 2000, XP Professional, and 2003/2008 systems have one local group policy object, and it's processed first when the system is started.** In a domain scenario, because the subsequent group policy objects are likely to overwrite these settings, this group policy object will probably have the least amount of effect on the local system when it's in a domain. On a stand-alone Windows system, it's usually the only group policy object processed; in this situation, it will have a large effect, if not the only effect.

2. **The next set of group policy settings that are processed are the settings for all and any site group policy objects.** These group policy objects are processed synchronously. (The domain administrator sets the order in which these will execute.) They're processed from the bottom of the list to the top, with the one at the top enforced last at this level.

3. **After all site group policy objects are run, the next set of group policy objects to be deployed are the ones set at the domain level.** These too are executed synchronously, processed from the bottom of the list to the top, with the one at the top enforced last in the event that there is more than one set to be deployed.

4. **The final set of group policy objects to be executed are any set at the organizational unit level.** All group policy objects linked to the upper-most (parent) organizational unit in the inheritance tree are executed first, followed by those in the next highest level, and so on, until you reach the local organizational unit, which is executed last. At each organizational unit in the hierarchy, there may be several group policies. They are processed in a specific order set by the domain administrator and are executed synchronously. This means that all group policy objects in the highest point of the inheritance tree are executed first in the specific order set by the domain administrator, and then all group policy objects at the next point of the inheritance tree are executed in the specific order set by the domain administrator, and so on all the way down to the local organizational unit.

Two rules apply when there are conflicting settings. At any particular group policy object, the computer setting prevails over the user configuration setting. For example, if GPO3 at the bottom of the list set at the domain level has a computer configuration setting set to do one thing and the same group policy object user section is set to do the opposite, the settings outlined in the computer configuration are enabled. The second rule is that anything executed next takes precedence. Following along with the preceding example, if the next group policy object set at the domain level (GPO2) has another setting that conflicts with a previous one, it takes precedence.

Here is an example:

1. The local system GPO says to remove Run from the Start menu. (It's removed.)

2. GPO2 at the domain level (bottom of the list) says to remove Run from the Start menu. (It's removed.) GPO1 at the domain level (top of the list) says to enable Run on the Start menu. (It's added.)

3. GPO2 at the parent OU level (bottom of the list) says to enable Run on the Start menu. (It's added.) GPO1 at the parent OU level (top of the list) says to enable Run on the Start menu. (It's added.)

4. GPO3 at the local OU level (bottom of the list) says to enable Run on the Start menu. (It's added.) GPO2 at the local OU level (middle of the list) says to enable Run on the Start menu. (It's added.) GPO1 at the local OU level (top of the list) says to remove Run from the Start menu. (It's removed.)

You're probably asking, "What does all this mean?" The example policy you create in the next section guides you through the setup.

Creating a group policy

Suppose you want to set a group policy to apply to all users in the domain. The policy will prevent the users from changing their passwords. Follow these steps to implement this new group policy:

1. **Open the Group Policy Management Console. (Choose Start⇨All Programs⇨Accessories⇨Run, and then type** gpmc.msc **and press Enter.)**

2. **In the console tree, select the forest name, expand the Domains branch, and then select the domain where you want to implement the policy.**

3. **Right-click the domain name and choose Create a GPO in This Domain and Link It Here.**

   The New GPO dialog box appears.

4. **Specify a name for the new GPO and then click OK.**

5. **In the right window pane, right-click the new policy name and choose Edit.**

6. **Navigate your way down through the left window pane to User Configuration⇨Administrative Templates⇨System⇨Ctrl+Alt+Del Options, as shown in Figure 11-7.**

7. **Double-click the Remove Change Password object in the right pane.**

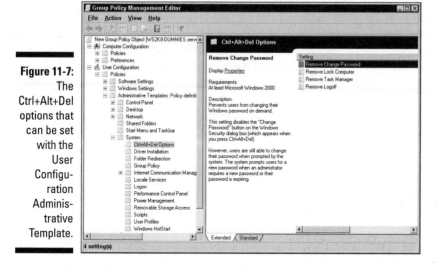

Figure 11-7:
The
Ctrl+Alt+Del
options that
can be set
with the
User
Configu-
ration
Adminis-
trative
Template.

8. **In the Setting tab, select Enabled, click the Apply button, and then click OK.**

This new policy affects all current and future user accounts in the domain because it's created and linked to the domain container. However, it doesn't affect those accounts that are logged on. The effect takes place after those users log out and then log back on to the system.

Notice when you opened the Group Policy tab and clicked the Edit button, you saw information relating to computer configuration and also to user configuration. If there's a conflict between the two, the computer configuration takes precedence in Windows Server 2008.

The preceding steps allow you to add a group policy and then edit the policy using the administrative templates that were visible to you. Other templates are available but simply not loaded. To add another template for use, go back to the left window pane under User Configuration and right-click Administrative Templates. Next, select Add/Remove Templates to display a list of policies. Click the Add button to view other available templates.

You'll find a lot of useful policies already preconfigured for you in Computer Configuration⇨Windows Settings⇨Security Settings. For example, there's a template for setting a policy to force unique passwords for accounts.

If you're concerned about security, you should employ an accounts policy that requires regular password changes (a new password every 30 days or so) and locks out accounts that fail to log on successfully after three tries.

Auditing for trouble

To look at the access control information for any given group policy, you can look at which locations are associated with the policy, who has permissions in the policy, and how it's audited (which is what we cover in this section). All this is accomplished by clicking the Properties button in the Group Policy dialog box.

Auditing information on the network allows you to track activities throughout your network. This process can help you locate configuration problems, security breaches, improper activity, and misuse of the system. To enable auditing on your local system, do the following:

1. **Open the Group Policy Object Editor. (Choose Start⇨All Programs⇨ Accessories⇨Run, and then type** gpmc.msc.**)**

2. **In the console tree, click Audit Policy.**

3. **Navigate the left results pane to select an event category that you want to change.**

4. **Double-click the option you want to audit.**

   The Security Policy Setting dialog box appears.

5. **Choose to audit either Success or Failure attempts (or both).**

   (This dialog box is displayed so that the administrator can choose to audit successful attempts, failed attempts, or both.)

6. **After making your selection, click OK.**

 You can add the Local Group Policy Object snap-in by opening Microsoft Management Console (MMC). Click Start and then in the Start Search text, type **mmc**. Press Enter when the appropriate entry on the Start menu is highlighted. From the File menu, click Add/Remove Snap-In to open the Add or Remove Snap-Ins dialog box. Under Available Snap-Ins, choose Local Group Policy Object and click Add to include it with selected snap-ins; then specify GPO properties and click Finish.

It's beneficial to audit failed attempts for certain objects, such as logon attempts and object access. This can warn you of an impending intruder.

The information obtained through auditing is recorded in the Event Viewer's Security Log. Launch the Event Viewer from the Administrative Tools menu and select Security Log. The right pane displays a list of the items you chose to audit. It's a good idea to check this log regularly, and then clear the log so it doesn't fill up.

Another point to remember is that this example uses the local security policy. If a domain policy is different, it takes precedence. For example, if you set to log all successes and all failures for all local security policy elements and the domain security policy is set to Not Configured, no logging is enabled because the domain security policy is enabled after the local security policy.

When Access Problems Loom . . .

User accounts govern who can access a computer system and what level of access that person enjoys. Sometimes, though, users run into problems that prevent the normal operation of the logon process.

Most logon problems center on an incorrectly typed password. Therefore, users should take the time to type their passwords correctly. This is good advice only if their accounts haven't been locked out because of failed logon attempts. If your user's account is locked out, it must be re-enabled. This can occur in one of two ways. If the lockout policy is set with a duration, you need to only wait until the time expires and try again. If the lockout policy requires administrative intervention, you have to reset that user's account.

When a user can't log on or communication with the network seems sporadic, check the following:

✔ Make sure that the network interface card (NIC) and other physical network connections are solid.

✔ On any Windows system — Windows NT Workstation, Windows 2000, Windows XP Professional, Windows Server 2003, and Windows Server 2008 — you must ensure that the computer is a member of the domain to log on to the domain with an account listed in Active Directory to access network resources.

✔ If using the Internet Protocol (IP) and a statically assigned IP address, check the configuration settings to ensure that the computer is using the correct IP address, subnet mask, and default gateway, and be sure that it has the proper DNS settings for the network.

✔ If your network employs Dynamic Host Configuration Protocol (DHCP) to assign IP settings from a small pool to a larger group of computers, you may be stuck as the last person standing when the music stops and all available connection addresses are in use. You can verify whether this would have happened by going to a command prompt, typing IPCONFIG /ALL, and reviewing the settings. If you have an IP address that falls in the 169.254.0.1 through 169.254.255.254 Automatic Private Internet Protocol Address (APIPA) range, it's possible that the DHCP server ran out of available addresses to assign, or your system had trouble communicating with the DHCP server.

If users can log on but can't access all the resources that they think they should be able to access, you need to verify several items:

✔ Group memberships

✔ Physical network connections to resource hosts (That is, check that a server's network cable isn't disconnected.)

✔ Presence of group policies restricting the user's action

If everything we mention checks out, you may have a fairly esoteric problem. Consult a Microsoft resource (online or through TechNet) to search for a solution. Yeah, that's weak advice, but it's the most valuable thing we can tell you. The Microsoft information database is expansive — if someone else has had the same problem, you can probably find information posted about its resolution.

Chapter 12

Managing Shares, Permissions, and More

*I*n large part, working with Windows Server 2008 means using the Windows NT File System, usually called NTFS. This file system's advanced features include attribute-level access control lists (ACLs) for objects, so you can control not only which users or groups can access a volume, directory, or file, but also which operations users or groups can perform against it.

Transactional NTFS and the kernel transactional technology called Transactional Registry are enhanced in Windows Server 2008. These transactions are necessary to preserve file system integrity and handle error conditions reliably.

Windows 2008 also supports FAT and FAT32 file systems (FAT stands for File Allocation Table), which don't include object-level access controls. However, FAT and FAT32 do support so-called *file shares* (shared directories with the files they contain) that support access controls. Understanding how shares work and how NTFS permissions combine with share permissions are major concerns in this chapter. We show how to figure out what a user can (and can't) do to files based on his or her account permissions, the groups to which he or she belongs, and the underlying defaults that apply to Windows Server 2008 itself.

Chapter 8 discusses this information as it applies to Active Directory.

More about Objects, Rights, and Permissions

Before you can revel in the details of the rights and permissions that apply to Windows Server 2008, you should ponder some technical terminology. That's why we take a brief detour to dictionary-ville — right here, right now.

An object lesson

Windows Server 2008 treats all user-accessible system resources — including users, groups, files, directories, printers, and processes — as objects. The term *object* has special meaning to programmers and tech-heads: This term refers to a named collection of attributes and values, plus a named collection of methods, which Microsoft calls *services*.

For example, a file object has a variety of attributes that you already know about, if you've spent any time at all around computers: Files have names, types, lengths, owners, plus creation and modification dates. For an object, each attribute also has an associated value; therefore, the attributes and values of an object that is a file might be as follows:

- **Name:** BCD (boot configuration data)
- **Type:** Boot configuration and boot environment settings
- **Contents:** Information on how to boot Windows Server 2008 (also used in Windows Vista; resides in $HOMEDRIVE\Boot)
- **Size:** About 32KB

Attributes identify individual objects of some specific type — in this case, a type of file — and define what they contain, where they're located, and so on.

However, it may not be so readily apparent why methods or services are important for objects. If you examine a file object, you can see that its methods describe operations that you would want to apply to a file. Therefore, the methods or services that apply to file objects include things such as read, write, execute, delete, rename, and other typical file operations. In short, *methods* define the operations that can be applied to a particular object. Among other things, this makes objects pretty much self-defining because they include in their attributes complete descriptions of themselves and include in their methods or services complete descriptions of what you can do to them. Other object types have different associated methods or services that reflect the objects' capabilities and the data that the objects contain.

When you examine the attributes for specific objects in Windows Server 2008, things start getting pretty interesting. Every single attribute of every single object has an ACL (this is sometimes pronounced *ackle,* to rhyme with *cackle*). ACLs identify those individual user accounts or groups that may access a particular object (or one of its attributes) and also indicate which services each user or group may apply to that object (or one of its attributes). Administrators use ACLs to control access to objects (and, logically, their attributes), giving themselves free rein to troubleshoot objects while limiting ordinary users' abilities to accidentally (or purposefully) harm the system.

When is a file not an object?

Windows Server 2008 uses objects for most everything in its operating environment that users can access. In fact, NTFS volumes, directories, and files are Windows Server 2008 objects with associated attributes and a set of well-defined services that may be applied to those objects. However, because older FAT file systems (and the newer Windows 98 FAT32) don't include built-in support for ACLs, FAT and FAT32 files are *not* objects. Therefore, even though FAT and FAT32 volumes, directories, and files still have attributes similar to those for NTFS files (namely, name, type, creation date, modification date, and so forth), FAT and FAT32 volumes, directories, and files aren't Windows Server 2008 objects, per se. The lack of built-in support for ACLs explains why FAT volumes and their contents are inherently insecure (because normal permissions don't apply to them).

More important, this also explains why default logon behavior for Windows Server 2008 is to deny everyone but server operators, administrators, backup operators, and printer operators the right to log on locally. That's because anyone who can access a FAT or FAT32 volume can do anything they want to it. By denying ordinary users the right to log on to a Windows Server 2008 at its keyboard and requiring them to log on only through the network, Windows Server 2008 can control access to FAT and FAT32 volumes through shares. Shares function as Windows Server 2008 objects and therefore have built-in access controls.

Users have rights; objects have permissions

In Windows Server 2008, standard usage is to speak of *user rights* and *object permissions*. Because object permissions are rather vague, permissions are commonly used to refer to a specific object class, such as *file permissions* or *printer permissions*.

A user's rights define what he or she can do to objects (or their attributes) in the Windows Server 2008 environment. A user obtains rights to objects in one of three ways:

- ✔ Those rights are explicitly assigned to an individual user account.

- ✔ Those rights are assigned to the groups to which the user belongs. This is where users can be granted privileges to perform specific tasks, such as backing up files and directories.

- ✔ Those rights are assigned through the Group Policy window. To access that window, open one of the Active Directory Administrative tools, right-click a site, an organizational unit, a domain, or a local computer. Choose Properties, click the Group Policy tab, and then click Edit. You edit user rights in the Group Policy window under Computer Configuration⇨Windows Settings⇨Security Settings⇨Local Policies⇨User Rights Assignment.

When a user logs on to a Windows Server 2008 domain (or a stand-alone system), a special key called an *access token* is generated. The *access token* represents the user's explicit individual rights and the groups to which the user belongs. It takes some time to generate an access token, which is one reason why logging on to Windows Server 2008 isn't instantaneous.

Every object (and its attributes) in the Windows Server 2008 environment includes an attribute called *permissions* (which is found on the Security tab of each object). This permissions attribute includes an ACL that identifies all users and groups allowed to access the object's attributes as well as services that each user or group may apply to the object's attributes.

Each time a user requests an object, Windows Server 2008 uses a built-in facility called the Security Reference Monitor (SRM) to check the user's access token against the permissions for that object. If the SRM finds that the user has permission, Windows Server 2008 fulfills the request; otherwise, the user is denied access. It's possible for users to have access to specific attributes of objects, but not other attributes. For example, Nancy may be granted access to view part of JoAnne's account information, such as her telephone number, but not JoAnne's street address.

Of Windows Server 2008 NTFS and Permissions

NTFS is a file system just as FAT and FAT32 (the 32-bit File Allocation Table used in Windows 98) are file systems. The difference between NTFS and these other file systems is that NTFS is *object-oriented*. Unlike FAT and FAT32, NTFS sees everything in NTFS partitions as objects of some specific type that have attributes and to which methods and services can be applied. The benefit of using NTFS is that you can set permissions for the volumes, files, and directories that use NTFS.

In fact, NTFS recognizes three types of objects:

- ✔ **Volumes:** The NTFS-formatted drive partitions that show up as disk drive icons. A volume object may contain files and directories.

- ✔ **Directories:** Named containers for files that occur in a volume or in some other directory. In fact, Windows Server 2008 allows you to nest directories however deep you want, which means that you can put as many directories within directories within directories as you like. (Although nested directories reach a point of diminishing returns fairly quickly.)

- ✔ **Files:** Named containers for data that include type, size, dates, and content among their attributes. Files are where information actually resides in NTFS.

To examine permissions for any object in NTFS, right-click that object in Windows Explorer, My Computer, or Active Directory Sites and Services. In the pop-up menu, select Properties and then click the Security tab. At the bottom of the Security dialog box, you see the Permissions section (as shown in Figure 12-1). From here, you can investigate a list of available permissions for this object (volume E on our hard drive, in this case) through the list that appears in the Permissions section in the lower half of the screen.

Figure 12-1:
The Permissions list shows you all the permissions that apply to the object.

Taking ownership of objects in NTFS

An owner of an object can always modify its permissions, no matter which permissions are already set for that object. This permission exists, at least in part, to sidestep the Deny trap that can occur when an object's owner mistakenly sets permissions for a general group, such as Everyone or Authenticated Users. (These two default groups are discussed further in Chapter 14.)

If the Everyone group is assigned Deny for all permissions of an object, that group includes anyone who may want to access that object. Unless an administrator or the object's creator (its owner, by default) resets permissions to be less restrictive, no one can access that object — or any objects that it contains.

Full Control is important because it grants the object's owner the power to change access to that object and to change services that apply to the object. In essence, Full Control is your get-out-of-jail-free card!

NTFS permissions

The Permissions list shows permissions for files, volumes, and directory objects in NTFS. NTFS file, volume, and directory permissions are similar. The only real differences are that container objects offer child inheritance options and a few permissions apply only to containers. We use the generic term *container* to refer to volumes and directories — in other words, objects that act as parents to child objects.

Windows Server 2008 has a slightly different method of permission assignments and permission restrictions than what is used in Windows NT, but the same method as used in Windows 2000. First and foremost, it doesn't have a No Access permission. Instead, all permissions are either granted or restricted using an Allow or Deny setting. Selecting Deny for all possible permissions for an NTFS object under Windows Server 2008 is the same as the No Access setting in Windows NT.

The standard or normal NTFS permissions are as follows:

- **Read** grants users the ability to view and access the contents of the folder or file.

- **Write** (folders) grants users the ability to create new folders and files within the folder.

- **Write** (files) grants users the ability to change the contents of a file and to alter its attributes.

✔ **List Folder Contents** (folders only) grants users the ability to see the names of the contents of a folder.

✔ **Read & Execute** (folders) grants users the ability to view and access the contents of the folder or file and to execute files.

✔ **Read & Execute** (files) grants users the ability to view and execute files.

✔ **Modify** (folders) grants users the ability to delete a folder and its contents, to create new files and folders within a folder, and to view and access the contents of a folder.

✔ **Modify** (files) grants users the ability to delete a file, change the contents of a file, alter a file's attributes, and to view and access a file.

✔ **Full Control** (folders) grants users unrestricted access to all of the functions of files and folders.

✔ **Full Control** (files) grants users unrestricted access to all of the functions of files.

Advanced permissions

Advanced permissions are detailed controls that can be used to create special access rights when the standard complement of permissions don't apply properly. Advanced controls are accessed by clicking the Advanced button on the Permissions tab of an NTFS object. This reveals the Advanced Security Settings dialog box, which has four tabs:

✔ The **Permissions** tab is used to define special-detail permissions.

✔ The **Auditing** tab is used to define the auditing scheme.

✔ The **Owner** tab is used to view the current owner or take ownership of an object.

✔ The **Effective Permissions** tab displays the permissions a user or group has on the current object, based on all applicable permission settings.

On the Permissions tab, users or groups can be added and their specific permissions defined. The possible selections are

✔ Full Control

✔ Traverse Folder/Execute File

✔ List Folder/Read Data

✔ Read Attributes

✔ Read Extended Attributes

✔ Create Files/Write Data

✔ Create Folders/Append Data

✔ Write Attributes

✔ Write Extended Attributes

✔ Delete

✔ Read Permissions

✔ Change Permissions

✔ Take Ownership

If you really must dig up all the details on special access rights, please consult Microsoft's TechNet CD and the Windows Server 2008 Resource Kit.

FAT and FAT32 Have No Permissions

Because the FAT and FAT32 file systems that Windows Server 2008 supports along with NTFS include no mechanisms for associating attributes with files and directories, files stored in a FAT or FAT32-formatted volume have no associated permissions, either. Anybody who's allowed to log on to a Windows Server 2008 Server with a FAT or FAT32 partition can access any files in that partition. This helps explain why you may want to restrict who's allowed to work on your servers, as well as why you should lock them up.

The reason that FAT partitions are still around is that a dual-boot machine that runs Windows 9*x* or some non-Windows operating systems (such as Linux or some version of UNIX) as well as Windows Server 2008 must include a FAT partition from which the other operating system can boot. This might be a FAT32 partition for Windows Server 98, but we recommend FAT because Windows Server 2008 can read that partition when it's running — and more operating systems can read FAT partitions than any other kind of file system.

Only Windows Server 2008, Windows Vista, Windows Server 2003, Windows XP, Windows 2000, and Windows NT can read NTFS partitions, so be careful when reformatting partitions on dual- or multi-boot machines! Plus, Windows Server 2008, Windows Vista, Windows Server 2003, Windows XP, and Windows 2000 all use NTFS version 5. Windows NT uses NTFS version 4 by default, but if you apply Service Pack 4 or later, Windows NT is upgraded to include NTFS version 5.

Share Permissions

When users access files on a Windows Server 2008 machine, they usually do so across the network, especially if you restrict who's allowed to log on to the server and limit physical access to the machine. Therefore, most users who access files on a Windows Server 2008 do so through a *network share,* which is a directory on a Windows Server 2008 that you've shared to the network for public access.

Shares are also objects for Windows Server 2008, so permissions do apply. The list of applicable permissions consists of the following entries, managed using the same Allow/Deny method as for direct NTFS object permissions:

- **Read** permits viewing of files in the share, loading of files across the network, and program execution.
- **Change** includes all Read permissions, plus creating, deleting, or changing directories and files within the share.
- **Full Control** includes all Change permissions plus changing permissions for and taking ownership of the share.

No Special Access exists for shares. Table 12-1 summarizes the basic permissions for shares.

Table 12-1	Share Permissions and Basic Permissions				
File	*Read*	*Write*	*Execute*	*Delete*	*Change*
Read	X		X		
Change	X	X	X	X	
Full Control	X	X	X	X	X

If you want to expose the contents of a FAT partition on a Windows Server 2008 to network users, doing so through a share automatically gives you some degree of access control, which is yet another advantage to using a network!

To create a share, right-click a directory in My Computer or Windows Server 2008 Explorer, and then choose share. The Properties window for that directory appears with the Sharing tab selected, as shown in Figure 12-2.

Figure 12-2:
The Sharing
tab provides
easy access
to a share's
name, user
limits,
permissions,
and caching
settings.

Click the Share button to open the new File Sharing window, which offers these options:

- ✓ **User name (input box):** You can manually type, select from a list, or search the network for applicable user names for this share.

- ✓ **Name (list box):** By default, you see an entry for the file or directory's original owner usually accompanied by an entry for the system administrator. This represents the active list of users who may utilize shared resources according to specified permissions.

- ✓ **Permission Level:** The Permission Level grants encapsulated rights — privileges defined by certain roles — to specified user names. Default definitions include reader (view-only), contributor (view all files, add, change, and delete new files), and co-owner (view, change, add, or delete all files). You may also remove entries here.

A more comprehensive method of managing shares and storage volumes is to navigate to Start➪Administrative Tools➪Share and Storage Management. This management application gives you a centralized perspective over all drives and drive shares on the system with more advanced properties and settings dialog boxes than the right-click context menu provides. Take any usual safety precautions when sharing files and data, ensuring that only appropriately shared data resides in such directories at all times.

Calculating Actual Permissions

Users have rights not only as a result of the NTFS permissions explicitly assigned to specific files or directories for their accounts but also by virtue of the groups to which they belong. Because NTFS shares exist, figuring out permissions can get pretty interesting when you have to combine NTFS and share permissions for a particular file or directory while also taking user settings and group memberships into account. To help you figure out what's what, we give you a recipe for calculation, plus a few rules to use, and then we walk you through an example to show you how things work.

The rules of calculation

To figure out which permissions apply to a share on an NTFS object, you must first determine which permissions apply to the NTFS object by itself. This could include inheritance features from parent to child object. (See Chapter 8 for a refresher on inheritance.) Next, you must determine the permissions that apply to the share. (The rules for this process appear in the following section.) Whichever of the two results is more restrictive wins and defines the actual permissions that apply to the file or directory in question. This process isn't difficult, but it may produce some counter-intuitive results.

You must apply these rules exactly as they're stated, or we can't guarantee the results. Here goes:

1. **Determine the permissions on the object.**

2. **Determine the permissions on the share.**

3. **Compare the permissions between the share and the object.**

   The *more restrictive* permission is the permission that applies.

Whenever you or your users can't obtain access to a particular file-system object through a share (or NTFS by itself, for that matter), always check group memberships and their associated permissions.

Figure this!

The formal explanation may not completely illuminate the process of figuring permissions, so this section provides a couple of examples.

Betty belongs to the Marketing Dept, Domain Users, and Film Critics groups. She wants to delete the file in an NTFS share named Rosebud.doc. Can she do it? Table 12-2 shows her individual and group permissions.

Table 12-2		Betty's NTFS and Share Permissions	
Type	*Membership*	*Name*	*Permission*
NTFS	User Account	BettyB	Read
	Group	Marketing Dept	Read
	Group	Domain Users	Change
	Group	Film Critics	Change
Share	User Account	BettyB	Read
	Group	Marketing Dept	Read
	Group	Domain Users	Read
	Group	Film Critics	Read

On the NTFS side, Read plus Change equals Change; on the share side, Read is the only game in town. The most restrictive of Read and Change is Read. Read doesn't allow Betty to delete, so Betty's out of luck! Maybe next time. . . .

Let the OS do it for you

Now that you know how to figure permissions manually, we show you a shortcut. In fact, we already told you about it earlier in this chapter. If you display the Advanced Properties dialog box from an object's Security tab, you can access the Effective Permissions tab. By selecting a specific user or group, this tab displays its effective permissions, as shown in Figure 12-3.

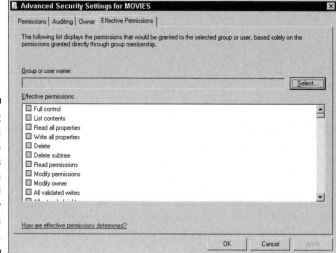

Figure 12-3:
The Effective Permissions tab from the Advanced Security Settings dialog box.

But What about Access Control with Active Directory Objects?

We talk about objects and access control, but with Active Directory, you must be aware of two more features: delegated access control and property-based inheritance. The following sections describe these two features in general; turn to Chapter 8 for the gory details.

Delegation of access control

You can enable others to manage portions of your network for you — otherwise, you'd be working 24/7! You can slice up the management by way of the domain, or you can give someone else rights to manage the organizational unit for you, depending on the functions you want that person to perform. This is accomplished through the Delegate Administration Wizard, which is in the Active Directory Users and Computers snap-in. (Choose Start⇨Administrative Tools⇨Active Directory Users and Computers, click a domain, and then choose Delegate Control from the Action menu.)

An *organizational unit* is an Active Directory container that holds other organizational units, computers, users, and groups. For more information on organizational units, see Chapter 7.

Before you can give others access to manage Active Directory objects, you must first have the proper permissions to delegate that object authority. In addition, you must give the proper permissions to others to manage that object. For more information on this, see Chapter 8.

Property-based inheritance

Just as you might inherit money from a relative, the lower levels of your network structure can inherit access control information set at a higher level of the structure. Inheritance, as its name suggests, always flows in a downward direction. We want to touch briefly on two methods of property-based inheritance. (For more information and detail on how this inheritance works, see Chapter 8.)

The first method is called *dynamic inheritance*. As the word *dynamic* suggests, the access control information for this type of inheritance is calculated on the fly every time a read/write to the object is requested. This results in some performance overhead (such as extra traffic) that should be considered on a busy network. (Extra traffic on a busy network can slow things down significantly.)

The second method is called the *static model,* also referred to as *Create Time Inheritance.* This means that the access control information for an object is set when the object is created by looking at the parent object permissions and combining those permissions with the new object permissions. Unless the new permissions are set at a higher level, the access control doesn't change for the object. Therefore, when a request is made to read or write to the object, no recalculation is necessary to determine the permissions. However, if permissions are changed at a higher level, these changes are propagated downward to change permissions or reset combined permissions at lower levels — similar to dominoes toppling over. The only time there's a recalculation is when the permissions at higher levels are set and the propagation is in progress.

Chapter 13

Preparing for That Rainy Day

· ·

· ·

A backup recovery scheme for your data is important because of the critical business applications and functions that typically reside on networks. Without a plan to protect data, disruptions to an entire organization's data and workflow process can occur, resulting in loss of revenue.

Unfortunately, many organizations place little emphasis on protecting their data until some actual loss occurs. In this chapter, you find out about different methods for protecting your organization's data to prevent losses.

Why Bother Backing Up?

Backing up is the process of copying data from one location to another — either manually or unattended. Copying data from one directory on a hard disk to another directory on that same hard disk is effective until the hard disk crashes and both copies of the data become inaccessible. Also, by copying data to the same drive, you neglect to copy any of its security or account information. This means you must re-enter that information manually. Don't you think it's a better idea to back up all files (such as system, application, and user data) to another physical medium (such as a tape, CD/DVD, or other backup device) and then rotate that device off-site periodically?

Many organizations place their critical business functions and data on the network, including e-mail, accounting data, payroll, personnel records, and operations. Loss of just one element of that collection hinders operations, even if it's just for a short time. Imagine if payroll information disappeared from the system and some employees didn't get paid on time. We wouldn't want to go there!

Data losses can be as simple as one corrupt file or as complex as the entire contents of a server's hard disk becoming unreadable. Organizations can avoid data loss problems almost entirely by backing up on a regular basis.

Considering potential threats

All kinds of threats pose danger to data. Anything from fires to computer viruses can obliterate data on a network. Planning for each type of disaster helps secure and restore your organization's data should that disaster occur.

Data loss on a network can occur in many ways. If you understand the potential threats and plan for them, you can prevent serious damage to your network and loss of data. We urge you to back up your network regularly and to rotate a recent copy off-site.

Here are some potential threats you and your network can encounter:

- ✔ **Hard disk crash:** Even if you've built fault tolerance (such as mirroring or duplexing) into a server, don't expect those methods to always work and recover everything 100 percent. We've seen mirrored drives go out of synch without notice until the hard disk crashes. Without backups, you can lose all your data or segments of it. It's a good idea to complement mirroring and duplexing with regular backups.

- ✔ **Ungraceful shutdown:** Every once in a while, you get a smart-aleck employee who hits the on/off switch to the server, causing it to shut down improperly. Most servers today come right back up — but not always. Shutting the server down in this manner can render its hard disks unreadable. You should put your servers in a secure location away from end users. And don't forget to back up on a regular basis!

- ✔ **Viruses:** Many organizations connect to the Internet, allowing employees to download all types of data to the local area network that could introduce viruses. Viruses pose a real threat to organizations. One virus can ruin an entire computer and render it useless in a short time. If this computer happens to be a server on your network, someone's going to be reading the employment classifieds. Installing virus protection software on the server allows you to check for viruses before they're stored on the server. Put a backup plan in place that allows you to restore the data on your network as it was before the introduction of the virus.

✓ **Environmental disasters:** We've seen many organizations lose data during environmental disturbances, such as bad storms. If lightning can zap the electronics in your home, it can do likewise to data on a network.

Some environmental disasters you should plan for include the following:

- *Fire:* One fire in a building or on a floor can annihilate an entire organization. If your organization loses everything in a fire, you'll be the savior if you produce a recent copy of the network stored safely off-site. If you store backup media on top of your server in the computer room, however, you'll be the one who's pounding the pavement.

- *Floods:* Placing a computer room, server, or backup equipment in the basement or first floor of a building is a bad idea, particularly in flood-prone areas. One flood can obliterate an entire organization. Even if a flood occurs, you're safe with backup media off-site — away from the flood zone.

- *Hurricanes:* Hurricanes bring high winds and rain with them. Don't put your server or backup equipment in a computer room with outside windows. You could come back and find everything strewn around and sopping wet — and have no backup media to restore.

- *Temperature:* Placing a server or a backup machine in a closed room lacking proper ventilation can cause problems. Don't put servers or backup equipment in small rooms with other heat-producing equipment, such as a copier, without forced air cooling. Buildings do shut down A/C systems on weekends and holidays, and heat can kill servers.

Some viruses have a gestation period; therefore, they can be inserted into your network but go unnoticed until after a set number of days. We've seen disgruntled employees place viruses on networks and then leave a company — 30 days later, a virus appears. Incorporate this thought into your backup plan by always backing up on a 30-day rotation scheme. If a virus like this is introduced onto your network, you can go back at least 30 days in your backup media to try to restore the network prior to the virus's introduction. If you have only a week's worth of backup, all the backups you have contain the virus.

How many backup types are there?

The computer world recognizes five types of backup methods, and the same is true with the Windows Server 2008 backup facility. The five types of backups available in Windows Server 2008 are:

✓ Normal

✓ Copy

- ✔ Daily
- ✔ Differential
- ✔ Incremental

Before you can truly understand backup methods, you must understand a little attribute called the *archive bit.* Files have *attributes,* which are the properties of a file. One of the attributes found in Windows Server 2008 is the archive bit. After a file is created or modified, its archive bit is automatically reset by the operating system. This *archive bit* indicates that the file needs to be backed up, even if backup software isn't installed or configured on the computer. Backup software looks for this bit to identify the status of files. Think of this as a seal on every file on your system. When the operating system, a user, or an application modifies the file, the seal is broken. The backup software then goes through the files and "re-seals" them by backing them up.

Normal

The *normal backup* copies all selected files and sets the archive bit, which informs the backup software that the files have been backed up. This type of backup is performed the first time computer data is backed up. With this type of backup, only the most recent backup image is needed to restore all files. (See the "Local backup" section, later in this chapter, for more information on normal backups.)

Copy

The *copy backup* is useful because it doesn't set the archive bit and, therefore, doesn't affect normal and incremental backups. It can be used to copy selected files between scheduled normal or incremental backups. (See the "Incremental" section later in this section for more information.)

Daily

The *daily backup* copies selected files that were changed the day the backup job started. A daily backup doesn't set the archive bit. This backup can be used to copy only those files that were changed on that day, and because the archive bit isn't set, the regular backup goes on as usual.

Differential

Like the copy and daily backups, the *differential backup* also doesn't set the archive bit. It copies all files that were created or modified since the last normal or incremental backup. One practice is to use a combination of normal and differential backups to configure the backup job for the computer. In this combination, a normal backup is performed weekly, and differential backups are performed daily. If this is the backup job used and a restore is being performed, only the last normal and the last differential images are required.

Incremental

The *incremental backup* is similar to the differential backup in that it backs up only those files that have been created or modified since the last normal or incremental backup. Unlike differential backups, however, incremental backups do set the archive bit, which indicates that the files have been backed up. A combination of normal and incremental backups can be used to configure a backup job. In this combination, a normal backup is used once a week and incremental backups are performed on a daily basis. To restore the files using this type of backup combination, the last normal and all incremental sets are required.

Configuring a backup job to use this combination is fast and utilizes storage space efficiently because only those files that were modified get backed up. However, it's important to note that restoration is more difficult and takes longer compared to a combination of differential and normal backups, simply because you have to use a whole set of incremental images. This type of backup combination or configuration is ideal for an enterprise in which an Automated Tape Library (ATL) can be used. Using an ATL, the backup software controls the entire restore operation, including the decision to load the correct tape sequence using its robotic arm.

An ATL is basically a software-controlled backup system in which loading or changing tapes isn't necessary. A typical ATL system is usually designed around a container/library, which can hold from just a few tapes to several hundred, with each tape identified by a unique bar code. Inside the library are one or several tape drives to read and write to tape. An ATL system also includes a mechanism responsible for moving the tape to and from the tape drive. This mechanism can be a robotic arm (in the case of large ATLs) or a simple system similar to those found in a cassette tape recorder. The backup software controls the entire operation by instructing the robotic arm to load a specific tape in a specific tape drive and start the backup or restore job.

Network versus local backup

When backing up information on a network, you have a choice between performing a network backup or a local backup. In this section, we cover the particulars of each option.

Network backup

Network backups are used in large network environments. When you use a network backup, a host computer is configured to back up remote computers attached to the host computer through the LAN. In this scenario, data travels from the remote computer over the network to reach the host computer — the one configured with backup storage. After data is off-loaded from the network interface to the computer's bus, the data is treated as if it were a local backup. (See "The Windows Server 2008 Backup Facility" section, later in this chapter, to find out how to configure your server to back up a remote computer.)

The transfer rate can be a problem with this type of backup because data must traverse and share the LAN with regular traffic. It's more than likely that the LAN is designed around a 10-Mbps Ethernet or a 100-Mbps Fast Ethernet. In any case, data speed would be greatly reduced, compared to the local backup. To deal with this problem and to accommodate the needs of an enterprise in which a large amount of data must be backed up each night, the industry has developed the storage area network (SAN). In this architecture, all computers and storage device(s) are attached directly to the loop using either 1,000 Mbps Gigabit Ethernet (GbE) links or a Fibre Channel Arbitrated Loop (FC-AL), with a bandwidth of 100 Mbps. Furthermore, only computers and the backup device(s) share this bandwidth. Such architecture is expensive, but its benefits for the enterprise more than justify its high cost.

Local backup

The local backup configuration consists of a local tape drive attached to or installed in the computer by means of an Integrated Drive Electronics (IDE) interface, a Small Computer System Interface (SCSI), or — as is most recently popular — Serial ATA (SATA) drives and connections. Local backup is fast because when you use these interfaces, backup storage is directly attached to the computer bus. On some of the new SCSIs, such as the Ultra-640 SCSI, the transfer rate can reach 640 Mbps. It's more likely that this transfer rate won't be achieved, however, because even fast hard drives can achieve only a fraction of that actual wire transfer rate, depending on the drive type. With today's advances in hardware, it's possible to get close to 30GB or more per hour with existing SCSI or SATA II gear.

Local backup is relatively inexpensive because it involves the price of only the backup storage and its interface (and media, where applicable). Most computers are already configured with extra SATAs or SCSIs that can be used for this purpose. One additional cost is the price of a license for the backup software, if third-party software is used. However, Windows Server 2008 comes with powerful backup software that's free!

Understanding the technology

Regardless of whether you choose a network or local backup, and regardless of how often you decide to back up, you must understand some terminology and technology used in backup systems and the different methods involved.

Online, nearline, offline

You hear a lot of buzz about online, nearline, and offline storage options. Choose the method that suits your organization's retrieval time and effort, depending on how often you find yourself restoring data and how fast you want data retrieved. Descriptions of these three backup types follow:

- ✔ **Online:** This type of backup is typically performed on your server, usually in the form of a second hard disk that is mirrored or duplexed. Data is readily available to users through their desktops with no intervention from you except that you must regularly check the status of this fault tolerance. Drives can go out of synch without notice unless you monitor the drives manually or through software.

- ✔ **Nearline:** This type of backup is performed on a device attached to the network. A nearline backup requires some work on your part because it usually uses some method unknown to the user, such as compression techniques. The data is there, but your users won't know how to perform functions, such as decompressing the files, to access the data.

- ✔ **Offline:** This type of backup involves devices that include their own software and hardware and are separate from the server. You need to know how to operate these devices because the users won't know how or might not have the security access to do so. These devices are typically the slowest because data must go from the server to another device. Many organizations place these devices on the network backbone and connect them through fiber-optic cable for higher transmission rates.

As you progress downward in the preceding bulleted list, options become more expensive, it takes longer for you to retrieve information, and more interaction on your part is required. In return, capacity and capability increases dramatically.

What's in the hardware?

Backup systems are composed of backup units, backup media (where applicable), and software components (oh, and you, the operator). These systems come in all sizes, shapes, and dollar signs, depending on your needs. In this section, we describe the most common ones you encounter so you can talk with your vendor about meeting your network needs.

Backup units

A *backup unit* is hardware that can be as simple as a tape device with one slot or a single network-attached storage device, or as complex as a jukebox platter system with mechanical arms or an entire storage area network. If you have low data-storage requirements, a simple backup unit with more capacity than your server will suffice. These units aren't terribly expensive and are available at local computer stores. Some of these units can be daisy-chained if you need more space.

If your organization has lots of data to back up, you might consider a jukebox approach or a sizable network-attached storage device. A *jukebox* is a device that looks like a little computer tower with a door. Inside, it has several slots plus a mechanical arm that can insert and move around tapes or CDs. With this type of system, you typically can insert a week's worth of backup tapes and let the system back up unattended. A network-attached storage device is basically a specialized server with LOTS of hard disks. Its sole function is to store and retrieve files and disk images upon request.

Backup media

Backup media means tapes, cartridges, CD-WORMs (write once, read many), erasable CD or DVD discs, diskettes, and more. Any device on which a backup unit stores data becomes the medium. Backup media come in many shapes and sizes. You want to make sure that you follow the manufacturer's recommendation for purchasing the right medium for your unit.

Don't buy video-grade tape cartridges at your local discount store for your backup purposes. Purchase data-grade tapes, which cost more but are designed for more rugged use.

Backup media come not only in different physical sizes but also in different capacities. Some tapes store as much as 800GB of uncompressed data. Erasable CD-ROMs store as much as 700MB in uncompressed mode and up to 1GB or more of textual data in compressed mode. Better yet, high-definition DVD-ROM storage capacities reach upwards of 25GB per disc using raw, uncompressed formatting. Regardless of which unit and medium you select, get plenty of them so you can work on a rotational scheme without continually using the same medium. We've seen folks who buy just one tape and use that tape over and over until it's time to restore from that tape. And guess what, the tape was defective; therefore, there was no backup! Spread out your backups over multiple tapes to minimize putting all your eggs in one tape basket!

Software

You can use the Windows Server 2008 built-in backup software on a third-party backup device, or you can use the software that comes with the device. We prefer to use third-party software because it's designed to work with certain manufactured devices, and the drivers are always readily available — and sometimes offer greater flexibility or features over native tools. However, that's not to say these native backup facilities aren't worth your time — there are plenty of compelling reasons why you should use Windows Server 2008 Backup, including faster backup technology using Volume Shadow Copy Service, simplified restoration and recovery, improved scheduling, backup capability for applications, support for DVD media, and much more.

One caveat, however small or large, is that you can't back up to tape in Windows Server 2008 Backup. Be prepared for a bumpy ride if you've been using `ntbackup.exe` for all your archival tasks — so much has changed that configurations and interfaces are entirely incompatible. Backup settings will not be upgraded, images created in ntbackup can't be recovered in Backup, and you need a separate disk to run scheduled backups. However, you may download a copy of ntbackup for Windows Server 2008, but you can utilize only legacy ntbackup images — you can't create new ones. For more details, visit `http://go.microsoft.com/fwlink/?LinkId=82917`.

Installation of the devices goes much smoother when you use the recommended software. Always keep a copy of the backup software off-site in case of a fire or other disaster. If you lose all your equipment, you'll need to reload this software on another machine before you can restore data. And this brings up another new feature to Windows Server 2008 Backup: offsite backup removal for disaster protection. Now you can save backup data to multiple participating disks and sites, enabling scheduled backup locations to automatically seek the next disk in the event a primary selection fails or becomes inaccessible. Isn't that nice?

Beep! Beep! Planning Backups

One of the most important tasks that you can perform is to plan your backup. Some of the best backup systems and methods can still fail, so it's smart to always test them first.

Storing backup tapes off-site

It's common for companies to store their backup tapes in a fire-proof safe — usually in the computer room where the fire might occur. These safes are great for one thing, and one thing only: paper. They're designed to withstand enough heat so paper doesn't burn. This heat, however, is more than sufficient to melt any tapes that may be stored in them.

For this reason, smarter companies store tapes off-site on a daily, weekly, or monthly basis, depending on how often data changes. Companies that use drives instead of removable media often make arrangements with Internet backup services to copy their backups to a remote site across the wire. Storing data off-site ensures data availability in case of a disaster, such as a fire or a flood. If a disaster were to occur, a new system could be installed, and data could be restored.

There are companies that provide off-site data vaulting for a fee. The tapes are picked up periodically and transferred to an off-site safe facility for vaulting. If needed, customers can call to get the required tapes for a restore. Such companies might have different service contracts. Although it's more costly to have this service 24 hours and 7 days a week, spending the extra funds to ensure access to tapes might be justifiable, depending on the operation and how critical the data is.

Documenting your hardware and its settings

It's especially important to document your hardware and its settings because it saves time that would be spent guessing and trying different configurations to get the system back up and ready for data to be restored from tape. Generally, accurate and comprehensive documentation ensures fast and reliable recovery.

Document all important settings, such as the following:

- The size of volumes or drives
- The type of file system used
- Whether the file systems are File Allocation Table (FAT) or NT File System (NTFS)
- Whether you've been using any kind of fault tolerance on your disk subsystem, such as mirroring or some type of Redundant Array of Inexpensive Disks (RAID)
- The part numbers of all the components installed in your systems
- All the vendors and your contacts. If the components in your system are from one of the large server manufacturers, such as Compaq or Hewlett Packard, they might loan you a system to recover your data.

Finally, have all your device drivers readily available.

Practicing disaster recovery for your system

It's wise to practice disaster recovery periodically to ensure its success whenever it's required after a real disaster. In large companies, it's normal practice and, in fact, mandated by management. Whereas it's easy to make this statement, actually implementing this practice is harder than you may think. The problem is that you can't attempt to recover your data on a *production system* (which is a system already used for another function). If you do and the backup is corrupt, your live data will become corrupt as well.

Many organizations purchase a second system with the same specifications as the production system as a backup. These systems tend to get "borrowed" for other pilot projects and come into production.

Windows Server 2008 has a new feature that makes disaster recovery much easier. This feature is similar to a third-party solution in which a total system recovery is possible with a few diskettes. Search for *disaster recovery* in the Windows Server 2008 Help and Support Center for more information.

The Windows Server 2008 Backup Facility

Microsoft used to include a backup program called ntbackup with its Windows NT operating systems. Windows Server 2008 ceases this tradition, opting instead for a much revised (and entirely incompatible) and optional Backup facility. The Windows Server 2008 version of Backup retains the capability to back up to nontape media and access network resources, and it includes built-in scheduling capabilities. These features were present in the Windows 2000 and Windows Server 2003 version of ntbackup but absent from the Windows NT version.

Great features of Windows Server 2008 Backup

As mentioned earlier, Windows Server 2008 Backup doesn't use tape storage devices. It opts instead to use internal and external disks, shared folders, and — perhaps most impressive of all — DVD media. Windows Server 2008 still supports tape storage drivers, which may be utilized in custom or third-party archival applications.

Backup's simplified design is ideal for medium-sized organizations or individuals not working as IT professionals, such as small business owners, but it can work for just about anyone. IT analysts and planners, early platform adopters, and security architects are chief among this collective who are often responsible for safekeeping or archiving various types and amounts of data in a number of occupational capacities.

Removable Storage Manager (RSM) — now an aspect of Server Manager — is an integrated part of the Windows Server 2008 operating system. This service is responsible for managing tasks such as the mounting and dismounting of storage devices on behalf of Windows Server 2008 Backup software. Relieving the backup software of these tasks and making them part of the operating system, unlike previous versions of Windows NT, makes the software much more reliable and robust.

Finally, you can back up (and restore) using the Backup Wizard. The wizard will ask you all the questions that you need to answer for a backup to be completed properly. See the "Scheduling backup jobs" section in this chapter for more details on the Backup Wizard.

Looking at the big picture

Windows Server 2008 ships with a completely new Backup facility that includes two methods for backing up your server: a GUI interface (Start⇨Administrative Tools⇨Windows Server Backup) and command line execution (\WINNT\system32\ntbackup). We prefer the advanced mode of the GUI interface (shown in Figure 13-1) for quick manual backups and the command line interface for batched and scheduled backups.

These methods aren't exactly unattended because you have to start them to run manually — unless you set them up with a scheduler task to run automatically at a preset time. Although somewhat crude and not so fancy, Windows Server 2008 Backup is better than nothing. If your budget is low and you can't afford to purchase a solution from a third-party vendor that specializes in backup software, this is the way to go. And the best part is that it's free! (It's included in the price of Windows Server 2008.)

Before purchasing a third-party backup product or using the Windows Server 2008 built-in backup program, search the Microsoft Knowledgebase (support.microsoft.com) for known bugs and problems regarding backup issues. Be specific in the search (that is, search for **Windows Server 2008 BACKUP**). Also, always install the latest service pack, which will correct most minor bugs known to Microsoft.

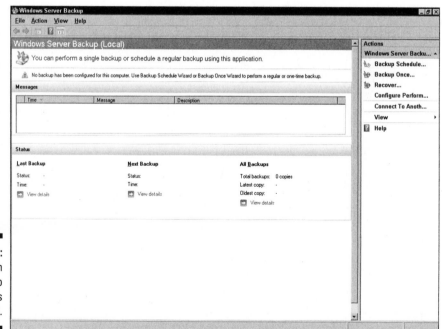

Figure 13-1:
The built-in GUI backup in Windows Server 2008.

You may install Backup through Windows Server 2008 Server Manager. Just follow these instructions:

1. **Choose Start⇨Server Manager.**

   The Server Manager console appears.

2. **Select Features Summary and then click Add Features.**

   The Add Features Wizard appears.

3. **Under Select Features, choose Windows Server Backup and then click Next.**

4. **After you reach the Confirm Installation page, click Install.**

5. **Click Close.**

This provides you with the basic ability to back up and recover Windows Server 2008 applications and data.

Performing command line backups

You execute ntbackup from the command prompt using the following syntax:

```
ntbackup backup [systemstate] "@bks file name"
/J {"job name"} [/P {"pool name"}] [/G {"guid name"}]
[/T { "tape name"}] [/N {"media name"}] [/F {"file name"}]
[/D {"set description"}] [/DS {"server name"}]
[/IS {"server name"}] [/A] [/V:{yes|no}] [/R:{yes|no}]
[/L:{f|s|n}] [/M {backup type}] [/RS:{yes|no}]
[/HC:{on|off}] [/SNAP:{on|off}]
```

Yikes, that looks complicated! But don't worry, it really isn't that bad. In most cases, you'll need only a handful of parameters rather than all of them. The best place to get more details on using ntbackup from a command line is the Command Line Reference, which you can access by typing **ntbackup /?** from the Run command. This displays a help window that contains the correct syntax for ntbackup, along with excellent descriptions, restrictions, requirements, and suggested uses of each parameter. Plus, several examples help you figure out how to use the command line syntax.

However, we really don't see much of a need for command line operation of ntbackup, especially because the GUI tool offers scheduling. But if you're really into batch scripts and would rather do things the hard way, be our guest.

Some files that are hard coded into ntbackup don't get backed up, and you can't change or alter this. Following are some of the files and other things that don't get backed up:

✔ **Open files:** Users can't have files open while the backup is running. Those files won't be backed up. Have the users log off the system and disconnect them from any shares.

✔ **Temporary files:** No temporary files, such as PAGEFILE.SYS, are backed up.

✔ **File permissions:** The account used to perform the backup must have permission to read files.

✔ **Other Registries:** Only the local Registry is backed up. Registries on other servers are not backed up.

Selecting targets and volumes

In the Windows NT version of ntbackup, you could choose the files that you want to back up only through the GUI. The Windows 2000 and Windows Server 2003 versions allow you to either select a root drive or directory from the command line or use the GUI to define a backup selection file (a .bks file). Windows Server 2008 changes the game slightly and permits you to select among the local drive volumes.

To create a Backup image of select volumes, follow these steps:

1. **Choose Start⇨Administrative Tools⇨Windows Server Backup.**

   The Welcome to the Backup or Restore Wizard screen appears.

2. **Under the Actions pane at right, choose Backup Once.**

   The Backup Once Wizard appears.

   The first time through, you may only choose Different Options. After you specify a default backup schedule, you can select the option The Same Options That I Use for Scheduled Backups.

3. **Click Next.**

4. **Under Select Items, choose Custom and click Next.**

5. **Select or deselect the selected volumes and click Next.**

   There may be several to choose from, and you may also select whether this should be a recovery image, which is selected by default. (See Figure 13-2.)

6. **Under Specify Destination Type, select the appropriate target(s) and click Next.**

   The options are Local Drives or Remote Shared Folder.

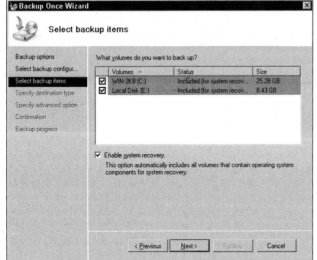

Figure 13-2:
Selecting
volumes to
be backed
up.

7. **Click the Start Backup button to back up to the location you selected in Step 6.**

   Windows Server Backup will create images of all the drives you selected in Step 5.

   If you prefer to use the Windows Backup and Restore center, please read the next section for information on using that version instead.

Specifying backup destination and media settings

Now that you've selected the files that you want to back up, you can choose the backup destination. If you don't have a tape drive installed on your system, the ntbackup program defaults to a file as its backup destination. Otherwise, simply select the backup device to which you'd like to back up the information as follows:

1. **Choose Start➪All Programs➪Accessories➪System Tools➪Windows Server Backup.**

   The Welcome to the Backup or Restore Wizard screen appears.

2. **Click Advanced Mode.**

3. **Click the Backup tab.**

4. **Choose the backup destination (File or Tape):**

   - *File:* Choose File in the Backup Destination drop-down list. In the Backup Media or File Name box, type the full path and filename (or click the Browse button to find it).

   - *Tape:* Choose a tape from the Backup Destination drop-down list.

5. **Click the Start Backup button.**

Scheduling backup jobs

As mentioned previously, scheduling backup jobs is a built-in feature of Windows Server 2008 Backup. Scheduling backup jobs is as simple as following these steps:

1. **Choose Start⇨All Programs⇨Administrative Tools⇨Windows Server Backup.**

2. **In the Actions pane at left, choose Backup Schedule.**

3. **Click Next.**

4. **Choose whether to create a Full Server (Recommended) or Custom Backup selection.**

5. **Answer the questions presented to you by the wizard.**

   You'll notice that you're prompted for a username and password. The user performing the backup (probably you) must be either an administrator, a member of the Backup Operators group, or have equivalent rights of these groups.

6. **Under Specify Backup Time, specify the frequency of the job and click Next.**

   The options are Once a Day or Multiple Backups Every Day. If you choose the second option, select the appropriate time slots.

7. **Continue through to the Confirmation dialog box to complete this task.**

   The calendar in the Schedule Jobs tab changes to reflect the jobs.

Restoring from a Backup

Backing up your data is only half the picture. The other half involves restoring files on the network. We hope that you have to restore only a few files for users from time to time. Making regular backups along the way makes this task friendly and easy. However, in a fire or other disaster, you might lose your data and computer equipment, including the server to which you need to restore. We hope that you heed our advice when we say to rotate tapes off-site each week to plan for this catastrophe. If you also lose the server, we hope that you have a good working relationship with your local vendors so you can get equipment in a hurry.

The most important thing to remember when restoring your network is to practice the restoration process when you aren't under the gun. This not only gives you confidence in performing the task, but also periodically tests the integrity of your backup. Although you can examine log files each morning, it's better to perform real restore tests — just like a dress rehearsal. When disaster does strike and you need to perform a real restore, all sorts of people will be looking over your shoulder asking you when things will be up and running. If you confidently know your backup system, you can perform this task under extreme pressure. Don't wait until the last minute to test and learn the system.

Always restore the system files (\SYSTEM32\CONFIG and Registry files) first, reboot, and then take a peek at the system to make sure everything looks like it's in place. Then restore the data files. If you plan your network directory and volume structure to segment system and data files, this task is much easier. Know ahead of time whether certain business departments require that their data be restored first. Sometimes this isn't necessary, but in instances where a customer service department exists, they usually want the network back up right away with immediate access to their data. Why? Because they're servicing the external customers that generate the revenue for your organization! Before restores become necessary, try to devise a restoration order plan for your network and practice it.

Note that sometimes you can't restore Windows Server 2008 system files; you may have to reinstall Windows Server 2008 and then restore the system files.

Third-Party Backup Options

Because Windows Server 2008 is such a new operating system, currently no third-party options are specifically designed for it. Rest assured, however, that this won't remain so for long.

We always recommend going with well-recognized, name-brand, third-party companies to ensure good compatibility with Windows Server 2008 and other network operating systems. Most of the popular packages support the capability to back up several different network operating systems at one time and contain easy-to-use interfaces for backup and restore options.

Finding third-party packages

One easy way to find other third-party backup software is to visit popular search engines on the Internet, such as `www.search.com`, and enter the keywords *Windows Server 2008 Backup*. Discount Internet shops, such as CDW (`www.cdw.com`), provide information about various backup devices in one handy location. On the CDW Web site, go to the Hardware section, click the Data Storage option, and look at how much information you have.

The backup market has two types of vendors: small-business backup solutions and enterprise backup solutions. We list the top vendors in each category to get your search started:

- ✔ **Small business:**

  - Exabyte, `www.exabyte.com`

  - ADIC (Advanced Digital Information Corporation), `www.quantum.com/AboutUs/ADIC/Index.aspx`

  - Hewlett-Packard, `http://welcome.hp.com/country/us/en/prodserv/storage.html`

- ✔ **Enterprise business:**

  - Symantec Veritas, `www.symantec.com/enterprise/theme.jsp?themeid=datacenter`

  - Legato, `www.software.emc.com`

Search the backup vendors' Web sites for white papers and cost of ownership documents. This information is free, and a lot of research has been compiled. You can use this information to convince management of your backup requirements.

Evaluating backup systems

Regardless of which vendor you choose, the following checklist provides some helpful criteria in evaluating tape systems. Determine the requirements for your organization and query the vendor as to whether their product has the features you desire — and whether you have to pay extra for some add-on modules.

This list should give you a good idea of what you may need when choosing a tape backup system:

✔ **Critical system files:** An essential feature in any tape system that you purchase is that it can back up the Windows Server 2008 system files — such as the Registry and event logs, security information, user accounts, and access control lists — in addition to the actual data.

✔ **Fast media index:** When backing up large amounts of data, it's critical that during the restore process you're able to obtain a catalog of the media contents within a minute or two. You don't want to wait 30 minutes each time you need to see the contents of a particular medium.

✔ **Multiplatform support:** Networks that support multiple platforms, such as Novell, Microsoft, and UNIX, are easier to back up if one backup system can support more than one platform.

✔ **Client backups:** Some users simply refuse to store files on the network. In this case, look for a package that automates client workstation backups across the network to your tape backup system. Some popular systems already include this option. Ask which client operating systems it supports — for example, Macintosh, UNIX, Windows, and OS/2.

✔ **Unattended operation:** Some tape systems work like jukeboxes and have a mechanical arm that inserts and removes tapes, so you can go home while the backup runs. These systems are expensive, but if you have a lot of data to back up and don't want to insert tapes all night, look for this feature.

✔ **Scheduling features:** If you want to perform incremental and full backups on different days, look for a system that is flexible and allows you to automate the scheduling features based on the day of the week.

✔ **Open files:** *Open files* are files in use during the backup operation. Not all backup systems are designed to back up open files, and some even halt when they get to one that's open. Most systems skip over the file and write an exception to a log file. More than likely, you want a backup system that backs up open files.

✔ **Security and encryption:** For small operations, this feature may not be as critical. For larger environments, ask the vendor how its system handles passing information through the network, such as passwords and account information.

✔ **Hierarchical Storage Management (HSM):** You want to make sure the vendor's product supports online, nearline, and offline storage and can manage using all three at one time.

✔ **Data storage size:** You want to find out how much data you can back up to the system (MB or GB), the size of the tapes the system uses (4mm, 8mm, DLT, or others), and whether it compresses data.

✔ **Remote management:** Getting to monitor backup status and progress remotely instead of being in front of the console is a handy feature.

✔ **Scalability:** Find out whether this system can be scaled to a larger environment should your network grow.

✔ **Security access:** Running an unattended backup means that a device must either log on to the network while you're gone or remain logged on with the keyboard locked. Check with the vendor as to how the product logs on to the network and maintains security.

The Backup Operator

Before a user is allowed to back up or restore the system, he or she must be a member of the Backup Operators group. This group is the same as the Backup Operators group in Windows NT, but Windows Server 2003 (and by extension, Windows Server 2008) has changed the procedures for adding users to the group and changing the group's policies. Depending on whether you're running Windows Server 2008 with Active Directory, the steps involved in adding a user to the Backup Operator group will be slightly different.

By default, the Backup Operators group doesn't have any members. It's simply an empty container or a placeholder for when you need to assign backup and restore rights to users.

To modify the membership of the Backup Operators group when Active Directory isn't installed (in other words, when your server is configured as a normal server instead of a domain controller), follow these steps:

1. **Choose Start➪All Programs➪Administrative Tools➪Computer Management.**

2. **In the left pane, expand the System Tools icon and highlight the Local Users and Groups icon.**

   If you don't see Local Users and Groups, it's probably because that snap-in hasn't been added to the Microsoft Management Console, or it may be that you're working on a domain controller, which is strictly controlled through Active Domain Users and Computers. If you're not working on a domain controller, you can type **dsadd.exe** into the Search box that pops up above the Start button when you click it. If you are working on a domain controller, you must use the Active Domain Users and Computers utility, which you can launch by typing **dsa.msc** into the aforementioned Search box instead.

3. **In the right pane, double-click the Groups option.**

   At this point, all the groups that currently exist on your system are displayed in the right pane.

4. **Highlight and right-click the Backup Operators group and choose the Add to Group option.**

5. **Click the Add button and type the username that you'd like to become a member of the Backup Operators group.**

6. **Click Check Names and then click OK.**

To modify the membership of the Backup Operators group when Active Directory is installed, follow these steps:

1. **Choose Start⇨All Programs⇨Administrative Tools⇨Active Directory Users and Computers.**

2. **In the left pane, double-click the tree to expand it.**

3. **In the right pane, double-click the Builtin folder.**

4. **In the right pane, double-click the Backup Operators group.**

5. **Click the Members tab.**

6. **Click the Add button to add users.**

Chapter 14

Network Security Management

*I*n the ever-changing world of information technology, protecting private data from prying eyes is becoming increasingly important. Maintaining a solid security posture that prevents access to internal information, processes, and resources is critical to sustaining a competitive edge and to ensure self-preservation in hostile environments. In this chapter, we discuss how to impose tight security on Windows Server 2008.

When you install Windows Server 2008 out of the box, it doesn't provide a totally secure environment, although it's much more secure than previous editions. You must customize security details on Windows Server 2008 to best suit your operating environment. This process involves executing multiple steps, careful planning, double-checking your settings, and a few noncomputer activities. If you don't care about the security of your data, you can skip this discussion entirely, though we can't imagine this applies to too many of our readers.

The goal of security isn't to create a system that's impossible for a hacker or misguided user to compromise. Instead, the goal is to erect a sufficiently imposing barrier against intruders so that the difficulty they encounter while attempting to break in is significantly higher than on someone else's system. It's kind of like building a brick wall around your yard so tall that it discourages an intruder from climbing over — so that the intruder goes into your neighbor's yard instead. Your goal is to convince attackers to go after easier targets. By following the prescriptions in this chapter, you can deploy a Windows Server 2008 system that's not only harder to crack than your neighbors' but also nearly watertight!

Protecting proprietary and private electronic property defends against outside attackers, but it also involves erecting a barrier against inside assaults and taking precautions against other threats to your data as well.

Network Security Basics

The basic precepts of network security require you to keep unauthorized people out of your network, to keep unwanted data out as well, and to keep wanted data in. Leave it to us to point out the obvious!

Creating a secure environment requires you to pay attention to three key areas, or martial canons:

- ✔ Understanding the operating system (or systems)
- ✔ Controlling physical access to the computer
- ✔ Educating human users

These three areas are like legs on a barstool. If any one of these legs is weak, the person on the stool will hit the floor. Nobody wants to be that person. It hurts!

In this section, we briefly discuss the issues involved with maintaining physical control and educating users. The third leg, the operating system itself, is our subject for the remainder of this chapter.

Getting physical

Controlling physical access means preventing unauthorized people from coming into close proximity to your computers, network devices, communication pathways, peripherals, and even power sources. A computer system can be compromised in several ways. Physical access is always the first step in breaking into a system. Remember that physical access doesn't always mean a person must be in your office building. If your network has dial-up access, someone can gain access remotely.

Controlling physical access means not only preventing access to keyboards or other input devices but also blocking all other means of transmitting to or extracting signals from your computer system. You want to exercise great care over what goes into and flows out of your network, thereby safeguarding everything within it.

Protecting the computer room and operating environment

Some physical access controls are obvious to everyone:

   ✔ Locking doors

   ✔ Using security badges

   ✔ Employing armed guards

   ✔ Using locking cases and racks

If you address only these items, you still leave other access methods wide open. You must think about the architecture, structure, and construction of your building. Can ceiling or floor tiles be removed to gain entry over or under the walls? Do ventilation shafts or windows provide entry into locked rooms? Are you feeling paranoid yet?

A person getting into your computer room isn't the only concern you should have. You also must think about the environment in which computers operate. Most computers operate properly across only a limited range of temperatures. Therefore, if intruders can gain access to thermostat controls, your system can become compromised. What is the one thing that all computers need? Electricity. Is your power supply secure? Can it be switched off outside your security barriers? Do you have an uninterruptible power supply (UPS) attached to each critical system? Did you install a backup phone line independent of the regular land line in case of emergency?

Even after preventing entrance into the computer room and protecting the operating environment, you still haven't fully secured your computers physically. You need to think about your trash — yes, the trash! You would be amazed at what private investigators and criminals can learn about you and your network from information discarded in your trash. If you don't shred or incinerate all printouts and handwritten materials, you may be exposing passwords, usernames, computer names, configuration settings, drive paths, or other key data. Trust us, this happens more often than you'd care to know, occasionally with enough oomph to make the nightly news.

Do you think we've covered everything now? Wrong! Ponder these issues:

   ✔ Does the nightly cleaning crew vacuum and dust your computer closet?

   ✔ Is that crew thoroughly screened and properly bonded?

   ✔ How often does the crew unplug computer systems to plug in cleaning machines?

   ✔ Is the key that unlocks your front door also the key that unlocks the computer room?

   ✔ How do you know that the cleaning crew isn't playing with your computer systems?

   ✔ How do you know that the members of the cleaning crew are who you think they are?

   ✔ Are floppy drives installed on servers and other critical systems?

✔ Can systems be rebooted without passwords or other authentication controls (for example, smart cards)?

✔ Do servers have extra ports ready to accept new attachments?

✔ Are your backup tapes stacked beside the tape drive?

✔ Are your backup tapes protected by encryption and passwords?

✔ Are all backup tapes accounted for? If some are missing, do you know what information was stored on them?

✔ What really happens in your office building after business hours? Are the doors locked every night?

If you can still sleep at night, you probably have most of these items under control. If you can't answer some of these questions with a solid, reassuring response, you have work to do. Get going!

Guarding against notebook theft

So far, physical access issues we've discussed focus on stationary computers. But what about mobile machines? Remember that expensive notebook system you purchased for the boss, that manager, and a system administrator so they could work while traveling and connect to the network over the phone? Should one of those notebooks fall into the wrong hands, somebody might have an open door through which they could access your network and take or ruin whatever they please.

Notebook theft is becoming the number one method for gaining access to company networks. Most notebooks are stolen at the airport. (We bet you could've guessed that one!) Although most travelers are smart enough not to check notebooks as luggage, there's one common location where notebooks and their owners are separated — the metal detector. All it takes is a few moments of delay while waiting to walk through the metal detector after you've placed a notebook on the x-ray conveyer, and poof — the notebook is gone by the time you reach the other end.

And despite all the precautions taken while traveling with notebooks, lapses in routine or procedures can allow opportunistic miscreants to take advantage: leaving one unattended. It may be in the car while retrieving out-of-town mail piling up at the post office, or making a quick stop at a corner store on the way home. In such unguarded moments, notebooks can and will disappear, and their absence may go completely unnoticed until you arrive home to collect your travel gear.

Controlling physical access in the workplace is also important because without access to a computer system, hackers can't break in. If you fail to manage physical access to your network, you're relying on operating-system-supported software security to protect your data. In that case, there's another glaring problem to contend with — if you've failed to properly educate network users, your security may already be compromised.

Informing the masses about security policies

The most secure network environment is useless if users don't respect the need for security. In fact, if left alone, most humans find the path of least resistance when performing regular activities — like leaving a notebook unattended in an unlocked car. In other words, users will do anything to make traversing security simple — such as automating password entry, writing down passwords in plain view, mapping unauthorized drives, installing unapproved software, transferring data to and from work and home on flash drives, and attaching modems to bypass firewalls or proxy servers. If you use software-based or operating-system-based security measures, users often find ways around them, or to reduce their effectiveness.

User education is a two-pronged process:

- First, network users must understand what security means, why it's important, and what measures are in place on your network.
- Second, violations of security policy and practice must be dealt with swiftly and strictly.

Educating network users

In most cases, educating network users means preparing an official document that details and explains all security restrictions, requirements, and punishments. This document, known as a *security policy,* serves as a network constitution, or its governing body of regulations. It also helps maintain network security and lets violators know they'll be prosecuted.

So, what does a user need to know about security imposed on an organization's network? Here's a brief list of highlights:

- Use passwords properly and choose them wisely. (Don't use an obvious name or number, such as a pet's name or your birth date.)
- Never write down or share passwords.
- Never share security badges and smart cards or leave them unattended.
- Restrict network access to authorized employees only.
- Don't share user accounts with other employees or with anyone outside the organization.

- Don't distribute data from the network in any form outside the organization.

- Don't step away from your workstation while you're logged on to the system.

- Understand the various levels of security in place on the network and the purpose of the stratification.

- Don't install unapproved software.

- Make it clear to all employees that tampering, subverting, or bypassing security measures is grounds for termination of employment.

- Respect the privacy of the organization and other users.

- Deal with violations of the security policy in a swift and severe manner without reservation or exemption.

Punishing users for violating the security policy

If a user violates a significant clause in the security policy, a severe punishment must be applied. In most cases, firing the individual is the only form of punishment that controls the situation effectively and prevents other users from making the same mistake. The repercussions of violating the security policy must be detailed in the policy itself. And if you spell out the punishment, you must follow through. Even if your top programmer is the culprit, he or she must receive the same punishment as a temporary mail handler.

Most analysts have discovered that deploying a severe security policy results in a common pattern — a short-term improvement in security, followed by a brief period of laxness, which results in violations, causing several users to be fired, which then results in an overall sustained improvement in security. Companies have reported that the loss of manpower because of violations was negligible in comparison to the prevention of security breaches.

You should create your own security policy that includes details about physical control, user education, and operating-system-level security measures. Remember the adage about the ounce of prevention. (It beats a pound of cure, every time.)

Windows Server 2008 and Security

Windows Server 2008 security adheres to several significant principles, chief among which is access control. Access control depends on user identity, and normally attaches to user accounts. To access a Windows Server 2008 computer or network, users must possess a user account with a valid username and password. But then, anyone who knows a valid username and password combination can gain access. Thus, both usernames and passwords for user accounts must be protected.

Windows Server 2008 includes several new features and functions to help make it more robust, secure, and reliable than its predecessors. Its services can be componentized into discrete roles necessary to sustain specific network functions such as DHCP or DNS, and they're hardened against various forms of remote attack. Windows Server 2008 also incorporates Network Access Protection, Federated Rights Management, and Read-Only Domain Controller capability to further strengthen its security posture to help protect your organizational assets.

Let's briefly define what some of these features do:

- ✔ **Network Access Protection** isolates noncompliant computers that violate organizational policy to provide restriction, remediation, and enforcement.

- ✔ **Federated Rights Management** services provide persistent protection for sensitive information, reduce risk, enable compliance, and deliver comprehensive data protection.

- ✔ **Read-Only Domain Controller** capability enables Active Directory Domain Services deployments with restriction to replication of the full Active Directory database for stronger protection against data theft.

The following paragraphs define and detail the fundamental principles, policies, and procedures behind a solid security posture. These apply equally to any organization, no matter how large or small its operational capacity.

Usernames are more than just names

Protecting usernames isn't always simple, but a little effort subverts easy attacks. Here are a few precautions you can take:

- ✔ **Make usernames complex.** Don't create usernames that employ just the first or last name of a person. Combine two or more elements to create a name, such as first name, last name, initials, department code, or division name. You should also avoid using users' e-mail addresses to name accounts. This makes guessing user names a bit more difficult. Even if a hacker knows your naming convention, making usernames complex makes *brute-force attacks,* in which every likely or possible password is attempted, more difficult. (See Chapter 11 for more information on naming conventions.)

✔ **Rename common accounts.** These include the Administrator, Guest, and IUSR_<*servername*> (created by Internet Information Services, or IIS) accounts. Rename these to something descriptive but not easily guessed. Then, create new dummy accounts with the original names that have absolutely no access. This serves as a decoy for hackers, effectively wasting their time and giving you more opportunity to discover who they are. You can even monitor access to these accounts to observe when would-be attackers are seeking unauthorized access.

✔ **Include a restriction to prevent users from employing their network logon usernames as logon names anywhere else.** In other words, a user's network logon name shouldn't be used as a logon name for Web sites, File Transfer Protocol (FTP) sites, or other external systems. If users don't use the same logon names everywhere, they'll be less tempted to use the same passwords everywhere as well.

Even with these precautions, usernames can be discovered. The important issue here is to make obtaining any data item needed to log on to your network as difficult as possible. After a username is known, the responsibility of protecting your network rests on the strength of its associated password.

Passwords and security

Passwords are the primary means by which unauthorized access to a system is prevented. The stronger the password, the more likely security will remain intact. As part of your security policy, you must require that strong passwords be used by each and every user. (See the upcoming "A few more things about passwords" section for guidelines for crafting strong passwords.) A single account compromised can result in unfettered access to entire systems.

Strong passwords can be enforced using built-in controls in Windows Server 2008. By employing all system-level controls that force strong passwords, little additional effort is required to ensure that users comply with the security policy. New to Windows Server 2008 is password-setting granularity: You may implement password settings on a user or group basis. No longer are you restricted to single, all-encompassing settings for a whole domain, which requires separate domains for separate settings. This occurs commonly where an organization requires different password settings that affect multiple, different administrative accounts.

Accounts Policies define restrictions, requirements, and parameters for the Password, Account Lockout, and Kerberos policies. To access Accounts Policies, follow these steps:

1. **Choose Start⇨Run.**

2. **Type** gpmc.msc **into the Start Search field and press Enter.**

3. **Double-click your forest name to expand its settings.**

4. **Expand Domains, select your domain name once more, and double-click to expand.**

   The Group Policy Management Console appears. An additional dialog box may also appear, stating that you've selected a link to a Group Policy Object (GPO) and that any changes made here are exercised globally wherever this GPO is linked (except for changes to link properties).

5. **Right-click the Default Domain Policy entry and choose Edit.**

   The Group Policy Object Editor appears.

6. **Under the Computer Configuration node, expand the Windows Settings item.**

7. **Under the Windows Settings node, expand the Security Settings item.**

8. **Under the Security Settings node, expand the Account Policies item.**

   Now you can see the Password, Account Lockout, and Kerberos policies in the right pane of the Local Security Settings window, as shown in Figure 14-1.

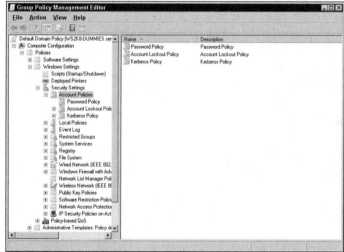

Figure 14-1:
The
Password,
Account
Lockout and
Kerberos
Policies
appear on
the right.

Password Policy

After you've found the Account Policies option, you can access the Password Policy by choosing Account Policies⇨Password Policy. The six options shown in Figure 14-2 allow you to control the requirements for user passwords. The higher you raise the bar in each of the six options, the stronger the password requirements become, thereby making it increasingly less likely that brute-force attacks will succeed against your system.

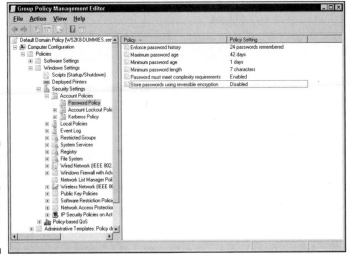

Figure 14-2:
The Group
Policy
editing tool,
Password
Policy.

In the following list, we briefly explain each option, spell out the default setting, and recommend the most appropriate settings for general use:

- **Enforce Password History:** We recommend a setting of 5 or greater, which means that the system remembers the last five passwords used so he or she can't reuse any of them.

- **Maximum Password Age:** Use this option to define when passwords expire and must be replaced. We recommend settings of 30, 45, or 60 days.

- **Minimum Password Age:** Use this option to define how long a user must wait before changing his or her password. We recommend settings of 1, 3, or 5 days.

- **Minimum Password Length:** Use this option to define the smallest number of characters that a password must include. We recommend at least eight characters for best results.

- **Passwords Must Meet Complexity Requirements:** (Astute observers may notice that this was disabled by default in previous versions.) Complexity requirements are rules, such as, requiring both capital and lowercase letters, requiring use of numerals, and requiring nonalphanumeric characters. If native password requirements aren't sufficient, we recommend that you research complexity requirements further by using the Windows Server 2008 Help and Support feature or the Windows Server 2008 Resource Kit.

- **Store Password Using Reversible Encryption for All Users in the Domain:** By enabling this attribute, you can use Shiva Password Authentication Protocol (SPAP), which is a security authentication mechanism for the Point-to-Point Protocol (PPP) developed by Shiva Corporation. Leave this disabled unless SPAP is required by a client.

Account Lockout Policy

The next policy in Account Policies is the Account Lockout Policy, which governs when user accounts are locked out because of repeated failed logon attempts. (Choose Account Policies⇨Account Lockout Policy.) Lockout prevents brute-force logon attacks (in which every likely or possible password is attempted) by turning off user accounts. The options are as follows:

✔ **Account Lockout Duration:** Use this option to define how long to lock out an account. A setting of Forever requires an administrator to unlock an account. We recommend a setting of 30 minutes or more.

✔ **Account Lockout Threshold:** Use this option to define how many failed logon attempts result in lockout. We recommend a setting of 3 to 5 invalid logon attempts.

✔ **Reset Account Lockout Counter After:** Use this option to define the time period after which the failed logon count for an account is reset. We recommend a setting of 15 minutes.

Kerberos Policy

The last policy in Account Policies is the Kerberos Policy, which governs the activity of secured communication sessions. (Choose Account Policies⇨ Kerberos Policy.) Kerberos is an advanced network authentication protocol. Using Kerberos, clients can authenticate once at the beginning of a communications session and then perform multiple tasks during that session without having to authenticate again. Kerberos is used to prove the identity of a client and a server to each other. After such identity verification occurs, communications can occur without repeating this process (or at least until the communications link is broken).

The options for this policy are specified in the following list with their recommended settings:

✔ **Enforce User Logon Restrictions:** *Enabled*

✔ **Maximum Lifetime for Service Ticket:** *600 minutes*

✔ **Maximum Lifetime for User Ticket:** *10 hours*

✔ **Maximum Lifetime for User Ticket Renewal:** *7 days*

✔ **Maximum Tolerance for Computer Clock Synchronization:** *5 minutes*

For more information on establishing a secure baseline in Windows Server 2008, please download the Microsoft Windows Server 2008 Security Guide and visit the Microsoft Security Web site (www.microsoft.com/security/ default.mspx).

A few more things about passwords

Whether you enable software controls to restrict passwords, we recommend that you include the following elements in your organization's security policy regarding passwords:

- ✔ Require a minimum of six characters; longer is better.
- ✔ Prevent the e-mail address, account name, or real name from being part of the password.
- ✔ Don't use common words, slang, terms from the dictionary, or other real words in passwords.
- ✔ Don't write passwords down, except to place them in a vault or safety deposit box.
- ✔ Don't use words, names, or phrases associated with users, such as family, friends, hobbies, pets, interests, books, movies, or workspace.
- ✔ If real words are used, garble them using capitalization, numbers, or nonalphanumeric characters — for example, Go7Ril-la instead of gorilla.
- ✔ Use numbers or nonalphanumeric characters to replace letters — for example, ALT3RN8 L3TT3R1N9 (or "alternate lettering").
- ✔ Use at least three out of four types of characters: uppercase, lowercase, numerals, nonalphanumeric (symbols, punctuation).
- ✔ Create acronyms to use as passwords from sentences — for example, Fifty-five dollars will pay a parking ticket = 55DwPaPt.

Through a combination of Windows Server 2008–enforced password restrictions and company security policy rules, you can improve the security of your system through the use of strong passwords.

A Look into the Future: Service Packs

Microsoft regularly releases updates and fixes for its products, called *patch releases*. It did so for Windows NT 4.0 and Windows 2000/2003, and will do so for Windows Server 2008. Because patches from Microsoft correct all kinds of bugs, problems, and other issues, it's inevitable that some of these patches address security problems. Therefore, it's vital to keep informed about the release and content of such patches.

Microsoft releases patches in two forms:

- ✔ **Hotfixes:** A *hotfix* is a patch for a single problem. Hotfixes aren't fully tested or supported by Microsoft. A hotfix should be applied only if you're actually experiencing the problem it corrects because a hotfix can sometimes cause other problems.

✔ **Service packs:** A *service pack* is many hotfixes, tested and combined into a single Band-Aid. Service packs are cumulative, meaning that each new release of a service pack includes the previous service pack plus all hotfixes and other improvements since that time. You need to apply only the most current service pack and any required hotfixes.

Service packs are thoroughly tested and therefore safer for deployment than hotfixes. However, we recommend that you delay application of a new service pack until it's about two months old. This gives the rest of the Windows Server 2008 community the time to install and test the patch for you. It's always better to learn from the mistakes of others than to fall into the pit yourself.

Before you apply any patch to Windows Server 2008, you should read the documentation included with the patches. Then make the following preparations:

✔ Back up the system — or at least your data and the Registry.

✔ Reboot the system.

✔ Close all applications and stop any unnecessary services.

If you don't know which level of a service pack you applied, you can check by looking at the Help⇨About page from some native Windows Server 2008 applications (such as Windows Internet Explorer).

In the past, the Microsoft Web site has been secretive about the location of service packs and hotfixes, but recently they've been much more forthcoming. The best place to find service packs is through the Windows Update tool. (It's in the All Programs section of the Start menu and appears as a command in the Tools menu of Internet Explorer.) You can also check out the download section of the Windows Server 2008 Web area at www.microsoft.com/windowsserver2008/default.mspx.

Copping an Attitude

To maintain a secure networking environment, you must be a pessimist. View every user as a potential security leak. The key to this philosophy is to grant only the exact level of access that users or groups need to perform their work tasks and absolutely nothing more. To take this to its logical end, you need to deal with the Everyone group and user rights. This is called the *principle of least privilege,* and you should exercise it rigorously.

The Everyone group

The Everyone group is a default group created by the system that includes all defined users and all anonymous users. Although it isn't the catchall group it was in Windows NT 4.0, the expansive nature of the Everyone group can still cause security problems because Windows Server 2008 defaults to grant Read access to the Everyone group on new volumes and new shares. This means that you should watch closely where this group appears in your system. You may be granting blanket access where you really don't want any snuggling going on.

The Everyone group might seem hard to track down. It doesn't appear in the list of built-in groups as viewed through Active Directory Users and Computers, for example. However, it does appear in the list of groups when setting security on objects. The Everyone group can't be removed from the system, but it can be effectively managed with a little effort. See Chapter 11 for more information on the Everyone group.

The Authenticated Users group is a standard feature of Windows Server 2008. It contains all defined users but doesn't contain anonymous users. Generally, you want to use the Authenticated Users group instead of the Everyone group when you need to grant blanket access. The Everyone group must remain on your system for backward compatibility and system-level requirements (such as allowing your system to boot).

Don't set all permissions for the Everyone group to Deny because you'll prevent anyone from accessing resources. Instead, just remove the Everyone group from the list of users and groups granted access.

Each time you create a new drive or a share, remove the Everyone group and then add only those users or groups that need access to the resource. Just as you don't want everyone gaining access to your computer, you don't want "everyone" to be allowed access to areas where it isn't required.

User rights

User rights are system-level privileges that control what types of activities can be performed. The default setting for user rights is reasonably secure, but you can make a few improvements. The User Rights management interface is accessed using the Group Policy editor. (See the "Passwords and security" section earlier this chapter.) The User Rights Assignment is located under Security Settings⇨Local Policies⇨User Rights Assignments. Through this interface, user rights are granted or revoked. Here are some changes you should consider making:

✔ **Remove the Guests group from the Allow Log on Locally right:** This inhibits nonauthenticated users from gaining unauthorized access.

✔ **Remove the Everyone group from the Access This Computer from the Network right:** This inhibits nonauthenticated users from gaining access to hosted resources over the network.

✔ **Remove the Everyone group from the Bypass Traverse Checking right:** This inhibits nonauthenticated users from jumping into subdirectories when they don't have access to parent directories.

✔ **Remove the Backup Operators group from the Restore Files and Directories right:** This inhibits nonadministrators from restoring files from backup tapes. Because files can be restored to file allocation table (FAT) partitions where access control lists (ACLs) are lost, this is an important security modification.

After you make these changes, double-check that regular users still have the capabilities they need to perform their required tasks. You may need to grant a few users or groups added user rights. For example, if you want users to access resources on a server from across the network, you should add a group, such as Users, to the Access This Computer from the Network user right.

Plugging Common Mouse Holes

Windows Server 2008 has a handful of common security holes that you need to look for and fill. Fortunately, we crawled around on our hands and knees so you don't have to. Just follow our advice, and you'll be all snug and secure.

Unseen administrative shares

Each time Windows Server 2008 boots, a hidden administrative share is created for every drive. These shares are backup paths for the system just in case direct access to system files is somehow interrupted. In other words, it's a redundancy you don't need! The administrative shares are disabled by adding AutoShareServer to the following Registry key:

```
HKEY_LOCAL_MACHINE\System\CurrentControlSet\Services\LanMa
        nServer\Parameters
```

A value of 0 turns administrative shares off, and a value of 1 turns them back on. Consult Microsoft TechNet for info about disabling administrative shares.

A hidden share is just like any other share, except a dollar sign appears as the last character in its name. This tells the system not to display that share in standard browser share listings. You can use the System Manager to view hidden shares. You can create your own hidden share just by adding a dollar sign to the end of the share name.

The problem with administrative shares is that they offer unrestricted access to every file on a drive. If the username and password of an administrator account ever get compromised, anyone can map to any administrative share on the network. Therefore, it's a good idea to turn off the administrative shares just as a precaution.

Decoy accounts

Everyone knows the name of the most important user account on your system. Because Windows Server 2008 creates the Administrator account when Windows Server 2008 is installed, everyone already knows that you have such an account and exactly what its name is. Therefore, you must change it!

Don't just change the name. Go one better and create a new dummy account with absolutely no access or privileges and name it Administrator. This dummy account can serve as a decoy to lure hackers away from real access.

Creating decoys for other common accounts, such as the Guest account and IUSR account (the one created by IIS), is also a good idea.

Last logged on username

By default, when Ctrl+Alt+Delete is pressed, the logon dialog box displays the username of the last person to log on successfully. This is insecure. To prevent this dialog box from appearing, enable the option titled Interactive Logon: Do Not Display Last User Name Policy. This option appears in the Security Options area of the Group Policy. (See the "User rights" section for details on finding this area.)

When good floppies go bad

A nifty tool called NTFSDOS v3.02 (which you can find by searching your favorite search engine) enables anyone to read NTFS files after booting from a DOS floppy. (This utility was once part of Winternals, now owned by Microsoft, which has since been abandoned and all traces removed from the Microsoft site.) The NTFSDOS drivers make possible what Microsoft once claimed was impossible. Now, anyone with physical access to your system can reboot with a floppy and copy files right from NTFS-protected drives. If you value your data (and your job), remove floppy drives from critical systems.

Security Equals Vigilance

Maintaining a secure environment is an ongoing process. Keeping up with security fixes, system changes, user activity, and a security policy is often a time-consuming task. In your efforts to protect Windows Server 2008, take the time to review the following Web sites, newsgroups, and other resources:

- **Microsoft Security & Privacy Web page:** www.microsoft.com/security/default.mspx

- **Microsoft Security Partners:** partner.microsoft.com/global/program/competencies/securitysolutions

- **Windows & .NET Magazine:** www.windowsitpro.com

- **Somarsoft:** www.somarsoft.com

- **CERT Coordination Center:** www.cert.org

- **Xtras, Inc.:** www.xtras.net

- **Microsoft TechNet:** http://technet.microsoft.com/en-us/default.aspx

Here are some books you may find helpful, too. (Yes, most of these titles have *Windows 2000* in them. In most cases, the information applies to Windows Server 2003, and to some extent 2008. But keep an eye out for new editions focused on Windows Server 2008.)

- *Microsoft Windows 2000 Security Handbook,* by Jeff Schmidt (published by Que)

- *Configuring Windows 2000 Server Security,* by Thomas W. Shinder, Stace Cunningham, D. Lynn White, Syngress Media, and Garrick Olsen (published by Syngress Media)

- *Windows 2000 Security Little Black Book,* by Ian McLean (published by Coriolis Group)

- *Maximum Security,* by various authors (published by Sams.net)

- *Firewalls and Internet Security: Repelling the Wily Hacker,* by William R.Cheswick, Steven M. Bellovin, and Aviel D. Rubin (published by Addison-Wesley)

- *Building Internet Firewalls,* by D. Brent Chapman and Elizabeth D. Zwicky, and Simon Cooper (published by O'Reilly & Associates)

Part IV
Serve It Yourself

The 5th Wave   By Rich Tennant

"The divorce was amicable. She got the Jetta, the sailboat, and the recumbent bike. I got the servers and the domain name."

In this part . . .

Those computer-friendly folks who aren't afraid of PC
hardware, or who revel in their sense of adventure,
are likely to find the prospect of building their own
servers both fun and interesting. But even those of you
who might be more amenable to saving money than going
boldly where you've never gone before can get something
out of this part of the book, wherein we explore what's
involved in putting together your own server PC on which
to run Windows Server 2008.

The adventure begins with a review of what goes into a
low-end server PC and what makes it different from an
ordinary desktop. You explore the key components of a
server from its motherboard to its processor and memory
to its storage and network connections as you find out
what makes servers special and what kinds of hardware
they thrive best upon.

After that, you get the chance to walk down the two primary paths to server hardware. First, you take the Intel
path and look at that company's server processors and
the motherboards, memory, and other parts that building
an Intel-based server is likely to incorporate. Second, you
repeat this exercise with AMD components and check out
their processors, motherboards, and so forth that harmo-
nize with their use. Either way, you discover how to roll
your own server and put it to work at sometimes
considerable savings over store-bought models.

Chapter 15

How to Be a DIY Guru

*T*here is perhaps no greater satisfaction and no better sense of pride of ownership than in being a do-it-yourselfer. A properly motivated individual can get the job done and seeks out the appropriate resources when his capability or experience falls short of what's needed to get the job done. A tremendous amount of knowledge and personal gratification comes from the experience garnered from doing it yourself.

Instead of wasting too much time backpedaling mentally in search of probable causes or guilty parties, you formulate plausible solutions or workarounds and scramble to put your own plans into action. You are a budding PC guru, a veritable technology ninja. Okay, maybe nobody else in your office sees it quite that way, but an undeniable pleasure comes from doing things yourself. Just remember the old saying, "Everything is easy when you know how to do it!"

Of course, it often takes an advanced degree from The School of Hard Knocks to become a competent DIY guru. But we know of only one surefire way to acquire the necessary experience — just do it! The following chapters cover material for both Intel (Chapter 16) and AMD (Chapter 17) components and configurations to give you a fair assessment of the construction phase for both products.

Server Requirements Revisited

Windows Server 2008 challenges the notion that you always need more hardware to keep pace with new Microsoft software platforms, an assumption that otherwise rings true. Windows Server 2008 has some interesting tricks up its technical sleeves that actually make it possible to operate using *fewer* resources — not more — than even an existing Windows Server 2000 or Windows Server 2003 installation.

Although you must still meet the minimum processing requirements (memory, CPU, storage capacity, and so on as outlined in Chapter 1), Windows Server 2008 features an installation option called Server Core that lets you establish a minimal server operating environment that contains only enough programs to support specific service roles. These core roles, such as DNS or DHCP, export only a few functions to the connected world and therefore need very little local capability, such as desktop or multimedia applications. In addition to reduced management, improved maintenance, and a smaller attack surface, the Server Core option enables you to proffer a server tailored to deliver only a certain set of capabilities and components. Because it's remotely manageable, you can skip a full-time keyboard or heads-up display after you've completed the installation process.

With that in mind, consider the operational capacity of your server and its services. Will these include only DNS and DHCP, or will it service e-mail clients as well? When you begin processing higher volumes of data for a given service or set of services, you must increase hardware resources to accommodate predictable upswings in demand, which can change dynamically and geometrically on any given workday.

Processors: Cores, counts, and options

Keep score on your core count. Traditionally, only high-end server processors had any concept of multiple CPUs or cores working in tandem. Originally this meant having a multiple of two processors per motherboard all operating in concert, usually on portions of the same data or separate streams of data for a similar service. Recent designs have taken on an entirely new approach, using multiples of two cores per CPU die, which increases processing power within about the same footprint. Today, it's common to see desktop computers using multiple multicore CPUs to handle compute-intensive tasks (perhaps video editing, multimedia processing, and — yes it's true — high-end multiplayer 3-D games).

You can, therefore, combine multiple multicore processors into a single multiple-socket motherboard. Crazy concept, yes? But *multiplicity* is a guiding principle for many modern computer components and subsystems, especially on servers. These include dual integrated networking interfaces, dual on-board disk array controllers, dual redundant power supplies, and matched-pair memory modules in doubled-up memory slots . . . and the list keeps growing. There are even dual separate 12 V power rails in many top-of-the-line power supply units (PSUs). Nowadays even desktop processors receive dual-core processor treatment from the likes of AMD and Intel.

Furthermore, there is another dividing line: processor bits. Typically, the modern CPU in your garden-variety desktop or workstation computer is a 32-bit little endian processor, which means it reads 32-bit words backwards (so that "ABCD" would appear "DCBA", if you didn't apply what you know about order when retrieving register contents). These words are the chunks of basic information that your processor processes in a single processing cycle, and the real distinction here is that newer makes and models increasingly offer 64-bit capability. This doubles the word length, acquires an entirely different designation (x64), and can support both 32-bit and 64-bit software.

Windows Server 2008 supports 32-bit and 64-bit operation with Intel's Itanium 64 (IA-64) platform fully supported in the Datacenter Edition, which is optimized for high-workload scenarios (as opposed to file or media services). Incidentally, Windows Server 2008 will also be Microsoft's last 32-bit Windows Server platform.

Motherboards can support anywhere from one to 32 processors depending upon make and model, so choose the right ones to meet your business needs.

Memory: You can't have too much

Main system memory is the intermediate workbench upon which all large-scale data is placed and used. Several computer applications may find themselves underserved and competing for a limited amount of resources, which will be highlighted and underscored during intense durations of heavy utilization. Memory is one of a few components you really can't "outsource" — like external drive storage arrays — and you absolutely should not skimp on it, regardless of the cost of acquisition. There's simply no justification for running the bare minimum in anything bigger than a small office.

That said, you can never really have too much memory because utilization spikes should never exceed current capacity anyway. It's better to have more headroom for all that data jumping around than to give it a glass ceiling to bump its head on.

There are also features found in the server memory that may or may not be required, depending on the hardware and software applications involved. Soft errors commonly occur in system memory, particularly where large volumes of data are processed in rapid succession. All this hyperactivity can cause subtle changes in the representation of data, which can potentially corrupt mission-critical information in a very bad way. Error Correcting Code (ECC) memory is an expensive, fault-tolerant variant of normal memory that can detect and correct soft errors as they occur, or *on the fly*. Contrasted with the *unbuffered* memory that desktops typically use, ECC memory is more robust and reliable, which explains why it's typically used with servers and server applications. See the nearby sidebar for more about system memory.

Weigh these options carefully and consider carefully whether you should use ECC memory in your servers, especially if they handle large volumes of (or any) mission critical data. (Hint: Most servers use buffered, ECC memory to maximize accuracy and reliability.)

Disk space: Look out, it's a RAID!

Redundant Arrays of Inexpensive Disks (RAID) remain a bastion of server-oriented data storage. Considering that, can you select the correct answer to this question: RAID combines several disks in a variety of ways that better serve data and its users by making it: A) faster, B) fault tolerant, or C) faster and fault-tolerant?

If you answered "faster *and* fault-tolerant," you're correct. RAID physically combines several separate disks into a single logical unit, which is then logically perceived and utilized by end-users as if it were a single storage volume and not a consolidation of multiple drives. This feat requires at least specialized software, and — at the very best — specialized hardware *and* software working as a cohesive unit capable of handling RAID capabilities. We won't delve into the finely-detailed distinctions and advantage hierarchies of the many RAID variations here. Just know that software and hybridized integrated chipset solutions operate at nowhere near the performance and reliability level that dedicated add-in RAID controller cards can deliver. If you're running a business that's sustained by timely and accurate data, don't waste time on second-best options. Protect your data with the very best coverage money can buy.

That said, RAID configuration subtly influences performance as follows:

✔ Increased disk count improves chances of single-disk failure.

✔ Error Checking Code (ECC) offers reliability with performance penalties.

✔ Mirroring data speeds up read access but slows down write operations.

✔ Striping enhances performance at the cost of reliability.

✔ RAID system design is a constant compromise in performance and reliability.

Much ado about memory

There are three types of main system memory, and you might have to know which type is most appropriate for your motherboard and processor selection. All three items must match for compatibility purposes, so check with the motherboard for ECC support if that's what you need.

✔ **Unbuffered memory** uses a chipset controller that deals directly with main system memory. No buffers or registers withhold

data, and unbuffered memory is the choice for desktop and workstation computers.

✔ **Registered or buffered memory** uses additional chips to delay passing of data to retain integrity for data in transit.

✔ **ECC (Error Correcting Code) memory** provides greater data accuracy and runtime durability by preventing soft errors from occurring in the first place.

Some of the best RAID solutions support *hot-swappable drives* — that is, they allow you to extract a defective drive from the array and insert a new one — while the system remains online. Less capable systems require a full shutdown and offline processing of data, which is a personal choice you make according to your business needs. Hot-swappable hardware costs more and is more flexible and reliable. If continued operation and data availability are worth the added cost, look into such systems. If not, skip them.

Network access: Internal, add-in, and counts

Network interfaces are another area in server design that tends to incorporate the power of two. Dual network interfaces integrated onto the motherboard layout are becoming increasingly common, generally with Gigabit Ethernet (GbE) capability. Add-in cards also appear with two or four network RJ-45 ports, each capable of servicing thousands of connections.

Network connections occur across the Internet in the millions; locally, a domestic network may generate thousands of internal connections. Individual endpoints may generate several hundred connections by themselves. The point we're trying to illustrate here is that the number of connections increases easily and geometrically in proportion to available bandwidth, line speed, and interface thresholds. It's better to have more operational capacity to deal with any sudden increase in processing overhead than to be underserved by under-performing hardware that just manages to squeak by under normal load.

Levels of RAID

No discussion of RAID capability is complete without at least a cursory breakdown and fundamental examination of its inherent properties and native advantages. There are many variations on the RAID theme that can easily confuse those of you who come from modest computing backgrounds, with no real exposure to high-end storage concepts.

A number of standard schemes, called *levels,* have evolved into a series of nested and (in some cases) nonstandard variations that seek to divide and/or replicate data among multiple drives to achieve increased reliability, enhanced performance, or both. The three elemental concepts to RAID include the following:

✔ **Mirroring:** The simultaneous duplication of data to more than one disk

✔ **Striping:** The splitting of data across several participating disks

✔ **Error correction:** The native ability to detect and possibly correct data errors

RAID systems employ one or several of these elements in combination, depending on the intended results and final application. A system delivering video-on-demand services may opt for striping but not mirroring, whereas an SQL database server might be interested in both data replication and striped access for speed.

Here are the most commonly used RAID levels:

✔ **RAID 0:** Minimum of two disks; striped set without parity for improved performance and additional storage without fault tolerance.

✔ **RAID 1:** Minimum of two disks; mirrored set without parity for improved fault tolerance against disk errors and failure, with increased performance toward read operations but slower writes.

✔ **RAID 2:** Minimum of three disks; uses non-standard bit-level striping techniques with ECC hamming parity; cost and complexity make it impractical (see RAID 3/5 for replacements).

✔ **RAID 3 and RAID 4:** Minimum of three disks; striped set with dedicated parity for improved performance with fault tolerance using a dedicated parity disk.

✔ **RAID 5:** Minimum of three disks; striped set with dedicated, distributed parity, which creates an array with fault tolerance against single drive failure.

✔ **RAID 6:** Minimum of four disks; striped set with doubly-distributed parity for fault tolerance against double drive failure.

Also, various nested RAID levels combine many of these features within layers. For example, a RAID 0+1 system is a mirrored (RAID 1) array whose segments are striped (RAID 0) arrays, which has a benefits structure similar to RAID 5.

Multiple interfaces facilitate better failover servicing for high-availability servers and server applications. The presence of a second, third, or fourth network interface enables meaningful reliability, such as the following:

✔ A backup network connection in the event that a primary interface fails

✔ Load-balancing features that help maintain optimal operational efficiency under heavy loads

✔ Specially screened traffic that may impose separate rules on different interfaces.

These are only a few concepts currently in daily use in networking environments around the world.

Case and power supply

After the CPU and graphics card, case design and form-factor are other crucial components in the case/power supply equation. You may have some prior experience with desktop and workstation PSU (power supply unit) designs; they're relatively predictable and boxy and lack any truly distinguishing features (until you get into the designer PSUs that are typically designated for gaming or enthusiast applications). However, the same source of power varies quite differently from most desktop and workstation units.

Much can be said about server case design without specifically citing the innumerable examples that all qualify in this category. Server cases can be reissued desktop enclosures, or they can be special designs custom crafted for particular environments or purposes, like Sun's Blade servers or any 1U, 2U, or 4U rack-mount design. (Space in equipment racks is measured in terms of equipment units, which translate into just under 3 inches high and 19 inches wide, just right for standard rack dimensions.)

Some embedded server platforms have the dimensions of a pack of gum, whereas others are large enough to fill a 1950 Cadillac's trunk. In any case, a server case design must include at least three major elements:

✔ Adequate airflow (for ventilation)

✔ Easy accessibility (for servicing)

✔ Simple extensibility or scalability (for upgrading)

These properties change from one case design to the next, incorporated in about as many ways as there are case designers, but they remain constant fixtures for any well-crafted server case design.

Case design should reflect the motherboard and CPU choice because of the direct correlation between a suitable case and its internal components. A standard ATX form-factor motherboard won't fit in a Mini-ITX enclosure, no matter how cleverly you repurpose all the other hardware and software to run as a server platform. There are specific, fixed mount points for every form-factor, with only a few deviations in the arrangement of motherboard components. Be sure to shop for cases in the appropriate category. Mixing and matching (for example, pairing an ATX case with a BTX motherboard or vice versa) simply doesn't work.

Server power supply units, or PSUs, are manufactured in various dimensions and designs, some of which aren't used in the desktop/workstation scene. Rack-mount PSUs are built in various sizes to meet small-footprint requirements in those environments. As such, they lack the mount points for a typical PSU case and are thus incompatible with conventional computer cases. Likewise, a standard workstation PSU doesn't make a viable substitute for the much smaller 1U, 2U, or 4U designs (all incompatible amongst themselves). Pick your form-factors wisely and consistently!

Perhaps more important is an uninterruptible power supply, or UPS, which is more important for servers than for desktops or workstations. As the power source for any computer, a power supply provides the vital energy it needs to operate all its parts. Without power, nothing works at all. In power sag or spike condition, this means critical business applications may not be available, which may not be in the best interests of your business operation. A UPS includes a built-in battery that can take over from the power company when power gets wonky or goes missing. (Small units usually offer 15 minutes of reserve power, enough to shut down systems gracefully; large units extend that time frame and may be integrated with backup power delivery from diesel or gasoline generators.)

You should consider purchasing a UPS rated for a specific load (expressed in volts, amps, and watts). Such units are often guaranteed to protect a specific maximum dollar amount of equipment. Also make note of the rated runtime for a UPS, which varies according to the load — anywhere from 15 minutes to an hour or more. Quality UPS units also act as line or power conditioners and clean up surges or sags in power that may adversely affect connected hardware. All mission-critical hardware running business-critical applications should receive UPS coverage without question.

Use the following guidelines to calculate the power consumption needs for any given server you build or buy:

- Approximate 25 watts for every optical drive and around 30 watts for every disk drive.

- A CPU can range between 55–100 watts, with system memory drawing around 14 watts per 512MB memory bank. Then consider that multicore arrangements also increase this consumption from the PSU and that disk drives surge around twice their operational draw when starting up. That is part of the reason you can find disk controllers with staggered startup features.

- PCI add-in cards can draw around 5 watts on the low end, and some PCI-X and even PCI-E add-in cards vary in consumption trends. If you installed a graphics card, you might also check its wattage ratings — they vary between 20–60 watts on the low end and 60–100 on the high end.

Tally up this count and then aim for a PSU with at least two-thirds more headroom or greater.

What about graphics?

Indeed, what about them? Many kinds of server capacities, including Windows Server 2008's new Server Core installation method, can largely go without a proper graphics card, which is ideal anyway because who wants to spend extra money on a graphics card for a single display per server in a cluster or farm formation, especially where there isn't a proper desktop? In fact, it isn't entirely uncommon to forego the use of expensive video adapters on many kinds of server platforms because you don't have graphical user interfaces.

Ideally, you'd want to share at least one graphics card per several servers, even if it means having groups of servers all feeding off a single heads-up display. This can even be done remotely with server management tools and remote procedure calls, which require no graphics card on the remote end. However you want to work it is your business.

We recommend that you find either an integrated video solution for that first install or last-resort scenario and avoid buying anything fanciful or feature-rich for your server.

Important miscellany (cooler, fans, optical drive, monitor, keyboard, mouse)

We haven't yet mentioned some crucial components that are essential to good server design. For many of you, these items are no-brainers, but maybe we don't entirely appreciate the full beauty behind some of these necessities. Even though this bit is for the uninitiated crowd, you could benefit from reading the following paragraphs at any experience level.

An enormous amount of processing ability comes at an enormous cost: heat buildup. The thermal footprint of a given processor increases by surface area and increases geometrically with the inclusion of multiple cores and larger caches. Invisible heat pockets develop in these target areas where processing is most frequent and intense: CPU, memory, network interfaces, and drives. It is essential to cool these problem areas properly, which changes from one case design and component build to another.

Not only are CPUs passively and actively cooled through a series of heatsinks and ball-bearing fans, but memory is now produced with heat spreaders to better distribute heat over a wider surface that can be cooled easier than isolated chips on the silicon surface. Fan designs for server computing tend to be larger and produce greater airflow, which automatically implies higher noise levels. This is in stark contrast to quiet-running, more efficient desktop and workstation components designed not to distract their users.

Because there's no GUI — or not much use for one — on a server, there's no graphics adapter or even a monitor, nor will you find elaborate audio interfaces, joystick and gamepad connections, pluggable peripherals and other such elements, either. Likewise, peripheral input devices are much less necessary with all the centralized network-based management tools popularized and already present in Windows Server 2008. You should probably have a few spare keyboards and mice around in case you need to work on several servers simultaneously, but other than that you can get by nicely with a very small inventory of such items.

Building a Better Budget

Another powerful and potential cost-saving feature of Windows Server 2008 is its native operating system–level virtualization strategy. *Virtualization* utilizes a hypervisor at the operating system's kernel layer — at the very core of the system — that can partition a single installation into several independently working parts. Enabled this way, you can experience and share a single server hardware build among several server software instances.

There are two big caveats here:

- This functionality will not initially be part of the platform; it will actually arrive much later, around 180 days after the market release of Windows Server 2008.

- It will be available to only the 64-bit (x64) versions of Windows Server 2008, so be prepared to step up components (such as the CPU) and drivers (like the network interface) to capably handle x64 processing.

CPU speed is less critical on server platforms than for desktops and workstations, so don't be drawn to the idea that you need fast clock cycles to do intensive computing. You tend to get more done with two or more slower-clocked CPUs than an individual desktop processor operating at much higher frequencies, where applications are specifically designed to multithread and properly utilize several separate processors.

Also consider that, instead of drawing up specs for a bunch of different servers, you can virtualize several simultaneous instances of the operating system and effectively produce multiple servers from a single hardware build. The basic principle at work here is to emulate a larger number of smaller, less capable servers using a smaller number of larger, more capable ones. The budgeting trick is to figure out how to spend less money on those more powerful machines than you would on the combined total of a larger number of small, less capable ones. Fortunately, this is an eminently workable solution and explains why so many companies and organizations, large and small, are making increased use of virtualization in their day-to-day operations. If you're interested in finding out more about virtualization, check out *Virtualization For Dummies* by Bernard Golden (Wiley).

PC Component Shopping Tips

In the server shopping world, it sometimes pays to stay slightly behind the curve. By that, we mean you should purchase a few steps back from bleeding-edge or latest-and-greatest parts. Reserve most of your budget for all of the most crucial system components (CPU, memory, and storage) and tweak your leverage in those areas.

Perform a little capacity planning beforehand to get an idea of what scale of operation is needed. Will your network remain relatively static over a period of months or years, or do network loads and demand change dynamically on a daily basis? Will interruptions to power or service have costly adverse effects on business? Know in advance what sorts of challenges you face and the sorts of solutions you desire.

When shopping for server hardware, you might notice an entire cottage industry built around specialty applications and designs that incorporate proprietary protocols, hardware, or various combinations thereof. We recommend that long-term strategists stick with reputable industry leaders like Dell, Compaq, or HP instead of leaning on smaller companies that specialize in proprietary solutions. That's not to say they're entirely bad — but what would happen if an up-and-comer goes belly up two years before you find out that a critical piece of hardware needs their specialized treatment? It's also by no means a bad thing to use the parts list for a commercial turnkey server when picking components for a do-it-yourself server that you may seek to build on your own.

Also consider the footprint for any given server you build. Sure, opting for rack-mount server hardware may save you some space, but it'll cost you more for components specifically tailored for rack-mount use. In that regard, there's always a substantial trade-off worth considering. Also consider that quad-core CPUs may be more beneficial in enterprise computing environments than in moderate or small office environments with up to a few hundred users, so you can definitely hit a point of diminishing returns with CPU speed and numbers. However, there really isn't a foreseeable excess of memory because that's the veritable workbench upon which all significant CPU tasks and projects are completed. Maybe a trade-off in CPU clock cycles/numbers versus memory capacity is your answer.

Dual network interfaces are almost a standard in today's world, but that doesn't mean you'll always get double-duty pulling power on the wire. You need solid GbE capability all around to adequately sustain high levels of bandwidth utilization, where a large part of the business environment hosts rich presentations, distance learning courses, and meetings online from a number of remote sources. In short, there's little justification for building 100 Mbps Fast Ethernet networks when GbE is so readily available and affordable.

Assessing Windows Server 2008 Compatibility

Microsoft gives you two options to perform a quick compatibility check that applies equally to Windows Vista and Windows Server 2008 (because the two openly share a common code base). These two tests are a clean installation of Windows Server 2008 or an upgrade to Windows Vista from Windows XP (SP2) on the target hardware. If you encounter any errors, you'll know that your hardware is in some way unfit for operating both Windows Server 2008 and Windows Vista.

We would like to see a much stronger solution made generally available for the public to examine hardware fitness for suitability with Windows Server 2008, but there doesn't appear to be a straightforward answer at the time of this writing. Currently, you can use the Microsoft Application Compatibility Toolkit (ACT) to roughly gauge the compatibility for certain builds, even though it's actually designed for software. You may explore the ACT and other compatibility toolkits and information at the Microsoft Web site at `http://technet.microsoft.com/en-us/windowsvista/aa905066.aspx`.

ACT utilizes compatibility evaluators to collect application, device, and hardware information from your desktop without interruption to any users. It then returns this information for your analysis prior to deployment of Windows platforms. Such is the case with Windows Vista's Hardware Assessment inventory tool, which examines an organization's readiness to run Vista. Best of all, you can use one PC to investigate an entire network of Windows computers and create a comprehensive report specific to individual computers and their respective recommendations. ACT also has the Vista Upgrade Advisor, a downloadable Web application that helps XP users identify upgrade path options, but more importantly makes suggestions as to what (if any) hardware changes are necessary for certain editions of Windows Vista. You may obtain the Vista Upgrade Advisor at `www.microsoft.com/windows/products/windowsvista/buyorupgrade/upgradeadvisor.mspx`.

There's a huge difference between true workstation and true server hardware. What works on a workstation may work as a server, but what's designed specifically for server use won't likely work on the desktop. Using these Vista-specific tools only gives a false sense of readiness for Windows Server 2008 for those of you using specialty hardware; otherwise a workstation-turned-server will do just fine with these evaluators. Perhaps the one true, time-tested compatibility evaluator really is the actual installation medium itself. So far, it remains that way.

Chapter 16

Servers the Intel Way

. . . .

. . . .

*W*e maintain the politically correct position that there is no inherently superior hardware component or server build. In our view, there's no need for religious debate or fanatical proselytizing about the advantages or benefits of one platform or part over another — we generally view those who engage in such behavior as having an agenda to push. The plain fact of the matter is this: Whatever works for you in your situation with your conditions and considerations is the *best* or *perfect* solution — for you!

Lots of unsubstantiated claims, anecdotal advice, and assumed truths about server solutions are floating around. After you discount all the superimposed mysticism, empty marketing rhetoric, and bad suggestions, there's usually not much left behind. We tend to stick to what we know holds true, both universally and for ourselves.

AMD processors, whatever you may hear, are just as good for most server computing tasks as Intel processors. Reading about benchmarks only tells you about the performance ratings a given system achieves in some particular test-environment scenario for an isolated set of variables and individual enhancements. What those benchmarks don't tell you is how well-suited or well-constructed your hardware is as it applies to your environment and its unique conditions. Especially when it comes to entry-level or low-end servers, neither AMD nor Intel enjoys a lasting or definite advantage, perhaps apart from what readers may know best or be most comfortable with.

In this chapter, we offer you the build-up walkthrough on an Intel server, not that it's that much different from our AMD procedure in the next chapter. The process is pretty much identical, although the parts are quite different.

Get geared up and ready to roll out on your new server hardware hog, easy rider. We're about to take a Sunday cruise through the build phase.

Choosing a CPU and Motherboard First

Although most of us don't make car-buying decisions based on the engine and chassis, a well-trained computer hardware hound sniffs out these traits much like a sports enthusiast shops for a Sunday speedster. You know that only high-performance equipment is capable of handling the power curve and dynamically changing conditions on a busy raceway circuit. In the same vein, server computers aren't garden-variety grocery getters with a sports package added on; they're certifiable performance platforms around which all else is designed, built, and implemented.

But our analogy stops there. Unlike true sports cars, server computers usually don't match or beat the fastest production quality products on the market, and that's because they don't aim to win that kind of race. Rather, servers are the cornerstones of business computing; they're the stable-kept workhorses that plow the fields and sow the land. They aren't show horses meant for exhibition. In fact, deep down a lot of server hardware is unassuming, perhaps even ugly to people who see only the most visible machines used in business operations: workstation computers.

The short of it is, the CPU and motherboard are the most important elements in your server foundation. They should be scrutinized and carefully selected according to their business value and processing power.

Intel first stabilized low-voltage chip designs, which is one of the compelling reasons Apple Computer switched platforms from the Freescale PowerPC core. Intel has an enormous production capacity and prides itself on creating stable processing platforms for workstation and server computing tasks. We see low-voltage parts as one small stride in the direction of greener computing environments, which you should consider in the design phase of your server build. Excess electricity and air conditioning cost more.

Low-cost Intel-focused motherboards are comparably less impressive, feature-wise, than comparable AMD-based motherboards, but they typically aim at more business-like uses. Even Intel's own business-class motherboards follow a similar form and format: a typical green plank loaded with unassuming chips and controllers.

Newer Intel processor types typically range from the Celeron D and Pentium 4 to the Pentium D and Core 2 Duo platforms, each with its own unique advantages and disadvantages. There are also enterprise-worthy Xeon and Itanium processor platforms for servers, plus high-efficiency Pentium and Celeron M cores and bleeding-edge Pentium Extreme Edition (EE) processors to choose from. Each CPU has its own corresponding set of requirements for compatible memory, core chipsets, and device controllers that provide varying degrees of capability and integrated features. That's why you must shop around for a platform to suit your business needs.

Intel processor packages also come in a variety of formats, sizes, and pinouts. There are pinned and *pinless* CPUs in 90 or 65nm die sizes reaching nearly to 4 GHz speeds, with varying on-board cache sizes. Some are even finished in 64-bit trim with dual and quad-core processing capabilities. In general, we recommend simple single- or dual-processor server mother- boards with basic graphics, ports, and connectors, with an emphasis on disk drive support and memory capacity.

Selecting and Sizing Memory

Imagine having a workspace the size of your footrest. You can build and complete small projects in it just fine. You can even complete lots of little projects in that small footprint over a period of time — but that's entirely the point. Other projects are lined up, waiting to advance through the task queue, hoping to get processed in an orderly and timely manner. Their frequency may be regular or sporadic, occurring at any given time in various numbers, but every one must be completed in turn and on time.

Next, imagine you're a factory worker assembling lots of little pieces into slightly larger combinations that then contribute to another, much larger project that may or may not involve other completed workbench projects as well. You couldn't possibly assemble that massive monstrosity in your tiny workspace! This is precisely the analogy we use to convey the working rela- tionship of your RAM to your CPU.

A large workspace offers you more than capacity: It also delivers confidence from knowing you can handle tasks of any size along with a large series of smaller, easily completed tasks, all within the same workspace, often around the same time. Main system memory offers your CPU a temporary residence for information in active use, providing room for intermediate building blocks in larger applications and processes. Imagine your server is the factory floor of a massive assembly plant where you oversee the production line. You want all the factory floor space you can get, right?

Memory not only needs to be available in the right quantity, but it must be of the proper type as well. There are several types of memory, none of which are interchangeable, all suited for particular products and specific purposes. There is memory in buffered and unbuffered flavors that can correct errors on the fly, and it's packaged in various formats that include Rambus Dynamic

RAM (RDRAM), synchronous Dynamic RAM (DDR and DDR2 SDRAM), SODIMM (Small Outline Dual Inline Memory Module, the type used in most notebook PCs), and others we won't even mention. What we will say is that you must be keen to match your memory selection to your motherboard and processor.

In our case, the Intel server motherboard uses two socket 771 bases and requires buffered, error correcting (ECC) DDR2 memory that works at speeds up to 667 MHz. For that motherboard, we chose 4GB of Kingston Value RAM, pictured in Figure 16-1, and it's an excellent bang for the buck choice rated as PC2 5300 (runs at 667 MHz).

Figure 16-1:
Kingston
Value RAM
DDR2
memory
modules
with ECC.

Selecting and Sizing Disk Space

Remember, Windows Server 2008 minimum requirements demand at least 10GB — unless you're using 16GB or more of RAM — and recommend 40GB of free drive space for server installation alone. That doesn't include all the extraneous applications and data you'll invariably need, either.

Realistically, you should probably include at least two drives of at least 200GB in size for system use and anywhere from three to six drives from 320GB to 1TB each for data. Nowadays, pricing on SATA drives has dropped below 25 cents per gigabyte, so there's no excuse for equipping a server with too little storage space.

Accessing current needs and anticipating future growth

When you outfit your server with storage, be sure to make allowances for long-term growth and expansion to support maximum flexibility and scalability. Only you can know what kinds of data and how much must be stored and processed on your servers, so make a rough guesstimate to quantify all that data. Let's assume this, for example: Your server processes audio sound bites from a department of journalists. These files average around 5MB per clip, with a single user processing perhaps hundreds at any given time for any given project. If you impose a cap of 5GB (or approximately 1,000 audio clips) per user directory and you have 20 active users on that server, you require at least 100GB of storage space. Subject each key application to the same metrics. (E-mail, project documents and spreadsheets, and graphics files may all be sized using the same kind of approach.) Let's say you come up with a grand total of 800GB of storage space required.

Next, assume you must mirror all these presumably valuable files so that they may be recovered in the event of disk failure or data corruption. You now need 1.6TB of storage space just to house user data alone. See how easily that adds up? And this naïve example takes into account only a narrow and specific selection of data — these same users are also likely to have other written records, annotated quotes, reference materials, citations, and other research data stored alongside these sound bites. You also haven't considered any video footage that may be necessary for the same user group, or taken into account other roles this same storage server may take on throughout its lifetime.

Planning for RAID

You must also plan carefully for any RAID server storage technologies you wish to employ on your server. These schemes generally require at least two disks (or some multiple thereof) and in some cases additional third or odd-numbered drives for checksum storage. There is also just a bunch of disks (JBOD), which creates a single logical storage volume from multiple physical drives that you can use to expand server with different-sized drives.

For RAID use, make certain that all drives are identical (including make, model, size, and interface). There are several types of hard disk interfaces, none of them compatible, from SCSI to SATA. Some use serial connections, others parallel, but what matters is that you identify and acquire the appropriate interface type for your motherboard or add-in drive controller.

Lastly, when purchasing new drives, be aware of the distinction between our decimal definition system reference and actual disk capacity that a computer reads as a binary number. In human terms, one gigabyte equals 1,000 megabytes; however, a computer sees one gigabyte as 1,024 megabytes, which makes a considerable difference at very large capacities.

Making Network Connections

You must decide if your server can do its job properly using built-in network interfaces. (Server motherboards generally include them in pairs. Our SuperMicro X7DAE extended ATX motherboard includes two Intel-based gigabit Ethernet interfaces.) Or you may need to install and use additional Ethernet interface cards instead. This would generally occur if you expect your server to handle huge volumes of network traffic, where you could benefit from a TCP/IP Offload Engine, or TOE, on the interface card.

For our test purposes — and for most home office/small office situations — the built-in network interfaces are perfectly okay. Given that TOE cards usually cost at least $100 each (and as much as $250) this represents a considerable savings — but only if you don't need the extra networking horsepower. When you do need it, such cards tend to pay for themselves pretty quickly.

Picking the Right Case and Power Supply

Cases and power supplies are generally closely associated, for multiple reasons. First, when you purchase a case, it may include a built-in power supply. Second, cases tend to dictate the size, shape, and set of features (or their orientation) that can or should be present on the power supply. To many, this seems only natural because these two parts are analogous to the skeleton and the heart, crucial for sustaining form and function for other internal organs — err, components.

Case designs vary so wildly you wouldn't recognize many modern examples as even having sufficient operating room for a proper server installation. Units can be as small as or smaller than your cell phone to larger than your refrigerator. For our build, we used a so-called bench case: It's really an open platform where the motherboard simply rests on the top shelf and the wire and cable cards emerge at the back. There is room underneath the top shelf and on a bottom shelf for the power supply, optical drive, and as many disk drives as you care to stack within its confines. We also chose a quiet, capable, and efficient Seasonic S12 650-watt power supply (which retails for about $165).

For ordinary business use, most SOHO buyers purchase either mid-tower or full-size tower cases. We've had good luck with the Antec Atlas and Titan models (which include their own power supplies in sizes from 550 to 650 watts), and the SuperMicro 743T case, which has the advantage of coming from the same company that made the motherboard, so you can be sure of a good fit (it also includes a built-in 650-watt power supply). All of these cases retail for between $100 and $200, which is about typical for a good-quality server case with a built-in power supply.

Testing as you go

Make sure that you're well-grounded when handling any computer components. Discharge any static electricity that may linger on your person by grasping some unpainted metal surface such as your toolbox, a nearby computer case, or an enclosure part. Basically, physical contact with anything grounded will draw static away from you and discharge safely.

Negligible though it may seem, sufficient static discharge can easily incapacitate hardware on first contact. We've yet to seriously damage any new hardware ourselves, but we can attest to occasions where all it took was a little discharge to do a lot of damage to well-worn or in-use parts — often resulting in their premature and untimely passing.

Grounding yourself regularly lets you test hardware for fit and function as you proceed through the build process. One common issue that causes initial lift-off failure is an improperly plugged or incompletely seated component. (Memory modules are particularly prone to this kind of fault.) Here are some areas to pay particular attention to:

- Be mindful of every beginning and end of every cable.

- Be certain that each component connector is correctly oriented and snug; otherwise, a slight tug — perhaps as you reach across to fix something — can dislodge and disrupt your work.

- Make sure that socketed components — memory, CPUs, and motherboards — are snugly seated in their sockets and avoid too much force when checking them. (A surprisingly small amount of brute force, improperly applied, can also spell doom for fragile computer components, especially CPUs with hundreds of tiny and delicate metal pins.)

Building an Intel-Based Server from A to Z

Our examples in this section can be extrapolated to other server builds that incorporate different hardware components just on basic principles. The techniques and procedures you may encounter when installing foreign or nonstandard hardware will vary by the product and its peculiarities, but otherwise, these concepts remain largely the same.

We selected components you might expect to encounter in a common Windows Server 2008 networking environment. Our walkthrough is tailored to be generic enough to follow even if you're using entirely different components, such as SCSI rather than SATA drive interfaces or DDR instead of DDR2 memory.

Insert the PSU

On to the power supply, or PSU, veritable heart to the host body that is a server case. If the CPU is the brain and RAM acts as memory workspace for that brain, the PSU is the heart that drives energy into an otherwise inanimate server. Without its correct and proper fit, there can be no function. Critical issues arise when even a minor detail is amiss on the PSU — an unplugged connection or an under-powered voltage rail, for example. Take special care and pay close attention to connectors on your PSU and where they must plug in.

The following example assumes that your PSU is new and therefore likely to be free of defects or malfunctions. However, this might be yet another unwarranted assumption — you could conceivably get through an entire server build and never realize the PSU is kaput. We recommend putting the PSU through some formal or informal preliminary testing to make sure it delivers sufficient power. You can purchase basic CPU testers from companies like Antec or StarTech for between $10 and $15; we urge you to do so and put them to work when you start building.

Also consider that your motherboard and CPU selections will impose different demands and requirements on a PSU, so choose your PSU wisely. Server-specific motherboards often incorporate specialized plugs or power interfaces for multiple CPUs, enhanced graphics cards, and other advanced features. Explore these options thoroughly before making any buying decisions, so that all three of these critical elements match up.

Follow these steps to insert the PSU:

1. **Locate the mount point for the PSU.**

   Mount points on the case, usually indicated by threaded screw holes, should align perfectly with those bored into the PSU case. Correctly orient these holes to properly position the PSU before inserting any mounting hardware.

2. **Orient the PSU properly.**

   Power supplies come in a variety of shapes and sizes, so you should check for fit and identify any clearance or access issues, including cable reach. If your PSU includes an auxiliary fan on its bottom surface, with the exhaust out the back, as shown in Figure 16-2, be sure there is adequate clearance for the fan to move airflow properly (in the bottom, out the back).

3. **Securely fasten the PSU in place.**

   It doesn't matter what pattern you follow when screwing in the mounting hardware; we prefer making an X pattern, traveling diagonally to mount and tighten screws. Never tighten them enough to deform the metal enclosure or server case material.

Figure 16-2: A power supply unit with a large auxiliary fan resting on its top surface, exhaust outlet showing at the front, intake fan at the top.

4. Plug the primary 20- or 24-pin power plug into its socket.

This is by far the largest and most recognizable plug on the PSU harness. You should have the proper PSU selection for your motherboard.

5. Optionally, bind each of the cables.

This enables better airflow and encourages a clean workspace for other administrators, integrators, or technicians who may do follow-up work inside the case.

Seat the CPU and cooler

Easily, the most expensive single-item purchase is the CPU; that goes double for dual-CPU rigs like the one we chose for our build. The CPU also happens to be the least accessible component in a completed system build because to get at it you must open the case and remove the cooler (which sometimes poses its own unique challenges) to expose it to view. We've encountered some coolers that required removing some or all of the nearby hardware, including magnetic and optical drives, socketed memory, and add-in cards. You perform all that work, just to free up sufficient work space around the cooler so that it can be dismantled, removed, and the CPU made accessible for service.

Ideally, you should install the CPU and cooler onto the motherboard before affixing the motherboard inside your server case. It's much easier to ensure proper placement and adequate workspace for tools when your movement isn't restricted by interior elements of the server case and other neighboring components. Usually the CPU has a small footprint, so pulling or placing one into its socket is a non-issue; however, coolers aren't nearly as predictable as

CPUs. Some designs are either so large or the case so cramped that working in a confined space is virtually impossible, so please heed our advice — it's based on painful experience.

Depending on the make and model of your CPU, there may be delicate pins on its underside or integrated into the CPU socket itself. This latter design is a more modern concept that presumably saves on replacement costs because a single server CPU at market price can cover the cost of several server-worthy motherboards. In short, if you bend a pin out of place on a CPU socket, you must replace a less expensive motherboard; force the CPU into place and bend some pins, and you must pay for a more expensive processor, if you can't gently persuade those pins back into alignment.

Seating the CPU

To seat the CPU, follow these steps:

1. **Locate the CPU socket.**

   Specialty designs often feature multiple sockets for multiple processors, so you may in fact identify several sockets. Primary and secondary sockets on the motherboard may be protected by a graphite-colored plastic shield, which should be removed for installation, that protects the CPU socket from incidental damage.

   Take a look at Figure 16-3, where we show two Intel Xeon 5000-series processor sockets on an Intel server motherboard.

2. **Check the CPU socket.**

   Modern CPU sockets are frail enough that they can break on the slightest provocation, and the only surefire fix is motherboard replacement. Don't be clumsy or overly forceful when examining the socket for defects, or when seating the CPU in a later step. CPU handling calls for a careful, delicate touch.

3. **Unlatch and uncover the CPU socket.**

   The socket will be guarded by a pressure plate and latching swing arm. You should be gentle when working with the latch. It should never bind or demand significant exertion to operate. Closely observe Figure 16-4, where we unlatch the arm that holds a tension plate over the CPU to keep a snug fit.

4. **Check for proper CPU orientation.**

   Also check that the CPU is free from defect in workmanship or finish quality to avoid complications later during the build.

5. **Socket the CPU.**

   Work the CPU gently into its socket; it should fit into place without much pressure or persuasion. Don't force it to fit; any resistance should provoke immediate action, which means repositioning the CPU into its correct orientation.

Figure 16-3:
Intel Xeon
CPU
sockets on a
SuperMicro
X7DAE
mother-
board.

Figure 16-4:
Unlatching
the
processor
socket arm
on a
mother-
board.

6. **Repeat Steps 1 through 5 as necessary for multiple CPUs.**

7. **Identify motherboard power plug points for the CPU.**

The appearance and arrangement will change from one motherboard to the next. In most garden-variety single-processor boards, you'll have a 4-pin auxiliary cable plug situated near the CPU. This is a main (and necessary) source of power for the CPU. Multiple-core motherboards may have several such plugs; sometimes they require a special 8-pin plug instead, as with our SuperMicro X7DAE motherboard. See Figure 16-5.

Figure 16-5: CPU power socket, of which there may be one or more, depending on the design.

Seating the cooler

Follow these steps to seat the cooler into its socket:

1. **Locate the cooler mount points.**

   Identify placement for the cooler, noting any retention brackets, retainer clips, or pilot holes that correspond to the cooler hardware assembly. Also observe placement of the power connector for later use.

2. **Dry-fit the cooler once.**

   A *dry-fit* approach lets you check any clearance issues you may have with access or placement of the CPU and/or its cooler. Situate your CPU into the socket, but do not mount it in place yet.

   You should dry-fit the CPU cooler into its socket at least once to learn the proper fit and orientation.

3. **Check its orientation and airflow path. You may have to opt for a less favorable or reversed orientation to achieve optimal airflow.**

4. **Inspect the underside of the CPU cooler. Check for a patch of grayish, silvery, or whitish thermal paste underneath the copper or aluminum base. Where there isn't already one, you'll have to apply thermal paste, which we recommend be spread directly atop the processor. Follow these steps:**

   a. *Remove the CPU from the socket and set it on top of a folded-up paper or cloth towel or a foam pad.*

   b. *Apply a thorough, consistent layer of thermal paste. Use a credit card or business card to smooth the paste into a thin layer that covers the entire top of the CPU package.*

   c. *Reseat the CPU into its socket.*

If you need to apply thermal paste, use either a manufacturer-supplied single-shot portion or some other source for thermal paste. It often comes in plastic syringes from which you can extrude just a dab and then use a business or credit card to spread a thin, smooth layer across the surface. We're fond of the Arctic Silver brand, a well-known and widely used thermal paste.

5. **Securely fasten the cooler mount plate to the motherboard.**

   Retention clips or a retainer bracket may interface with the motherboard and cooler; assemble these in their correct orientations. There's almost always some clamp or screw that keeps the cooler securely in place.

6. **Connect the cooler power cable (see Figure 16-6).**

   Never omit this step or intend to connect it later — this isn't a minor detail that you can leave unfinished or overlooked. Otherwise your CPU will get overcooked!

   Our setup, pictured in Figure 16-6, shows that we have one power plug situated catty-corner just outside our main processor socket on the Intel motherboard.

Figure 16-6:
CPU cooler fan power plug located on an Intel server motherboard.

Seat the RAM modules

Memory modules all have their own distinctive and predictable footprints, and their actual formats can change in subtle ways that require a keen eye. For example, discriminating DDR from DDR2 memory takes a bit of basic product knowledge; differentiating ECC or registered from unbuffered memory takes a keen eye and *strong* product knowledge. We don't expect you to have that ability. Leave that for the propeller heads and, at the very least, the retail associates and sellers of such hardware.

You should already know what kind of RAM works with your CPU and motherboard. There are some dangerous (read: fiery) incompatibilities that can arise from mixing memory rated for different interfaces at different voltages. And despite the fact that memory designers and circuit engineers try to make it difficult to plug the wrong component into the wrong socket, some ingenious installer invariably finds a way to do so with lethal effect (for the RAM, not the installer). Pay attention to what you're doing.

To seat RAM modules, follow these steps:

1. **Locate the RAM banks.**

   Long, parallel rows of memory sockets stretch alongside or nearby the CPU socket.

2. **Identify socket keying for orientation.**

   Memory and memory banks are keyed for a specific fit and orientation. Carefully observe which way the memory fits. Selecting the proper memory type from the very beginning ensures no complications here. Match up the short segment of pin on the module with the short segment in the memory socket, and you're ready to go.

   In Figure 16-7, we install DDR memory into the Intel motherboard for our two-way Intel Pentium processors. Our memory banks on this motherboard aren't color coded in a manner that visually indicates matched banks, but some motherboards employ color-coding for your convenience.

Figure 16-7:
Banks of memory in our Intel server motherboard.

3. **Unlatch the toothed latches on each socket.**

   Each latch tooth corresponds to a groove cut into the sides of the memory module. These teeth lock into place to hold memory securely inside the socket.

4. **Gently press the memory modules into place.**

   Memory should slide into the socket with little resistance. You should never force-fit memory modules because they can break under pressure. If you encounter any resistance, rotate and retry.

5. **Repeat Steps 3 and 4 for multiple modules or multiple processor memory banks.**

   In a multiple-socket motherboard, you'll have to make special considerations as to how much memory you allocate per processor.

Install the hard disk drives

Disk drive formats haven't really changed much over the years. Disk platters have gotten increasingly dense while the overall width has remained constant. The interfaces have gone through many fundamentally different changes that both enhance and better the lifespan of our most precious storage long-term volumes, but overall the procedure for installing them remains unchanged.

Whether your hardware includes SCSI, Parallel ATA (PATA), or Serial ATA (SATA) cabling, it's all the same: You install a cable between the drive and the controller. It's really as simple as that. For the purposes of this demonstration, we use SATA because our motherboard (pictured in Figure 16-8) includes a SATA controller with connectors. But you can mentally substitute whatever interface you're currently working with and follow along with these steps:

Figure 16-8: SATA drive controller connection.

1. **Locate the nearest appropriate disk drive bay.**

   Disk drive bays are generally cages of stacked 3.5-inch drive slots that appear much smaller across than do 5.25-inch accessory drive bays. These may be self-contained cages capable of being extracted entirely from within the case, or they may use fixed or removable drive mounts or rails.

2. **Identify the nearest drive connector.**

Sometimes the best slot isn't in the most convenient or accessible location. Avoid stretching the drive cable. Reposition the drive as necessary to achieve an optimal distance from its controller connection.

3. **Insert the disk and fasten securely.**

   Slide the drive into its slot. It should take no persuasion. Be sure to use the screws that came with the drive because they're properly threaded, and never over-tighten any fastening hardware. An inappropriate thread count can strip the drive threads and lock the fastener in place or damage overly-tightened mount points.

4. **Cable the drive to the motherboard.**

   Always utilize the first drive slot designation — usually indicated as IDE0/IDE1, SATA0/SATA1, or SCSI0/SCSI1. (Check your motherboard reference manual.) Link all additional drives in sequence on the controller or motherboard, whichever is the intended target.

5. **Connect the drive to the power supply.**

   The standard power connector is a 4-pin Molex type that features beveled edges on only two corners so that you can never plug it in wrong. For SATA drives, a keyed power connector may be used instead. (It's also oriented to resist improper hook-ups.)

Install the optical disk

As with magnetic storage, little has changed so significantly that you'll find this new encounter unfamiliar. An optical disk, for all its apparent qualities, appears either as a tray or slot-loading device with an activity light (or several) and at least one button (eject) and possibly some decals (indicating drive capability and type).

Whatever underlies that façade can change randomly, for all we know — that's one yard we hardware hounds tend not to dig holes in. As long as we keep connecting their cables in a predictable, adaptable fashion, we don't much care either. Here are the steps for installing an optical disk:

1. **Locate the nearest appropriate optical drive bay.**

   In a multiple-slot or tower configuration, we recommend placement furthest away from nearby heat-producing parts. This can even mean staggering drive placement between slots (leaving an opening between each drive) so that heat has less chance to pocket and build up.

2. **Check for proper fit.**

   Whether going in from the front or pushing through the back, perform a dry-run once through so you can identify any potential hang-ups. This may include removing a faceplate or shield, clearing an obstruction, or relocating the drive. Also make sure all your drive mount holes line up properly.

3. Insert the drive into the bay.

It should slide easily and freely into place with little persuasion.

4. Fasten the drive securely in place.

Again, don't over-tighten the screws so that they deform any softer parts.

5. Cable the drive to the motherboard.

Identify the proper slot for your drive, typically *not* the first channel on the first drive controller bank of the motherboard. Drive connections on the motherboard are numbered sequentially from first to last, and we recommend you not interleave hard drives and optical drives.

When using an on-board RAID controller, use only those drives specifically involved in the RAID array on that controller. Where there are two separate controllers, use one RAID-specific setup for optical drives and the other for hard disks, no matter how many plugs may remain unused on the hard disk array.

6. Cable the power supply to the drive.

After establishing all other steps, connect power to the drive. Ensure proper fit.

Set up the hardware

After you have all the hardware seated, cabled, and primed for action, you can begin your crucial first boot-up. Assuming that you plugged in every cable and included every component, the system should at least show you the initial Power-On Self-Test (POST) warm-up phase — it's like calisthenics for computers.

If nothing happens, you should check your power source. Or if you observe a little activity and then nothing, that indicates some sort of component incompatibility or a faulty power source (among other possible causes). If you hear any beep codes, be aware that they provide audible indicators for various sorts of operational issues — memory isn't seated correctly, the CPU is missing or can't be detected, or a USB drive is plugged in and just isn't wanted there.

Barring any such complications, you'll be presented with a startup screen. This may flash instantly before your eyes, but hopefully you get a chance to see whatever key sequence is necessary to trigger the BIOS setup screen. From here, you must make all the necessary server-specific changes to settings that require them — such as any ECC memory settings, CPU identifiers, and the initial boot order. This is important for the next step, where you install Windows Server 2008.

Install the OS

We cover more detailed instructions governing the installation process, with a qualifying explanation of the entire procedure, in Chapter 5. There are a number of ways you can install Windows Server 2008 (or upgrade from an eligible software platform), so we can't reasonably cover them all. Here's a synopsis for the straightforward process, as described more thoroughly in Chapter 5.

If your server will include an earlier version of Windows kept alongside Windows Server 2008, install it first. This permits the Windows Server 2008 boot manager (which uses boot configuration data, or BCD, stores) to identify and utilize that installation.

After you complete the Initial Configuration Tasks setup (Chapter 6), spend some time getting to know the Server Manager interface and all its functionality. You'll be spending a considerable amount of your administrative time on the server managing, monitoring, and modifying attributes through this interface. Don't be afraid of trying new installation methods, either. You'll eventually want to perform a remote network install, an unintended install, or perhaps both. Try everything at least once!

Ready to Rock-and-Roll?

We've walked you through the process of installing the server hardware and software necessary for your first build, which we assume went smoothly. The next step is to purpose this server for your network and all its users by including features and functions that are vital to sustaining your business processes.

Now that you have your server hardware assembled and operating under the control of Windows Server 2008, you're ready to start adding users, network roles, and server responsibilities. Prepare to begin operation as *a newly-fledged* server administrator!

Chapter 17

Servers the AMD Way

· ·

In This Chapter

▶ AMD server hardware installation step by step

▶ AMD CPU and motherboard selection

▶ Sizing up your memory requirements

▶ Sizing up your disk utilization trends

▶ Case and power supply considerations

▶ Installing server hardware components

▶ Server software installation time

· ·

A s explored in more detail in the preceding chapter, we maintain an objective view regarding the relative advantages and benefits of Intel and AMD processors, including server models. At some times, Intel may enjoy an apparent advantage, at others, the balance tips toward AMD. But either way, when you've made your choice, you must live and work with the resulting system, and that's when the real effort gets underway.

To us, what's most important is an easy trio to remember. We call them the three Cs:

- ✔ **Comfort** refers to what you know and are familiar with and rests on the tendency, that all humans share, to repeat successful or positive experiences. Those who know Intel best usually stick with what they know, and those who know AMD best do likewise.

- ✔ **Cost** lets budget limits or thriftiness come to the fore. We know plenty of system builders and buyers who have opted to go with what they perceive to deliver the best bang for the buck at the time of purchase, even if that means leaving comfort behind to try something new.

- ✔ **Convenience** addresses the tendency to build or buy what's most readily available and, therefore, easiest to come by.

As you make your own server selections, whether you're choosing components to build a server yourself or evaluating turnkey server systems, you'll find all three Cs coming into play at one time or another. Comfort usually governs the big decisions (motherboard and CPU); cost usually governs how much you're willing to spend on parts both big and small; and convenience invariably rules when you put everything together and discover you need another fan, some cables, or other miscellany.

In this chapter, we offer you a build-up walkthrough on an AMD server, not that it's terribly different from the Intel procedure discussed in the previous chapter. We discuss component selections and take you through the assembly process.

Choosing the CPU and Motherboard First

As in the previous chapter, we maintain that choosing a motherboard and one or more CPUs to populate it are the key elements in any system build. After you've chosen those items, everything else follows naturally and nicely from that decision.

What we chose for our example build

For our AMD build, we selected a dual-processor motherboard with two mid-range processors from the company's second-generation dual-core Opteron family in its value-priced 2000 series — namely, two Opteron 2114 CPUs and a Gigabyte GA-3CCWV-RH motherboard to match.

Interestingly, the Gigabyte motherboard costs between $280 and $320 as we write this chapter — about $100–120 less than the SuperMicro X7DAE featured in the preceding chapter. The 2114 is a 2.2 GHz dual-core processor that retails in the neighborhood of $215, while the Intel 5110 we chose in the preceding chapter retails for about $220 and runs at 1.6 GHz. Thus, our AMD system clocks at about 30 percent faster and costs $110–130 less. Given Intel's commanding market position, especially in the server market, this is a very typical situation, where AMD comes out slightly ahead in price performance, and Intel comes out ahead in options and availability.

Exploring your options

An AMD CPU's real advantage — insofar as we're concerned here — is usually its price point. Apart from that difference, however, we find no significant advantage or disadvantage that should persuade you for or against AMD or Intel. We don't really care, as both are excellent choices. You just can't lose going either way.

AMD processor packaging appears in a few variations, depending which segment of the market you shop within — recent, near recent, or not-so-recent past. Today's server-worthy AMD processors range from 754 to 939 and 940 pinned sockets to a more recent unpinned socket AM2 design, all of which require different processors, memory types, and — in some cases — an almost entirely different component selection. As we write this chapter, the market includes K8 processor cores, which include everything from rock-solid server Opterons to cutting-edge desktop Athlon 64 FX processors and the low-cost Sempron and mobile Turion processors. Most of these come in 32-bit and 64-bit models, where some include dual-core processing, with quad-core models coming to market for the first time ever from AMD.

AMD processor dies also range from the relatively standard 90nm unit size to a smaller, more efficient 65nm unit size. Herein lies a crucial distinction: A smaller unit size is geared toward higher energy efficiency, which lessens the financial burden and overall power consumption impact on your business or organization. This can be a significant advantage for large-scale operations looking to reduce their operational energy footprint to conserve long-term costs owing to cumulative excessive heat build-up and increased cooling costs.

The logic that drives high efficiency circuitry works like this: It's okay to pay more for a lower-powered part upfront because you'll save more money in the long run on energy costs. Thus, for example, the Opteron 2114 we chose for our build also comes in a high efficiency model, the Opteron 2114 HE. The standard part is rated at 95 watts while the HE part is rated at 68 watts, indicating that, cycle for cycle, the HE part consumes about 30 percent less energy than the standard model. The price differential is a mere $20 or so and argues strongly in favor of buying a more power-efficient part not only because it saves energy but also because lower power consumption means cooler operation and a longer device lifetime.

Perhaps the most significant point to bring up is that when buying a server-oriented (as opposed to workstation-oriented) processor and motherboard combination, you'll generally have to step up all other parts to match, which costs more. If you want strong results on a smaller scale or at a lower price point, opt instead for high-end desktop components that also work as server hardware.

Selecting and Sizing Memory

Our Gigabyte GA-3CCWV-RH motherboard houses two Opteron 2000-class server processors, which require DDR2 ECC memory. That's the kind we must use. Because we're installing the 32-bit version of Windows Server 2008, we opt for two 2GB modules, the maximum memory that the 32-bit version supports.

Selecting and Sizing Disk Space

We repeat the same choice we made for the Intel build in Chapter 16 — namely, two 320GB Seagate 7200.10 perpendicular magnetic recording (PMR) hard disks. These offer an unbeatable combination of speed, quiet, and affordability (at about $80 each as we write this chapter). A production server build would probably add three or four more such drives, if not bigger ones. (The 7200.10 models also come in 400, 500, and 760GB sizes at prices in the $100, $120, and $210 range, which makes the 500GB models best buys in this product family.)

Making the Network Connections

As with the Intel motherboard in Chapter 16, the GA-3CCWV-RH motherboard includes two GbE RJ-45 ports in its rear port block. For most small office/home office environments, this is more than sufficient network connectivity. Only if you're serving a large number of users or hosting extremely network-intensive applications or services on your server will you need more networking horsepower. In that case, you'll want to investigate PCI or PCIe-x1 network interface cards with TCP/IP Offload Engine (TOE) capabilities. These generally retail for $100 to about $250 each for single- or dual-port GbE models. If you need them, you'll generally not be bothered much by the extra expense they entail.

Picking the Right Case and Power Supply

Cases and power supplies are closely linked for at least two reasons:

- ✔ When you purchase a case, it often includes a power supply.
- ✔ It's important to make sure that the case accommodates the type of power supply you wish to use. This won't affect your choices much if you build in a standard mid-tower or full-sized tower case, as we recommend — in that case, any modern ATX 12 V power supply rated at 550 watts or higher should do the trick. But if you're building in any kind of compact or rack-mount enclosure, matching PSU and case becomes a veritable mandate.

Please consult the section on case and power supply in Chapter 16 to get our recommendations for some good server cases in the $100–200 price range. Other good case vendors include Cooler Master, Thermaltake, and Athena Power.

Construction from A to Z

Our illustrated examples in this section can be applied to other server builds utilizing different hardware just on basic principle. The techniques and procedures you may have to call upon when installing foreign-made or nonstandard hardware will vary according to each product and its peculiarities, but the underlying concepts and sequence covered here remain largely the same.

We selected components you might expect to see in a common Windows Server 2008 networking environment. Our walkthrough is tailored to be generic enough to follow along even if you're using entirely different components, like SCSI instead of SATA drive interfaces or DDR instead of DDR2 memory.

Insert the PSU

On to the power supply. You'll begin by installing it inside your case, and then routing power leads to the motherboard connections. Before you do anything else with it, however, you may want to pick up a cheap PSU tester (models usually cost from $10 to $15 and plug into the same 20- or 24-pin connector that serves as the motherboard's primary source of juice) and check to make sure your PSU works properly. A green light at this stage simply means you can expend the time and effort necessary to mount the PSU inside the case and start stringing power leads.

The steps that follow assume that the PSU is new and therefore relatively free from defect or malfunction. However, this is yet another unsafe assumption — you could conceivably get through an entire server build and never realize that the PSU is defunct. We recommend putting the PSU through some formal or informal preliminary testing to make sure it at least delivers sufficient power.

If you buy a power supply rated at 550 watts or higher, it'll generally include the kinds of power leads you need for a server motherboard. (Generally, this requires a 20- or 24-pin ATX lead plus either a 4-pin or 8-pin motherboard lead, if not both varieties.) All of the 550-watt power supplies we looked at while researching this book (which included models from Gigabyte, Corsair, Zalman, NorthQ, Sea Sonic, and Antec) included at least two 4-pin leads, two 6-pin leads (used for SLI and CrossFire dual graphics card setups), and at least one 8-pin lead for auxiliary motherboard power. We reused the same power supply for our AMD system that we used for our Intel system — namely, a Sea Sonic S12 650-watt power supply (retails for about $145). Here are step-by-step installation guidelines:

1. **Locate the mount points on the PSU and case.**

   Mount points on the server case, usually indicated by threaded screw holes, should align perfectly with those bored into the PSU case. Orient these holes to properly position the PSU before inserting or tightening any fasteners. You may also want to look at sound insulation kits for PSUs available from vendors like Antec. These cost less than $15 and include silicon dampening materials on the mounting screws, as well as a form-fitting silicon gasket that slips between the PSU and your case. These serve to eliminate metal-to-metal contact and eliminate noise that vibration might otherwise induce.

2. **Orient the PSU properly.**

   Power supplies come in any number of treatments and a variety of shapes and sizes, so you should check for fit and identify any clearance issues including cable reach. If your PSU includes an auxiliary intake fan underneath, as most of them do, be sure there is adequate clearance for the fan to draw air into the PSU inside the case and for it to exhaust warm air out the back of the case.

3. **Securely fasten the PSU in place.**

   It doesn't matter what pattern you follow when screwing in the mounting hardware; we prefer making an X pattern, traveling diagonally to insert and tighten screws. Never tighten them enough to deform the enclosure or server case material.

4. **Plug the primary 20- or 24-pin power plug into its socket on the motherboard.**

   This is by far the largest and most recognizable plug on the PSU harness. Your PSU should include all the power cables your motherboard requires.

5. **Optionally, tie each of the cables down.**

   This enables better airflow and encourages a clean workspace for other administrators, integrators, or technicians who may do follow-up work inside. It's also a good idea to coil up unused cable strands next to the PSU, and then use cable ties to secure them out of the way as much as possible.

Seat the CPU and cooler

Easily, the most expensive single-item purchase for any computer is its CPU. For the motherboards we chose for these chapters, that goes double because each one accommodates two processors. The CPU also happens to be the least accessible component in a completed system because you must open the case and then remove the cooler to get at this device. We've encountered cooler designs that required us to remove some or all of the nearby hardware components, including magnetic and optical drives, socketed memory, and other adapter cards, just so we could get the cooler out and get at the CPU. That's a lot of extra work just to do what's really necessary. Try to pick the smallest workable cooler, and you probably won't have to go through such contortions yourself.

Ideally, you should install the CPU and cooler onto the motherboard before it's seated inside the server case. It's much easier to mount these parts when you have adequate workspace for tools, and when your movement isn't restricted by interior elements inside the server case and other neighboring components. Usually, the CPU has a small footprint, so pulling or placing one into its socket is easy. Coolers are nowhere near as predictable as CPUs. Some coolers are either so large or the case so cramped that working in confined spaces is virtually impossible, so please heed our advice — it's based on prior, painful experience.

Installing the CPU

Depending on the make and model of your CPU, it may include delicate pins on the underside of the processor die. Otherwise, such pins may be integrated within the CPU socket. Either way, you want to proceed with care and caution when seating, socketing, and locking the CPU into place. This is an extreme case, where a little brute force improperly expended can result in major replacement expenses, whether for a new CPU or another motherboard.

Here's our step-by-step guide for CPU installation:

1. **Locate the CPU socket.**

   Specialty motherboards often include multiple sockets for multiple processors, so you may identify several sockets. Some primary or secondary sockets on the motherboard may be protected by a graphite-colored plastic shield, which must be removed prior to installation, that protects the CPU socket from incidental damage.

   Take a look at Figure 17-1, where we zoom in on the AMD Opteron processor socket on a Gigabyte server motherboard.

2. **Check the CPU socket carefully.**

   Modern CPU sockets are sufficiently frail to break at the slightest provocation, where the only surefire fix is total replacement. Don't be clumsy while examining the socket for defects or problems.

3. **Unlatch and uncover the CPU socket.**

   The socket will be guarded by a pressure plate and latching swing arm. Be gentle when working the latch; it should never bind nor require significant effort to operate.

4. **Check for proper CPU orientation.**

   Also check that the CPU itself is free from defects in workmanship or finish to avoid complications much later during the build.

Figure 17-1:
AMD
Opteron
CPU socket
on a
Gigabyte
mother-
board.

5. **Socket the CPU.**

   Work the CPU gently into its socket; it should drop into place without much pressure or persuasion. Never force the fit; any resistance should provoke immediate action, which usually means repositioning the CPU in the correct orientation.

6. **Repeat Steps 1 through 5 as necessary for multiple CPUs.**

7. **Identify motherboard power plug points for the CPU (see Figure 17-2).**

   The appearance and arrangement of this will change from one mother-board to the next. In most garden-variety single-processor boards, you'll have a 4-pin auxiliary cable plug situated nearby the CPU. This is a main (and necessary) source of power for the CPU. Multiple-core mother-boards will have several, sometimes requiring a special 8-pin plug. See Figure 17-2 for an example. (In the figure, note the 4-pin cover designed to accommodate older 20-pin ATX cables; for modern 24-pin PSUs, you must remove this as well.)

Figure 17-2:
The 8-pin
CPU power
socket is
next to the
24-pin
mother-
board
power plug.

Installing the cooler

Follow these steps to install the cooler:

1. **Locate the cooler mount points.**

   Identify placement for the cooler, noting any retention brackets, retainer clips, or pilot holes that correspond to the cooler's hardware assembly. Also observe placement of the cooler's 3- or 4-pin fan power connector for later use.

2. **Dry-fit the cooler once.**

   A *dry-fit* approach lets you check any clearance issues you may have with access or placement of the CPU and/or its cooler. Situate your CPU into the socket, but do not mount it in place yet.

   You should dry-fit the CPU cooler into the socket at least once to learn its proper fit and orientation. Check its orientation and airflow path. You may have to opt for a less favorable or reversed orientation to achieve optimal airflow.

3. **Inspect the underside of the CPU cooler.**

   Check for a patch of grayish, silver, or white thermal paste beneath the copper or aluminum base. Where it's absent, you will have to apply thermal paste yourself, which we recommend you smear directly onto the processor. Follow these steps:

   a. *Remove the CPU from its socket and place it gently on a paper or cloth towel to protect delicate pins or contact points on its bottom surface.*

   b. *Apply a thin, consistent layer of thermal paste.*

   A couple of small blobs in the middle is usually enough, which you must spread out into a thin, smooth layer that covers the entire top surface of the CPU package. Use a credit card or cardboard business card to smooth the paste into a thin, even layer.

   c. *Reseat the CPU into its socket.*

 If you need to apply thermal paste, use either a manufacturer-supplied single-shot portion or some other source for thermal paste. It often comes in plastic syringes from which you can extrude just a dab and then use a business or credit card to spread a thin, smooth layer across the surface. We're fond of the Arctic Silver brand, a well-known and widely used thermal paste.

4. **Securely fasten the cooler mount plate to the motherboard.**

   Retention clips or a retainer bracket may interface with the motherboard and cooler; assemble these in their correct orientations. There's almost always some clamp or screws to keep the cooler securely mounted.

5. **Connect the fan power cable to the CPU fan block on the motherboard.**

Never omit this step or leave it for later — this isn't a minor detail that you want to leave unfinished or overlooked. Otherwise, your expensive CPU could wind up overcooked!

Our setup, pictured in Figure 17-3, shows one of the CPU fan power blocks situated just behind the main power plug on the Gigabyte motherboard. To power up the fan, simply slide the 3-pin connector over the three rightmost pins in the 4-pin block. (It's made to accommodate both 3- and 4-pin CPU fan power leads.) We chose a pair of common and popular Zalman CNPS 7000 coolers for our two Opteron processors; these retail for about $40 each.

Figure 17-3:
CPU cooler fan power plug on the Gigabyte server motherboard.

Seat the RAM modules

Memory modules all have distinctive and predictable footprints, but the actual format can change in subtle ways that require a keen eye to spot. For example, differentiating DDR from DDR2 memory takes a bit of basic product knowledge; differentiating ECC or registered from unbuffered memory takes a keen eye and *strong* product knowledge. We don't expect you to have that sort of ability. Leave that one for the propeller heads and at the very least the retail associates and sellers of such hardware.

By doing your homework in advance, you should've already identified and obtained appropriate RAM for your motherboard. There are some dangerous (read: fiery) incompatibilities that can arise from mixing memory rated for different interfaces at different voltages. And despite memory designers' and circuit engineers' best efforts to make it difficult to plug the wrong component into the wrong socket, some ingenious installers invariably find some way to do it, sometimes with lethal effects to the hardware itself. Please pay attention to what you're doing.

Testing as you go . . . redux

In Chapter 16, we exhort our readers to ground themselves before they handle any computer equipment, especially circuitry such as memory modules or CPUs. Consider that same request firmly but politely stated here, too.

This time around, we want to encourage you to check your work at each step along the way, as it makes sense to do so. A minimal operational PC consists of a power supply, motherboard, processor, and cooler (or multiples thereof, as on the server boards in these chapters), and memory. After you stick them inside your case and hook up the power and reset leads, you should flip the power switch and see if the board lights up and the cooler fan(s) begin to spin. If so, you can keep on building. If not, you need to

check your connections and wiring to make sure that the power leads from the PSU to the motherboard are all properly attached, and the control leads from case to motherboard likewise.

As you complete each additional step along the way — adding disk drives, optical drives, and so forth — repeat the power-up test to see if LEDs turn on, drives spin up, and so forth. If you test as you go, by the time you're ready to boot up for real, your chances of getting a splash screen and a set of POST messages will be pretty high. That means less time wasted getting the hardware working before installing Windows Server 2008. We think this is the right way to do it and hope that, with practice, you'll think so, too.

The quickest way to make sure everything is copasetic is to put the memory module next to the memory socket and make sure that the slots in the middle line up exactly. If so, please proceed with the following step-by-step guide; if not, get the right RAM and try again!

1. **Locate the RAM banks.**

   Long, parallel rows of memory sockets stretch alongside or nearby a CPU socket.

2. **Identify socket keying for orientation.**

   Memory modules and memory banks are keyed for a specific fit and orientation. Carefully observe which way the memory fits (or doesn't). Selecting the proper memory type from the get-go ensures no complications here.

   In Figure 17-4, we install DDR memory into the Gigabyte motherboard for our two-way AMD Opteron processors. This board contains color-coded memory banks as a visual indicator to match rows where you should insert the memory, which is by no means a standard feature. This lets you take advantage of the performance boost that dual-bank memory can deliver.

3. **Unlatch the toothed latches on each memory socket.**

   Each tooth corresponds to a groove fashioned into the memory module. These teeth lock into place to keep memory secure in the socket.

Figure 17-4:
It's best to insert memory modules pairwise, each into a same-colored slot.

4. **Gently press memory modules into place.**

   Memory should slide into its socket with little or no resistance. Never force-fit a memory module; it can break under pressure. If you encounter resistance, rotate and retry.

5. **Repeat Steps 3 through 4 for multiple modules or multiple processor memory banks.**

In a multiple-socket motherboard, you'll have to make special considerations as to how much memory you allocate per processor.

Installing hard disk drives

Disk drive formats haven't really changed much over the years. Disk platters have gotten increasingly dense, but overall width has remained constant. Interfaces have gone through many important changes that both enhance and improve the lifespan of our precious storage volumes, but overall the installation procedure remains unchanged.

Whether your hardware includes SCSI, Parallel ATA (PATA) or Serial ATA (SATA) cabling, it's all the same: You install one cable between drive and controller and another from a power supply cable to the drive itself. Simple as that. For the purposes of our demonstration, we assume you have SATA; our build (pictured in Figure 17-5) includes a SATA controller. Feel free to substitute whatever interface you're currently working with, if it's something other than SATA, and follow our step-by-step guide:

Figure 17-5:
SATA drive
positioned
with left-
facing SATA
connector.

1. **Locate the nearest appropriate disk bay.**

   Disk drive bays are generally cages of stacked drive slots that are narrower (3.5 inches versus 5.25 inches) than the accessory drive bays. These may be self-contained cages that you can extract from the case completely, or they may use a series of fixed or removable drive mounts, clips, or rails.

2. **Identify the nearest suitable drive connector.**

   Sometimes the best slot isn't in the most convenient or accessible location. Avoid stretching the drive cable. Reposition the drive as necessary to achieve optimal distance from its controller connection. Consult the motherboard manual to identify where the boot drive (or mirrored pair of drives) must connect.

3. **Insert the disk and fasten it securely.**

   Slide the drive into its slot. It should take no persuasion. Be sure to use the screws included with the drive because they'll be properly threaded, and never over-tighten any fasteners. A mismatched screw can strip the drive threads and lock the fastener in place. If in doubt, try the screws on the drive before you mount it in the case, and use only screws that thread in and out without resistance or binding.

4. **Cable the drive to the motherboard.**

   Always utilize the first drive slot designation — usually indicated as IDE0/IDE1, SATA0/SATA1, or SCSI0/SCSI1. (Check your motherboard reference manual.) Link all subsequent drives in an orderly fashion to the controller or motherboard, as your configuration dictates.

5. **Connect the drive to the power supply.**

   The de facto standard power connector is a 4-pin Molex type that features beveled edges on only two corners so that you can never plug it in wrong. SATA drives tend to use modular power connectors, like the one shown above the left-hand bank of SATA controller plugs on the motherboard in Figure 17-5.

Installing the optical disk

As with magnetic storage technology, little has changed where optical drive installation is concerned. An optical disk, for its apparent qualities, appears either as a tray or slot-loading device with an activity light (or several) and at least one button (eject) and possibly some decals (indicating drive capability and type). That said, with an increasing selection of SATA-attached optical drives available nowadays, we prefer those because SATA data cables are much more compact and easy to install than IDE data cables.

Whatever underlies an optical drive's front panel can change randomly, for all we know. As long as those drives keep working when we cable them up properly, we don't much care either. Here's a step-by-step guide to optical drive installation:

1. **Locate the nearest appropriate optical drive bay.**

   In a multiple-slot or tower configuration, we recommend placing your optical drive as far away as possible from heat-producing parts, such as disk drives. This often means staggering drive placement across slots (leaving an opening between drives) to give air more room to circulate within the server case.

2. **Check for proper fit.**

   Whether going in from the front or pushing through the back, make a dry-run to identify potential hang-ups. These may include removing a faceplate or media tray shield, clearing obstructions, or relocating the drive to a different 5.25-inch bay. Next, make sure all your drive mount screw holes line up with slots or mount points in the case.

3. **Insert the drive into the bay.**

   It should slide easily and freely into place with little persuasion.

4. **Fasten the drive securely in place.**

   Again, don't over-tighten the screws; snug is good enough.

5. **Cable the drive to the motherboard.**

   Identify the proper slot for your drive, typically not the first channel on the first drive controller bank of the motherboard. Drive connections on the motherboard are numbered sequentially from first to last, and we recommend you not interleave hard drives and optical drives. If you're using IDE cables, don't connect a hard drive and an optical drive to the same cable.

   When using an on-board RAID controller, use only those drives specifically involved in the RAID array on that controller. Where there are two separate controllers, isolate each RAID setup completely from any optical drives, no matter how many plugs may remain unused in the RAID array.

6. **Cable the power supply to the drive.**

   After establishing all other steps, connect the power to the drive.

7. **Make sure the drive tray opens and closes properly.**

   Ensure proper fit, especially in a case with front panel doors or built-in media tray covers. Sometimes, you may have to slide the drive forward or back a little (or a lot) so that the switch on the front of the case engages properly with the switch on the front of the drive.

Setting up hardware

When you have all your hardware seated, cabled, and primed for action, you can begin your crucial first real boot-up. Of course, this means you must hook up a monitor and a keyboard as well so that you can provide input and view output from your server. Assuming you've plugged in every cable and included every component you need, your system should at least show you the initial Power-On Self-Test (POST) warm-up phase — like calisthenics for computers.

If nothing happens at all, you should check the power supply and its various connections. A little activity and then nothing usually spells some sort of component incompatibility or a faulty power source (among other possible causes). If you hear beep codes, please note that they provide audible indications for various operational issues — memory isn't seated correctly, the CPU is missing or can't be detected, or a USB drive is plugged in and just isn't wanted.

Barring any such complications, you'll be presented with a startup screen. This may flash instantly before your eyes, but hopefully you get a chance to see whatever key sequence is necessary to trigger the motherboard's BIOS setup. From here, you must make all necessary server-specific changes to settings that require them — such as any ECC memory settings, CPU identifiers, and the initial boot order. This is important for the next step, where you finally install Windows Server 2008.

Installing the OS

We provide detailed instructions about the installation process, with a qualifying explanation of the entire procedure, in Chapter 5. There are many ways you can install Windows Server 2008 (or upgrade from an eligible software platform). We can't reasonably cover them all here (or in Chapter 5, either). Here's a synopsis for the straightforward process described more thoroughly in Chapter 5: We inserted the DVD, ran the install process, and got Windows Server 2008 up and running without encountering anything out of the ordinary. It found our drives, both optical and hard disks, without difficulty, and we were able to load drivers for key motherboard components without problem in the final, post-install configuration and networking phase. We can only hope your installation goes as well as ours did.

If your server will include an earlier version of Windows alongside Windows Server 2008, install that software first. This permits the new Windows Server 2008 boot manager to identify and offer that installation as a boot option as well.

After you complete the Initial Configuration Tasks setup (Chapter 6), spend some time getting to learn the Server Manager interface and all its functionality. You'll be spending a considerable amount of your administrative time on the server managing, monitoring, and modifying attributes through this interface. Don't be afraid to try new installation methods, either. You'll eventually want to perform a remote network install, an unintended install, or perhaps both. Try everything at least once!

Ready to Rock-and-Roll?

We've walked you through the process of installing server hardware and software necessary for your first build, which we anticipate went smoothly. You must now customize and configure this server for your network and all your users by including the accounts, features, and functions they'll need.

Now that you have your server hardware assembled and operating under the guidance of Windows Server 2008, you're ready to start adding users, network roles, and server responsibilities. Prepare to function as a *newly-fledged* server administrator!

Chapter 18

Taking Care of Your Own Issues

• •

• •

*A*ny proper troubleshooting process begins with a basic format or formal structure. Generally, from a technician's perspective, we envision a pyramid of prioritized checkpoints that we run through when investigating a problematic piece of hardware or software. This methodology remains roughly the same no matter how we apply it, even if the conditions and variables change considerably within the context of exercising that methodology.

When you troubleshoot a car engine problem, you don't normally check tire pressure or trunk contents. In the context of an engine bay issue, that just doesn't make any sense. Instead, you probably check engine fluid levels, battery terminals, spark plugs and distributor caps, serpentine belts, and various other interconnections. These things make perfect sense in the context of troubleshooting an engine problem. Now suppose you had some sort of tire traction or roadway handling problem, would you first check the engine bay? We don't think so.

Likewise, you need a proper format to approach server-related issues or problems. Even if you don't fully understand the nature of the problem, you need a working structure to begin analyzing and identifying a probable cause. If your server experiences some form of connectivity issue, the first thing we recommend checking is the cabling — it will fail on you more often than you'd like to think possible. The same applies to hard drive cables as well as network interface cables. Sometimes this is the only source of a seemingly critical error that, if overlooked, will confuse and baffle you into submission.

Equally important is your thoroughness and adherence to a formal diagnostic methodology or troubleshooting format — that is, never overlook any step, no matter how seemingly benign or unimportant it may appear to be. Such casual assumptions really can get the best of you, and we don't want to see you wipe egg off your face simply because you made an easily avoidable but utterly unwarranted assumption.

Troubleshooting Common Windows Server 2008 Problems

In the following sections, we sketch an informal methodology for approaching several troublesome Windows Server 2008 problems. We feel that giving you a more flexible framework or a set of universally-applicable procedures is more beneficial than citing a few narrow, specific examples.

Setup failures

Installation or setup failures are a common occurrence, but they won't normally recur with appreciable frequency. Unattended installations may be crippled by an incorrect parameter or incompatible setting, the network may become inaccessible during a remote install, or user error may cause failure during a manual installation procedure.

Generally, begin troubleshooting such an issue by checking the `Setupact.log` and `Setuperr.log` files, which will be located in one of two places according to when the installation failed: If setup only has sufficient time to copy files, these files are located in `$WINDOWS.~BT\Sources\Panther`; otherwise, if setup halted in the midst of expanding or implementing software, try `Windows\Panther` on the partition that contains the Windows Server 2008 installation.

Unavailable partition

A partition may become inaccessible to the installer for a number of reasons. Some of the known reasons are described in the following list:

- **Insufficient storage space:** An inadequate partition requires resizing (just click Extend) or another partition deleted to clear sufficient space.

- **Insufficient free space:** Again, adequate space must be cleared by deletion of unnecessary files and perhaps reclamation and reallocation of other partitions.

- ✔ **Invalid volume format:** If the designated partition is prepared as a non-NTFS format, Setup will invalidate its use as an installation target. Reformat as NTFS.

- ✔ **Invalid volume type:** If the target partition is neither a basic disk nor a simple dynamic volume, Setup will deem it ineligible as an installation medium. Create or select an appropriate volume type from your available storage media.

- ✔ **Initialized raw disks:** Your server may contain a single uninitialized raw disk; two or more require partitioning, which requires running Setup twice. Either partition and initialize disks prior to use, or (as with new builds) just endure the inevitable double-reboot setup process.

- ✔ **Invalid BIOS settings:** Disk and optical drives may be disabled or not flagged as bootable media in the BIOS. Reboot and trigger the BIOS setup menu, then flag the appropriate bootable disk volume.

You may encounter issues that aren't described here, but those are exceptional cases.

Restart failure

Occasionally, Windows Setup will fail to rediscover its installation source (for example, disk or optical drive). Often, this requires you to load a driver so that it can be identified after Windows Setup readies for first boot, much like what occurred with early Windows XP installations and SATA disk or optical drives.

Follow these steps to prepare Windows Setup with the appropriate drivers:

1. **Save the driver to an appropriate storage medium (such as a USB drive, CD or DVD, and so on).**

2. **Start the Windows Server installation DVD to invoke Windows Setup.**

3. **Under Disk Selection, click Load Driver and follow the onscreen instructions.**

If the system fails to start following this driver inclusion, it may not have been digitally signed. Where possible, try using only digitally-signed device drivers.

Startup failures

Windows Server 2008 may fail to start up for a number of reasons, with system failure occurring in a number of areas. Some startup errors are duly noted: Incompatible or incorrectly installed hardware might elicit a series of diagnostic BIOS beep codes, or state that it can't find a working boot volume. Other errors aren't so obvious, such as those that crash Windows as it attempts to bootstrap itself, which triggers an instant reboot, which repeats the process all over again.

Common causes of startup failure are ranked below in descending order of likelihood:

- ✔ Hardware failure
- ✔ Driver failure
- ✔ Corrupt file or volume
- ✔ Misconfigured setting
- ✔ Malware or viral infection

We explore these top-level topics in better detail throughout the following paragraphs.

Hardware failure

A server system can fail to initialize and start up due to hardware failures of all kinds (for example, a bad or disconnected plug or electrical damage). We've personally experienced such grief with developmental or experimental quality driver controllers that systematically and independently ruined drive after drive until we recognized them as the true source.

Chipset issues are probably the most difficult to diagnose without some specialized skills and toolsets. Some drive failures are self-evident (the sound of galloping coconuts suggests the drive arm is contacting the platters), and others are easily resolved, although just as easily overlooked (unseated or defective drive cable). For the most part, you can use most of your senses (including common sense) to diagnose many hardware issues.

Driver failure

Driver and system data updates can also be a source of run-time woes. Again, drawing on our recent experiences, we've seen seemingly benign processes result in total disaster, often repeatedly on the same or separate machines despite our best efforts.

Windows Update has occasionally triggered some series of unfortunate events that conspire to ruin mission-critical data and files, which fortunately affected only a few Windows XP installations — so far, no such bad luck with Windows Server products! The point is, it happens, and even we wouldn't believe it possible had we not directly experienced it ourselves.

Corrupt file or volume

Corrupted files and volumes are common and usually easily corrected. Windows Server 2008 has modified the entire boot infrastructure so that it no longer resembles its predecessors (except Windows Vista), but we're willing to wager any boot-time issues will be relatively similar. Granted, each solution will be entirely different.

Corruption happens any number of ways: A drive controller goes bad, a drive cable gets disconnected, a drive volume is unexpectedly taken offline when updating data, and so forth. You could be creating a backup image onto an external USB drive plugged into your Windows Server 2008 server when another administrator, unaware of your workload, unplugs it for use elsewhere. Experimental drive utilities could potentially make an incorrect write or overwrite to an incorrect place and make an entire volume unreadable.

Misconfigured settings

Misconfigured settings can occur anywhere, often in places you can't predict or expect and manifesting in ways you may not anticipate. Even a simple Group Policy setting can be overridden in some indirect manner that leaves you baffled as to why your Local Policy settings just aren't taking effect.

Important registry settings or other startup and run-time parameters may be altered in some manner that brings about chaos and disorder, which can happen with an installed or improperly installed application, an unassuming although disastrous configuration change, or some other unintentional and apparently innocuous act.

Malware or viral infection

On the malignant side of change lies malware and viral infection. These automata of anarchy seek to ruin stability and security stance for individual computers and entire organizations alike. They usually aren't coded with the best intentions or by the best programmers fully capable of what they're doing, and every so often you encounter one such beast that undeniably and perhaps irreparably damages something sacred.

Our intent isn't to leave you grief-stricken by all that can possibly go wrong; we just want to foster a healthy situational awareness about your server environment and its operating conditions. Lots of little things can go wrong, plenty of them can be fixed, and few are really worth losing sleep over.

Diagnosing startup errors

Here are the five senses you may use to diagnose a given problem:

- ✔ Sense of smell
- ✔ Sense of sound
- ✔ Sense of sight
- ✔ Sense of feel
- ✔ Common sense

We appropriately omit the sense of taste because you really shouldn't be found tasting your hardware components. It's just not right.

Sense of smell

Your sense of smell can alert you to an electrical or thermal issue. The smell of hot and burning hardware gives off a powerful smell that is very distinct, much like cooking in the kitchen. When you've been around hot hardware situated in poorly ventilated or inadequately conditioned environments, you'll know the kind of odor we're talking about.

Sense of sound

After you've become acclimated to the operational quirks and characteristic properties of your server hardware, it becomes like your daily commute. You notice when your car sounds a little out of tune, or emits a sound you haven't heard before. Sensing that *something is wrong* becomes second nature to you; the very server you operate is sufficiently familiar that you're fully aware of its baseline behavior and condition.

Sense of sight

Sometimes you have to crack open the case to investigate what's going on inside. How do things look? Is there sufficient dust buildup to impede airflow? Are any components showing visible signs of wear or tear? Simple observation can reveal many clues about what probably or potentially causes problems.

Sense of feel

Occasionally, you'll have to place your hand near or on hardware to see how it feels. Do you feel any excess heat or vibration? Any residues or particles that don't belong? Hot and humid operating environments can create unfavorable conditions inside a server case. Servers like to stay cool, much as we do, and appreciate around the same climate and temperature that keeps us humans comfortable, too.

Common sense

We say *common sense*, but these things really aren't that common until you experience them routinely and repeatedly. It's uncommon to instantly know all the particularities and oddities about the mechanical operation of your server prior to its construction. You can't know if "that clicking noise" is actually an acceptable byproduct or something to investigate. Common sense is a skill honed with experience. Just pay attention to the fundamental aspects of your server hardware so you can grow to understand what it does, and how to identify and mend what breaks before or as it happens.

Troubleshooting problems while in safe mode

Safe mode is a troubleshooting option for Windows that starts your computer with only basic services and functionality. If an existing problem doesn't reappear when you start Windows in safe mode, you can eliminate the default settings and basic device drivers as possible causes.

Should your computer automatically restart in safe mode, use the process of elimination to isolate the source. Individually start all commonly-used applications, including those contained in the system Startup folder, to identify the probable cause.

Run-time issues

After you get past all the setup and first-boot issues, there still remains a vast expanse of unforeseeable complications that may arise before you reach the desktop and after you log in. There are higher-level application or system configuration settings that manifest problems only in the user domain or when administering server operations.

We can't possibly conceive of every potential avenue of attack, but we do cover considerable ground in the first few subjects because they specifically concern Windows Server 2008 and not third-party or additional applications installed afterward.

User Account Control

Windows Server 2008 defaults to running applications as a standard user, even if you're currently logged in with an administrative group account. Users who attempt to launch applications marked with administrative properties will be asked to confirm their intentions, and only applications operating under administrative credentials may affect system-wide and global settings. All this is handled in User Account Control, or UAC.

Custom or in-house installers/uninstallers and software update programs may not be properly detected or permitted to run with administrative credentials. Standard user applications may fail to perform their tasks or be inaccessible, particularly if marked to require administrative privilege. Applications with insufficient credentials may run incorrectly or not at all, which can be manifested in any number of ways.

We highly recommend familiarizing yourself with the UAC's format and structure, learn how it does and does not function, and so forth. Teach applicable users to launch their privileged programs with the right-click context menu feature to run applications as administrator. Observe file and directory permissions and group memberships and reduce any restrictive Access Control Lists (ACLs) that prove prohibitive. Custom applications should be written to operate in a least-privileged environment scenario, require the lowest workable level of user credentials, and present the smallest window of exposure when operating under administrator rights.

Group Policy infrastructure

The Group Policy infrastructure delivers and enforces preferential configuration settings and organizational policy settings for a given set of targeted users and computers within the scope of an Active Domain unit. It comprises a Group Policy engine and multiple client-side extensions, responsible for reading and applying these settings for individually targeted client computers.

That level of complexity and interdependency can make troubleshooting Group Policy problems downright vexing. Thus we can only hope that Microsoft will update its Group Policy Diagnostic Best Practice Analyzer (GPDBPA), which currently works for Windows XP and Windows Server 2003, to do likewise for Windows Vista and Windows Server 2008. It's an extremely helpful tool designed to "help you identify Group Policy configuration errors or other dependency failures that may prevent settings or features from functioning as expected." (Microsoft's own wording is so appropriate, we just had to quote it here.) You can find this tool by visiting the Microsoft Download center at `http://support.microsoft.com/kb/940122`. Hopefully, by the time you read this, a similar tool for Vista and Windows Server 2008 will be available!

Printing infrastructure

The printing infrastructure for any Windows Server 2008 print server is organized into a hierarchy of managed entities that collectively permit local and remote users to utilize and manage printers and all print-related activities. This defining structure is shown in Figure 18-1, with each relevant aspect summarized in Table 18-1.

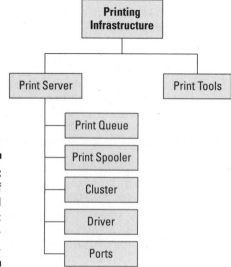

Figure 18-1: Hierarchy of Managed Entities: Print Infrastructure.

Table 18-1	Printing Infrastructure
Entity	*Description*
Print server	A computer attached to a print device that is accessible to other users locally logged on and remotely connected through the shared printers folder.
Print queue	The task list representation of a print device.
Spooler device	The governing server process, also called a *print spooler,* that manages all print jobs and print queues for any given server.
Cluster	A high-availability system distributed among two or more computers that share a given print queue workload in the event that one of the computers fails or becomes inaccessible.
Driver	The basic software instructions that make computer control possible over hardware devices.
Port	An input or interface type that enables communication between computer and device; typically a parallel, USB, or TCP/IP connection.
Print tools	All local and remotely-situated applications that are responsible for print queue management or printer-related tasks.
Physical printer	The actual device that processes information and produces documentation.

When you begin troubleshooting this hierarchy, start by eliminating all the most obvious and simple causes first. Check for paper feed or supply issues, cable connections, power and activity light illumination, and so on. Next, work your way to the computer, analyzing software settings and relevant configuration settings for remote connections, including networking properties. How you individually process these elements is entirely up to you; all we suggest is a regular, thorough sequence upon which to base your work.

Windows Activation

After installing Windows Server 2008 in evaluation mode, should you attempt to restart the computer in Diagnostic mode beyond its expiration you won't be able to log in. You'll receive a message that the activation period has expired. Try the following two solutions in this order:

1. Start `msconfig.exe`.
2. Under the General tab, select **Diagnostic Startup**.
3. Under the Services tab, choose **Plug and Play**.

4. Click OK and then click Restart.

This lets you to restart the computer in Diagnostic mode by configuring the Plug and Play service. Otherwise, you may recover from this issue by setting the computer to start normally. Follow these instructions:

1. **In the Windows Activation dialog box, select Access Your Computer with Reduced Functionality.**

   The Internet Explorer window appears.

2. **In Internet Explorer 7's address bar, type** %windir%\system32\msconfig.exe **and press Enter.**

   The MSConfig configuration utility appears.

3. **Click General and select Normal Startup.**

4. **Click OK and then click Restart.**

Hardware upgrades and software updates

You may encounter run-time errors long after installation, perhaps after introducing a new piece of hardware or upgrading an old one. If after installing a new device, your Windows Server 2008 install or the device itself fails to work, run through the following checklist:

- Ensure hardware device compatibility with both your server computer and Windows Server 2008.
- Install any necessary device drivers from their respective install media.
- Reboot the server to reinitialize or retry the driver.
- Reconnect any present USB devices to alternative ports.
- Check for update drivers through Windows Update.

Apart from checking Windows Update, always check the manufacturer's Web site for any updated driver versions, particularly those that might resolve the issues you experience. If installing a new driver is the source for instability or incompatibility, you can also restore a driver to its previous — presumably known-good — version (Device Manager⇨*Driver Category*⇨Driver⇨Roll Back Driver). You must be logged in as administrator when performing most driver-related tasks.

If you suspect Windows Update had something to do with your latest issue, or if you want to eliminate it as a possible cause, you may also remove updates. (Choose Control Panel⇨Programs⇨Installed Updates⇨*Update Entry*⇨Remove.) Generally, this isn't recommended because many updates address or enhance server security. Start by opening Windows Update and clicking View Update History to see a list of applied updates.

If you're prohibited from removing an update when connected to a network, there may be a Global Policy curtailing your activity, or it could be a security-specific update that can't be retracted. A network-wide Global Policy and Windows Automatic Update may automatically reinstall updates when you restart Windows Server 2008, so be prepared to handle such cases where necessary.

Last, always check Device Manager (click Start and type **device manager** into the search field) when you suspect a hardware and/or driver issue. An entry indicated by an exclamation point icon signifies a driver issue: Either an inappropriate or approximate match has been substituted in lieu of a proper or more recent driver. These devices may work in some cases yet fail in others; the only real remedy is to find, install, and use the right driver. Device Manager is always your looking glass into the hardware and driver subsystem.

Monitoring Server Operations

Put Server Manager high on your priorities list when it comes to gathering initial intelligence on the issue at hand. Server Manager consolidates several subsets of system management functionality that were otherwise spread among many independent and diverse applets. Along with some preexisting capability come new or newly-revised components that further facilitate system management tasks.

In many cases, Server Manager is the oracle into your server, a window through which you can peer and observe its innermost workings. Open Server Manager and expand your domain name to reveal a tree of entries where you'll find an appropriately-named Diagnostics subsection. In this sub-section, you'll encounter three categories: Event Viewer, Reliability and Performance, and Device Manager.

We recommend that you check applications and services logs, particularly any warnings or errors topics that are relevant to the problem you're currently investigating. Sometimes the most minute details will escape observation, only later found to be the culprit. As a matter of principle, you should at least eliminate any question that the cause left an electronic paper trail through the system's highly active logging and filing facilities, before digging into detailed research and diagnostics.

Event Viewer

Windows Server products have long included the Event Viewer application, which has remained relatively unchanged since its debut in Windows NT. Microsoft has redesigned this applet to supply a more aggregated view of system-wide events that previously appeared only in individual event logs. Each of the initial primary categories remains the same (Application, System, and Security logs), but Event Viewer (shown in Figure 18-2) now provides a consolidated perspective on the overall health of your server.

You may observe errors, warnings, and informational and successful audit details as they've occurred in the last hour and last 24 hours to gauge recent activity. Expand each container for in-depth coverage of each event. Underneath the Event Viewer category branch lurks a Windows Logs container, a storehouse for event logs that appear in their old, familiar format.

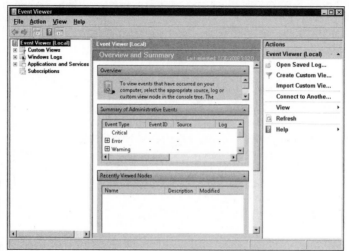

Figure 18-2:
The Event
Viewer.

Custom Views

Windows Server 2008 presents large amounts of data at your request. All Windows applications, components, and security parameters may be represented, so Event Viewer provides you with filters necessary for deep inspection. You may find that default methods for presenting such data doesn't suit your needs or preferences, which is what motivates the Custom Views dialog.

This container is designed to permit dynamic content filtering based on simple rules that you specify to Event Viewer for information display. Open a menu to select the Create Custom View dialog box by right-clicking the Custom Views container. Here, you can specify filters based on time period, event level (critical, error, warning, information, and verbose), event log, event source, include/exclude event IDs, task category, keywords, user, and computer entries.

Windows Logs

Two additional categories (Setup and Forwarded Events logs) are included with the standard entries (Application, Security, and System logs). Setup logs contain information relevant to any system configuration changes, but the information isn't always detailed or descriptive. Only a simple statement to the effect of a role being installed or uninstalled will appear. Forwarded Events logs contain entries based on subscriptions to remote system event log services, which are filtered against some criteria and sent here.

Applications and Services Logs

Application and Services logs are general events related specifically to the Windows operating system. Previously, you would browse the event logs for a particular issue you wanted to troubleshoot; Windows Server 2008 nicely categorizes and sorts events related to specific criteria (such as Active Directory).

When no events of interest appear in an event log, it's reasonable to suspect that logging has been disabled or log files have been cleared. Confirm that logging is indeed enabled (choose *Log*⇨Properties⇨Enable Logging) and — barring that — determine if logs have been cleared by searching the System log for event ID 104 — the value generated whenever a log is cleared. Analytic and debug logs aren't visible by default and must be specifically enabled for viewing. (Choose Event Viewer⇨View⇨Show Analytic and Debug Logs.)

Reliability and Performance

Windows Server 2008 also consolidates Performance Monitor and other such relevant run-time information into a single applet, also made accessible through the Server Manager interface. If you've spent any amount of time with Windows platforms, you may already be familiar with its Performance Monitor tool — we use it as a barometer for the general well-being of our workstations and servers.

Monitoring Tools

Expand this container category to view the resource utilization overview, which has that familiar line-graph illustration and real-time update activity you're already accustomed to seeing. CPU, RAM, disk, and network activity are summarized in frequency of activity and a graph illustrating peaks and valleys of activity throughout the observational time frame.

Each of these sub-elements in the performance dialog box can be further expanded to reveal more detailed information about operational parameters. Underneath the CPU section, for example, there appears a list of active processes and CPU time dedicated to each individual process, all of which makes up the utilization trends charted therein.

Performance Monitor

Apart from its integration into Server Manager, Performance Monitor appears similar in form and function since Windows Server 2003. This diagnostic utility facilitates troubleshooting hardware issues, primarily processor utilization. The line graph charts CPU activity history as a running track record, with spikes indicating surges in activity for the noted time period. A high percentage of processor utilization is indicative of overload and a potential bottleneck.

Performance monitoring consists of performance counters, performance logs and alerts, and the System Monitor. Counters provide utilization information regarding how well the platform or its applications, drivers, and services are performing. This helps you to identify bottlenecks and better fine-tune application performance through graphical charts and timeline indicators.

Performance logs and alerts generate alert notifications based on these counter thresholds. As an API, it can be used programmatically to query performance data, create event trace sessions, capture a configuration, and track API calls throughout some of the Win32 dynamic libraries. System Monitor is an API that enables you to view real-time data and track record performance counter data related to the CPU, RAM, and all of your disk drives.

Reliability Monitor

Windows Server 2008 is really good at keeping track of records for its daily operations and activities. It dutifully logs, dates, and sorts its entries and applies your specially-defined filtering rules so that information is presented in a manner you see fit. We've grow familiar with its form and become expectant of its function.

What happens when you work remotely or on a foreign system? Problem history and server history are usually two key issues that are addressed within the opening of a trouble-ticket field dispatch or on-site servicing procedure. You can't possibly know what that system's performance has been over any length of time, but the Reliability Monitor (shown in Figure 18-3) absolutely does know. This is an index into the running track record for system stability to include keeping tabs on software installs/uninstalls, application failures, hardware failures, windows failures, and a catch-all miscellaneous failures category.

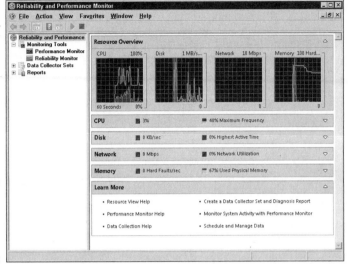

Figure 18-3:
The
Reliability
Monitor.

Steep drops, which level out again quickly, accompany installation of a new application. Any noteworthy event is detailed on the day of failure, and double-clicking a specific entry provides more detailed information about the event.

Data Collector Sets and Reports

Data collector sets are the cornerstones of performance monitoring and reporting within the new Windows Server 2008 Reliability and Performance Monitor. Data points are collected and organized into a single component to facilitate performance tracking and periodic review. Collector sets can be individually created and recorded or grouped with other collector sets and configured to generate alerts at specified thresholds. Sets contain performance counters, event trace data, and system configuration information.

You can create a collector set from existing templates or predefined collector sets, or through individual configuration. These sets enable you to better utilize the Windows Reliability and Performance Monitor to track overall system health and progress in a completely customizable way.

Device Manager

Underneath Reliability and Performance resides the Device Manager; click its label to produce the details pane for system-wide device properties. This is another holdover from Windows Server products past. This application is responsible for inventorying and reporting low-level hardware presence and facilitates troubleshooting problematic devices or drivers.

The Device Manager maintains a catalog of devices installed on the system so that you can identify any and all components. Use the Device Manager as a window into your system whenever a device is improperly functioning or not identified. Defective drivers are indicated by an exclamation point icon to signify where you should begin diagnosing issues. You can also centrally manage all drivers, versions, and updates.

Tweaking Windows Server 2008 for Efficiency

During the setup and install process, many additional components, packages, and language features are often included unnecessarily into your server build. When you discover a need to reclaim precious native storage space and begin a process of elimination for all but the more critical parts, start by cleaning out any leftover installation material. This includes any Microsoft Office suite products as well — they tend to generate a lot of supportive install-time files that tend to get left behind unless manually specified for removal when installation completes.

Managed entities

The hierarchy of managed entities is pictured in Figure 18-4. Each element is described briefly in Table 18-2.

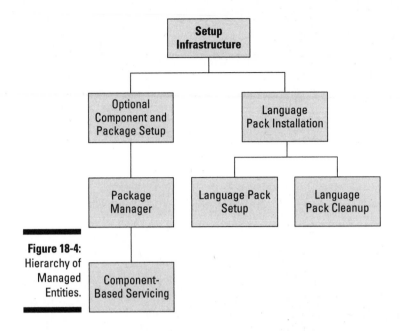

Figure 18-4:
Hierarchy of
Managed
Entities.

Table 18-2	Managed Entities
Entity	*Description*
Optional Component and Package Setup	OCSetup.exe is a command line tool that installs, updates, and uninstalls optional Windows components. We recommend using it for bare-bones Server Core installations; full-blown installs should use Server Manager.
Package Manager	This is the underlying tool that OCSetup.exe uses to install Windows components and particularly facilitates unintended installations and disabling options in an offline Windows image.
Component-Based Servicing	This is part of the *servicing stack* (files and resources required to service a Windows image or live OS) that provides APIs to client installers such as Windows Update or Windows Installer.

(continued)

Table 18-2 *(continued)*

Entity	Description
Language Pack Installation	Supplemental language support files make dialog boxes, menus, wizards, and built-in help topics accessible to non-native speakers.
Language Pack Setup	`Lpksetup.exe` installs and removes multilingual user interface (MUI) language packs and language interface packs (LIPs).
Language Pack Cleanup	This is an automatically-scheduled, run-once application that operates in silent mode on the first boot after installation completes, and then removes any unused language pack files.

Run-time optimization

Windows Server 2008 does a fair job of minimizing unnecessary components bundled with the default install. This confers several immediate advantages: It shortens the install phase, creates a more flexible minimal foundation upon which to build your specific features, and gives you greater control over setup aspects. Typically, there isn't a whole lot to the default install that you need to strip away to streamline your server.

Over time, or through a timeline of developmental periods or experimental phases, you may experience sluggish system performance owing to an abundance of unnecessary or resource-intensive system processes and components. We like to maintain a conservative profile and remove parts that aren't vital to system or business functions. In the sections that follow, we cite a few such examples to inspire your own excursions into the realm of server optimization.

Turn off Indexing Service

Windows Indexing Service generates search content properties for all files targeting local and network-attached storage volumes to optimize return-time for results. This service runs continuously and can potentially slow the PC's performance, particularly on servers with revolving data storage and continuous cyclic indexing.

If you don't need fast file searches, turn off Indexing Service by following these steps:

1. **Open Computer.**

2. **Select the target volume, right-click, and choose Properties.**

3. **Deselect the Allow Indexing Service to Index This Disk check box.**

4. **Click OK.**

Disable unnecessary services

Services run continuously in the background and even consume resources in their idle states awaiting some event or receipt of data. Not all that is loaded is needed, which is particularly why Microsoft wisely chose to componentize and modularize Windows Server 2008 into a Server Core build option.

Over time, you may find your system consumed by many services ravaging many shared resources, only to realize that some of those processes are no longer necessary. Either they've fallen into disuse, never found utilization, or since been replaced by the next best thing. Either way, you neither want nor need them there, so you should remove them.

To view startup services and statuses, open Start and type **services.msc** in the Start Search bar. Left-click a service entry to view its description and become informed of what other dependent functionality will be affected by its removal from operation.

To disable a service, follow these steps:

1. **Right-click the service and choose Properties.**

2. **Change its startup type to Manual.**

3. **Click Stop to halt the service.**

Schedule Disk Defragmenter

If not already set, schedule disk defragmentation at regular intervals that correspond to local usage. Disk defragmentation realigns file segments to optimize their arrangement on disk so that they may be read and written to most efficiently. This ensures optimal disk performance, especially for drives that process large numbers of files of various sizes.

Making the Most of Your Server

As you build your own body of experience in working with Windows Server 2008, you'll become more confident in using its tools and in tweaking, optimizing, and adjusting it to better fit your business needs. In the meantime, we hope these troubleshooting tips — and the rest of this book, in fact — will help you cultivate the skills and knowledge that you'll employ to keep things up and running.

Part V
The Part of Tens

The 5th Wave   By Rich Tennant

"It appears a server in Atlanta is about to go down, there's printer backup in Baltimore, and an accountant in Chicago is about to make level 3 of the game 'Tomb Pirate.'"

In this part . . .

When Moses came down from the mountain, how many commandments did he carry? Ten. How many fingers do most people have? Ten. On a scale of one to ten, what's a perfect score? Ten. We aren't entirely sure that all these things are necessarily connected, but that number shows up everywhere, even on the *Late Show with David Letterman*. Perhaps that's why The Part of Tens is a key ingredient in this and all other *For Dummies* books. Then again, it could just be a coincidence. . . .

Each chapter in this part includes a list of tips, tricks, techniques, reminders, and resources for inspired information about your Windows Server 2008 system and its network. We'd like to claim the same source of inspiration that Moses had for his commandments, but our Part of Tens comes only from the "School of Hard Knocks" next door.

These chapters are constructed to save you time, steer you around common networking potholes, and get you safely past common sources of chaos and confusion. The best part of tens, however, is one that doesn't appear directly in this part of the book — that's the part where you hold your breath and *count to ten* as you begin to lose your cool. If you try that part first, the other Part of Tens will do you a lot more good!

Chapter 19

Ten Tips for Installation and Configuration

*I*f you spend enough time working with Windows Server 2008, you undoubtedly will be required to install this software on multiple systems. This job can be more "interesting" than it has to be — not to mention that it can take more time than you want it to.

This chapter provides some fact-filled sources of information, some tried-and-true guidelines, and some great repair tools and techniques to help you successfully survive the Windows Server 2008 installation process. Knowing these tips and not needing them is better than not knowing but needing them.

Exceed the Minimum Requirements

Table 19-1 offers a quick rundown of the minimum requirements to run
Windows Server 2008 (and bonus realistic recommendations).

Table 19-1	Windows Server 2008 Minimum Requirements (Plus Realistic Recommendations)	
Item	Minimum Requirement	Recommended
CPU	1 GHz	2 GHz
RAM	512MB	4GB
Disk space	10GB	1TB
Optical drive	DVD-ROM	DVD-ROM
NIC	Integrated chip	Add-in card or two (TOE is best)
Display better	Super VGA (800 x 600)	Super VGA (800 x 600) or
Pointing device	MS Mouse or compatible	MS Mouse or compatible

To configure a production server to conform to minimum requirements
is a recipe for disaster. The performance (or lack thereof) you'd be able to
squeeze from such a machine would have a mob of users at your heels in
no time at all.

When building a Windows Server 2008 computer, more of just about everything is better: This applies to more powerful (and more) CPUs, more RAM,
and more powerful network interface cards (NICs). Servers do their jobs in
quiet obscurity in most cases, so you don't have to install a 512MB graphics
card, a fancy flat-panel monitor, or a top-dollar mouse or touchpad. You can
opt to skip the DVD player on the Windows Server 2008 computer as long as
you can access the server across the network from another machine where
the contents of the DVD-ROM have been copied to a hard drive.

If you install Windows Server 2008 on a machine that doesn't include a NIC,
you won't be able to install or configure any of its network-related aspects.
We're convinced that there's no point to installing a server that isn't attached

to a network, so don't install Windows Server 2008 on a machine unless it has a NIC. (Even better, use a NIC connected to a real, live network, if not multiple NICs, preferably with a TCP/IP Offload Engine, or TOE, to help max out network performance.)

Use Only Qualified Server Hardware

Before you even think about installing Windows Server 2008 on a machine, be sure that the hardware you're considering will make a good home for that software. Nevertheless, without a formal seal of approval or a guarantee from a vendor, how can you be sure that the software will work with your hardware?

Fortunately, you *can* be sure by checking the Windows Server Catalog. This is a comprehensive list of hardware that's been tested and certified to be compatible with Windows Server 2008 (or other server versions). This catalog is available online at `www.microsoft.com/whdc/hcl/default.mspx`.

You can also use the installation utility to automatically check your hardware for you. However, to use the latest catalog available, the system must also have Internet access. There are two ways to test your system for catalog compliance:

- Insert the DVD and let the auto-run mechanism start. (Or execute from `startup.exe` from the root of the DVD.) Click Check System Compatibility and then click Check My System Automatically.

- Execute the following from the command prompt or Run dialog box:

```
i386\win32 /checkupgradeonly
```

Both methods attempt to first download the latest hardware catalog and then test your system's hardware for compliance with the requirements of Windows Server 2008. If any problems or incompatibilities are found, you see an onscreen report.

Many hardware vendors offer server machines with Windows Server 2008 preinstalled. When you're buying new servers, price one that includes the Windows Server 2008 operating system and one that doesn't. You may be pleasantly surprised by the price breaks you can get when buying a preinstalled system.

Install from Your Network

The following may seem counterintuitive, but here it goes: Copying files from a hard drive elsewhere on a network is faster than copying files from a local DVD-ROM player (even a 36x or 40x player). Why? Because hard disks are as much as 40 times faster than DVD ROM drives.

Savvy network administrators create a set of directories on a network drive and install Windows Server 2008 across the network when they can. This tactic is fast, easy, and requires only that you load a DVD once, no matter how many times you install from it. In fact, network installation is what makes the next topic — automated installations — feasible.

Let the Software Do the Work: Automating Installation

Normally, user input drives the Windows Server 2008 installation program: from character-based prompts during the initial load phase and by user navigation of menus and input items during the later phases. As an alternative, text files called *answer files* may drive Windows Server 2008 installation, making it possible to automate installation more or less completely. Script-driven installation can be especially handy when you must install more than two or three copies of Windows Server 2008 at any given time.

Windows Server 2008 supports more methods for automating installation than previous implementations (such as Windows Server 2003 and NT 4.0), including the following:

- ✔ You can create a single variation or several variations of base installation material and deploy them in enterprise-wide computers all at once with company-specific applications, configurations, and data.

- ✔ You can create a set of automated commands to complete the Setup process without requiring human intervention (at least, as long as no errors are encountered).

- ✔ You can create a separate specialty recovery partition using the Windows Preinstallation Environment to create a Windows Recovery Environment for on-the-go or self-service users.

- ✔ You can even automate the first logon after Windows Server 2008's setup completes to install and configure selected applications, and then shut down the system thereafter — all from the magic of answer files!

How do you get a piece of this magic? Well, you can dig into the Windows Server 2008 Technical Library, available online at `http://technet2.microsoft.com/windowsserver2008/en/library`, and dig into the Server Manager entries available there. Or you can go straight to work with a utility called Server Manager command, also known as `Server ManagerCmd.exe`, which gets installed as part of the base Windows Server 2008 installation.

The Windows Server 2008 ServerManagerCmd utility supports scripting and unattended deployment of Windows Server 2008 roles using XML-based answer files. Their structure and syntax is explained in the Server Manager Technical Overview Appendix (available through the Server Manager entry through the preceding Technical Library link), along with complete documentation for the command line arguments available that determine how the answer file will be interpreted.

Windows Server 2008 also includes two utilities that are somewhat Ghost-like in their capabilities. (Ghost is a popular system-imaging utility for Windows computers that allows administrators to set up a single installation, take a snapshot, and then customize that same snapshot to install one machine or several machines at the same time.) These two utilities follow:

- **Sysprep:** A utility designed to duplicate disk contents when installing multiple, identically configured machines at the same time. First, you create a normal installation on a single machine, and then you install the applications you want to distribute. Next, you use Sysprep to distribute copies of this configuration to other identical systems elsewhere on the network. It doesn't get much easier than this!

- **Syspart:** A utility designed to clone installations across multiple machines where the hardware is dissimilar. It works as an extension of the unattended install facility with a default `unattend.txt` answer file.

You can also consult the Windows Server 2008 Resource Kit (published by Microsoft Press) or the TechNet CD or Web site to find out all you can about the various installation files before starting any big jobs. We also advise you to try a couple of trial runs using these tools before attempting to automate the installation of one or more production servers.

You can access Microsoft TechNet content by using the search engine available online at `http://technet.microsoft.com`. Check the Microsoft Press Web site at `www.microsoft.com/learning/books/default.mspx` for availability of the Windows Server 2008 Resource Kit.

Beat Installation Weirdness: Be Persistent

Despite your best efforts, and even if you've taken all the proper precautions, the occasional Windows Server 2008 installation will fail. We've seen causes of failure that range from defective media to network congestion (trying to copy files to too many machines at once) to boot sector viruses. (We hate when that happens!)

When an installation fails, take a deep breath, count to ten, and try any or all of the following corrections:

✔ **Restart the installation:** If you get past the initial parts of the character mode portion of the installation, the software is often smart enough to pick up where it left off and carry on from there. If you're that lucky, count your blessings and then go out and buy a lottery ticket!

✔ **If installation won't pick up where it left off, look for a directory named WIN_NT.~LS:** Delete this directory and its contents. The Windows Server 2008 installation program looks for these directories and attempts to save time by picking up where it left off. We include the DOS DELTREE command in our emergency install disk tool kit because it lets us dispatch these directories and their contents quickly and easily.

✔ **If all else fails, repartition and reformat the boot drive to remove all vestiges of your failed attempt:** You'll start over with a clean slate! Our emergency install disk toolkit also includes a DOS Fdisk and a handy utility called Delpart.exe, which can remove even non-DOS partitions (such as NTFS) from a PC hard drive. Delpart.exe is available for free download from several Web sites. Search your favorite search engine for *Delpart.exe*.

If the final technique doesn't work, recheck the Windows Server 2008 Hardware Catalog for potential sources of difficulty. (See the "Use Only Qualified Server Hardware" section earlier in this chapter for details on this catalog.) Otherwise, look for guidance on your problems on Microsoft's TechNet CD or the Windows Server 2008–related newsgroups on the news://msnews.microsoft.com news server.

Let Lo-Res Come to Your Rescue!

You'll find out that Windows Server 2008 doesn't care a bit whether the display on your Windows Server 2008 machine is working. Windows Server 2008 continues to chug along quite happily — even if you can't see what the system is doing because the screen is totally confusing or nothing is showing at all. The leading cause of display problems is loading a display driver that doesn't work with your graphics adapter, or your monitor, or both!

When this problem happens (and it's a common post-installation problem), don't panic. Simply reboot the machine. (Press the Reset button on the computer case if you can't read the screen at all.) When the boot menu shows up, press F8 to access the Advanced Options, and then select Enable Low-Resolution Video (640x480).

Doing so boots Windows Server 2008 with a plain-vanilla VGA driver. Then you can try a different driver (or troubleshoot the hardware). This time, use the test button to make sure the driver works before you change your display!

Use "Last Known Good" to Do Good!

After installation is complete, you must continue to configure your Windows Server 2008 to install additional software and add all types of information about system and user policies, account and group names, and so forth. If you encounter trouble along the way, or Windows Server 2008 balks for some reason and won't boot, you can always use the F8 technique described in the previous section to view and select from its advanced boot options. This time, pick the entry that reads "Last Known Good Configuration." Also known as the LKGC, this uses the last working set of startup settings to restart the machine, and usually suffices to escape the malign effects of a bad driver installation or faulty configuration setting. After using this option, you'll have to repeat everything you did since the last time you rebooted — and hopefully, fix whatever broke in the meantime — but at least you'll be able to keep chugging along in forward motion.

A Custom Installation Saves Systems!

The problem with Startup disks is that it takes six of them to boot older Windows Server 2003 installations. Using disks also forces you through a time-consuming set of steps to get a machine running. Fortunately, creative minds decided to develop a generic Windows Server 2008 and Windows Vista installation Windows Image Format (WIF) and a new disk-imaging tool called ImageX.

You can even install a preinstallation setup environment onto the target computer so that the DVD media needn't even be accessible for self-service and repair in the field by the system end-user. The Windows Recovery Environment (Windows RE) is an extensible recovery platform based on the

Windows Preinstallation Environment (PE), which is triggered any time Windows fails to startup. A Startup Repair tool automates system diagnosis and repair for the unbootable installation and serves as a starting point for manual troubleshooting and recovery.

Newer server hardware configurations may exclude floppy drives in preference for the now prevalent CD and DVD drives. However, the theory of preventive maintenance and a bootable recovery medium remains much the same. Server motherboards with compliant BIOS settings can even boot from USB drives and storage devices, which further increases your recovery options in the event of failure.

Every time you make a change to Windows Server 2008, those changes are recorded in the Windows Server 2008 Registry. Sometimes, those changes can have unforeseen side-effects — especially if you've been editing the Registry directly — and can make your machine falter or even fail to boot. When your machine does falter or fails to boot, always try reverting to the last working version of the Registry. When the boot menu shows up, press F8 to access Advanced Options, and then select Last Known Good Configuration. You roll back to the version of the Registry that was in use the last time your machine booted successfully. The good news is that your machine will probably boot; the bad news is that you'll lose all the changes you've made since the last time you rebooted the machine. Bummer!

When you make lots of changes, either back up the Registry or reboot frequently. This keeps the amount of work you can lose — from an ill-advised Registry change, a bad driver selection, and so on — to a minimum. Restore points include Registry backups as part of what they capture, so they're just as good as a Registry backup per se, only easier! Choose Start⇨Control Panel⇨System⇨System Protection, then click the System Restore button to create a restore point at any time.

Use the Windows Server 2008 DVD to Boot

The Windows Server 2008 DVD is bootable, which means that you can boot your server from the DVD. You no longer need to mess with startup boot floppies. To boot your system from the DVD, make sure your server BIOS includes the optical drive in its boot priority settings, preferably at or near the top of that list.

If your system won't boot from the DVD, it needs to boot from something. If that's the case for your system, there are ways to work around this problem. Worst case, you can create a minimum boot image on a USB flash drive and take that route, or do likewise with a USB-attached hard disk. Microsoft TechNet provides a helpful article that explains just how to do that at www.microsoft.com/technet/technetmag/issues/2006/10/Windows PE/default.aspx.

Microsoft soars to new heights with its latest bootable DVD media, but you have to experience this at work to appreciate the difference. For starters, the same installation DVD doubles as a diagnostic and troubleshooting disk that can boot a dead installation, perform basic startup repair, or enable an administrator to select from restore or backup options without booting into Windows. What isn't so obvious is the underlying Windows Image Format (WIF) that drives the entire installation — it's essentially a template image that you can recreate and custom tailor to suit your personal or business needs. Whether deploying a single workstation and server or several workstations and servers, the new WIF framework lets you customize Windows installations to meet your needs.

When in Doubt, Back Up!

Windows Server 2008 is a reliable operating system, but accidents do happen. Make sure you back up your Windows Server 2008 before you make any significant changes to that machine. Significant changes include adding *beaucoups* of new users or groups, making Active Directory changes, adding services or applications, or doing anything else that significantly updates the Registry. Then, if the server goes down after those changes are applied, you can always restore the backup after booting from your startup disks and reactivating the backup software to get back to where you started. Don't leave home without it!

Prepare for the Real Work!

Although installing Windows Server 2008 by itself is no mean feat, the real work begins when that job ends. Formulate and then translate your plans for domain and directory structures, machine names, usernames, group names, and disk structures from concept to reality. This is the real work that makes Windows Server 2008 usable to your audience and able to deal with the demands they'll put on your system. And again: **Remember to back up your system on a regular basis!**

Chapter 20

Ten Steps to Networking Nirvana with Windows Server 2008

*W*indows Server 2008 without a network is like a bicycle without wheels or chips without salsa. (Our apologies in advance to the unicyclists and fat-free members of our audience.)

Because Windows Server 2008 and networking go together like gangbusters, your gang (of users) may try to bust you whenever the network stops working. Try as you might to avoid it, it will happen from time to time. When the network goes on vacation but you're still in the office, read over these tips and tricks to get things shipshape again.

Never Overlook the Obvious

The number one cause for failed networks is — you guessed it — loose connections. Always check a server's network interface cards (NICs) to make sure that cables are still plugged in or otherwise attached. Also, check all hubs, routers, the Integrated Services Digital Network (ISDN) box, the modem, and anywhere else those cables go (including client machines).

Networking experts often talk about a troubleshooting pyramid that follows the progression of network capabilities up from the hardware and cables through the protocol stack to the applications that request network services. In this analogy, the base of the pyramid is far bigger than the top. This pyramid illustrates that problems are most likely to occur at the physical level of networking. Why? Because that's where the cables and connections are. Go ahead — check them again.

Check Windows Server 2008 Routing

Windows Server 2008 happily lets you insert two or more network adapters or other devices that can carry network traffic — such as modems, Fibre Channel interfaces, or even Channel Service Unit/Data Service Units (CSU/DSUs) for high-speed digital networking. Doubling up on network adapters (or other network traffic handling devices) lets Windows Server 2008 move traffic from one connection to another. This capability, known as *routing,* enables Windows Server 2008 to interconnect separate pieces of a network.

The most exposed and important part of many networks is the link that ties a local network to the Internet (or at least, to your local Internet Service Provider). If Windows Server 2008 fills that role on your network, be prepared to perform regular troubleshooting rituals to keep this all-important link to the outside world running.

If you can, you should isolate this function on a separate computer or a network appliance designed for that role. This is a good idea for two reasons:

- Adding the burden of routing traffic and managing an Internet interface requires additional software and services that can tax (and possibly overburden) a Windows Server 2008 system.

- Limit the impact of system failure to as few services as possible. Chances are that your users will be less unhappy if they lose only Internet access or only access to shared files and applications, rather than losing both at the same time.

If you do use a Windows Server 2008 system as a router, especially if an Internet link is involved, think about installing or using firewall software, such as Microsoft's Windows Firewall and Network Access Protection (NAP), on that machine. A firewall protects your network from interlopers and allows you to monitor and filter incoming (and outgoing) content and information, while NAP lets you quarantine remote users who don't meet your security policy requirements (current anti-virus software, OS patches, and so forth).

Open Your TCP/IP Toolkit

If you're going to attach to the Internet (and who isn't, these days?), you want to build a TCP/IP toolkit to help with the inevitable troubleshooting chores involved in keeping a TCP/IP network working properly.

Fortunately, Windows Server 2008 includes a fine collection of TCP/IP tools and utilities that you can use immediately. Table 20-1 includes some prime candidates for your IP troubleshooting toolbox. Given this arsenal of tools, you should be well prepared to shoot TCP/IP troubles before they shoot you!

Table 20-1	TCP/IP Diagnostic Utilities
Utility	*Description*
arp	Displays the address translation tables used by the IP Address Resolution Protocol (ARP). Helps detect invalid entries and ensure proper resolution of numeric IP addresses to Media Access Control (MAC) addresses.
hostname	Displays your IP host name onscreen. Use this to check your machine's current name.
ipconfig	Displays all current network configuration values for all interfaces. Use this to check address assignments for your machine, the default gateway, and the subnet mask.
nbtstat	Shows protocol statistics and active connections using NetBIOS over TCP/IP. Use this to troubleshoot Microsoft naming issues.
netstat	Shows active TCP and User Datagram Protocol (UDP) connections. Use this to check TCP/IP network connections and statistics.
nslookup	Displays information about known DNS servers.

(continued)

Table 20-1 *(continued)*

Utility	Description
ping	Verifies basic connectivity to network computers. Type PING loopback to check internal capabilities first, and then check local and remote machines to check overall connectivity.
route	Displays network routing tables and enables you to edit entries; useful primarily when static routing is in effect.
tracert	Determines the route from the sender to a destination by sending Internet Control Message Protocol (ICMP) echo packets that cause all stations between sender and receiver to announce themselves.

Use One or More Fast Server Network Adapters

On a Windows Server 2008 Server, performance is the name of the game. In networking, because network traffic tends to congregate at the server, spending extra bucks on a fast, powerful network adapter makes sense. At a bare minimum, you want a Peripheral Component Interconnect (PCI)–based NIC, if not a PCI-e x4 or x8 card or a PCI-X 133 MHz card. Other hardware enhancements worth purchasing for Windows Server 2008 network adapters include the following:

✔ **TCP Offload Engine (TOE):** Permits the network adapter to handle TCP packet processing without requiring the CPU to get involved very much. This requires a network adapter that supports the Windows Server 2008 TCP Chimney with a driver that can handle TCP offload functions, but such cards are widely available. (See Appendix A for details.)

✔ **Direct Memory Access (DMA):** Enables the network adapter to transfer data directly from its onboard memory to the computer's memory without requiring the CPU to mediate.

✔ **Shared adapter memory:** Enables a network adapter's onboard RAM to map into computer RAM. When the computer thinks it's writing (or reading) to its own RAM, it's writing (or reading) straight to (from) the card. Shared system memory works the same way, except the card reads from and writes to the computer's RAM instead of its own onboard RAM. Extra memory for network adapters is almost as good as more RAM on Windows Server 2008 PCs!

> ✔ **Bus mastering:** Lets the network adapter manage the computer's bus to coordinate data transfers to and from the computer's memory. Bus mastering enables the CPU to concentrate on other activities and can improve performance by 20 to 70 percent. This is the most worthwhile of all the enhancements mentioned here.

The idea is to put the processing power and speed where it does the most good: on the network adapter with which all users interact to obtain data from (or move packets through) a server. A high-speed backbone (Gigabit Ethernet or better) is also an extremely good idea for modern networks.

Know When to Divide and When to Conquer

When traffic reaches high levels on a network segment, traffic jams occur just like they do at rush hour on the highway. When this happens, you need to improve the existing roads (switch to a faster network technology) or add more roads (break up the existing network and put one subset of users on one new piece, another subset on another piece, and so on).

How can you figure out when traffic is starting to choke your network? Easy! Windows Server 2008 includes a service called Network Monitor (affectionately called NetMon) that you can install on your server to monitor the traffic moving into and out of your server (and on the cable segment or segments to which that server is attached).

NetMon doesn't install on Windows Server 2008 by default, but it's easy to add. Choose Start⇨Control Panel⇨Add or Remove Programs⇨Add/Remove Windows Components⇨Management and Monitoring Tools. Then click the Details button, select the Network Monitor Tools check box, and click OK. After you follow the instructions from there, NetMon shows up in the Administrative Tools folder (Start⇨Administrative Tools⇨Network Monitor).

Get to know NetMon, and you get to know your network much better!

When in Doubt, Check Your Services

What do network servers do? They provide network services. When things get weird with Windows Server 2008 and you can't find anything wrong with the network, visit the Services tool, as shown in Figure 20-1.

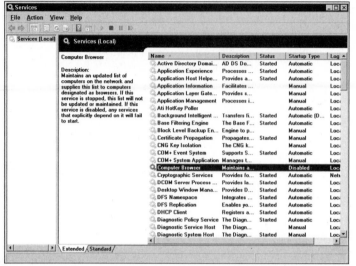

Figure 20-1:
The
Services
tool
indicates
the status
for all
services
installed on
Windows
Server 2008.

To view this display, follow this menu sequence: Start⇨Administrative Tools⇨Services. Then click the Services entry to view the list of services currently installed on Windows Server 2008.

Be sure to check the entries for key services such as Computer Browser, the Server service, and the Workstation service. Make sure that the Status field says Started and that the Startup field is properly set. (It should read Automatic for services that are supposed to launch upon startup.)

Many times, when the network shows no obvious problems, you may find that a key service has been paused or stopped or has simply quit for some reason. If a service has stopped, refer to the Event Viewer to find out why because a stopped service usually indicates a serious problem that will recur.

Handle Names and Addresses Efficiently

The only way to find something on a network is to know its address. Alas, human beings are better at remembering symbolic names than numeric addresses (or worse yet, the arcane bit patterns that computers use to address one another).

This means a lot when you operate a working network, but two primary concerns from a troubleshooting perspective are:

✔ The services that provide name-to-address translation must be properly configured and working correctly for users to use a network effectively.

✔ Network addresses, subnet masks, and related information (such as default gateways, router addresses, and so on) must be unique, properly specified, and in substantial agreement for computers to use a network properly.

Symptoms of trouble in this area are many and varied. Duplicate addresses usually cause all holders of the same address to drop off the network. Invalid names or addresses simply can't be reached and may require serious troubleshooting to correct. Active Directory may be unavailable or not working for some reason or another. (In general, check the spelling of names carefully and the numeric values for addresses equally carefully.)

Fortunately, problems in this arena usually make themselves known during initial configuration or when settings change. If you simply check your settings and assumptions against a known, working set of values, you can usually undo such woes quickly and painlessly.

Ask What's New or Different

When troubleshooting a network, what's new or what's changed is often a source of trouble. Thus, when you investigate network snafus, be sure to ask yourself, "What's new?" and "What's different?" right away, and then answer in as much detail as possible. While digging up those gory details, you will often uncover the source of the trouble and can determine its solution, all in one swift fell swoop.

Savvy network administrators keep a log of changes and additions to servers on their networks, so when those key questions get asked, answers are immediately forthcoming. You could do worse than to emulate these professionals!

If You Need Help, Ask

Occasionally, when troubleshooting a system, you run into problems that are so mysterious or baffling that you won't have a clue about how to correct them. When that happens, don't tear out your hair — ask for help instead.

If you're having a problem with Windows Server 2008, your first (and hopefully, last) source of support should be the various Microsoft Web pages on the product. The Microsoft Small Business Center is a good place to start (`www.microsoft.com/smallbusiness/support/technical-overview.aspx`). If you get stuck, you can always visit the online forums where other Windows Server 2008 users and experts congregate. You can also check the TechNet CD (you can order it from `www.microsoft.com/technet`) or the Microsoft Developer Network (which you can join at `www.msdn.microsoft.com`).

If the problem is with a piece of hardware, check the manufacturer's Web site or bulletin board for a driver update. If that doesn't lead to a happy dance, you may have to pay that vendor's tech support operation for some advice, too. If you can determine a problem's root cause, you can often get help from those who know that root the best. Even if it costs you, think of the valuable time (and aggravation) you'll save. Better to light a candle than curse the darkness!

Watch Network Trouble Spots

The best way to shoot network trouble and other types of system problems is to stop them before they happen. The only way to prevent problems and keep your network running is to study your network environment closely and carefully and figure out where its weak points are. Do this before your network demonstrates its weaknesses to the world at large by breaking.

If you keep an eye on potential trouble spots and perform regular maintenance and upkeep activities (such as scheduled backups, file-system cleanups, upgrades, service packs, and hotfixes), you can prevent problems. And believe us, preventing problems isn't just less work, it's also the cause of far less unwanted notoriety than fixing things after they break. Don't feel compelled to learn this the hard way!

Part VI
Appendixes

The 5th Wave   By Rich Tennant

©RICHTENNANT

"They can predict earthquakes and seizures, why not server failures?"

In this part . . .

Consider this part of the book a no-charge added bonus to the preceding primary chapters, and you'll get a good sense of why this stuff is in here. We want to provide our readers with some additional information and background to help them appreciate why server PCs are different from desktops, and we want to help them adapt to the brave new world of Windows Server 2008–based networks.

In one of our appendixes, we tackle networking components and technologies most likely to be of interest to those who work with network servers, such as TOE (not those little wrinkly things at the end of your feet, rather special hardware called a TCP/IP Offload Engine, which is designed to take the work involved in processing network packets from your CPU and turn it over to your network interface card instead — and you thought you didn't need this, eh?). And last but by no means least, we provide peerless pointers to nonpareil sources for Windows troubleshooting. You may not find them interesting to read for entertainment value, but when you need them, you'll be glad you have them!

Appendix A

Server Components and Technologies

●●●

*L*ike most server operating systems, Windows Server 2008 performs at its best if equipped with more of everything: more CPUs (and more CPU power), more RAM, more storage, and more and faster network interfaces. In this appendix, we cover key server components, explain briefly how they work and what kinds of options you have available, and describe price and performance tradeoffs you'll encounter when pondering spending more or less money to acquire more or less performance.

In the sections that follow, we discuss the following topics as they relate to server platforms and hardware:

- ✔ **Server motherboards:** What makes them different and special as compared to their desktop brethren

- ✔ **Processors:** Why more CPUs with more cores get more work done, as well as what makes server processors different from desktop CPUs

- ✔ **Memory (RAM):** Why more is nearly always better, and what makes server RAM different from desktop RAM

- ✔ **Disk drives, controllers, and RAID arrays:** High-speed disk drives, special-purpose disk controllers, and disk arrays all combine to give servers a decidedly different take on storage than is typical for desktops.

- ✔ **Network interfaces:** TCP/IP Offload Engines (also known as TOE), higher speeds, and multiple interfaces put servers on a different networking path than most desktops or workstations walk.

Our goal is to describe what kinds of things are available and how much they cost, what kinds of features and functions you should look for, and what kinds of tradeoffs you'll have to make between cost and performance.

Server Motherboards

Your choice of server motherboard will determine most of the other components that go into a server, so in many ways, it's both heart and soul of any resulting server. The motherboard

- ✔ Includes one or more CPU sockets (which determine what kind of central processor you use) and memory sockets (which determine how many and what kind of memory modules you use).
- ✔ Includes (usually) two GbE network interfaces and sets the foundation for networking capability.
- ✔ Defines base-level RAID support.
- ✔ Includes bus slots to accommodate additional network interfaces or RAID controllers you may decide to use instead.

Table A-1 describes the basic options to which you should attend when choosing a server motherboard.

Table A-1	Windows Server Motherboards	
Item	*Number (Low–High)*	*Notes*
CPU sockets	1–4	For low-end servers, one or two CPU sockets usually suffice.
CPU types	Varies	Important to check what kinds of CPUs will fit, both for matching and to meet performance requirements.
Bus speed	800–1333 MHz	Faster buses provide better performance but require more expensive hardware devices.
Chipsets	Varies	Determine memory handling, disk I/O, graphics, and bus access.
Disk controllers	Varies	Look for SCSI and RAID or SATA and RAID support.
Memory (RAM)	4–8 slots	Look at number of slots, maximum size and speed per module, also look for dual-channel and ECC support.

Item	Number (Low–High)	Notes
PCI Express slots	1–3	Look for one or more 8x slots, plus one or more additional PCI-e x1, PCI-e x4, and PCI-X slots.
Built-in graphics	1	Nice to have, but not strictly required as long as one PCI slot is available for a graphics card.
Ports/connectors	Varies	You need at least two USB ports, plus the means to connect a mouse and keyboard.

Whereas very few desktop and only some workstation motherboards include two or more CPU sockets, many server motherboards support two or more. And whereas $300 is a lot for a desktop motherboard and $400 is a lot for a workstation motherboard, many server motherboards cost $500 or more. You'll want to make sure the motherboard supports the type of disk drives you wish to use and can accommodate enough memory to meet your performance requirements.

Good server motherboard manufacturers are many but the best-known players include Intel Corporation, Tyan, and Asus. On the Intel side, look for motherboards that support Socket 771 for one or two Xeon processors; on the AMD side, look for 2000 or 8000 series Socket F processors.

Server Processors

You'll want to attend to many things when choosing CPUs for server use. Chief among those are the number of *cores* per processor, which defines the number of independent working units inside each processor package, or *chip*. We recommend at least two cores per processor and at least four cores per server, which means you can purchase a motherboard with a single socket as long as you're willing to buy a quad-core processor; if you buy a two-socket motherboard, you can go with two dual-core units. See Table A-2 for more on our recommendations for Windows server processors.

Table A-2	Windows Server Processors	
Item	*Number (Low–High)*	*Notes*
CPU cores	1–8	For low-end servers, two or four cores per processor usually suffice.
CPU speed	1.8–3.0 GHz	Faster processors perform better but also consume more power and produce more waste heat.
Maximum memory speed	266–667 MHz	Faster memory performs better but costs more.

For most of the readers of this book, the AMD 1000 and 2000 series Opteron processors and the Intel Xeon 3000 series processors will probably make the most sense. These come in single, dual, and quad-core models, and prices range from a low of around $120 to as much as $300 each. Count on buying two, and your budget will be appropriately conservative.

Server Memory (RAM)

The kind and amount of memory that servers use differs drastically from that found in most desktop and workstation PCs. All of these kinds of PCs use memory modules, which are usually called DIMMS (double inline memory modules), that indicate support for a 64-bit-wide data path to the memory chips onboard. To begin with, most servers use a special type of random access memory (RAM) that's called *registered ECC*. Each of these words has a special meaning:

- **Registered:** This means that the memory uses a special storage area called a *memory register* (register, for short) in which it stores information to be written to the memory module. This slows down memory access by one clock cycle to access the register (instead of directly reading from or writing to memory locations), but ensures that data is both stable and reliable, which are eminently desirable characteristics for server use.

- **ECC:** This stands for Error Checking and Correction, which basically uses additional memory chips to hold error check data about values stored in memory. As values are read, error check data makes sure the data is correct, and when a single-bit error is detected, this kind of memory can fix such errors. ECC memory generally runs a little bit slower (two percent slower, according to some estimates) than conventional non-ECC memory, but it ensures that data is correct and error free, which are also eminently desirable characteristics for server use.

ECC memory modules must be purchased as such and generally cost anywhere from two to three times as much as non-ECC memory of the same speed. Is it worth it? For server use, most definitely. Typical price ranges for DDR2 ECC memory appear in Table A-3.

Table A-3		Windows Server Memory		
Speed	*Size*	*Low $*	*High $*	*Designation*
400 MHz	1GB	$35	$70	PC2-3200
400 MHz	2GB	$100	$130	PC2-3200
533 MHz	1GB	$55	$90	PC2-4200
533 MHz	2GB	$100	$150	PC2-4200
667 MHz	1GB	$60	$100	PC2-5300
667 MHz	2GB	$200	$300	PC2-5300

When it comes to buying server memory, get the fastest that your motherboard will support. Experience has also taught us that you should fill slots in pairs (to make best use of dual-bank capabilities) and that you should fill as many slots as you can afford when you put your system together. (Because memory technology changes rapidly, newer, faster memory often costs less than older, slower memory.) We recommend nothing less than 4GB for a Windows Server 2008 32-bit system and nothing less than 8GB for a Windows Server 2008 64-bit system.

Disk Drives, Controllers, and RAID

When it comes to choosing storage for a server, one fundamental selection drives the rest of the process. Modern servers tend to use either the SCSI (Small Computer Systems Interface) or SATA (Serial Advanced Technology Attachment, also known as Serial ATA) hard drives. Each type of drive requires its own unique disk controller, so choosing SCSI means that you must also use a SCSI controller, and choosing SATA means that you must also use a SATA controller.

Windows servers also have another typical wrinkle — namely, a typical setup approach where one drive, or a pair of mirrored drives, is used for operating system files and information, and other drives (often in a RAID array) are used to store data and applications for user access. Thus, it isn't unusual to use two disk controllers on a server: one to handle the operating system image and related files and the other to handle data drives.

Windows distinguishes between two primary sets of disk structures related to any Windows system, including a Windows server. The *system volume* (also known as the *system partition* or *system drive*) contains the hardware-specific files needed to start Windows up, including `Ntldr`, `Boot.ini`, and `Ntdetect.com`, among others. The *boot volume* (also known as the *boot partition* or *boot drive*) contains the Windows operating system and supporting files (which typically reside in the . . . `\WINDOWS` and . . . `WINDOWS\System32` folders, respectively).

Because most modern server motherboards usually include both SCSI and SATA controllers (although not always with RAID for both types of drives), it's a fairly common practice to use SATA for the Windows operating system drive, and SCSI for the data drives, usually in a RAID 5 or RAID 10 array. (We explain these terms later in this section.) Sometimes, you'll use a pair of mirrored drives for the Windows operating system to ensure extra reliability and improved performance.

SCSI versus SATA drives

The short version of this discussion is that SCSI is faster and more expensive than SATA. The longer version gets a little more complicated. Let's start by looking at typical drive speeds for the two technologies, as shown in Table A-4. Because 3.5" drives are invariably used in servers nowadays, we restrict ourselves to that form-factor. (Other form-factors are smaller and slower anyway, the laws of rotational physics being what they are, but smaller drives are used far more frequently in notebook PCs than any other kind, and almost never in servers.)

Table A-4		Typical SCSI and SATA 3.5" Drive Speeds		
Type	*RPM*	*Cost/GB (Low–High)*	*Capacity (Low–High)*	*Remarks*
SATA	7,200	$0.20–$0.40	40GB–1TB	Larger, more capable drives cost more; sizes range from 80GB to 1TB.
SATA	10,000	$1.33–$2.02	74–150GB	WD Raptor models, available in only two sizes, are the only 10,000 RPM SATA drives available.

Type	RPM	Cost/GB (Low–High)	Capacity (Low–High)	Remarks
SCSI	10,000	$1.48–$2.45	146–434GB	Most major drive manufacturers offer such drives but none in sizes larger than 4xxGB.
SCSI	15,000	$4.10–$8.97	36–46GB	Same as for 10K RPM SCSI drives, except sizes top out at 146GB.

There's a very interesting moral to be drawn from the foregoing table. Unless your server must absolutely scream with disk speed, the best storage value comes from 7,200 RPM SATA drives. With Seagate now offering perpendicular magnetic recording (PMR) drive technologies that basically stand bit regions sideways on the disk platter and therefore cram data into hitherto unheard-of data densities, you can get very good performance from drives that range from 320 to 750GB in size, at prices from 25 cents to 28 cents per GB.

High-performance junkies will often use a WD 10,000 RPM Raptor or a 10,000 or 15,000 RPM SCSI drive for the Windows system drive, but even these folks are increasingly turning to 7,200 RPM SATA drives for data RAID arrays.

The whole SCSI versus SATA subject continues to be a raging debate in server hardware circles. Some of the most interesting outlooks on this subject come from well-known system builder Puget Custom Computers. Its "SCSI vs SATA, Which is Faster?" article includes fascinating explanations and test results to back up its contention that SATA is more or less edging SCSI out of the server storage game. Find it online at www.pugetsystems.com/articles. php?id=19.

SCSI versus SATA controllers

The other side of the storage equation is the disk controller. Those who need fast storage usually also opt to purchase add-in disk controller cards, and eschew controllers and RAID circuitry built into most modern server mother-boards. Those who can stomach the higher costs of 10,000 or 15,000 RPM SCSI drives should also prepare to swallow additional costs for suitable disk controllers.

Even modest SCSI RAID controller cards (like the Adaptec 2246200-R) cost more than $300, and a high-end version (like the Adaptec 2185900) costs more than $700. A minimal RAID array usually requires at least three disk drives, where it isn't unusual for them to include as many as seven drives. (The max for most SCSI controllers is 15 devices per SCSI channel.) On the SATA side, costs are pretty similar: Low-end RAID controllers start at about $200 (like the Adaptec 2220300-R) and approach $700 at the high end (like the Adaptec 2251600). SATA controllers can typically handle many more devices, however, where high-end controllers top out at 128 devices in total.

When choosing a disk controller for your server, two additional selection factors come into play:

- **Bus slot:** A disk controller is an interface card and, therefore, must plug into an interface slot. Most servers come equipped with one or more of each of the slot types described in Table A-5. Be aware that the faster the bus speed for a given slot, the more a controller card that uses such a slot typically costs.

- **Slot contention:** When designing a server, multiple interface cards may end up competing for scarce slot space. This makes the number and type of slots available on a motherboard an important consideration for its purchase, and putting some thought into what kinds of cards you want to put in your service is equally important. You may have to balance the need for fast storage — which requires a disk controller card — against the need for fast network access — which may mandate one or two high-speed TCP/IP Offload Engine (TOE) network adapters.

This can force some tough choices, and may occasionally appear to argue for the wisdom of Solomon in choosing faster storage versus faster networking.

Table A-5	Server Bus Slot Speeds and Feeds			
Name	*Bus Speed*	*Bit Width*	*Maximum Throughput*	*Remarks*
PCI	33 MHz	32 bits	132 MB/s	Common PC utility bus.
PCI64	133 MHz	64 bits	1066 MB/s	Occasionally found on server motherboards.
PCI-e x1	33 MHz	1 bit	250 MB/s	All PCI-e buses are *bidirectional.* (Throughput shown is one-way only; total possible amount is double.)

Name	Bus Speed	Bit Width	Maximum Throughput	Remarks
PCI-e x4	33 MHz	4 bits	1.0 GB/s	Used for some disk controllers.
PCI-e x8	33 MHz	8 bits	2.0 GB/s	Used for many disk controllers and TOE network adapters.
PCI-X	66–133 MHz	64 bits	1.08 GB/s	Popular server bus technology.

Typically, you find between one and three PCI-e x8 slots on a server motherboard, and one or two PCI-X slots as well. If the numbers permit, you can use either one for disk controllers and network adapters. The important thing is to purchase a motherboard that has enough of the right kinds of slots to meet your needs.

There's also a case to be made at the low end of the server spectrum that you should try to use built-in controllers and adapters first and move to more expensive add-in cards only if built-ins don't cut it. But because this means you still need the right number and kind of bus slots to add any adapters you need, it's wise to pay attention to bus slots even if you don't intend to stuff them immediately after the purchase of the motherboard on which they reside.

Building RAID arrays

The full expansion for the RAID acronym holds the meat of its technology story: A *redundant array of inexpensive disks* uses conventional disk drives in a group and achieves performance, reliability, and availability gains by doing so. Using RAID of any kind requires multiple drives to work — at least two and as many as six (for the various types of RAID we're about to explain, compare, and contrast in this very section) drives are needed to support different RAID schemes.

RAID schemes go by the numbers, starting with 0 through 6, plus 10, 50, and other designations. Here we examine only those types of RAID most often used on Windows servers (but we do provide a couple of pointers at the end of this section to where the curious or the technically motivated can learn about "missing numbers" if they like). For convenience, we list them in numerical order in Table A-6, starting with zero.

Table A-6		RAID Schemes and Characteristics		
Name	**Minimum Disks**	**Typical**	**Failure**	**Remarks**
0	2	3–5	0	Striping across multiple drives; no redundancy or fault tolerance; offers best performance improvement; easy to implement.
1	2	2	1	Also known as *disk mirroring* or *duplexing,* copies everything onto each drive in a pair; easiest recovery from failure; hardware controller recommended.
0+1	4	4–10	1	Stripes across mirrored pairs; expensive with high overhead but offers very high data transfer performance.
5	3	5–7	1	Striping with parity, 1/*n* overhead (*n* = number of drives); keeps running even if a single drive fails; hardware controller required.
10	4	6–10	1	Combines striping with *mirroring* (all drives are in mirrored pairs and all pairs are striped); expensive and high overhead but high reliability and performance.
50	6	6–10	2	Combines parity and striping across two or more RAID 3 (parity) sets; very expensive but very resilient to drive failure.

In RAID arrays, all disks are usually the same kind, make, and model to permit them to work together most effectively. Another technology, called JBOD (just a bunch of disks), works like RAID 0 to stripe data across any number of disks (2 to 15, practically speaking) where the disks need not be the same. *Striping* essentially distributes data across all drives in an array so that reads and writes can be broken up and distributed across all of them. This provides a nice boost to overall performance. People usually use RAID 0 or JBOD for a performance boost, but because it confers no added reliability, these technologies aren't used very often on servers.

Disk mirroring or duplexing requires 100 percent overhead in exchange for increased reliability. Essentially, two drives each contain a copy of the same thing so that if one fails, the other one can keep chugging right along.

- ✔ **Mirroring** generally refers to "two drives, one controller," so that if the controller fails, the whole array goes down.

- ✔ **Duplexing** refers to "two drives, two controllers," so that if one drive or controller fails, the working drive and controller keep on truckin'.

When RAID 1 is used on servers, it's most often used for the Windows system/boot drive, because that allows it to keep working even if one of the drives fails with little or no downtime for repairs and reconstruction. When both drives are working, two reads are possible for the set, which effectively doubles read speed as compared to a single drive. Write speed remains unchanged because data must be written to both drives to keep the mirror synchronized.

Disk striping with parity enables control data about a collection of data blocks to be written to the only drive where none of that data resides. If a single drive fails, this lets any single stripe be reconstructed from the portions on the still-working drives that are intact, plus the parity data on the parity drive for that stripe. The controller mixes things up so that no single drive failure results in the loss of parity data needed to reconstruct missing stripe elements. RAID 5 also offers the highest read data transaction rates and medium write data transaction rates, and it's widely used on servers that need improved performance and reliability.

RAID 0+1, 10, and 50 are all pretty complex and expensive, and they're used more often in high-end, high-volume environments than on servers in small businesses or SOHO situations. You'll see that many of the disk controllers that support RAID offer these options, but they aren't as applicable for low-end to medium-demand server situations.

High-End Network Adapters

As with disk controllers, network adapters for various server buses are available. You can find versions of such adapters for the PCI, PCI-e x1 and x4, and the PCI-X buses. When shopping for such cards, make sure that Windows Server 2008 drivers are available for them, or you won't be able to put them to work on your server.

Vendors who offer TCP Offload Engine adapters invariably also require installation of the Windows TCP Chimney Offload on those Windows Server 2008 systems on which they're to be used. This essentially equips the driver to hand over TCP processing, including IP address information, ports in use, packet sequence numbers, and so forth, without requiring the server CPU(s) to get involved. For any kinds of connections that persist over time and use large packet payloads — such as network storage access, multimedia streaming, and other content-heavy applications — TCP Chimney Offload reduces CPU overhead by delegating network packet processing, including TCP segmentation and reassembly, to the network adapter. In turn, the CPU is freed up to do other things, such as handle additional user sessions or process application or service requests more quickly.

Vendors that offer network adapters that work with Windows operating systems are listed in Table A-7, along with price ranges, product descriptions, and URLs.

Table A-7		Windows TOE Network Adapters		
Vendor	*Product*	*Prices*	*Description*	*URL*
Alacritech	SENxxxx	$449–849	1–4 ports, fiber & copper, PCI, PCI-X	www.alacritech.com
Chelsio	S30xx	$795–1,495	2–4 ports, copper, PCI-e x1, x4, PCI-X	www.chelsio.com
Dell	NetXtreme II	$100	Model 5708, 1 port, PCI-e x1	www.dell.com
HP	Bladesystem	$225–400	1 or 2 ports, PCI-X, NC370i, NC373m	www.hp.com

For servers that support less than 25 simultaneous users, a network adapter with TOE capability is overkill. If servers support 25–100 users, a network adapter with TOE becomes increasingly helpful, and when handling over 100 users, it helps to keep the server available to handle other tasks as well as managing its network connections.

Appendix B

Windows Troubleshooting Resources

*W*indows Server 2008 is something of a world unto itself. In fact, it's a large, complex, and pretty interesting world, as the attached collection of recommended Windows Server 2008 resources in print and online illustrate.

In the sections that follow, we look at books and magazines that address Windows 2008 topics, as well as a plethora of Web sites, forums, newsgroups, and more. We start with a series of enthusiastic nods to the source for Windows Server 2008 and a whole raft of additional information and resources — namely, Microsoft itself. After that, we trip over numerous third parties in print and online. Along the way, you should find some fabulous goodies to help you learn more about Windows Server 2008, understand it better, and deal with troubles, trials, and tribulations related to that operating system as and when they should happen to come up.

Marvels from Microsoft

As the company that built the Windows Server 2008 operating system, it's only natural that Microsoft should also have a lot of information to share about this product. And it doesn't disappoint in any way, either in terms of volume, coverage, technical depth, and more, more, more than many will ever want to know about Windows Server 2008. We present all of the important online links at the Microsoft sites in Table B-1, each of which includes a name so we can also expand a little on this content in a bulleted list of explanations that follows the table.

Table B-1 Microsoft Windows Server 2008 Resources Online

Name	URL
Blogs	www.microsoft.com/communities/blogs/PortalHome.mspx
Microsoft Press	www.microsoft.com/mspress/hop
TechNet forums: Server 2008	forums.microsoft.com/TechNet/default.aspx?ForumGroupID-161&SiteID=17
TechNet SysInternals Web page	www.microsoft.com/technet/sysinternals/default.aspx
Windows Server 2003 newsgroup	https://www.microsoft.com/technet/prodtechnol/windowsserver2003/newsgroups.mspx
Windows Server 2008 home page	www.microsoft.com/windowsserver2008/default.mspx
Windows Server 2008 Learning Portal	www.microsoft.com/learning/windowsserver2008/default.aspx
Windows Server 2008 TechCenter	http://technet.microsoft.com/en-us/windowsserver/2008/default.aspx
Windows Server 2008 Technical Library	http://technet2.microsoft.com/windowsserver2008/en/library/

✔ **Blogs:** Important categories include Windows Server 2008, Windows Longhorn Beta 1, and Windows Longhorn Beta 2. This is where you can find developers, trainers, and key "idea people" from Microsoft explaining what's up and what's going on with Windows Server 2008.

✔ **Microsoft Press:** This organization publishes lots of materials about the company's platforms, most notably the Resource Kit titles that act as general technical encyclopedias for the company's operating systems. This Web page tells you what's coming down the pike from the press, and while we see numerous interesting Windows Server 2008 resource kit titles on IIS 7.0, Group Policy, Active Directory, productivity solutions, and more as we write this list, we don't see a single monolithic *Windows Server 2008 Resource Kit.* (These sometimes take 6–12 months after product release to arrive in print, however.)

✔ **TechNet forums:** TechNet is the Microsoft Technical Network, itself a huge compendium of technical information on Microsoft offerings. Among those offerings are online forums, including those for Windows

Server 2008 mentioned in the URL (but you can find information about anything and everything Microsoft-related through TechNet).

✔ **TechNet SysInternals Web page:** SysInternals is a formerly independent company that's now part of Microsoft, and its outstanding library of Windows administration tools is still available online. Check out the free tools available at this URL in all of these covered categories: file and disk utilities, security utilities, networking utilities, system information tools, process utilities, and miscellaneous stuff. You'll find a surprising number of real gems here. (We're especially fond of TCPView, BgInfo, ProcessMonitor, and the Registry defragmentation tool, PageDefrag.)

✔ **Windows Server 2003 newsgroup:** As we write this, no official Windows Server 2008 newsgroups are defined yet, but we expect them to show up in a windowsserver2008 directory like the windowsserver2003/ newsgroups entry we include by way of indirect reference here.

✔ **Windows Server 2008 home page:** This is the primary jumping off point in the Microsoft Web pages for all things related to Windows Server 2008. You'll find pointers to all the other Microsoft resources mentioned here, and more, on this Web page.

✔ **Windows Server 2008 Learning Portal:** This is where you can turn for access to official Microsoft Windows Server 2008 training materials and information. At present, Microsoft is offering a free e-book and a free four-part introductory online course on Windows Server 2008 to all comers, but by the time you read this, you'll probably find different offers and information there instead.

✔ **Window Server 2008 TechCenter:** This is home to the Windows Server 2008 Technical Library, related community resources online, links to popular downloads and recent Knowledge Base articles, and additional resources as well. It's an outstanding clearinghouse for technical Windows Server 2008 information. Elements of the Technical Library are also available in convenient downloadable form from the Windows Server 2008 Step-by-Step Guides page (`www.microsoft.com/down loads/details.aspx?FamilyID=518d870c-fa3e-4f6a-97f5-acaf31de6dce&DisplayLang=en`). We also provide a direct link to the Windows Server 2008 Technical Library, which is starting to flesh out significantly as this new OS is readied for release.

Windows Server 2008 Books

A quick hop up to your favorite online bookstore will no doubt augment this list immediately, but here are a couple of titles we've heard good things about as we're working on our own book (and as Microsoft continues to ready Windows Server 2008 for its commercial release).

✔ *Administering Windows Server 2008 Server Core*, by John Paul Mueller (Wiley Publishing, February 2008) is designed to serve as both a tutorial and a desk reference for administrators. This book includes a discussion of the new interface, describes how to perform all kinds of tasks, and provides a complete reference for relevant Server Core commands. Topics included cover performing essential maintenance, executing registry hacks, automating routine tasks, managing hardware, managing the network, working with TCP/IP, working with applications and data, monitoring system events and performance, managing users, and securing your system. Mueller's book makes an excellent supplement to this one.

✔ *Windows Server 2008 Implementation and Administration*, by Barrie Sosinsky (Wiley Publishing, February 2008). This book provides a concise instruction for IT professionals already trained to use earlier versions of Windows Server. It dispenses with common networking Windows technology and concepts that administrators already know, such as DHCP, DNS, and basic Active Directory to concentrate on the crucial features of the new operating system. This book seeks to bridge the old to the new without making readers relearn familiar material. Thus, this book contains topics that might be found in other Windows Server 2008 books, but it's organized to enable the reader to use these technologies more quickly. As much as possible, the book presents instructional how-to material with an eye toward teaching administrators to use Windows Server 2008 in new and more productive ways.

Server-Friendly Publications

The entire computer trade press always covers Microsoft, to a greater or lesser extent. Table B-2 points you to publications where you're most likely to find information relevant to the needs and interests of system or network administrators, and other IT professionals, who are among the people most likely to work with Windows Server 2008 on a day-to-day basis.

Table B-2	Windows Server Publications
Name	**URL**
Microsoft Certified Professional Magazine Online	www.mcpmag.com
Windows IT Pro Magazine	www.windowsitpro.com
Redmond Magazine	www.redmondmag.com

✔ *MCP Magazine*, as this publication is better known, caters to certified Microsoft professionals, most of whom manage Windows systems and servers for a living. This isn't an exclusively server-focused publication, but it provides lots of useful information about Microsoft operating systems and technologies.

✔ *WindowsITPro Magazine* is probably the best and most highly regarded of the specialty publications that focus on Windows-oriented IT professionals. This publication does a great job of covering server hardware, software, and operating systems and should continue to be a great source of information on Windows Server 2008 for interested professionals.

✔ *Redmond Magazine* is another publication that caters to the needs of working IT professionals with a Windows focus. This publication also does a good job of covering server hardware, software, and operating systems, and it's also devoting increasing coverage to Windows Server 2008.

Other Third-Party Windows Server 2008 Sources

To some extent, we appreciate the existence and variety of third parties who also provide information about Windows Server 2008. That's because Microsoft sources must toe the company line and can't always be as exact (or as direct) when it comes to identifying trouble spots and how to work around them. Typically, that's where the third parties really come into their own, and it's what makes them so worth attending to, as listed in Table B-3.

Table B-3	Other Third-Party Windows Server Resources
Name	*URL*
Windows Server Troubleshooting	`http://teamapproach.ca/trouble`
WindowsNetworking.com	`www.windowsnetworking.com`
ZDNet Troubleshooting Windows Server 2003	`http://downloads.zdnet.com/download.aspx?docid=172733`

✔ **Windows Server Troubleshooting:** The Canadian Team Approach group has put a stellar server troubleshooting guide together here. Although it doesn't yet include many Windows Server 2008 specifics, we expect them to remedy this in the near future. It's one of the best general troubleshooting references we've ever seen anywhere.

✔ **WindowsNetworking.com:** This is a Web site that caters to professional IT administrators who manage Windows servers, among other elements of the IT infrastructure. Among this site's many attractions are articles on current and emerging technologies, a large collection of information and tips under an "Admin KnowledgeBase" heading, plus tutorials on all kinds of subjects bound to be of interest to anybody who manages a Windows Server of just about any vintage, including Windows Server 2008. See a collection of Windows Server 2008 articles and tutorials at `www.windowsnetworking.com/articles_tutorials/Windows_Server_2008`.

✔ **ZDNet Troubleshooting Windows Server 2003:** The editors at ZDNet have done a great job of assembling a detailed, thorough Windows Server 2003 troubleshooting guide. While we hope they'll do likewise for Windows Server 2008 ASAP, there's a lot in here that remains fresh and relevant, even for those who use Windows Server 2008 instead.

Index

• *T* •